say cheesy

Other Books by Darby Conley

The Dog Is Not a Toy (House Rule #4)

Fuzzy Logic: Get Fuzzy 2

Groovitude: A Get Fuzzy Treasury

The Get Fuzzy Experience: Are You Bucksperienced

I Would Have Bought You a Cat, But . . .

Blueprint for Disaster

Bucky Katt's Big Book of Fun

Say Cheesy

A GET FUZZY Collection

by darby conley

**Andrews McMeel
Publishing**

Kansas City

Get Fuzzy is distributed internationally by United Feature Syndicate.

05 06 07 08 09 BBG 10 9 8 7 6 5 4 3 2 1

ISBN: 0-7407-4663-4

Library of Congress Control Number: 2005923962

Get Fuzzy can be viewed on the Internet at

www.comics.com/comics/getfuzzy.

for my mom

again

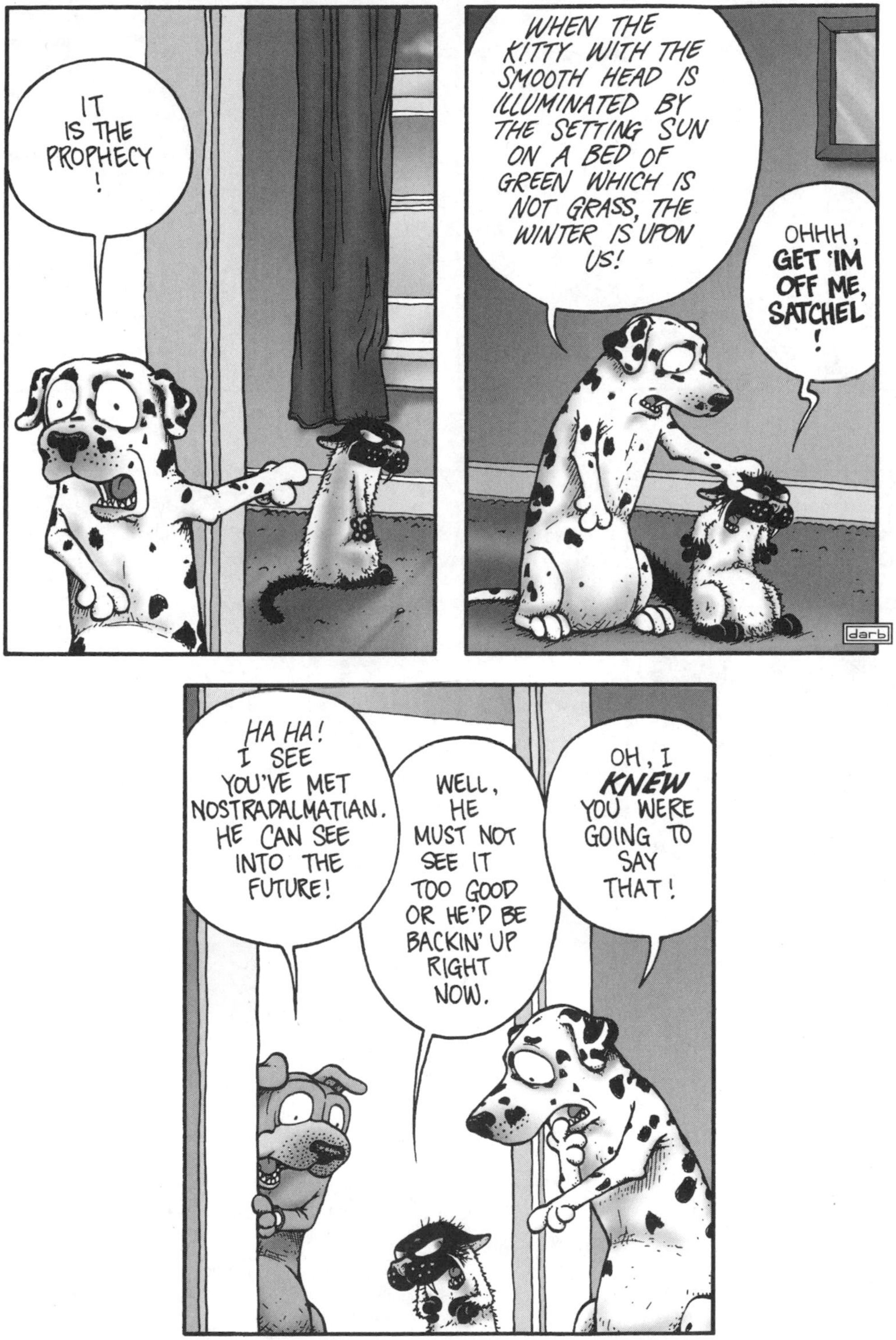
IT IS THE PROPHECY !
WHEN THE KITTY WITH THE SMOOTH HEAD IS ILLUMINATED BY THE SETTING SUN ON A BED OF GREEN WHICH IS NOT GRASS, THE WINTER IS UPON US!
OHHH, **GET 'IM OFF ME, SATCHEL** !
darb
HA HA! I SEE YOU'VE MET NOSTRADALMATIAN. HE CAN SEE INTO THE FUTURE!
WELL, HE MUST NOT SEE IT TOO GOOD OR HE'D BE BACKIN' UP RIGHT NOW.
OH, I ***KNEW*** YOU WERE GOING TO SAY THAT!

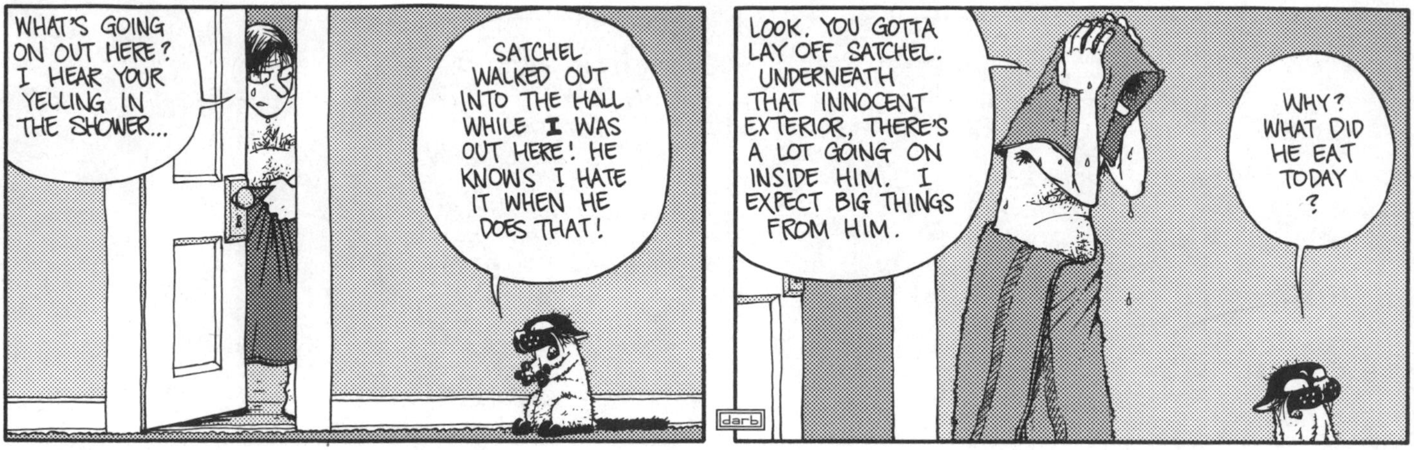
WHAT'S GOING ON OUT HERE? I HEAR YOUR YELLING IN THE SHOWER...
SATCHEL WALKED OUT INTO THE HALL WHILE I WAS OUT HERE! HE KNOWS I HATE IT WHEN HE DOES THAT!
LOOK. YOU GOTTA LAY OFF SATCHEL. UNDERNEATH THAT INNOCENT EXTERIOR, THERE'S A LOT GOING ON INSIDE HIM. I EXPECT BIG THINGS FROM HIM.
WHY? WHAT DID HE EAT TODAY?
darb

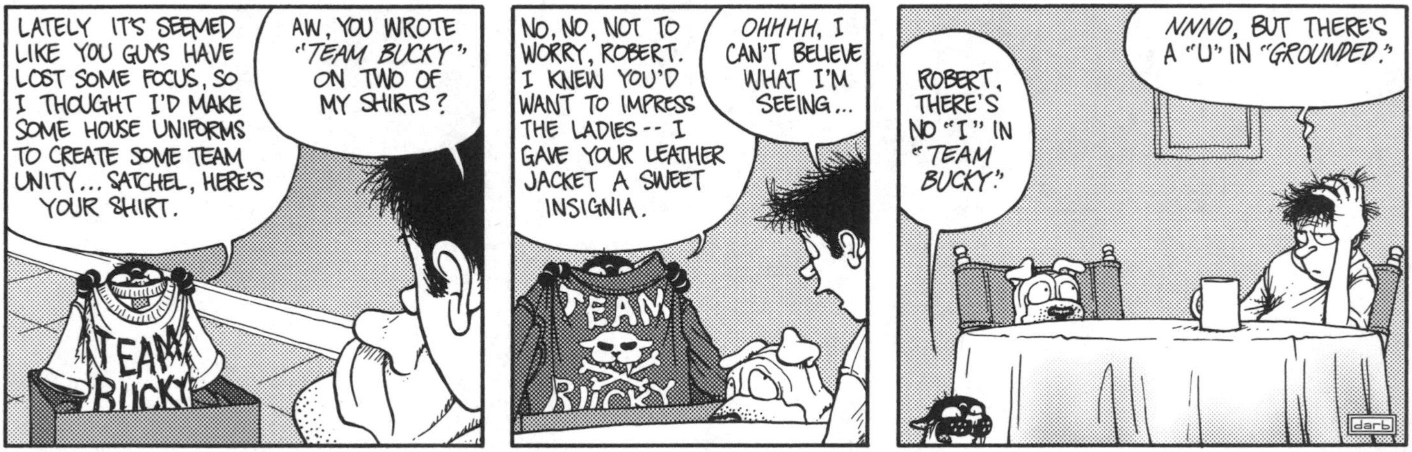
LATELY IT'S SEEMED LIKE YOU GUYS HAVE LOST SOME FOCUS, SO I THOUGHT I'D MAKE SOME HOUSE UNIFORMS TO CREATE SOME TEAM UNITY... SATCHEL, HERE'S YOUR SHIRT.
AW, YOU WROTE "TEAM BUCKY" ON TWO OF MY SHIRTS?
TEAM BUCKY
NO, NO, NOT TO WORRY, ROBERT. I KNEW YOU'D WANT TO IMPRESS THE LADIES -- I GAVE YOUR LEATHER JACKET A SWEET INSIGNIA.
OHHHH, I CAN'T BELIEVE WHAT I'M SEEING...
TEAM BUCKY
ROBERT, THERE'S NO "I" IN "TEAM BUCKY."
NNNO, BUT THERE'S A "U" IN "GROUNDED."
darb

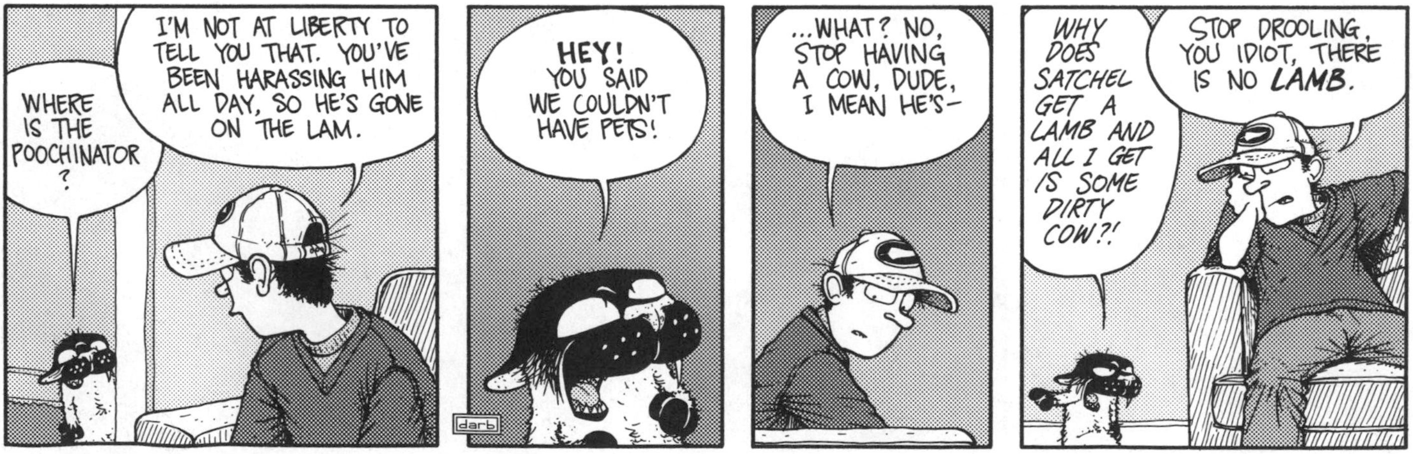
WHERE IS THE POOCHINATOR?
I'M NOT AT LIBERTY TO TELL YOU THAT. YOU'VE BEEN HARASSING HIM ALL DAY, SO HE'S GONE ON THE LAM.
darb
HEY! YOU SAID WE COULDN'T HAVE PETS!
...WHAT? NO, STOP HAVING A COW, DUDE, I MEAN HE'S—
WHY DOES SATCHEL GET A LAMB AND ALL I GET IS SOME DIRTY COW?!
STOP DROOLING, YOU IDIOT, THERE IS NO LAMB.

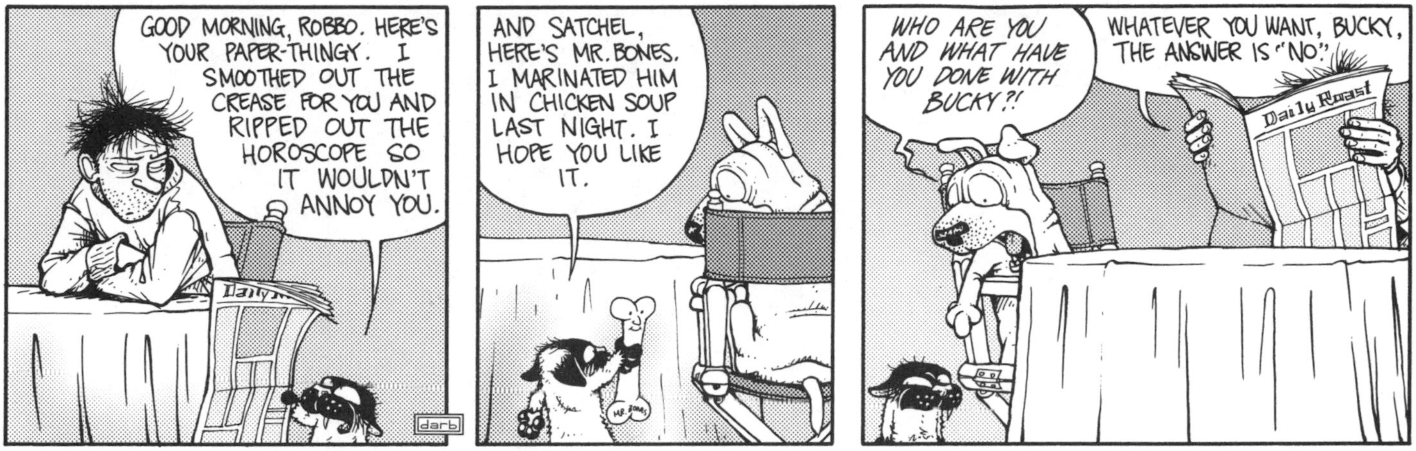
GOOD MORNING, ROBBO. HERE'S YOUR PAPER-THINGY. I SMOOTHED OUT THE CREASE FOR YOU AND RIPPED OUT THE HOROSCOPE SO IT WOULDN'T ANNOY YOU.
AND SATCHEL, HERE'S MR. BONES. I MARINATED HIM IN CHICKEN SOUP LAST NIGHT. I HOPE YOU LIKE IT.
WHO ARE YOU AND WHAT HAVE YOU DONE WITH BUCKY?!
WHATEVER YOU WANT, BUCKY, THE ANSWER IS "NO."
Daily Roast

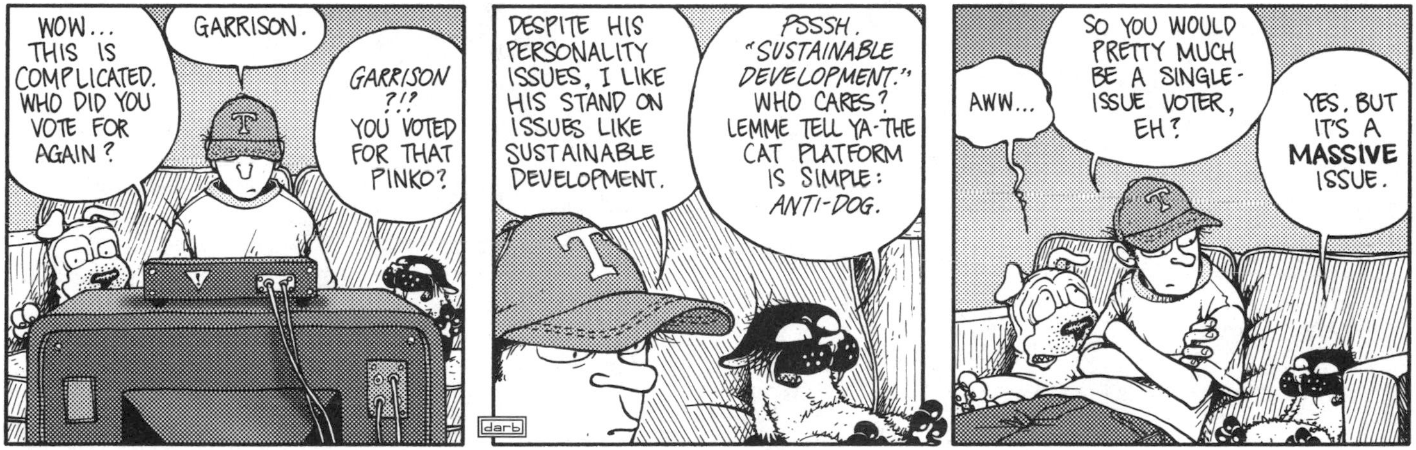
WOW... THIS IS COMPLICATED. WHO DID YOU VOTE FOR AGAIN?
GARRISON.
GARRISON?!? YOU VOTED FOR THAT PINKO?
DESPITE HIS PERSONALITY ISSUES, I LIKE HIS STAND ON ISSUES LIKE SUSTAINABLE DEVELOPMENT.
PSSSH. "SUSTAINABLE DEVELOPMENT." WHO CARES? LEMME TELL YA-THE CAT PLATFORM IS SIMPLE: ANTI-DOG.
AWW...
SO YOU WOULD PRETTY MUCH BE A SINGLE-ISSUE VOTER, EH?
YES. BUT IT'S A MASSIVE ISSUE.

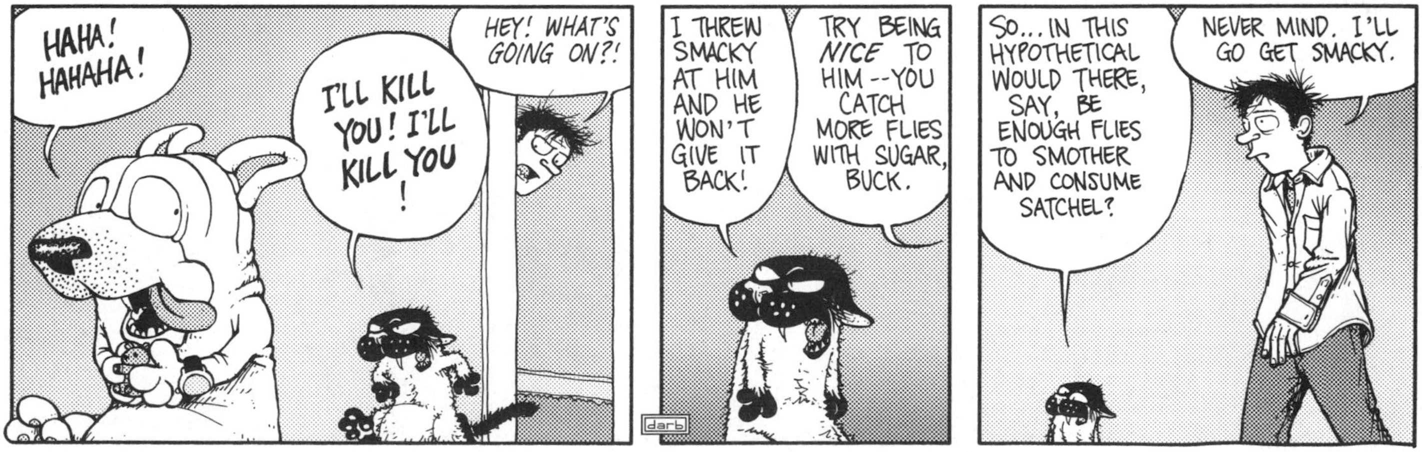
HAHA! HAHAHA!
I'LL KILL YOU! I'LL KILL YOU!
HEY! WHAT'S GOING ON?!
I THREW SMACKY AT HIM AND HE WON'T GIVE IT BACK!
TRY BEING NICE TO HIM--YOU CATCH MORE FLIES WITH SUGAR, BUCK.
SO... IN THIS HYPOTHETICAL WOULD THERE, SAY, BE ENOUGH FLIES TO SMOTHER AND CONSUME SATCHEL?
NEVER MIND. I'LL GO GET SMACKY.

THAT'S MY LATEST SCREENPLAY. IT'S A REMAKE OF THAT OLD GORILLA MOVIE. I UPDATED IT TO GIVE IT RELEVANCE TO A MODERN AUDIENCE.
"CHINCHILLAS IN THE MIST"?
IT'S THE TRUE-LIFE STORY OF MY HEROIC YET LITTLE-KNOWN DEALINGS WITH SUBURBAN WILDLIFE.
BUCKY, IN THE LAST SCENE YOU BITE OFF ALL THE CHINCHILLAS' HEADS! THAT'S NOT HOW "GORILLAS IN THE MIST" ENDED!
darb
SATCHEL, THIS IS A REMAKE. I UPDATED IT. I DON'T CARE HOW THE GORILLA MOVIE ENDED, I'VE NEVER EVEN SEEN IT!
HOW DO YOU DO A REMAKE OF A MOVIE YOU'VE NEVER SEEN?
NO, MAN, THIS IS A DIFFERENT MOVIE. I DON'T--HEY, WHERE ARE YOU GOING? YOU DIDN'T READ THE WHOLE THING!
AND YET... I'M STRANGELY COMFORTABLE WITH THAT.

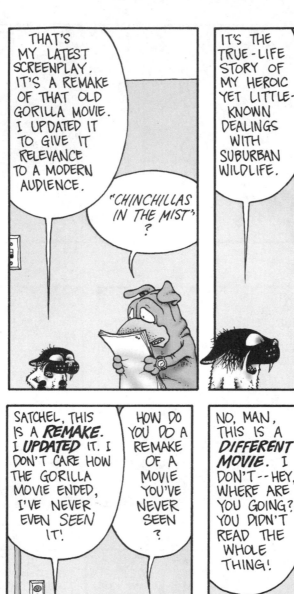

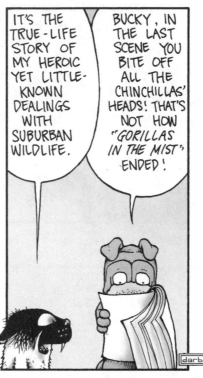

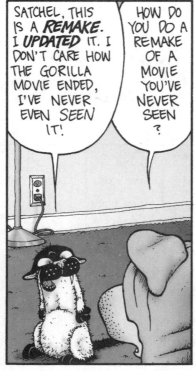

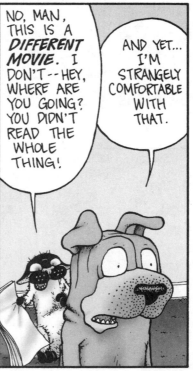

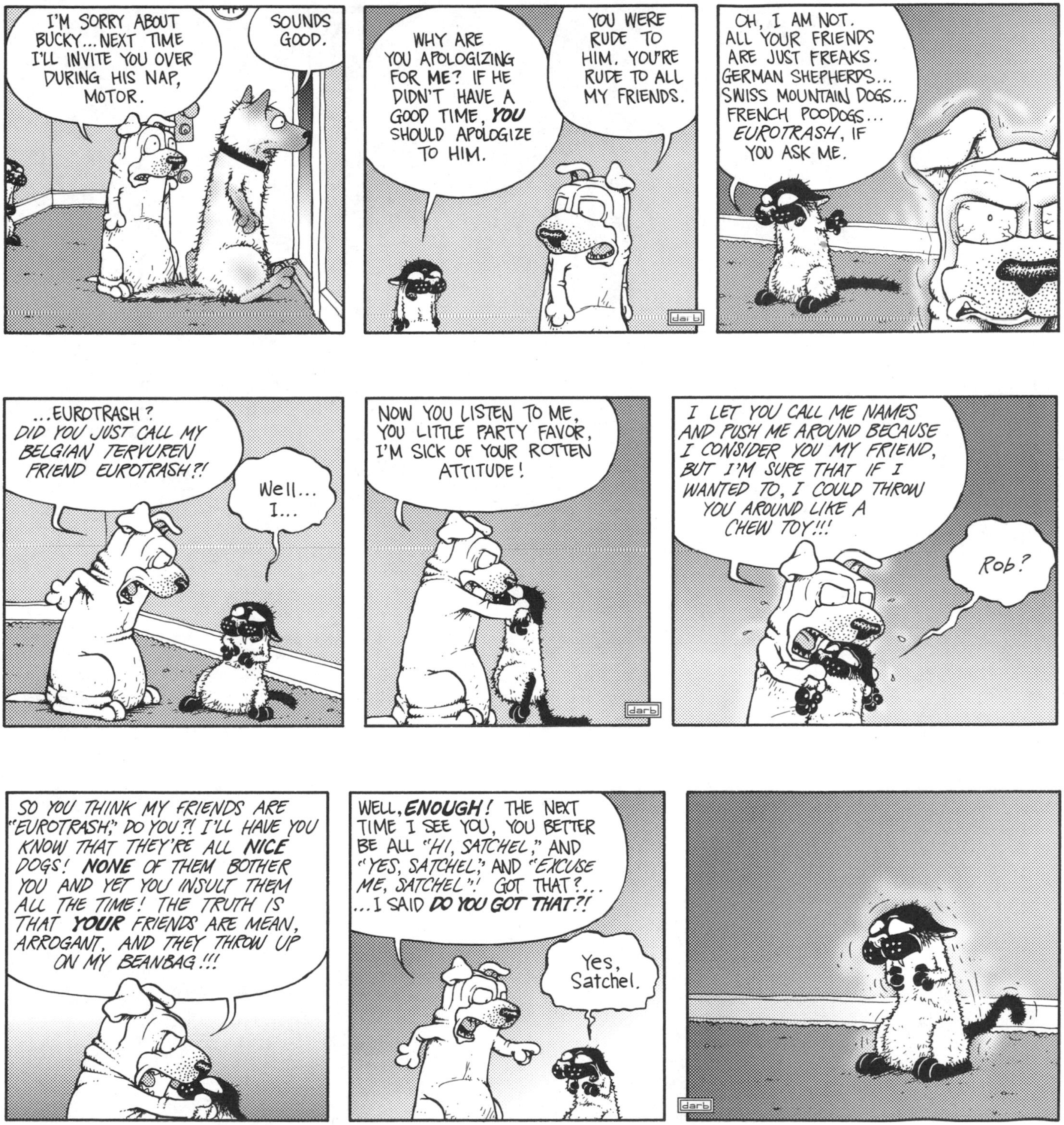
I'M SORRY ABOUT BUCKY... NEXT TIME I'LL INVITE YOU OVER DURING HIS NAP, MOTOR.
SOUNDS GOOD.
WHY ARE YOU APOLOGIZING FOR ME? IF HE DIDN'T HAVE A GOOD TIME, YOU SHOULD APOLOGIZE TO HIM.
YOU WERE RUDE TO HIM. YOU'RE RUDE TO ALL MY FRIENDS.
OH, I AM NOT. ALL YOUR FRIENDS ARE JUST FREAKS. GERMAN SHEPHERDS... SWISS MOUNTAIN DOGS... FRENCH POODOGS... EUROTRASH, IF YOU ASK ME.
...EUROTRASH? DID YOU JUST CALL MY BELGIAN TERVUREN FRIEND EUROTRASH?!
Well... I...
NOW YOU LISTEN TO ME, YOU LITTLE PARTY FAVOR, I'M SICK OF YOUR ROTTEN ATTITUDE!
I LET YOU CALL ME NAMES AND PUSH ME AROUND BECAUSE I CONSIDER YOU MY FRIEND, BUT I'M SURE THAT IF I WANTED TO, I COULD THROW YOU AROUND LIKE A CHEW TOY!!!
Rob?
SO YOU THINK MY FRIENDS ARE "EUROTRASH," DO YOU?! I'LL HAVE YOU KNOW THAT THEY'RE ALL NICE DOGS! NONE OF THEM BOTHER YOU AND YET YOU INSULT THEM ALL THE TIME! THE TRUTH IS THAT YOUR FRIENDS ARE MEAN, ARROGANT, AND THEY THROW UP ON MY BEANBAG!!!
WELL, ENOUGH! THE NEXT TIME I SEE YOU, YOU BETTER BE ALL "HI, SATCHEL," AND "YES, SATCHEL," AND "EXCUSE ME, SATCHEL"! GOT THAT?... ...I SAID DO YOU GOT THAT?!
Yes, Satchel.
darb

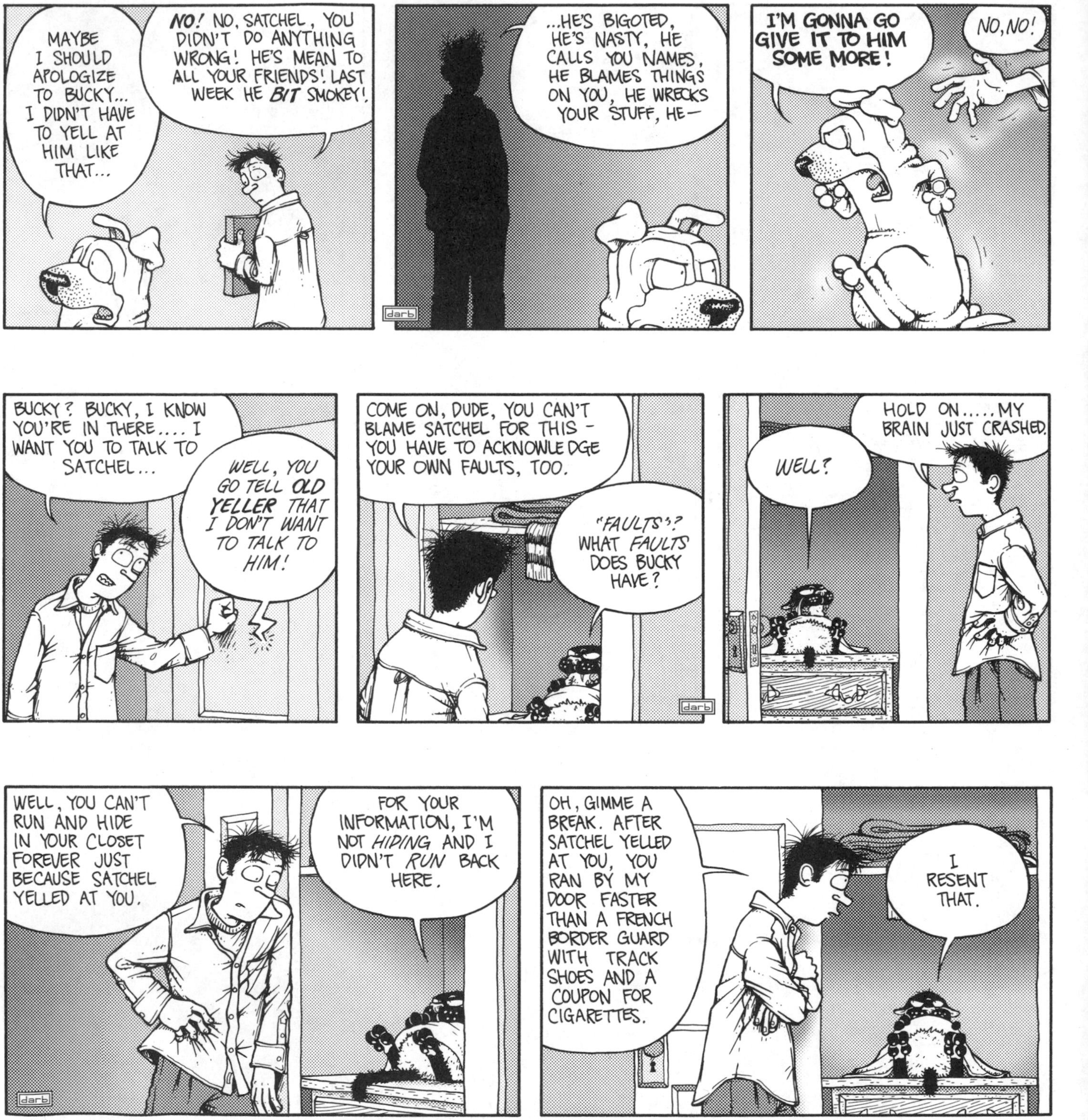
MAYBE I SHOULD APOLOGIZE TO BUCKY... I DIDN'T HAVE TO YELL AT HIM LIKE THAT...
NO! NO, SATCHEL, YOU DIDN'T DO ANYTHING WRONG! HE'S MEAN TO ALL YOUR FRIENDS! LAST WEEK HE BIT SMOKEY!
...HE'S BIGOTED, HE'S NASTY, HE CALLS YOU NAMES, HE BLAMES THINGS ON YOU, HE WRECKS YOUR STUFF, HE—
I'M GONNA GO GIVE IT TO HIM SOME MORE!
NO, NO!
BUCKY? BUCKY, I KNOW YOU'RE IN THERE.... I WANT YOU TO TALK TO SATCHEL...
WELL, YOU GO TELL OLD YELLER THAT I DON'T WANT TO TALK TO HIM!
COME ON, DUDE, YOU CAN'T BLAME SATCHEL FOR THIS - YOU HAVE TO ACKNOWLEDGE YOUR OWN FAULTS, TOO.
"FAULTS"? WHAT FAULTS DOES BUCKY HAVE?
WELL?
HOLD ON..... MY BRAIN JUST CRASHED.
WELL, YOU CAN'T RUN AND HIDE IN YOUR CLOSET FOREVER JUST BECAUSE SATCHEL YELLED AT YOU.
FOR YOUR INFORMATION, I'M NOT HIDING AND I DIDN'T RUN BACK HERE.
OH, GIMME A BREAK. AFTER SATCHEL YELLED AT YOU, YOU RAN BY MY DOOR FASTER THAN A FRENCH BORDER GUARD WITH TRACK SHOES AND A COUPON FOR CIGARETTES.
I RESENT THAT.

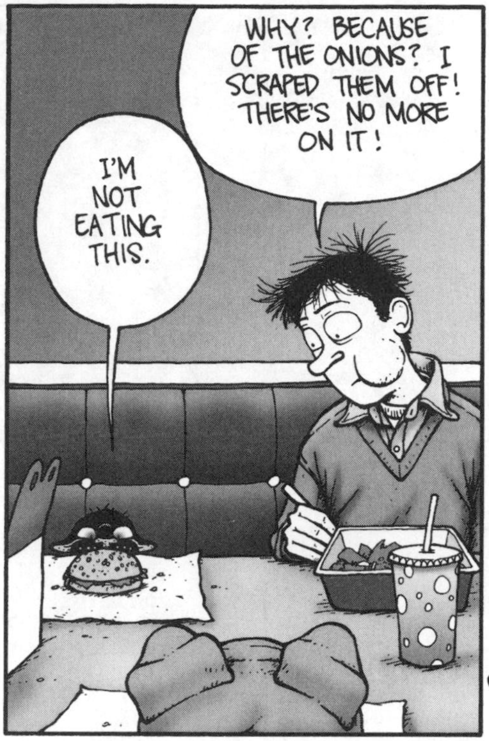
I'M NOT EATING THIS.
WHY? BECAUSE OF THE ONIONS? I SCRAPED THEM OFF! THERE'S NO MORE ON IT!

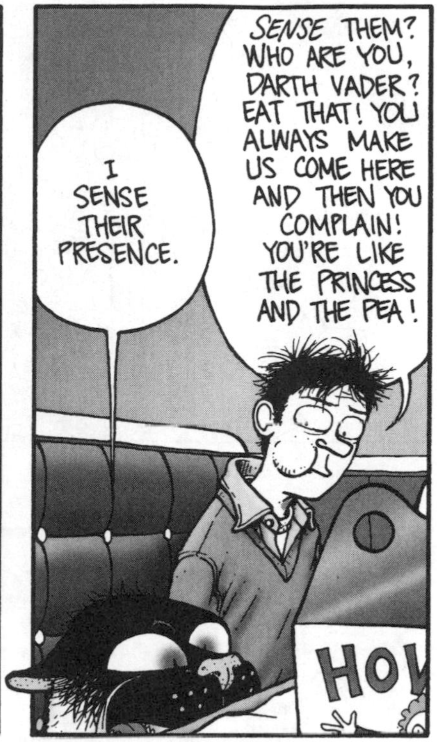
I SENSE THEIR PRESENCE.
SENSE THEM? WHO ARE YOU, DARTH VADER? EAT THAT! YOU ALWAYS MAKE US COME HERE AND THEN YOU COMPLAIN! YOU'RE LIKE THE PRINCESS AND THE PEA!
HOW

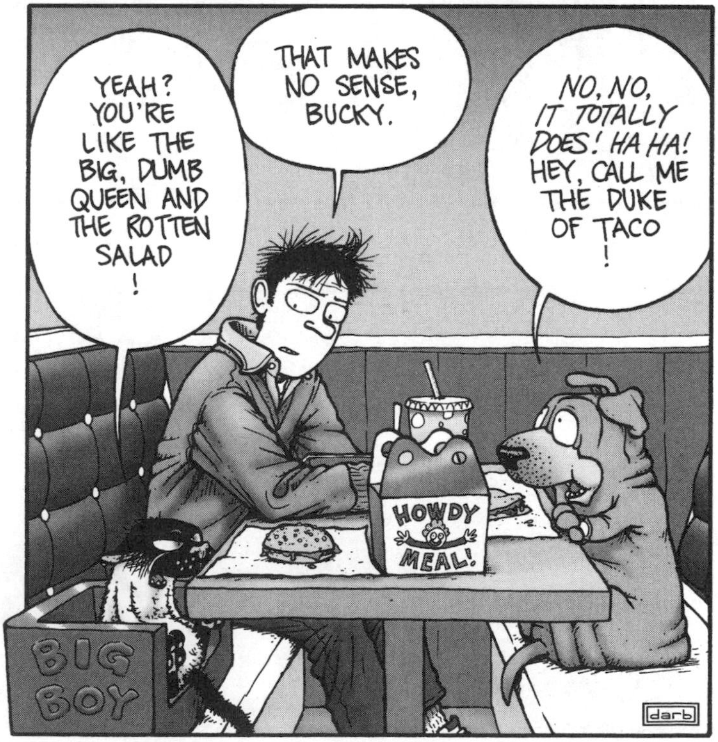
YEAH? YOU'RE LIKE THE BIG, DUMB QUEEN AND THE ROTTEN SALAD!
THAT MAKES NO SENSE, BUCKY.
NO, NO, IT TOTALLY DOES! HA HA! HEY, CALL ME THE DUKE OF TACO!
HOWDY MEAL!
BIG BOY
darb

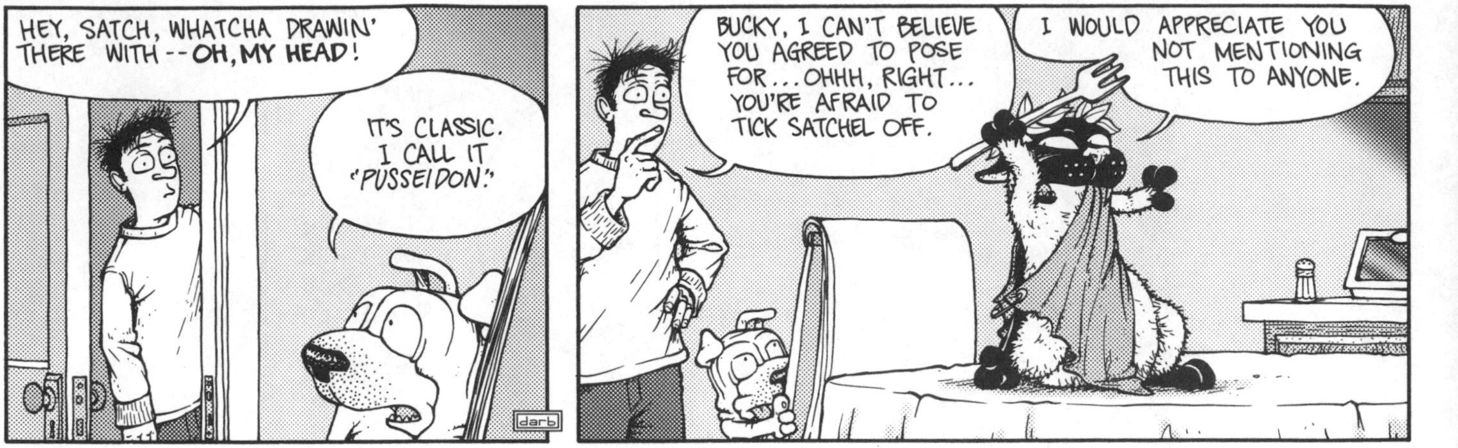
HEY, SATCH, WHATCHA DRAWIN' THERE WITH -- **OH, MY HEAD**!
IT'S CLASSIC. I CALL IT "PUSSEIDON."
BUCKY, I CAN'T BELIEVE YOU AGREED TO POSE FOR... OHHH, RIGHT... YOU'RE AFRAID TO TICK SATCHEL OFF.
I WOULD APPRECIATE YOU NOT MENTIONING THIS TO ANYONE.

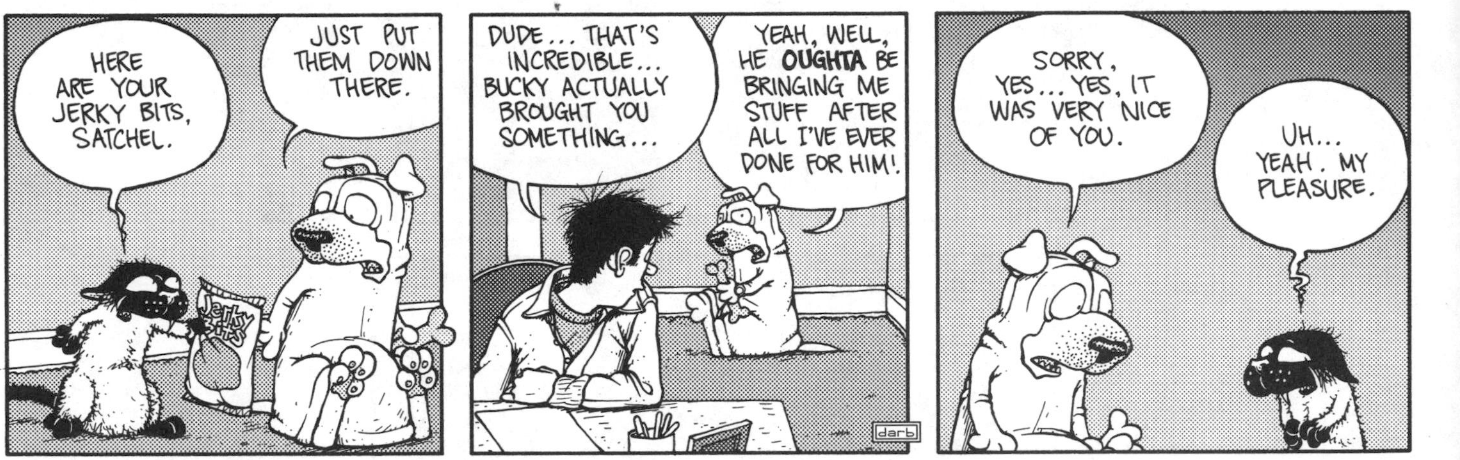
HERE ARE YOUR JERKY BITS, SATCHEL.
JUST PUT THEM DOWN THERE.
JERKY BITS
DUDE... THAT'S INCREDIBLE... BUCKY ACTUALLY BROUGHT YOU SOMETHING...
YEAH, WELL, HE **OUGHTA** BE BRINGING ME STUFF AFTER ALL I'VE EVER DONE FOR HIM!
SORRY, YES... YES, IT WAS VERY NICE OF YOU.
UH... YEAH. MY PLEASURE.

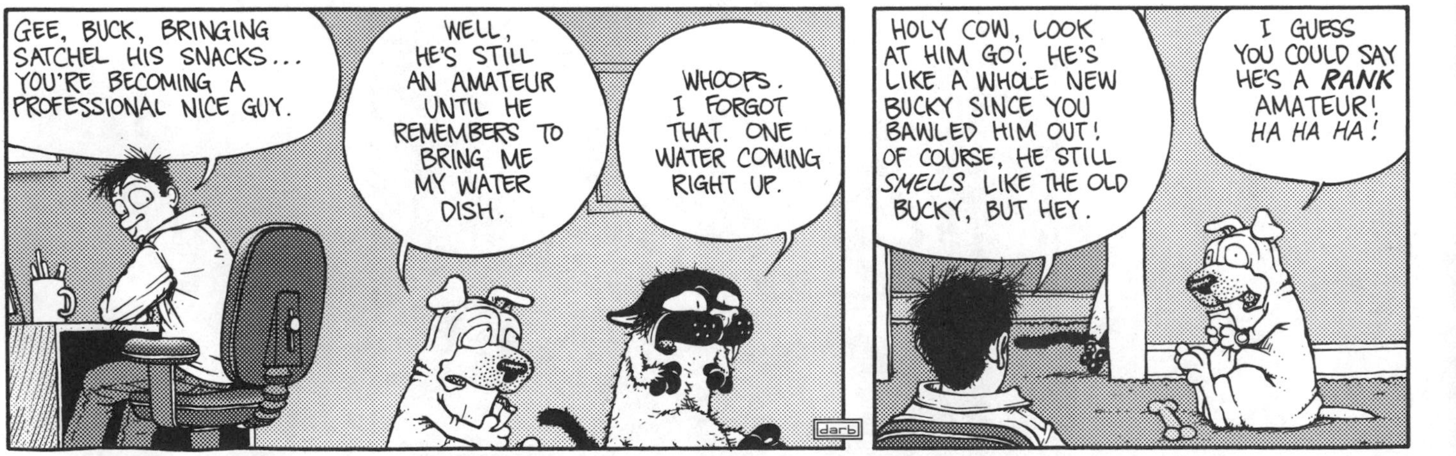
GEE, BUCK, BRINGING SATCHEL HIS SNACKS... YOU'RE BECOMING A PROFESSIONAL NICE GUY.
WELL, HE'S STILL AN AMATEUR UNTIL HE REMEMBERS TO BRING ME MY WATER DISH.
WHOOPS. I FORGOT THAT. ONE WATER COMING RIGHT UP.
HOLY COW, LOOK AT HIM GO! HE'S LIKE A WHOLE NEW BUCKY SINCE YOU BAWLED HIM OUT! OF COURSE, HE STILL *SMELLS* LIKE THE OLD BUCKY, BUT HEY.
I GUESS YOU COULD SAY HE'S A ***RANK*** AMATEUR! *HA HA HA!*

ROB! THERE'S A STRANGE CAT OUT HERE IN THE HALLWAY DEMANDING MONEY!
AW, SATCHEL, THAT'S JUST BUCKY.
NO, NO, I NOT "BUCKY." MY NAME EES *FILIPO.*
MM-HM. AND WHY DO YOU WANT MONEY, FILIPO?
EES NOT FOR ME, EES FOR- HOW YOU SAY- "*BUCKY KATT*"? STREET GANG OF FEELTHY DOGS KEEDNAP HIM. THE LADS ARE DEMANDING A WEE $20 FEE TO RETURN HIM...
MM-HM. MM-HM. YOUR ACCENT IS SWITCHING BETWEEN SPANISH AND SCOTTISH, THERE, FILIPO.
YOU ARE VERY PERCEPTIVE. I HAPPEN TO COME FROM **EXACTLY** BETWEEN THE TWO, MATE.
MM-HM. SEE, NOW IT'S AUSTRALIAN, DUDE.
YOU SPEAK VERY GOOD ENGLISH THOUGH, FILIPO.
ITALIA
EXIT

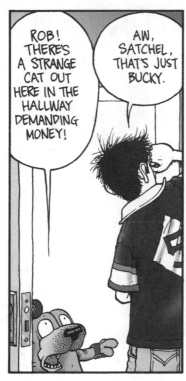

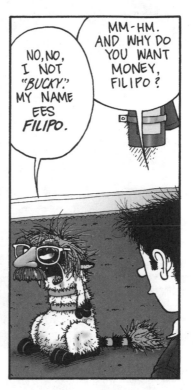

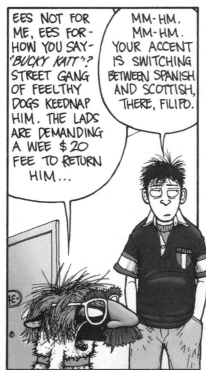

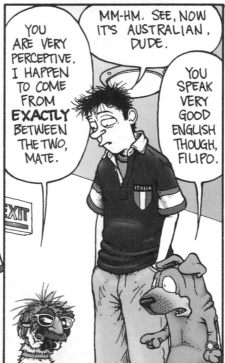

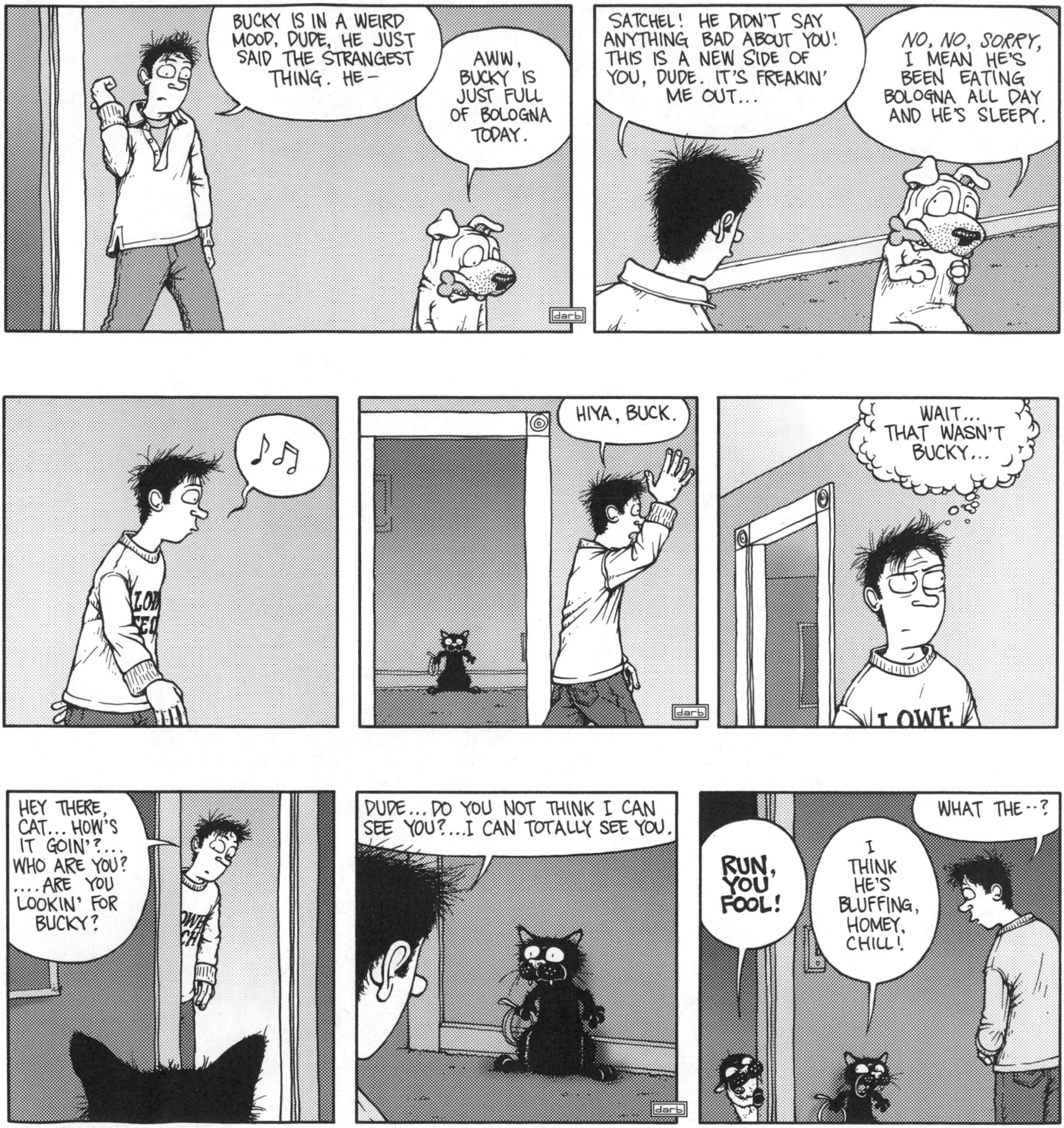
BUCKY IS IN A WEIRD MOOD, DUDE, HE JUST SAID THE STRANGEST THING. HE-
AWW, BUCKY IS JUST FULL OF BOLOGNA TODAY.
darb
SATCHEL! HE DIDN'T SAY ANYTHING BAD ABOUT YOU! THIS IS A NEW SIDE OF YOU, DUDE. IT'S FREAKIN' ME OUT...
NO, NO, SORRY, I MEAN HE'S BEEN EATING BOLOGNA ALL DAY AND HE'S SLEEPY.
HIYA, BUCK.
darb
WAIT... THAT WASN'T BUCKY...
HEY THERE, CAT... HOW'S IT GOIN'?... WHO ARE YOU? ....ARE YOU LOOKIN' FOR BUCKY?
DUDE... DO YOU NOT THINK I CAN SEE YOU?...I CAN TOTALLY SEE YOU.
darb
WHAT THE--?
RUN, YOU FOOL!
I THINK HE'S BLUFFING, HOMEY, CHILL!

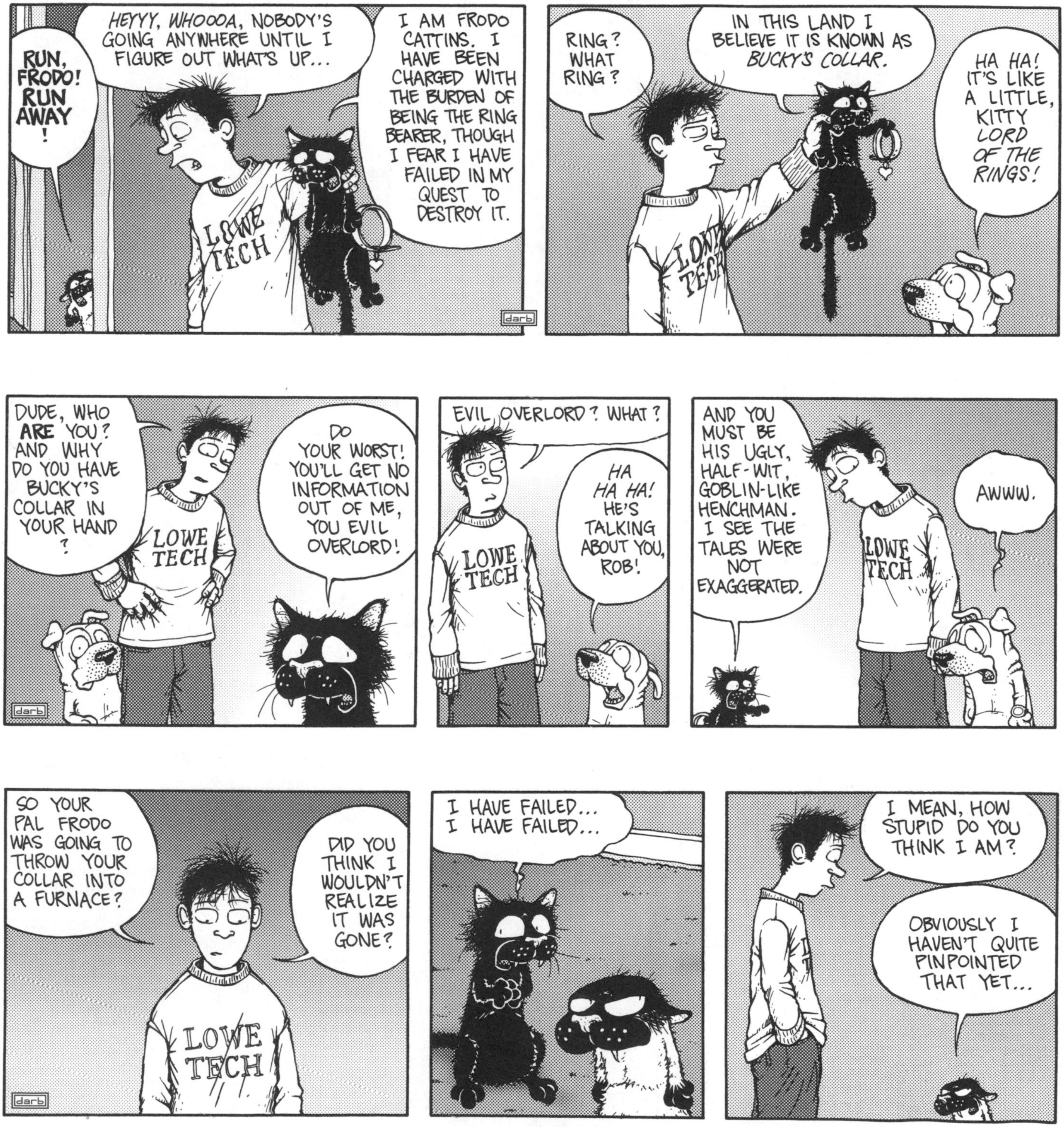
RUN, FRODO! RUN AWAY!
HEYYY, WHOOOA, NOBODY'S GOING ANYWHERE UNTIL I FIGURE OUT WHAT'S UP...
I AM FRODO CATTINS. I HAVE BEEN CHARGED WITH THE BURDEN OF BEING THE RING BEARER, THOUGH I FEAR I HAVE FAILED IN MY QUEST TO DESTROY IT.
LOWE TECH
darb
RING? WHAT RING?
IN THIS LAND I BELIEVE IT IS KNOWN AS BUCKY'S COLLAR.
HA HA! IT'S LIKE A LITTLE, KITTY LORD OF THE RINGS!
LOWE TECH
DUDE, WHO ARE YOU? AND WHY DO YOU HAVE BUCKY'S COLLAR IN YOUR HAND?
DO YOUR WORST! YOU'LL GET NO INFORMATION OUT OF ME, YOU EVIL OVERLORD!
LOWE TECH
darb
EVIL OVERLORD? WHAT?
HA HA HA! HE'S TALKING ABOUT YOU, ROB!
LOWE TECH
AND YOU MUST BE HIS UGLY, HALF-WIT, GOBLIN-LIKE HENCHMAN. I SEE THE TALES WERE NOT EXAGGERATED.
AWWW.
LOWE TECH
SO YOUR PAL FRODO WAS GOING TO THROW YOUR COLLAR INTO A FURNACE?
DID YOU THINK I WOULDN'T REALIZE IT WAS GONE?
LOWE TECH
darb
I HAVE FAILED... I HAVE FAILED...
I MEAN, HOW STUPID DO YOU THINK I AM?
OBVIOUSLY I HAVEN'T QUITE PINPOINTED THAT YET...

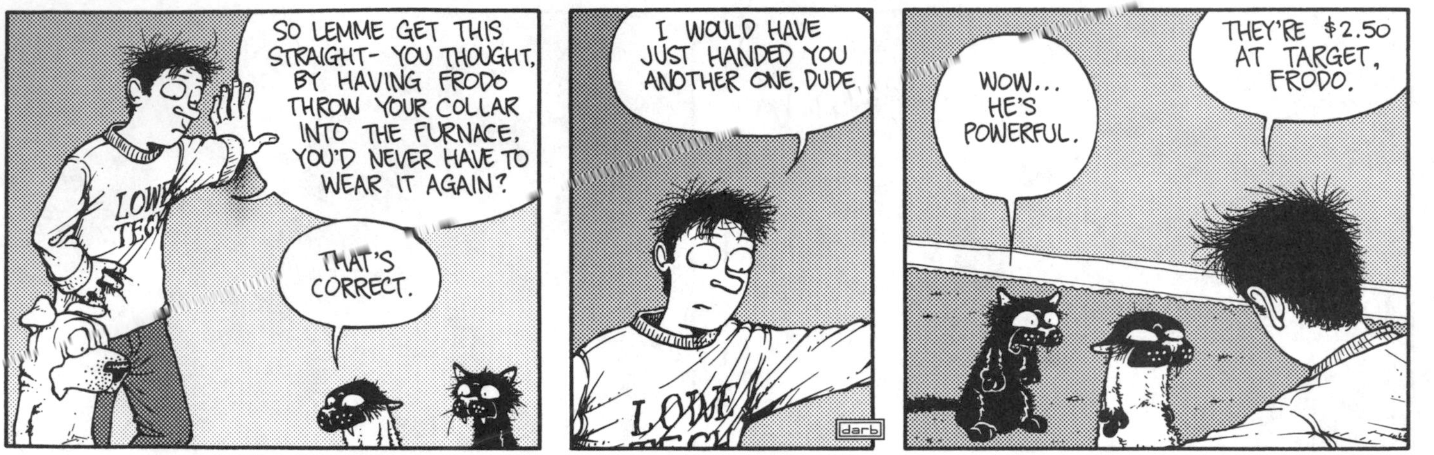
SO LEMME GET THIS STRAIGHT- YOU THOUGHT, BY HAVING FRODO THROW YOUR COLLAR INTO THE FURNACE, YOU'D NEVER HAVE TO WEAR IT AGAIN?
THAT'S CORRECT.
I WOULD HAVE JUST HANDED YOU ANOTHER ONE, DUDE.
WOW... HE'S POWERFUL.
THEY'RE $2.50 AT TARGET, FRODO.
LOWE TECH
darb

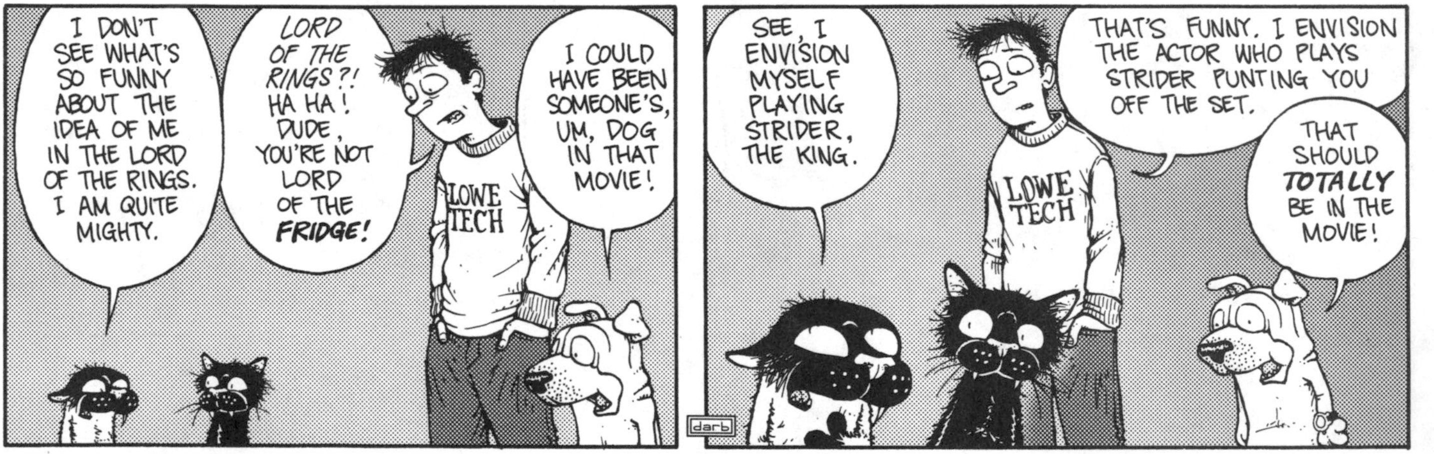
I DON'T SEE WHAT'S SO FUNNY ABOUT THE IDEA OF ME IN THE LORD OF THE RINGS. I AM QUITE MIGHTY.
LORD OF THE RINGS?! HA HA! DUDE, YOU'RE NOT LORD OF THE ***FRIDGE!***
I COULD HAVE BEEN SOMEONE'S, UM, DOG IN THAT MOVIE!
SEE, I ENVISION MYSELF PLAYING STRIDER, THE KING.
THAT'S FUNNY. I ENVISION THE ACTOR WHO PLAYS STRIDER PUNTING YOU OFF THE SET.
THAT SHOULD ***TOTALLY*** BE IN THE MOVIE!
LOWE TECH
darb

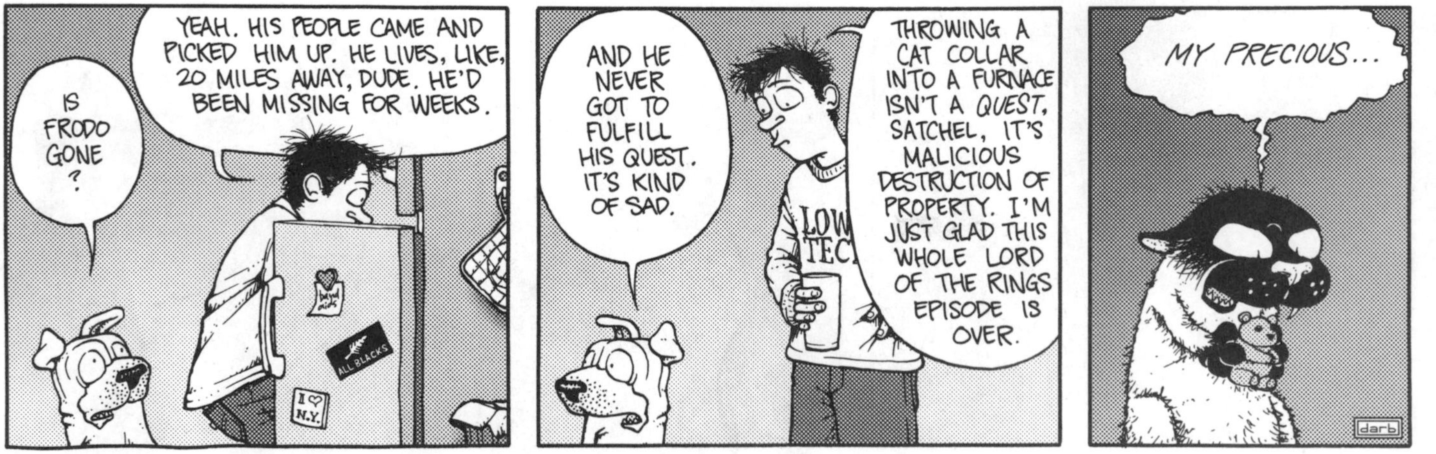
IS FRODO GONE?
YEAH. HIS PEOPLE CAME AND PICKED HIM UP. HE LIVES, LIKE, 20 MILES AWAY, DUDE. HE'D BEEN MISSING FOR WEEKS.
ALL BLACKS
I ♥ N.Y.
AND HE NEVER GOT TO FULFILL HIS QUEST. IT'S KIND OF SAD.
THROWING A CAT COLLAR INTO A FURNACE ISN'T A *QUEST*, SATCHEL, IT'S MALICIOUS DESTRUCTION OF PROPERTY. I'M JUST GLAD THIS WHOLE LORD OF THE RINGS EPISODE IS OVER.
MY PRECIOUS...
darb

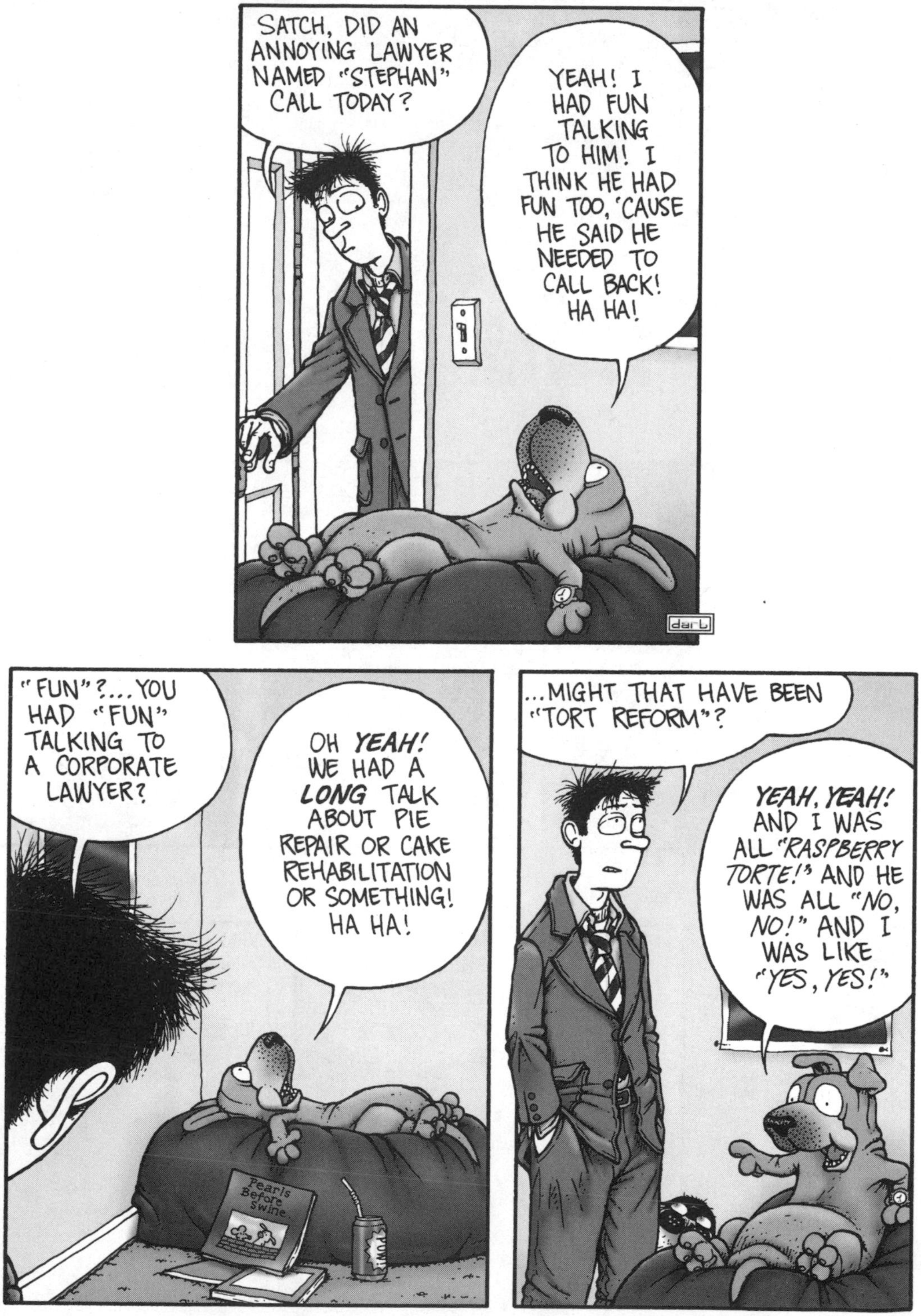
SATCH, DID AN ANNOYING LAWYER NAMED "STEPHAN" CALL TODAY?
YEAH! I HAD FUN TALKING TO HIM! I THINK HE HAD FUN TOO, 'CAUSE HE SAID HE NEEDED TO CALL BACK! HA HA!
darb
"FUN"?... YOU HAD "FUN" TALKING TO A CORPORATE LAWYER?
OH *YEAH!* WE HAD A ***LONG*** TALK ABOUT PIE REPAIR OR CAKE REHABILITATION OR SOMETHING! HA HA!
Pearls Before Swine
...MIGHT THAT HAVE BEEN "TORT REFORM"?
YEAH, YEAH! AND I WAS ALL "*RASPBERRY TORTE!*" AND HE WAS ALL "*NO, NO!*" AND I WAS LIKE "*YES, YES!*"

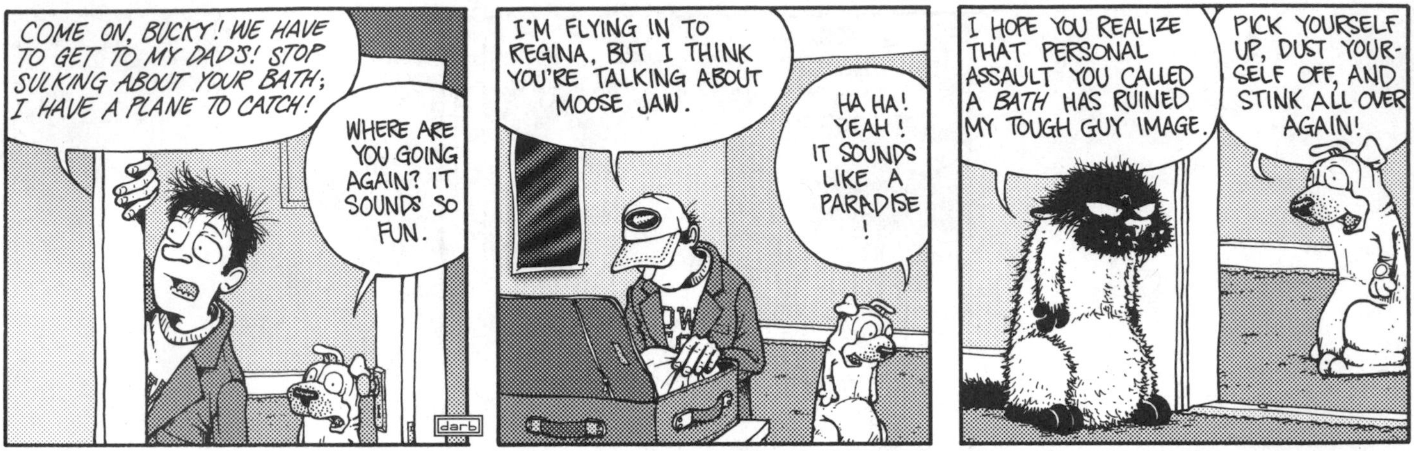
COME ON, BUCKY! WE HAVE TO GET TO MY DAD'S! STOP SULKING ABOUT YOUR BATH; I HAVE A PLANE TO CATCH!
WHERE ARE YOU GOING AGAIN? IT SOUNDS SO FUN.
I'M FLYING IN TO REGINA, BUT I THINK YOU'RE TALKING ABOUT MOOSE JAW.
HA HA! YEAH! IT SOUNDS LIKE A PARADISE!
I HOPE YOU REALIZE THAT PERSONAL ASSAULT YOU CALLED A BATH HAS RUINED MY TOUGH GUY IMAGE.
PICK YOURSELF UP, DUST YOURSELF OFF, AND STINK ALL OVER AGAIN!
darb

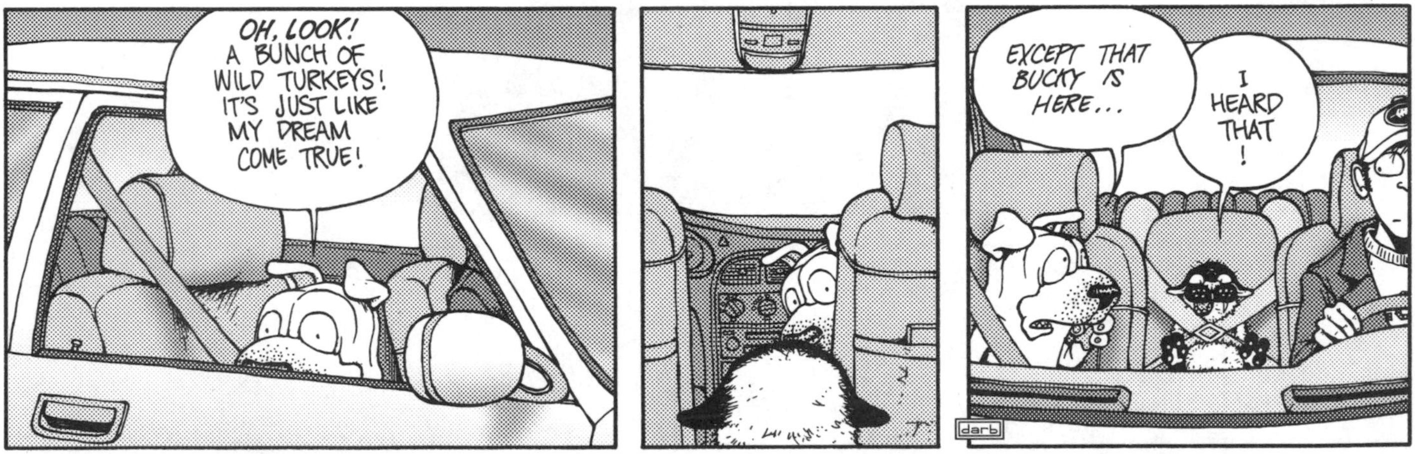
OH, LOOK! A BUNCH OF WILD TURKEYS! IT'S JUST LIKE MY DREAM COME TRUE!
EXCEPT THAT BUCKY IS HERE...
I HEARD THAT!
darb

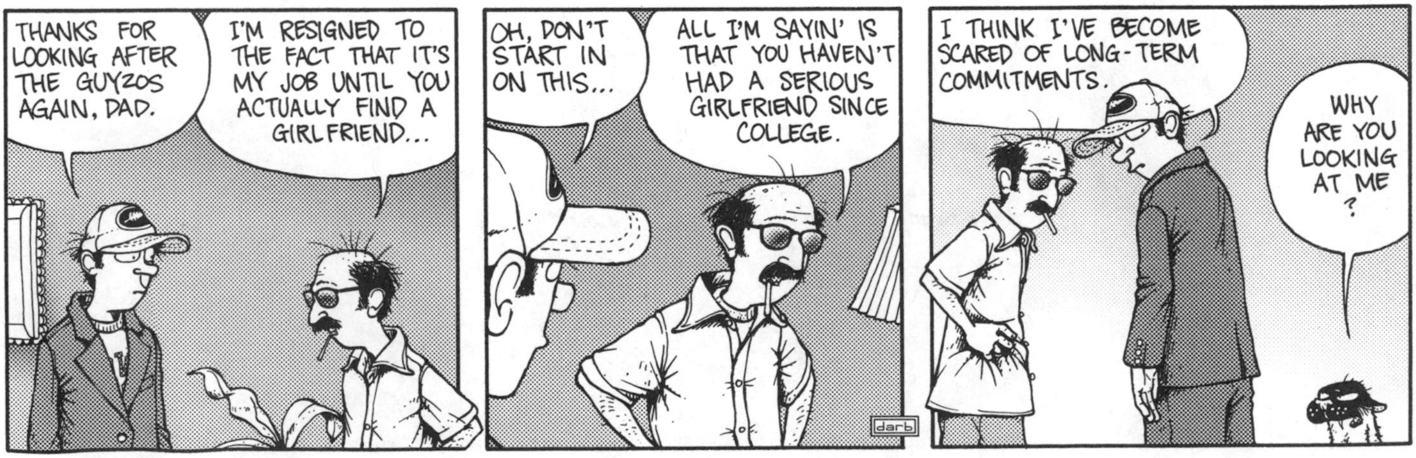
THANKS FOR LOOKING AFTER THE GUYZOS AGAIN, DAD.
I'M RESIGNED TO THE FACT THAT IT'S MY JOB UNTIL YOU ACTUALLY FIND A GIRLFRIEND...
OH, DON'T START IN ON THIS...
ALL I'M SAYIN' IS THAT YOU HAVEN'T HAD A SERIOUS GIRLFRIEND SINCE COLLEGE.
darb
I THINK I'VE BECOME SCARED OF LONG-TERM COMMITMENTS.
WHY ARE YOU LOOKING AT ME?

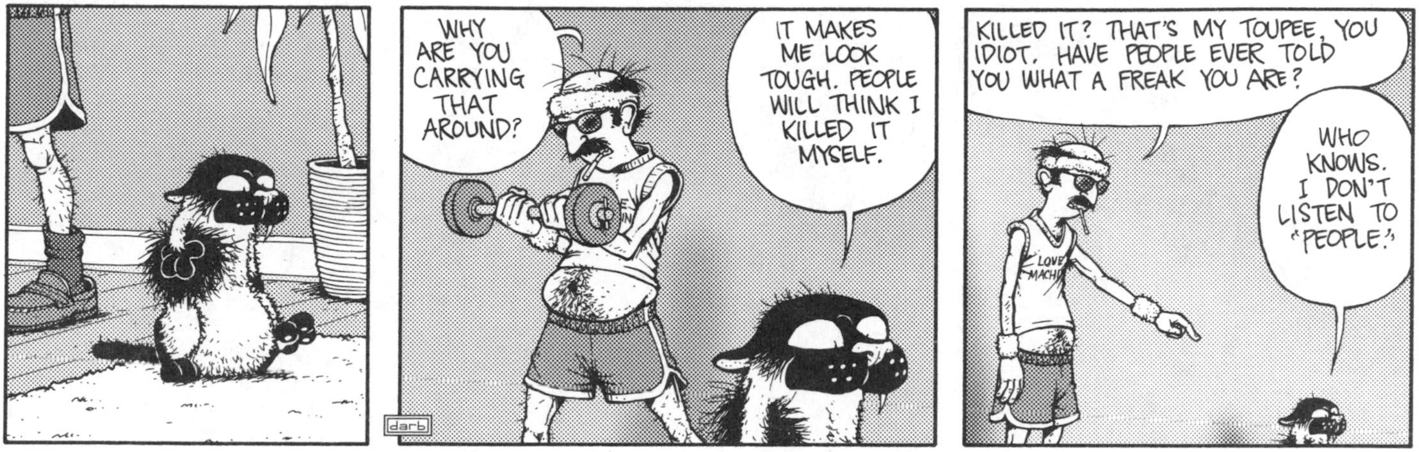
WHY ARE YOU CARRYING THAT AROUND?
IT MAKES ME LOOK TOUGH. PEOPLE WILL THINK I KILLED IT MYSELF.
darb
KILLED IT? THAT'S MY TOUPEE, YOU IDIOT. HAVE PEOPLE EVER TOLD YOU WHAT A FREAK YOU ARE?
WHO KNOWS. I DON'T LISTEN TO "PEOPLE."

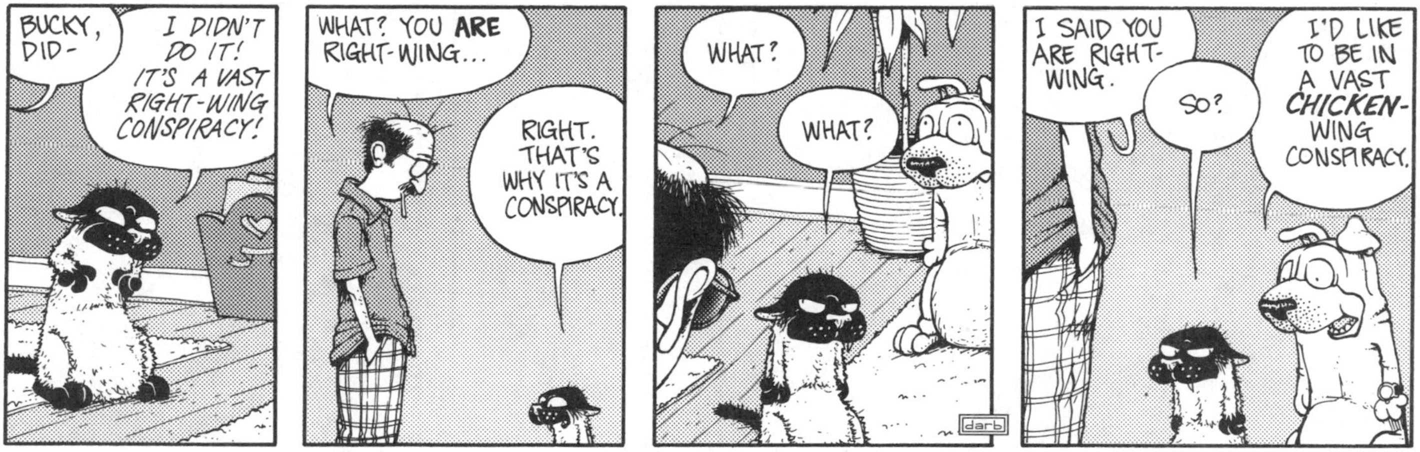
BUCKY, DID-
I DIDN'T DO IT! IT'S A VAST RIGHT-WING CONSPIRACY!
WHAT? YOU **ARE** RIGHT-WING...
RIGHT. THAT'S WHY IT'S A CONSPIRACY.
WHAT?
WHAT?
darb
I SAID YOU ARE RIGHT-WING.
SO?
I'D LIKE TO BE IN A VAST **CHICKEN-**WING CONSPIRACY.

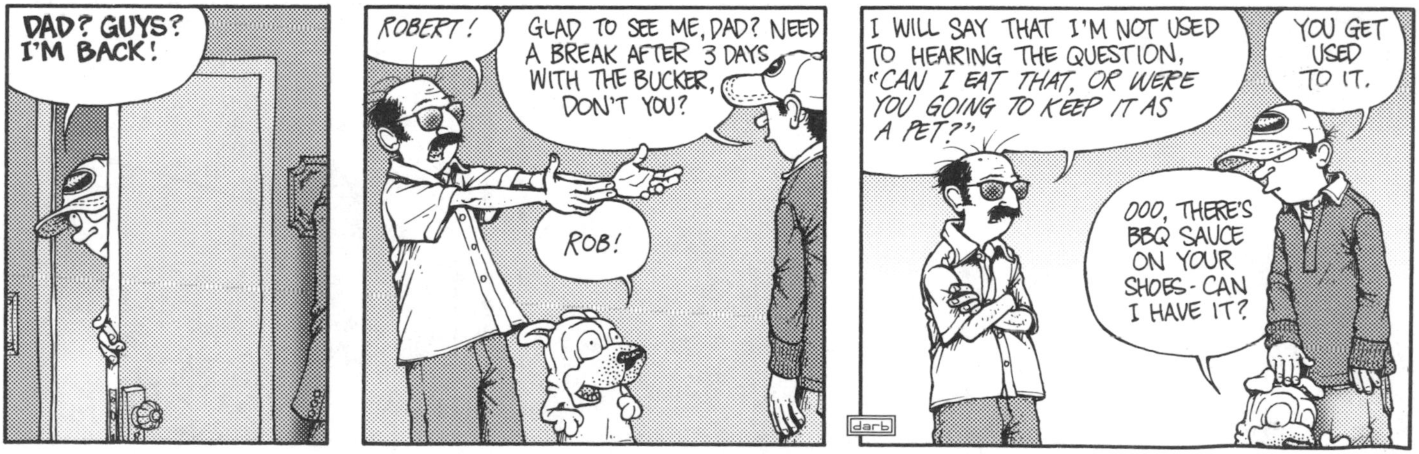
DAD? GUYS? I'M BACK!
ROBERT!
GLAD TO SEE ME, DAD? NEED A BREAK AFTER 3 DAYS WITH THE BUCKER, DON'T YOU?
ROB!
darb
I WILL SAY THAT I'M NOT USED TO HEARING THE QUESTION, "CAN I EAT THAT, OR WERE YOU GOING TO KEEP IT AS A PET?"
YOU GET USED TO IT.
OOO, THERE'S BBQ SAUCE ON YOUR SHOES- CAN I HAVE IT?

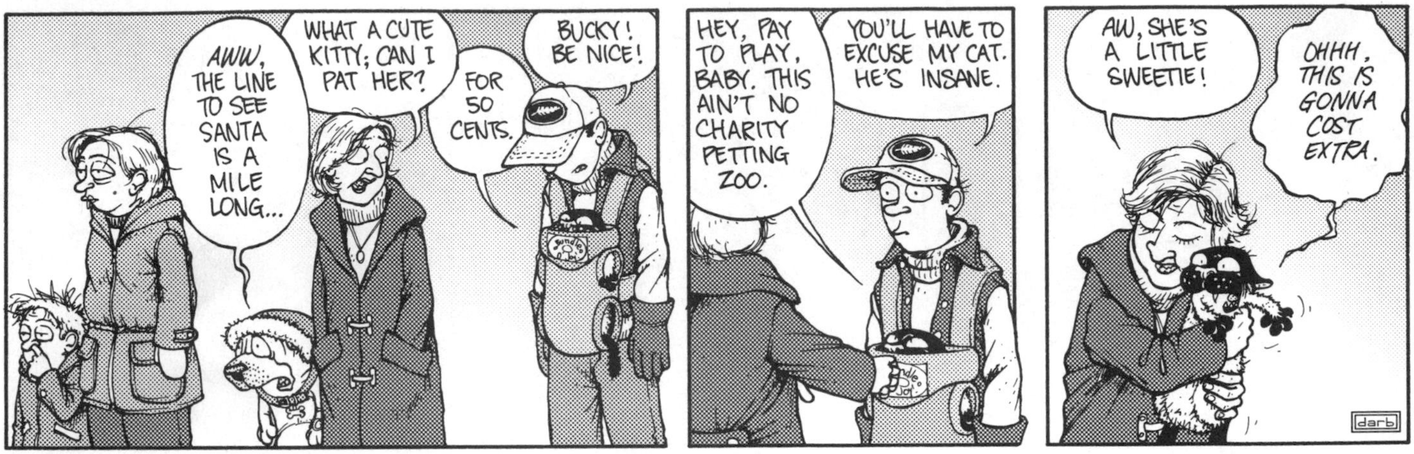
AWW, THE LINE TO SEE SANTA IS A MILE LONG...
WHAT A CUTE KITTY; CAN I PAT HER?
FOR 50 CENTS.
BUCKY! BE NICE!
HEY, PAY TO PLAY, BABY. THIS AIN'T NO CHARITY PETTING ZOO.
YOU'LL HAVE TO EXCUSE MY CAT. HE'S INSANE.
AW, SHE'S A LITTLE SWEETIE!
OHHH, THIS IS GONNA COST EXTRA.
darb

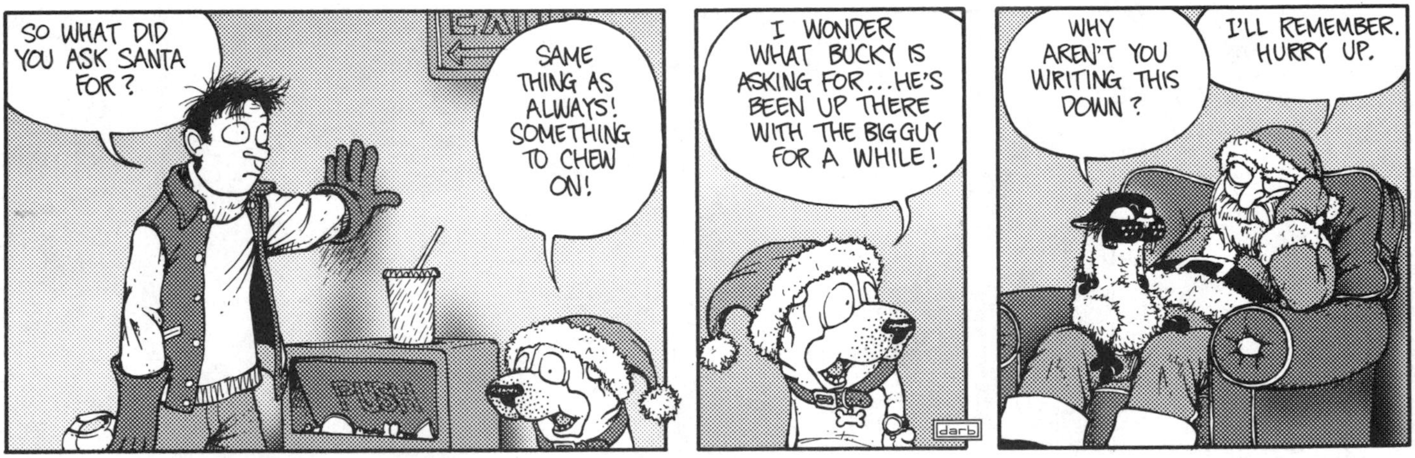
SO WHAT DID YOU ASK SANTA FOR?
SAME THING AS ALWAYS! SOMETHING TO CHEW ON!
I WONDER WHAT BUCKY IS ASKING FOR...HE'S BEEN UP THERE WITH THE BIG GUY FOR A WHILE!
darb
WHY AREN'T YOU WRITING THIS DOWN?
I'LL REMEMBER. HURRY UP.

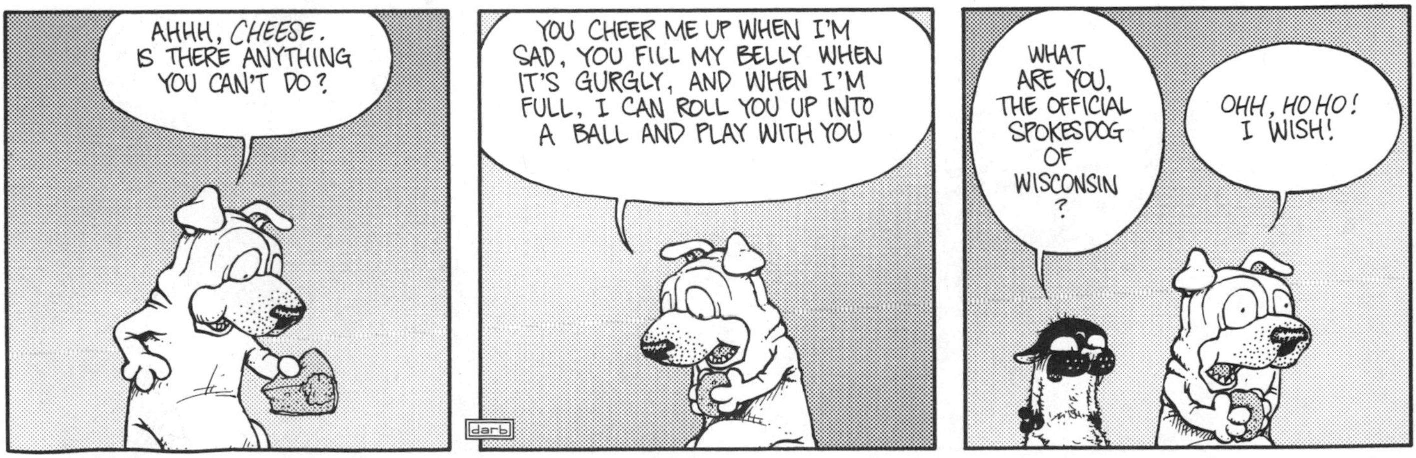
AHHH, CHEESE. IS THERE ANYTHING YOU CAN'T DO?
darb
YOU CHEER ME UP WHEN I'M SAD, YOU FILL MY BELLY WHEN IT'S GURGLY, AND WHEN I'M FULL, I CAN ROLL YOU UP INTO A BALL AND PLAY WITH YOU
WHAT ARE YOU, THE OFFICIAL SPOKESDOG OF WISCONSIN?
OHH, HO HO! I WISH!

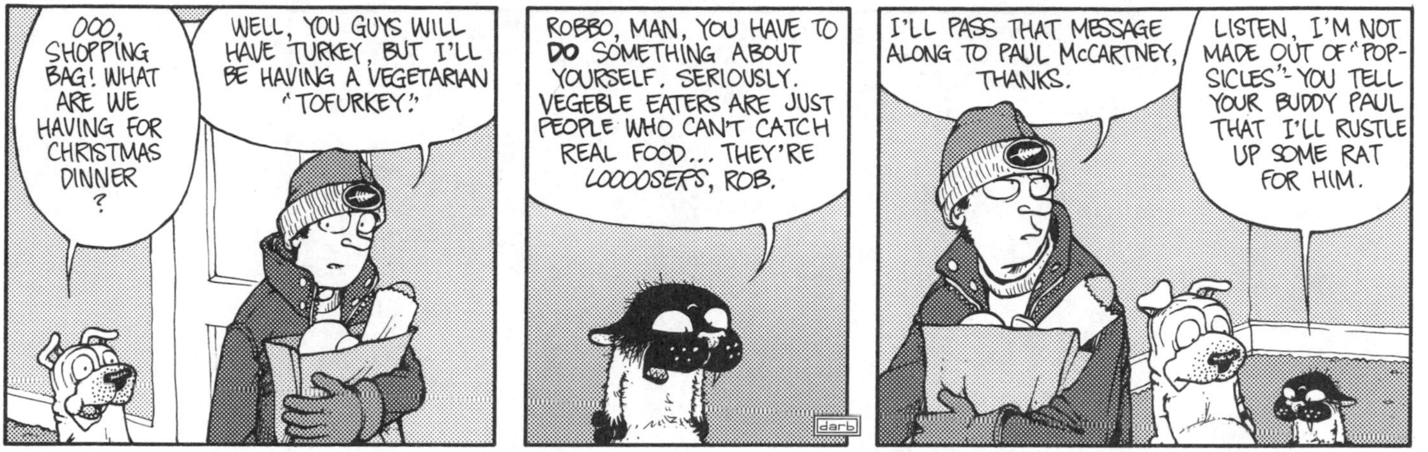
OOO, SHOPPING BAG! WHAT ARE WE HAVING FOR CHRISTMAS DINNER ?
WELL, YOU GUYS WILL HAVE TURKEY, BUT I'LL BE HAVING A VEGETARIAN "TOFURKEY."
ROBBO, MAN, YOU HAVE TO DO SOMETHING ABOUT YOURSELF. SERIOUSLY. VEGEBLE EATERS ARE JUST PEOPLE WHO CAN'T CATCH REAL FOOD... THEY'RE LOOOOSERS, ROB.
I'LL PASS THAT MESSAGE ALONG TO PAUL McCARTNEY, THANKS.
LISTEN, I'M NOT MADE OUT OF "POP-SICLES"- YOU TELL YOUR BUDDY PAUL THAT I'LL RUSTLE UP SOME RAT FOR HIM.

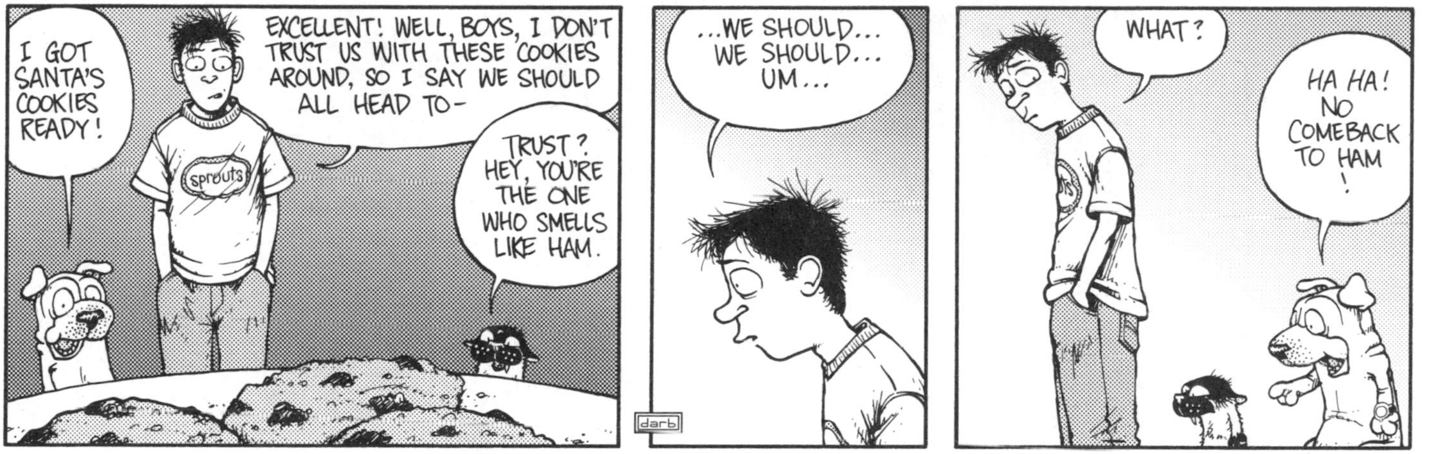
I GOT SANTA'S COOKIES READY!
EXCELLENT! WELL, BOYS, I DON'T TRUST US WITH THESE COOKIES AROUND, SO I SAY WE SHOULD ALL HEAD TO-
TRUST? HEY, YOU'RE THE ONE WHO SMELLS LIKE HAM.
...WE SHOULD... WE SHOULD... UM...
WHAT?
HA HA! NO COMEBACK TO HAM !

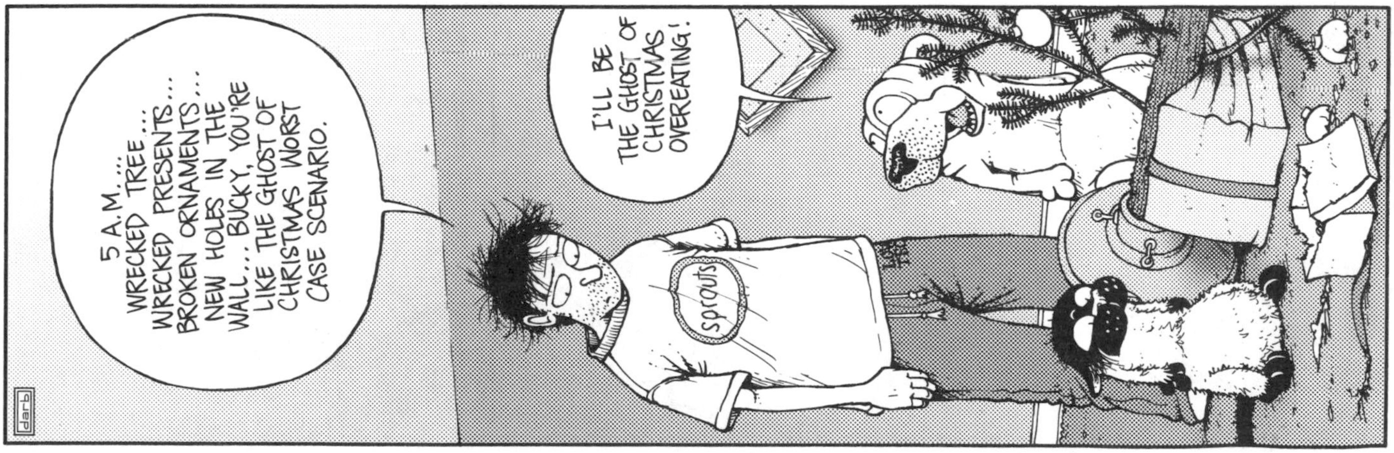
5 A.M.... WRECKED TREE... WRECKED PRESENTS... BROKEN ORNAMENTS... NEW HOLES IN THE WALL... BUCKY, YOU'RE LIKE THE GHOST OF CHRISTMAS WORST CASE SCENARIO.
I'LL BE THE GHOST OF CHRISTMAS OVEREATING!

DUDE, WHAT ARE YOU EATING? I GAVE YOU THAT $10 TO BUY SATCHEL'S CHRISTMAS PRESENT, NOT SOME CAT SNACK.

HIS WHAT? OH, YEAH. NO SWEAT. I GOT HIS, UM, THING.

I DON'T THINK YOU EVEN REMEMBER WHAT YOU WERE SUPPOSED TO GET HIM... HOW **BIG** WAS THIS "THING" YOU GOT HIM?

OH, YOU KNOW HOW BIG THOSE THINGS ARE...LIKE YAY BIG.

MM-HM. SO... WHAT COLOR WAS IT?

UHH... IT WAS MONKEY.

"MONKEY" IS NOT A COLOR, BU—

ALRIGHT, ALRIGHT! I DIDN'T GET IT!

darb

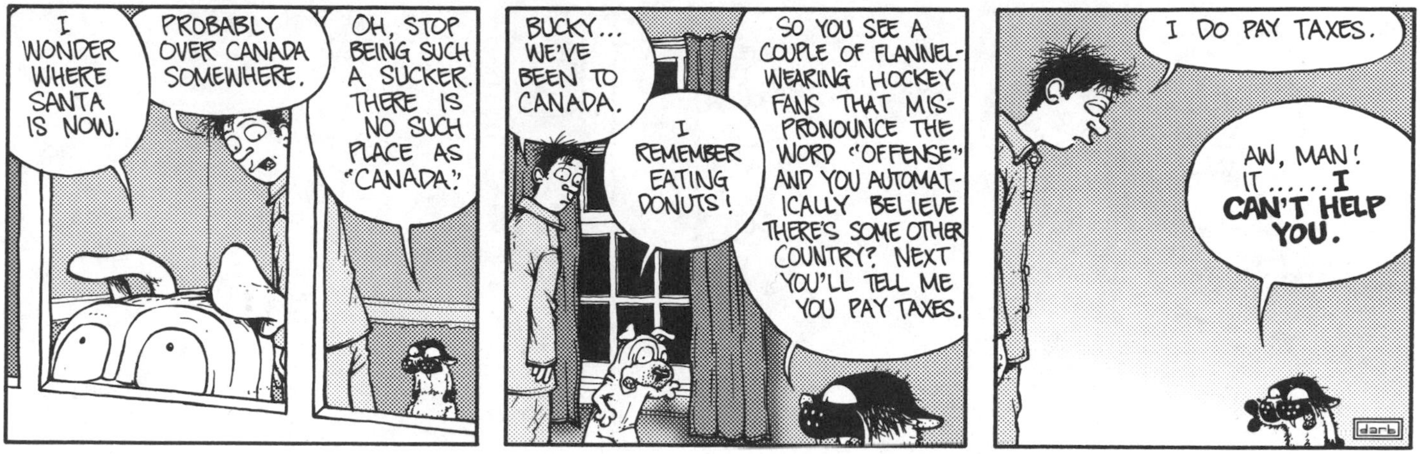
I WONDER WHERE SANTA IS NOW.
PROBABLY OVER CANADA SOMEWHERE.
OH, STOP BEING SUCH A SUCKER. THERE IS NO SUCH PLACE AS "CANADA."
BUCKY... WE'VE BEEN TO CANADA.
I REMEMBER EATING DONUTS!
SO YOU SEE A COUPLE OF FLANNEL-WEARING HOCKEY FANS THAT MIS-PRONOUNCE THE WORD "OFFENSE" AND YOU AUTOMAT-ICALLY BELIEVE THERE'S SOME OTHER COUNTRY? NEXT YOU'LL TELL ME YOU PAY TAXES.
I DO PAY TAXES.
AW, MAN! IT......I CAN'T HELP YOU.
darb

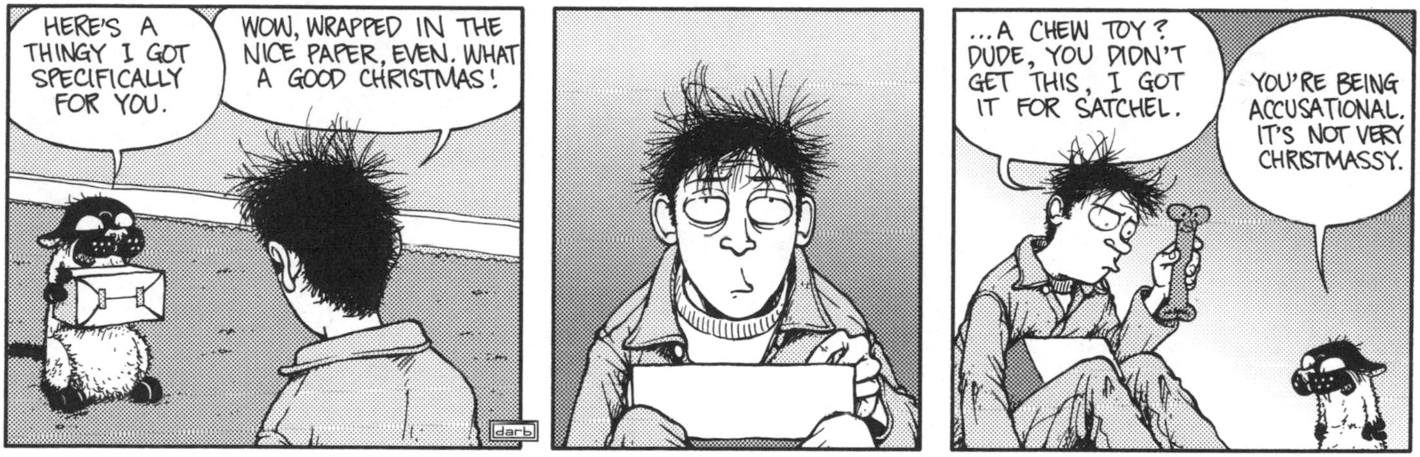
HERE'S A THINGY I GOT SPECIFICALLY FOR YOU.
WOW, WRAPPED IN THE NICE PAPER, EVEN. WHAT A GOOD CHRISTMAS!
darb
...A CHEW TOY? DUDE, YOU DIDN'T GET THIS, I GOT IT FOR SATCHEL.
YOU'RE BEING ACCUSATIONAL. IT'S NOT VERY CHRISTMASSY.

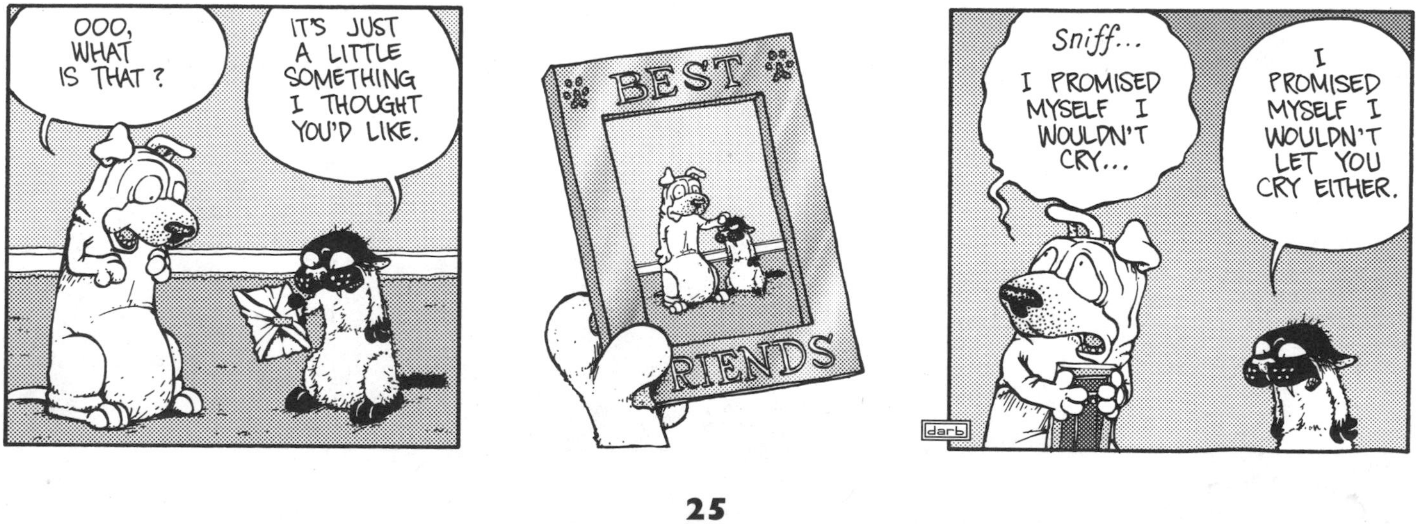
OOO, WHAT IS THAT?
IT'S JUST A LITTLE SOMETHING I THOUGHT YOU'D LIKE.
BEST FRIENDS
Sniff...
I PROMISED MYSELF I WOULDN'T CRY...
I PROMISED MYSELF I WOULDN'T LET YOU CRY EITHER.
darb

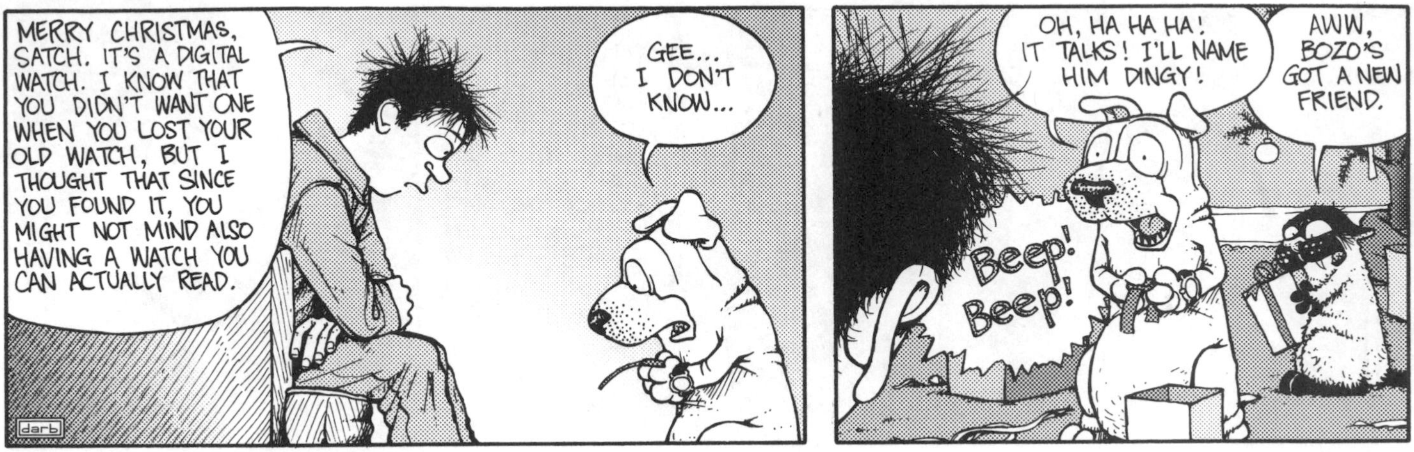
MERRY CHRISTMAS, SATCH. IT'S A DIGITAL WATCH. I KNOW THAT YOU DIDN'T WANT ONE WHEN YOU LOST YOUR OLD WATCH, BUT I THOUGHT THAT SINCE YOU FOUND IT, YOU MIGHT NOT MIND ALSO HAVING A WATCH YOU CAN ACTUALLY READ.
GEE... I DON'T KNOW...
OH, HA HA HA! IT TALKS! I'LL NAME HIM DINGY!
Beep! Beep!
AWW, BOZO'S GOT A NEW FRIEND.

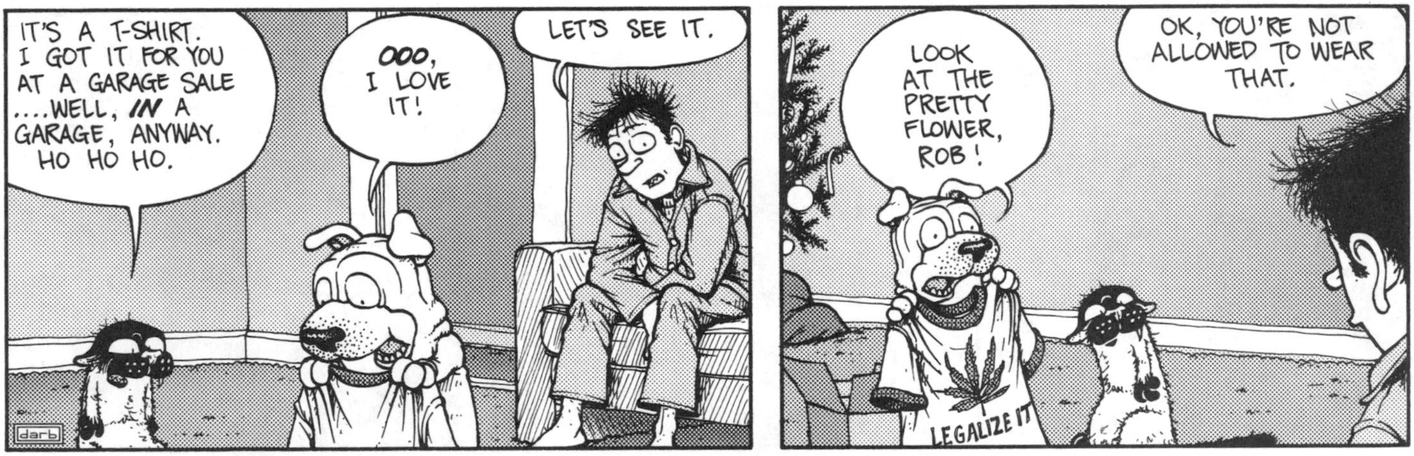
IT'S A T-SHIRT. I GOT IT FOR YOU AT A GARAGE SALE ....WELL, IN A GARAGE, ANYWAY. HO HO HO.
OOO, I LOVE IT!
LET'S SEE IT.
LOOK AT THE PRETTY FLOWER, ROB!
OK, YOU'RE NOT ALLOWED TO WEAR THAT.
LEGALIZE IT

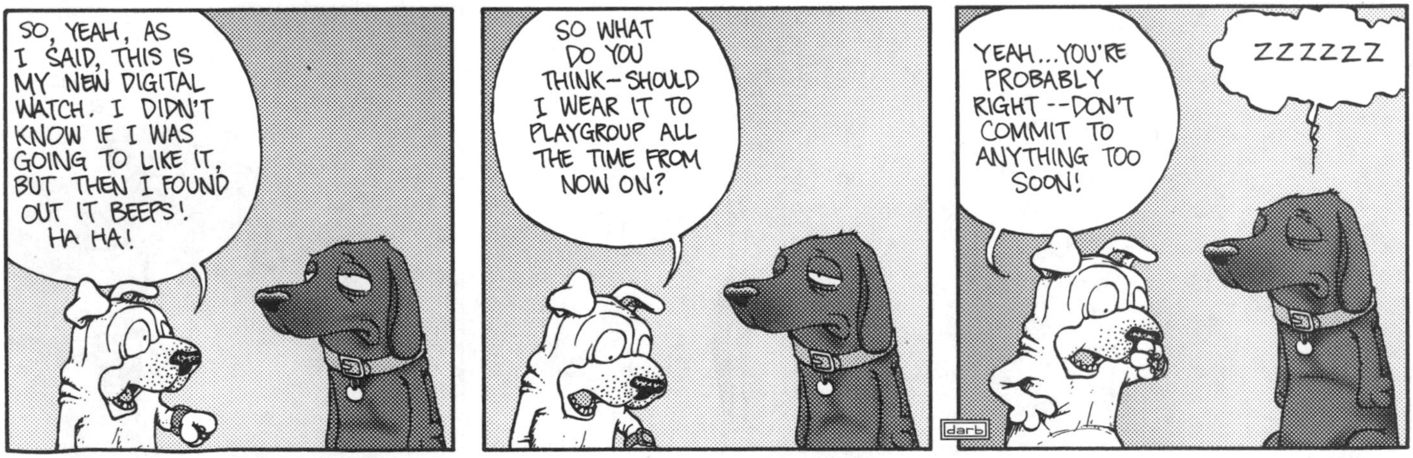
SO, YEAH, AS I SAID, THIS IS MY NEW DIGITAL WATCH. I DIDN'T KNOW IF I WAS GOING TO LIKE IT, BUT THEN I FOUND OUT IT BEEPS! HA HA!
SO WHAT DO YOU THINK—SHOULD I WEAR IT TO PLAYGROUP ALL THE TIME FROM NOW ON?
YEAH...YOU'RE PROBABLY RIGHT--DON'T COMMIT TO ANYTHING TOO SOON!
ZZZZZZ

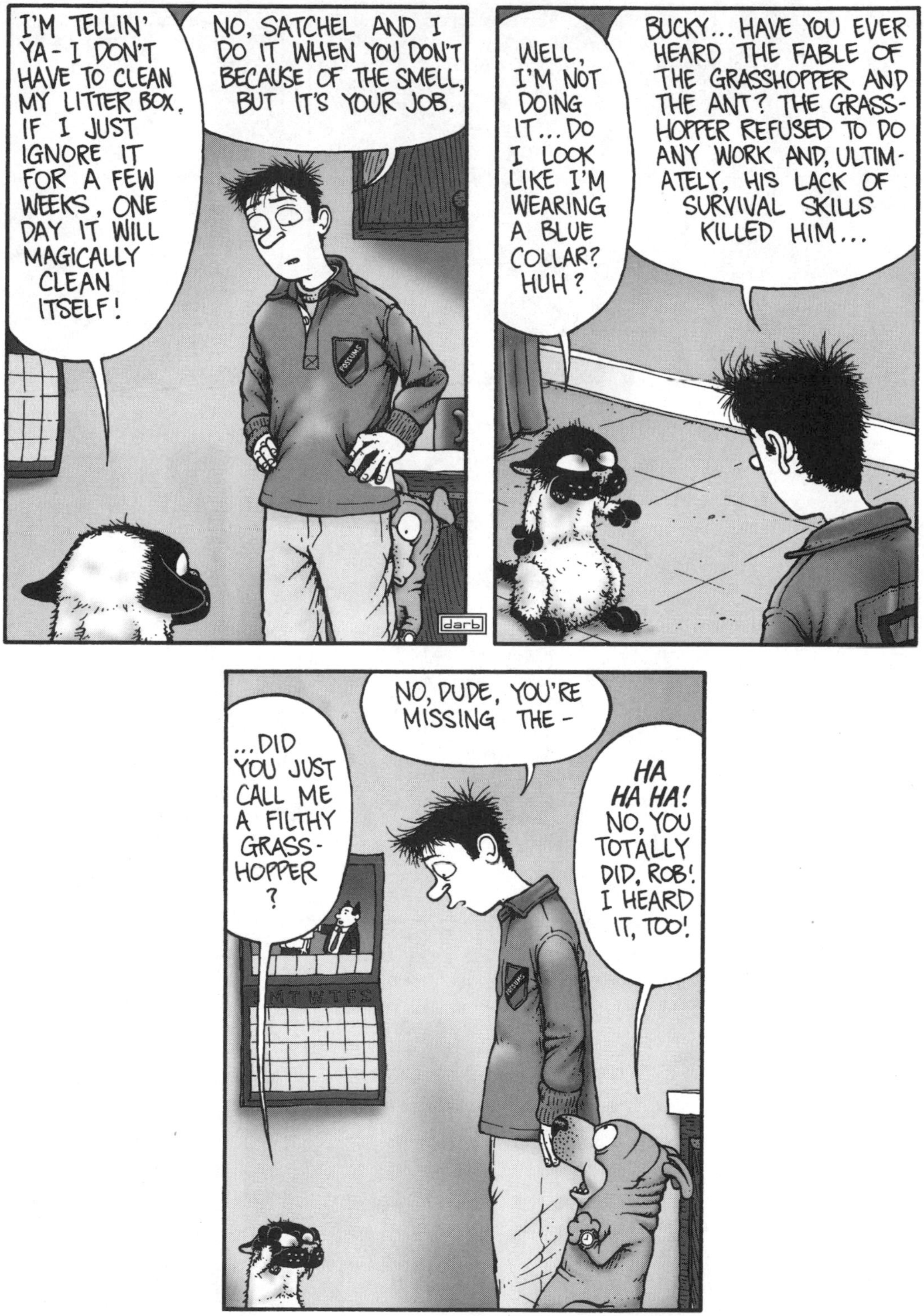
I'M TELLIN' YA- I DON'T HAVE TO CLEAN MY LITTER BOX. IF I JUST IGNORE IT FOR A FEW WEEKS, ONE DAY IT WILL MAGICALLY CLEAN ITSELF!
NO, SATCHEL AND I DO IT WHEN YOU DON'T BECAUSE OF THE SMELL, BUT IT'S YOUR JOB.
POSSUMS
darb
WELL, I'M NOT DOING IT... DO I LOOK LIKE I'M WEARING A BLUE COLLAR? HUH?
BUCKY... HAVE YOU EVER HEARD THE FABLE OF THE GRASSHOPPER AND THE ANT? THE GRASS-HOPPER REFUSED TO DO ANY WORK AND, ULTIM-ATELY, HIS LACK OF SURVIVAL SKILLS KILLED HIM...
NO, DUDE, YOU'RE MISSING THE-
...DID YOU JUST CALL ME A FILTHY GRASS-HOPPER?
HA HA HA! NO, YOU TOTALLY DID, ROB! I HEARD IT, TOO!
POSSUMS

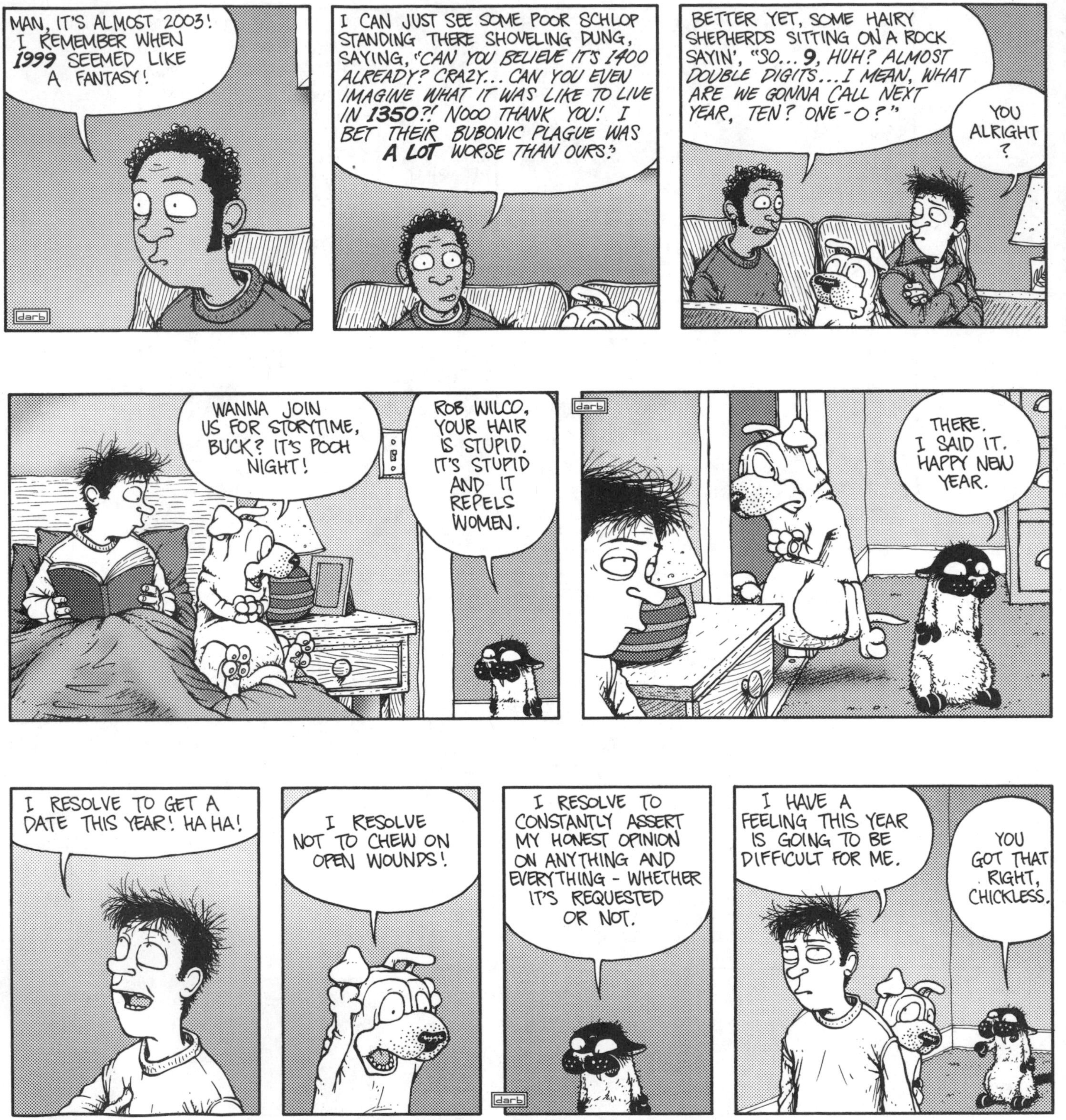
MAN, IT'S ALMOST 2003! I REMEMBER WHEN 1999 SEEMED LIKE A FANTASY!
I CAN JUST SEE SOME POOR SCHLOP STANDING THERE SHOVELING DUNG, SAYING, "CAN YOU BELIEVE IT'S 1400 ALREADY? CRAZY... CAN YOU EVEN IMAGINE WHAT IT WAS LIKE TO LIVE IN 1350?! NOOO THANK YOU! I BET THEIR BUBONIC PLAGUE WAS A LOT WORSE THAN OURS."
BETTER YET, SOME HAIRY SHEPHERDS SITTING ON A ROCK SAYIN', "SO... 9, HUH? ALMOST DOUBLE DIGITS... I MEAN, WHAT ARE WE GONNA CALL NEXT YEAR, TEN? ONE-O?"
YOU ALRIGHT?
WANNA JOIN US FOR STORYTIME, BUCK? IT'S POOH NIGHT!
ROB WILCO, YOUR HAIR IS STUPID. IT'S STUPID AND IT REPELS WOMEN.
THERE. I SAID IT. HAPPY NEW YEAR.
I RESOLVE TO GET A DATE THIS YEAR! HA HA!
I RESOLVE NOT TO CHEW ON OPEN WOUNDS!
I RESOLVE TO CONSTANTLY ASSERT MY HONEST OPINION ON ANYTHING AND EVERYTHING - WHETHER IT'S REQUESTED OR NOT.
I HAVE A FEELING THIS YEAR IS GOING TO BE DIFFICULT FOR ME.
YOU GOT THAT RIGHT, CHICKLESS.
darb

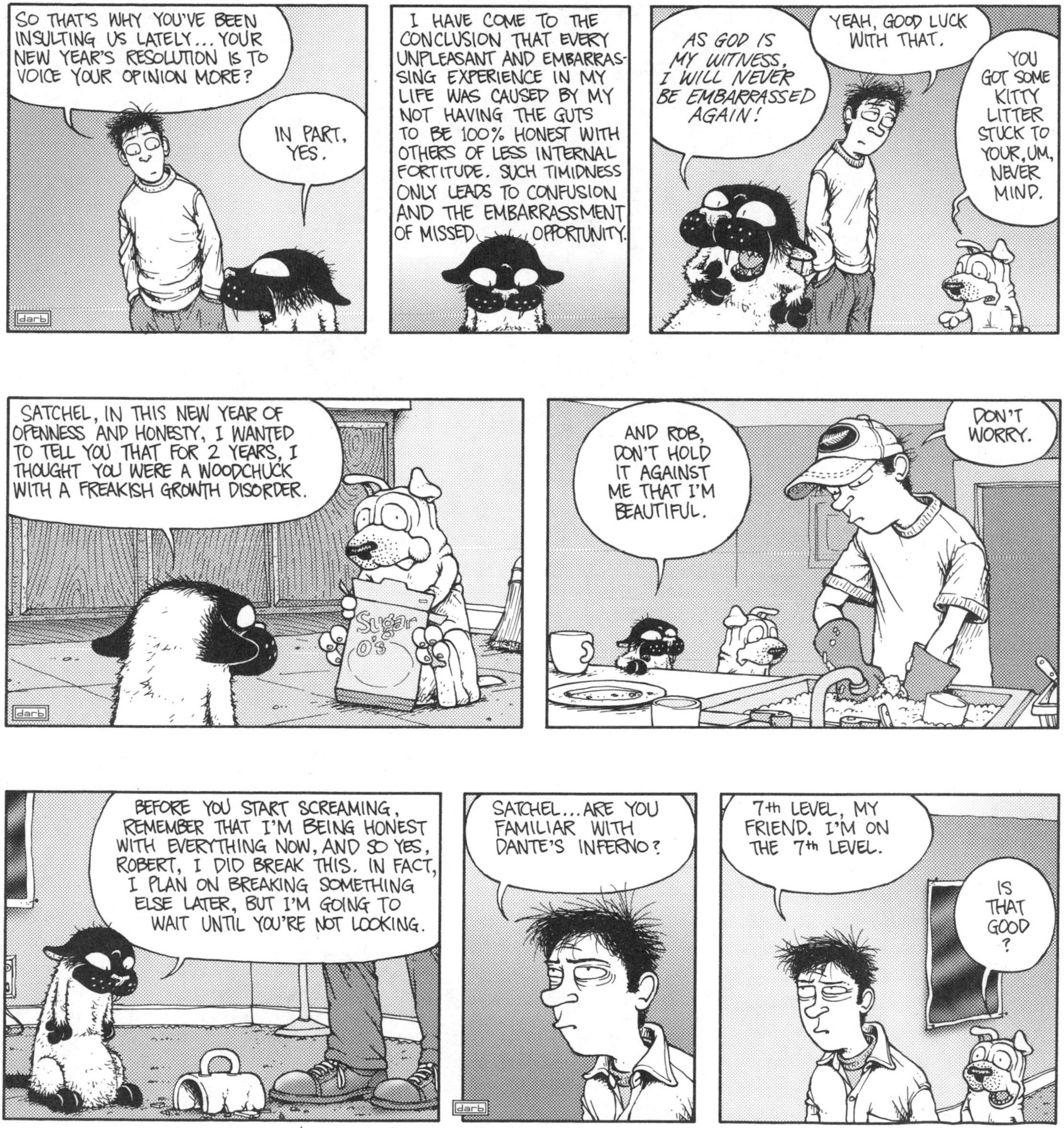
SO THAT'S WHY YOU'VE BEEN INSULTING US LATELY... YOUR NEW YEAR'S RESOLUTION IS TO VOICE YOUR OPINION MORE?
IN PART, YES.
I HAVE COME TO THE CONCLUSION THAT EVERY UNPLEASANT AND EMBARRASSING EXPERIENCE IN MY LIFE WAS CAUSED BY MY NOT HAVING THE GUTS TO BE 100% HONEST WITH OTHERS OF LESS INTERNAL FORTITUDE. SUCH TIMIDNESS ONLY LEADS TO CONFUSION AND THE EMBARRASSMENT OF MISSED OPPORTUNITY.
AS GOD IS MY WITNESS, I WILL NEVER BE EMBARRASSED AGAIN!
YEAH, GOOD LUCK WITH THAT.
YOU GOT SOME KITTY LITTER STUCK TO YOUR, UM, NEVER MIND.
SATCHEL, IN THIS NEW YEAR OF OPENNESS AND HONESTY, I WANTED TO TELL YOU THAT FOR 2 YEARS, I THOUGHT YOU WERE A WOODCHUCK WITH A FREAKISH GROWTH DISORDER.
Sugar O's
AND ROB, DON'T HOLD IT AGAINST ME THAT I'M BEAUTIFUL.
DON'T WORRY.
BEFORE YOU START SCREAMING, REMEMBER THAT I'M BEING HONEST WITH EVERYTHING NOW, AND SO YES, ROBERT, I DID BREAK THIS. IN FACT, I PLAN ON BREAKING SOMETHING ELSE LATER, BUT I'M GOING TO WAIT UNTIL YOU'RE NOT LOOKING.
SATCHEL... ARE YOU FAMILIAR WITH DANTE'S INFERNO?
7th LEVEL, MY FRIEND. I'M ON THE 7th LEVEL.
IS THAT GOOD?

WHOA, THERE YOU ARE. WHERE HAVE YOU BEEN?
I SNUCK IN TO THE FÜD SHØPPE LOOKING FOR SQUID HEADS BUT I WAS RAVAGED BY LOVE-STRUCK DAMES WANTING A PIECE OF BUCKY MAGIC.
DID... DID YOU JUST SAY "*DAMES*"?
YOU KNOW- BROADS, SKIRTS. CHICKADEES. THAT JOINT WAS LOUSY WITH 'EM. THEY WERE DRIPPING OFF ME.
darb
"DAMES DRIPPING OFF ME?" WHAT **YEAR** IS THIS?
SOUNDS LIKE THE YEAR OF THE **CAT!** HA HA!
DON'T TOUCH ME.

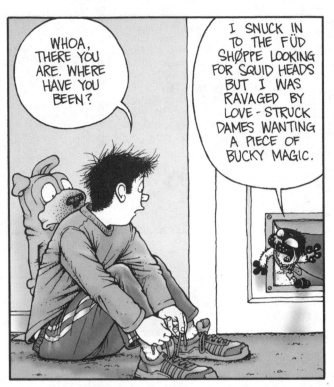

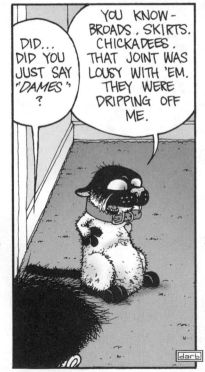

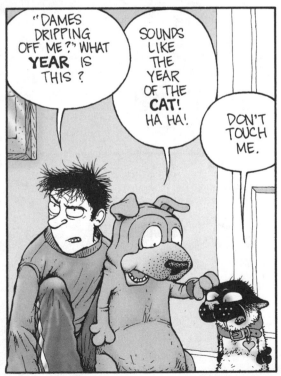

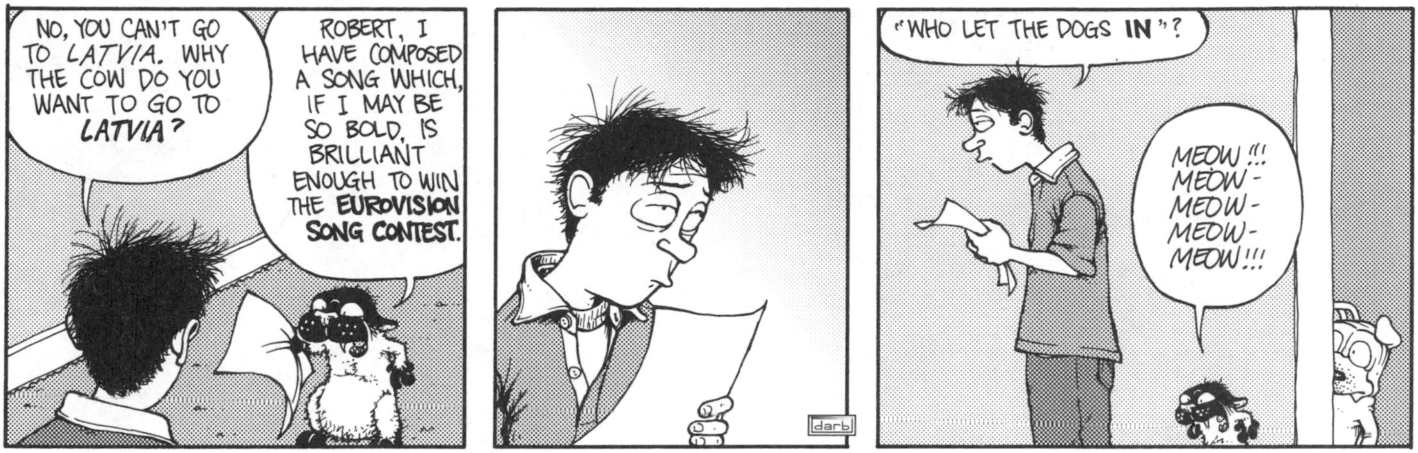
NO, YOU CAN'T GO TO LATVIA. WHY THE COW DO YOU WANT TO GO TO LATVIA?
ROBERT, I HAVE COMPOSED A SONG WHICH, IF I MAY BE SO BOLD, IS BRILLIANT ENOUGH TO WIN THE EUROVISION SONG CONTEST.
darb
"WHO LET THE DOGS IN"?
MEOW!!! MEOW-MEOW-MEOW-MEOW!!!

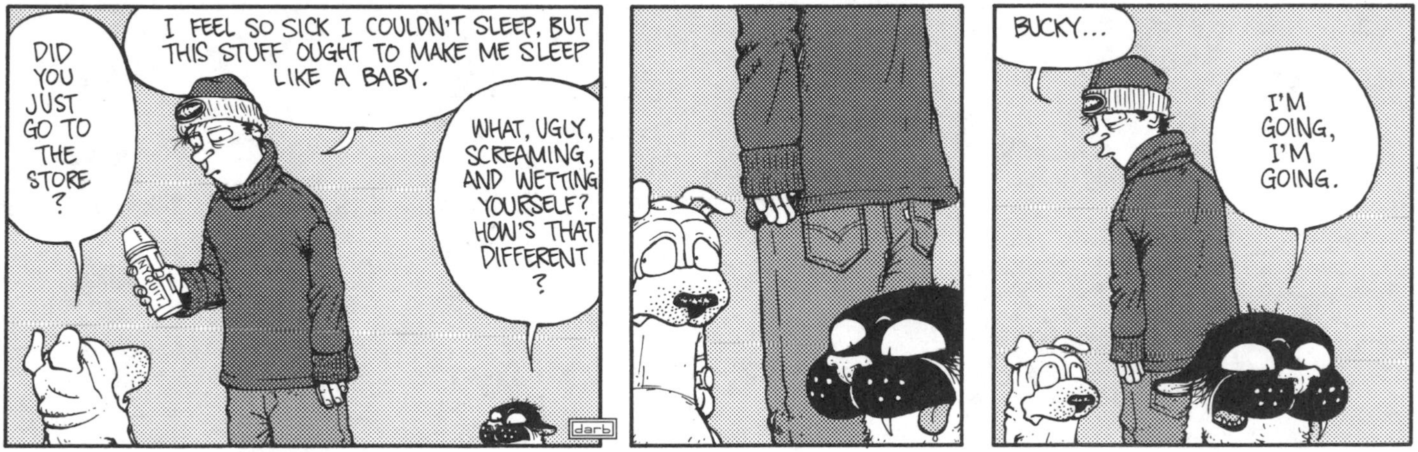
I FEEL SO SICK I COULDN'T SLEEP, BUT THIS STUFF OUGHT TO MAKE ME SLEEP LIKE A BABY.
DID YOU JUST GO TO THE STORE?
WHAT, UGLY, SCREAMING, AND WETTING YOURSELF? HOW'S THAT DIFFERENT?
darb
BUCKY...
I'M GOING, I'M GOING.

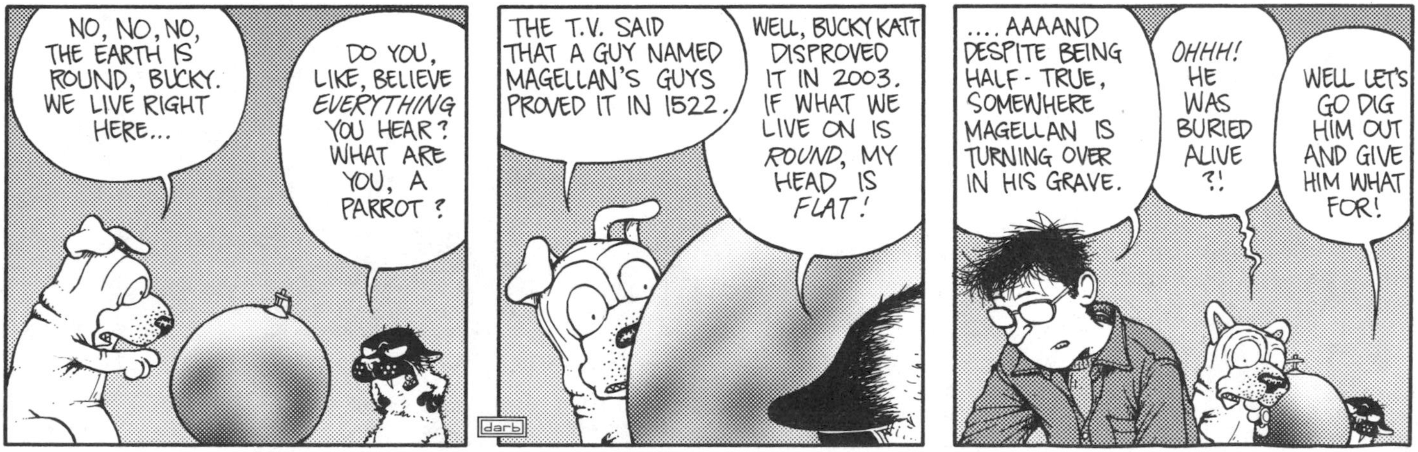
NO, NO, NO, THE EARTH IS ROUND, BUCKY. WE LIVE RIGHT HERE...
DO YOU, LIKE, BELIEVE EVERYTHING YOU HEAR? WHAT ARE YOU, A PARROT?
darb
THE T.V. SAID THAT A GUY NAMED MAGELLAN'S GUYS PROVED IT IN 1522.
WELL, BUCKY KATT DISPROVED IT IN 2003. IF WHAT WE LIVE ON IS ROUND, MY HEAD IS FLAT!
....AAAAND DESPITE BEING HALF-TRUE, SOMEWHERE MAGELLAN IS TURNING OVER IN HIS GRAVE.
OHHH! HE WAS BURIED ALIVE?!
WELL LET'S GO DIG HIM OUT AND GIVE HIM WHAT FOR!

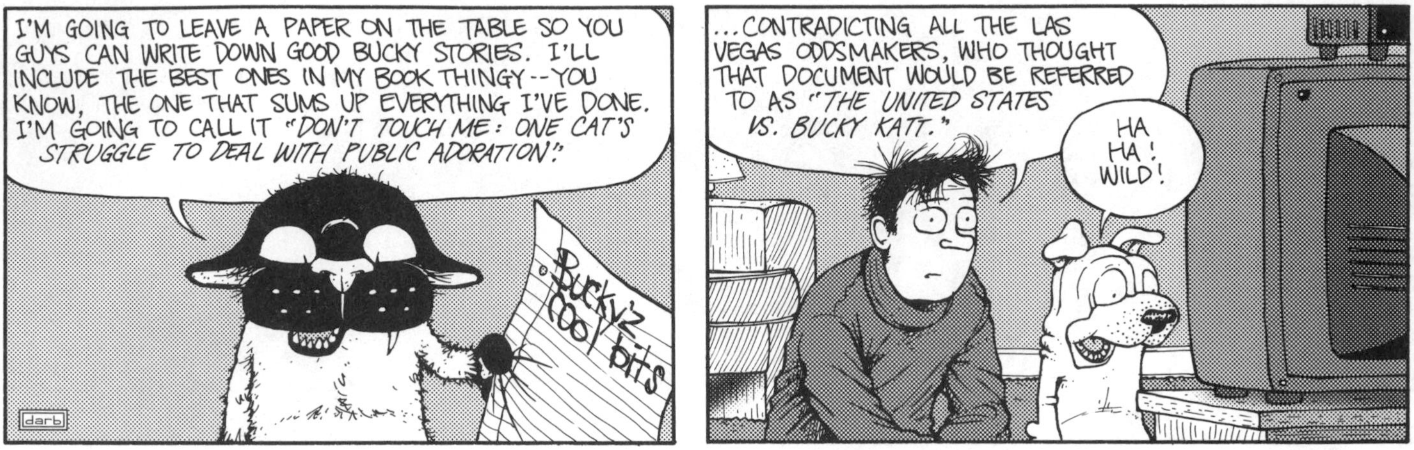
I'M GOING TO LEAVE A PAPER ON THE TABLE SO YOU GUYS CAN WRITE DOWN GOOD BUCKY STORIES. I'LL INCLUDE THE BEST ONES IN MY BOOK THINGY--YOU KNOW, THE ONE THAT SUMS UP EVERYTHING I'VE DONE. I'M GOING TO CALL IT "DON'T TOUCH ME: ONE CAT'S STRUGGLE TO DEAL WITH PUBLIC ADORATION."
Bucky'z Cool bits
darb
...CONTRADICTING ALL THE LAS VEGAS ODDSMAKERS, WHO THOUGHT THAT DOCUMENT WOULD BE REFERRED TO AS "THE UNITED STATES VS. BUCKY KATT."
HA HA! WILD!

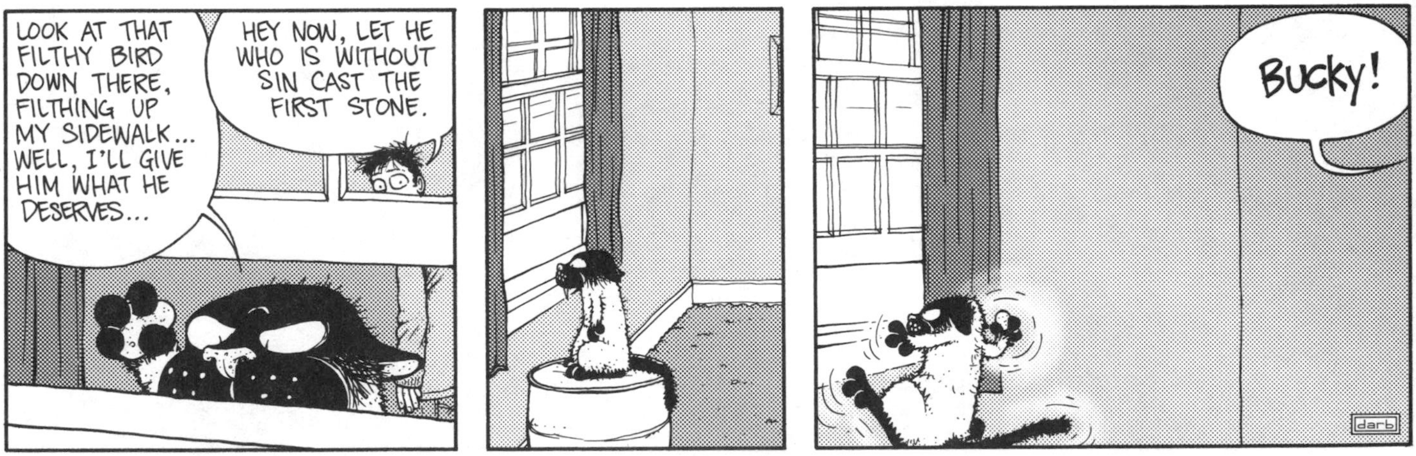
LOOK AT THAT FILTHY BIRD DOWN THERE, FILTHING UP MY SIDEWALK... WELL, I'LL GIVE HIM WHAT HE DESERVES...
HEY NOW, LET HE WHO IS WITHOUT SIN CAST THE FIRST STONE.
BUCKY!
darb

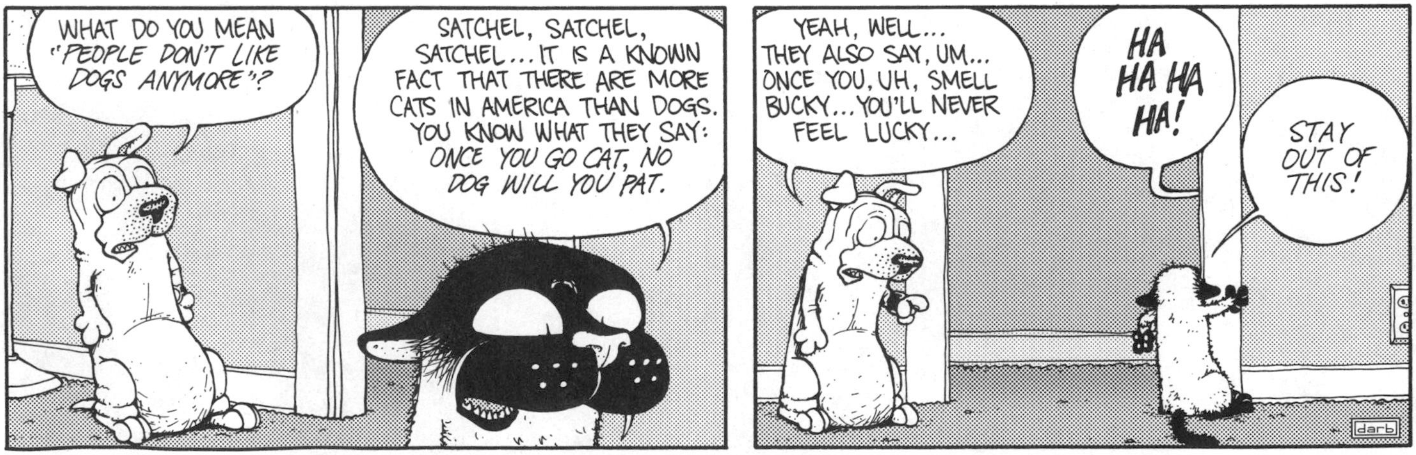
WHAT DO YOU MEAN "PEOPLE DON'T LIKE DOGS ANYMORE"?
SATCHEL, SATCHEL, SATCHEL... IT IS A KNOWN FACT THAT THERE ARE MORE CATS IN AMERICA THAN DOGS. YOU KNOW WHAT THEY SAY: ONCE YOU GO CAT, NO DOG WILL YOU PAT.
YEAH, WELL... THEY ALSO SAY, UM... ONCE YOU, UH, SMELL BUCKY... YOU'LL NEVER FEEL LUCKY...
HA HA HA HA!
STAY OUT OF THIS!
darb

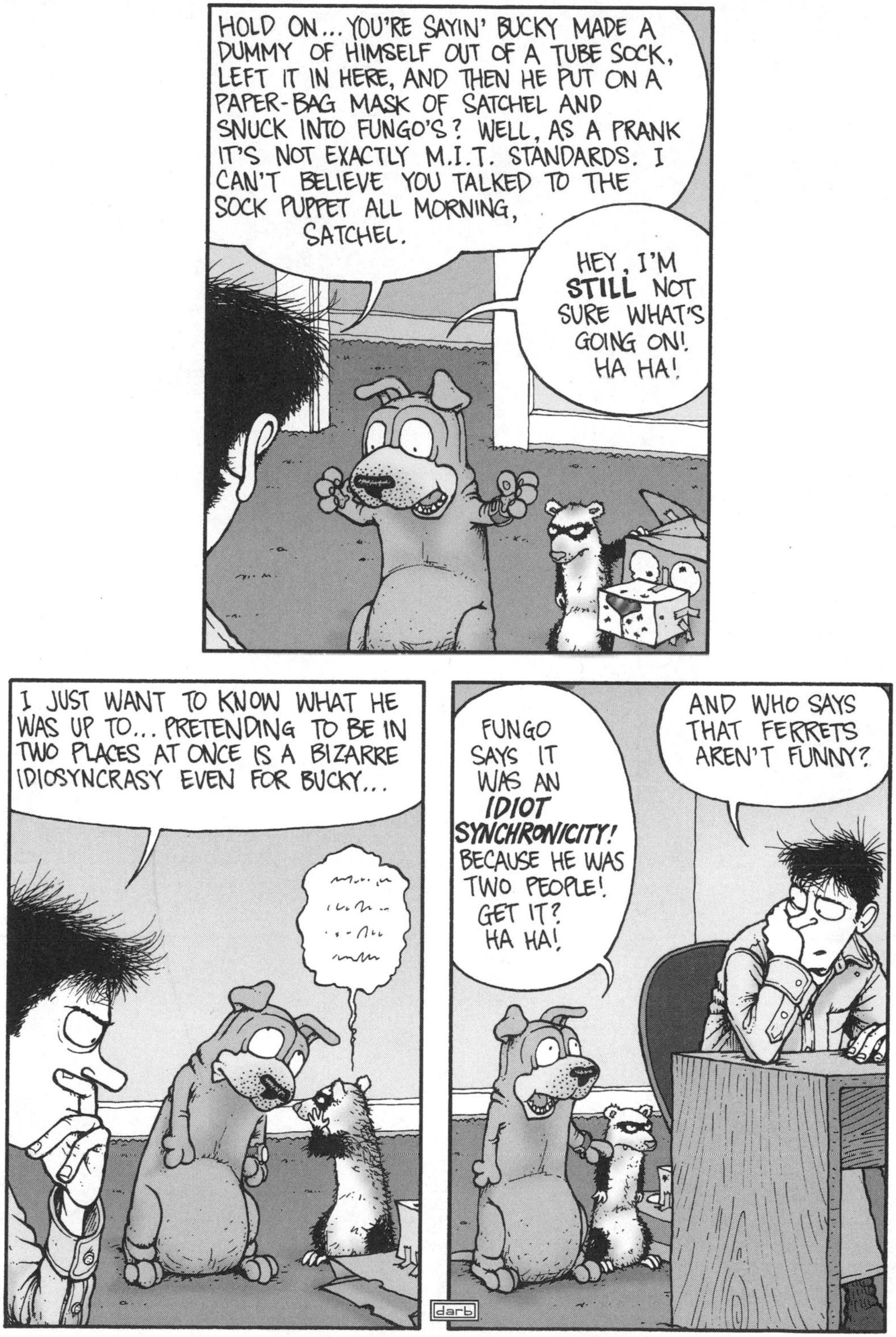
HOLD ON... YOU'RE SAYIN' BUCKY MADE A DUMMY OF HIMSELF OUT OF A TUBE SOCK, LEFT IT IN HERE, AND THEN HE PUT ON A PAPER-BAG MASK OF SATCHEL AND SNUCK INTO FUNGO'S? WELL, AS A PRANK IT'S NOT EXACTLY M.I.T. STANDARDS. I CAN'T BELIEVE YOU TALKED TO THE SOCK PUPPET ALL MORNING, SATCHEL.
HEY, I'M **STILL** NOT SURE WHAT'S GOING ON! HA HA!
I JUST WANT TO KNOW WHAT HE WAS UP TO... PRETENDING TO BE IN TWO PLACES AT ONCE IS A BIZARRE IDIOSYNCRASY EVEN FOR BUCKY...
FUNGO SAYS IT WAS AN ***IDIOT SYNCHRONICITY!*** BECAUSE HE WAS TWO PEOPLE! GET IT? HA HA!
AND WHO SAYS THAT FERRETS AREN'T FUNNY?
darb

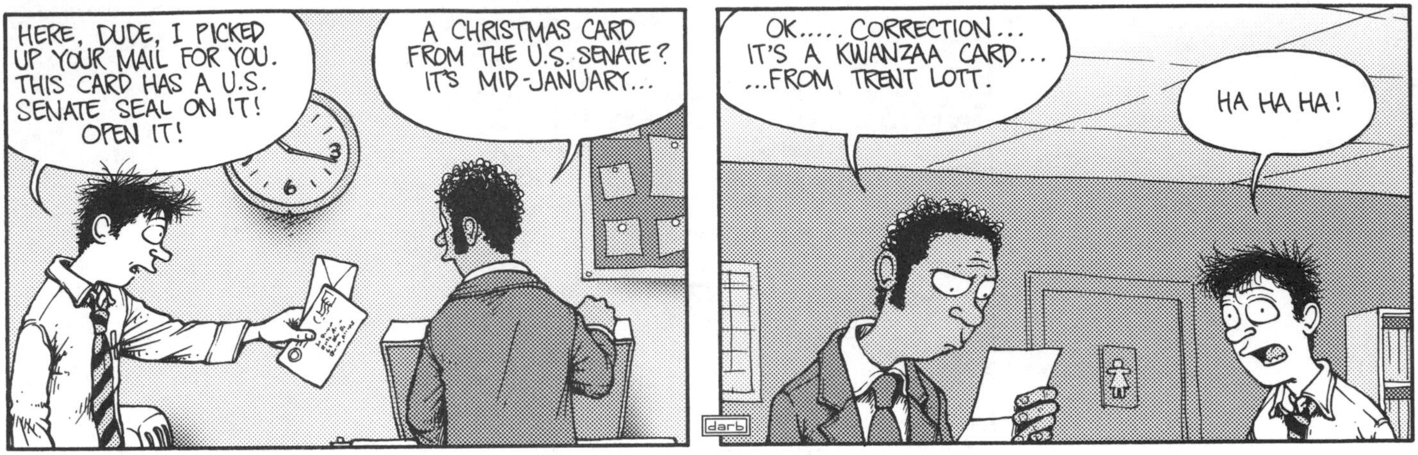
HERE, DUDE, I PICKED UP YOUR MAIL FOR YOU. THIS CARD HAS A U.S. SENATE SEAL ON IT! OPEN IT!
A CHRISTMAS CARD FROM THE U.S. SENATE? IT'S MID-JANUARY...
OK..... CORRECTION... IT'S A KWANZAA CARD... ...FROM TRENT LOTT.
HA HA HA!

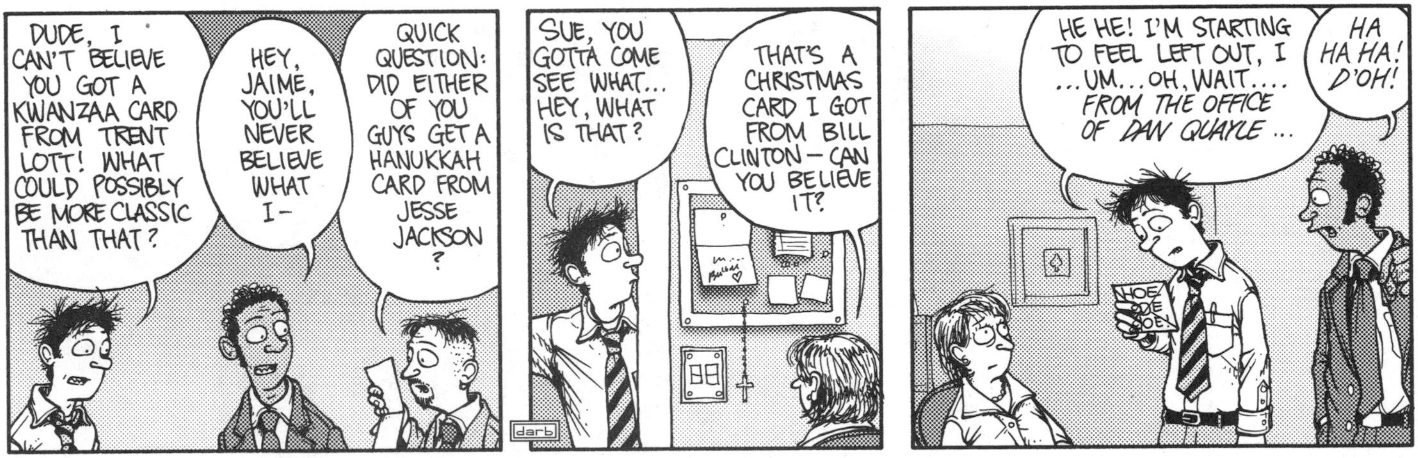
DUDE, I CAN'T BELIEVE YOU GOT A KWANZAA CARD FROM TRENT LOTT! WHAT COULD POSSIBLY BE MORE CLASSIC THAN THAT?
HEY, JAIME, YOU'LL NEVER BELIEVE WHAT I-
QUICK QUESTION: DID EITHER OF YOU GUYS GET A HANUKKAH CARD FROM JESSE JACKSON?
SUE, YOU GOTTA COME SEE WHAT... HEY, WHAT IS THAT?
THAT'S A CHRISTMAS CARD I GOT FROM BILL CLINTON—CAN YOU BELIEVE IT?
HE HE! I'M STARTING TO FEEL LEFT OUT, I ...UM...OH, WAIT.... *FROM THE OFFICE OF DAN QUAYLE...*
HA HA HA! D'OH!

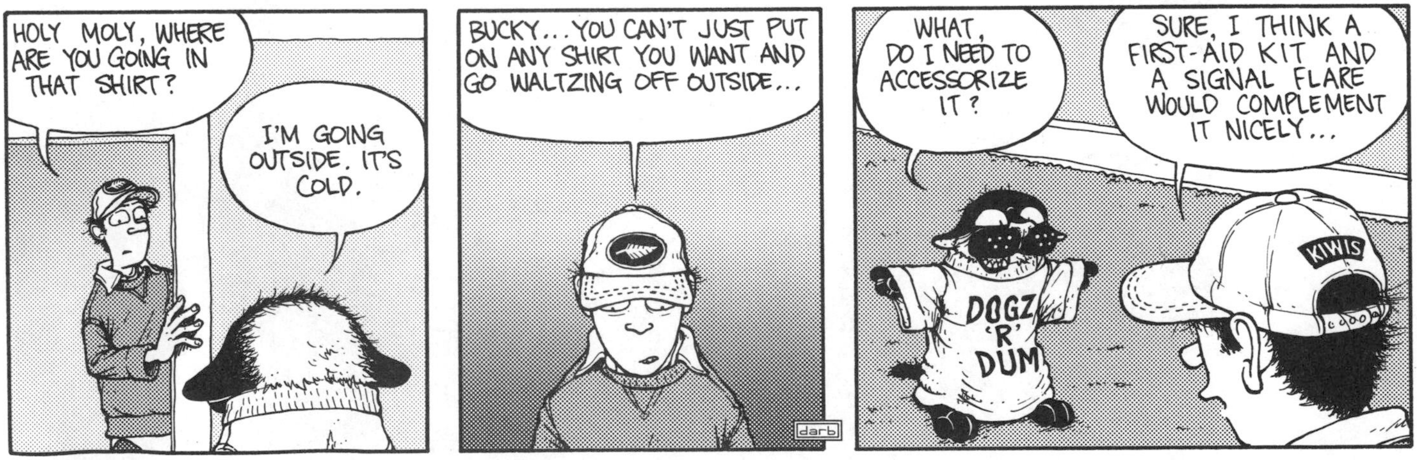
HOLY MOLY, WHERE ARE YOU GOING IN THAT SHIRT?
I'M GOING OUTSIDE. IT'S COLD.
BUCKY... YOU CAN'T JUST PUT ON ANY SHIRT YOU WANT AND GO WALTZING OFF OUTSIDE...
WHAT, DO I NEED TO ACCESSORIZE IT?
SURE, I THINK A FIRST-AID KIT AND A SIGNAL FLARE WOULD COMPLEMENT IT NICELY...
DOGZ 'R' DUM
KIWIS

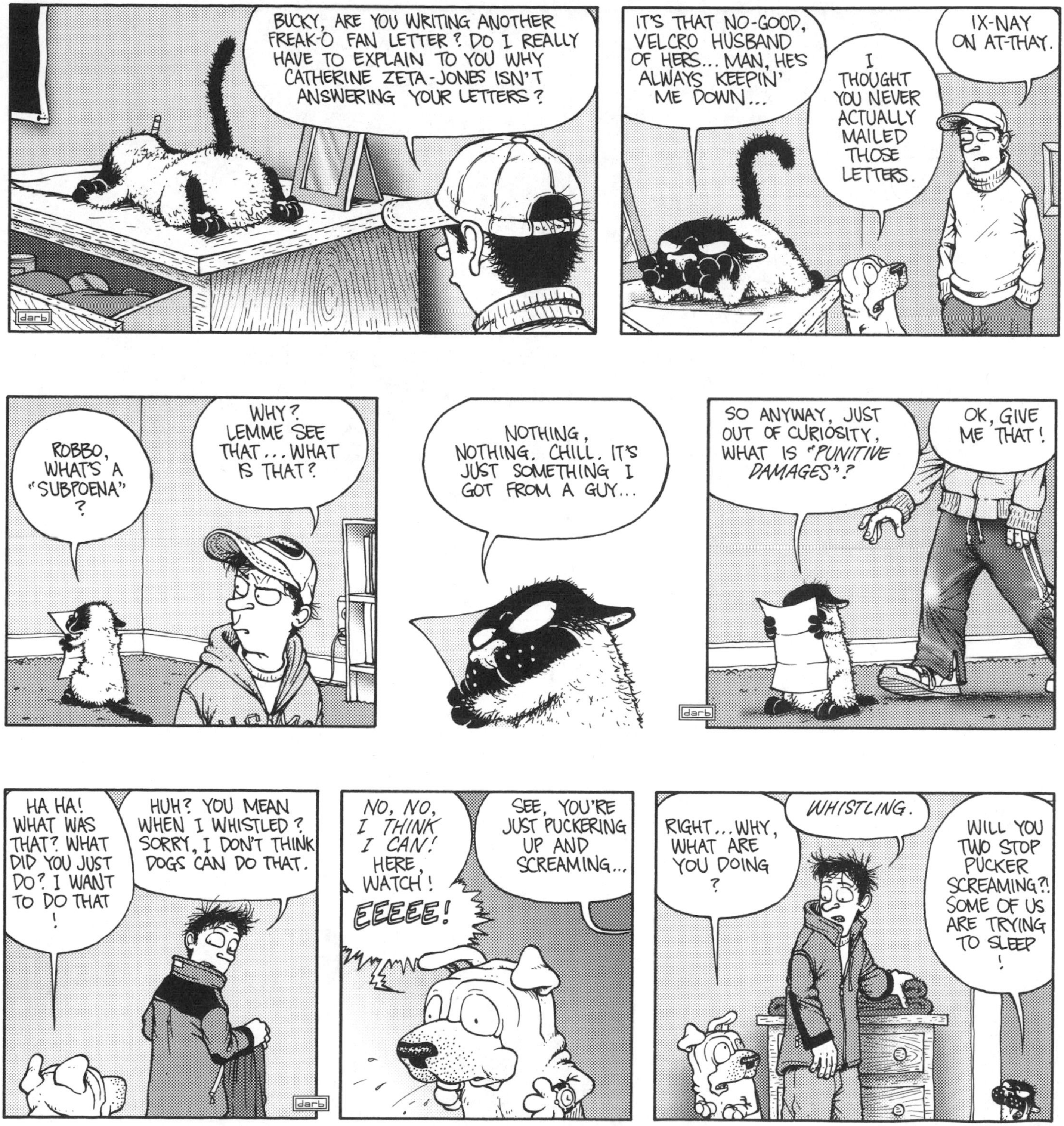

BUCKY, ARE YOU WRITING ANOTHER FREAK-O FAN LETTER? DO I REALLY HAVE TO EXPLAIN TO YOU WHY CATHERINE ZETA-JONES ISN'T ANSWERING YOUR LETTERS?
darb
IT'S THAT NO-GOOD, VELCRO HUSBAND OF HERS... MAN, HE'S ALWAYS KEEPIN' ME DOWN...
I THOUGHT YOU NEVER ACTUALLY MAILED THOSE LETTERS.
IX-NAY ON AT-THAY.
ROBBO, WHAT'S A "SUBPOENA"?
WHY? LEMME SEE THAT... WHAT IS THAT?
NOTHING, NOTHING. CHILL. IT'S JUST SOMETHING I GOT FROM A GUY...
SO ANYWAY, JUST OUT OF CURIOSITY, WHAT IS "PUNITIVE DAMAGES"?
OK, GIVE ME THAT!
darb
HA HA! WHAT WAS THAT? WHAT DID YOU JUST DO? I WANT TO DO THAT!
HUH? YOU MEAN WHEN I WHISTLED? SORRY, I DON'T THINK DOGS CAN DO THAT.
darb
NO, NO, I THINK I CAN! HERE, WATCH!
EEEEE!
SEE, YOU'RE JUST PUCKERING UP AND SCREAMING...
RIGHT... WHY, WHAT ARE YOU DOING?
WHISTLING.
WILL YOU TWO STOP PUCKER SCREAMING?! SOME OF US ARE TRYING TO SLEEP!

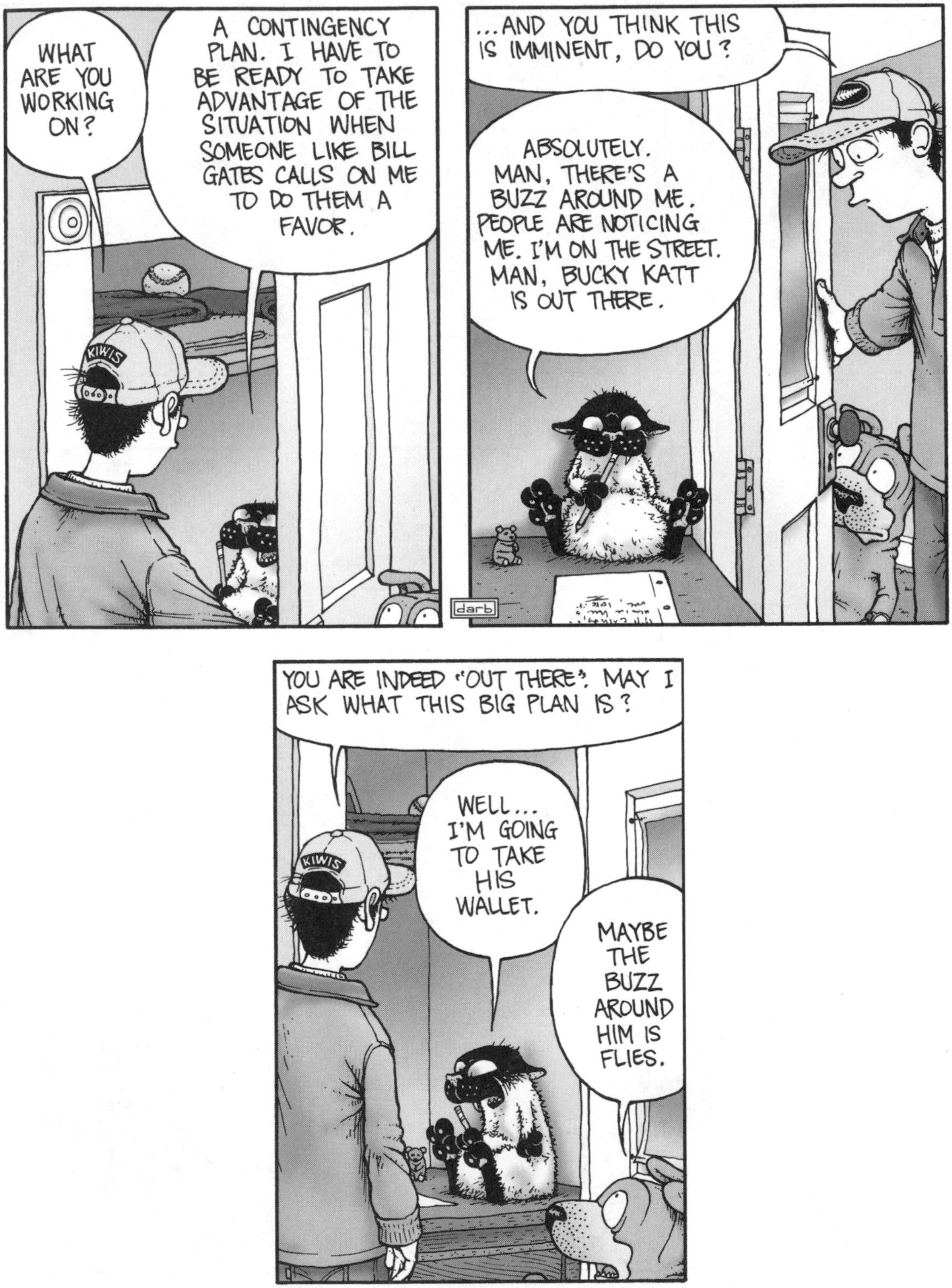
WHAT ARE YOU WORKING ON?
A CONTINGENCY PLAN. I HAVE TO BE READY TO TAKE ADVANTAGE OF THE SITUATION WHEN SOMEONE LIKE BILL GATES CALLS ON ME TO DO THEM A FAVOR.
darb
...AND YOU THINK THIS IS IMMINENT, DO YOU?
ABSOLUTELY. MAN, THERE'S A BUZZ AROUND ME. PEOPLE ARE NOTICING ME. I'M ON THE STREET. MAN, BUCKY KATT IS OUT THERE.
YOU ARE INDEED "OUT THERE". MAY I ASK WHAT THIS BIG PLAN IS?
WELL... I'M GOING TO TAKE HIS WALLET.
MAYBE THE BUZZ AROUND HIM IS FLIES.

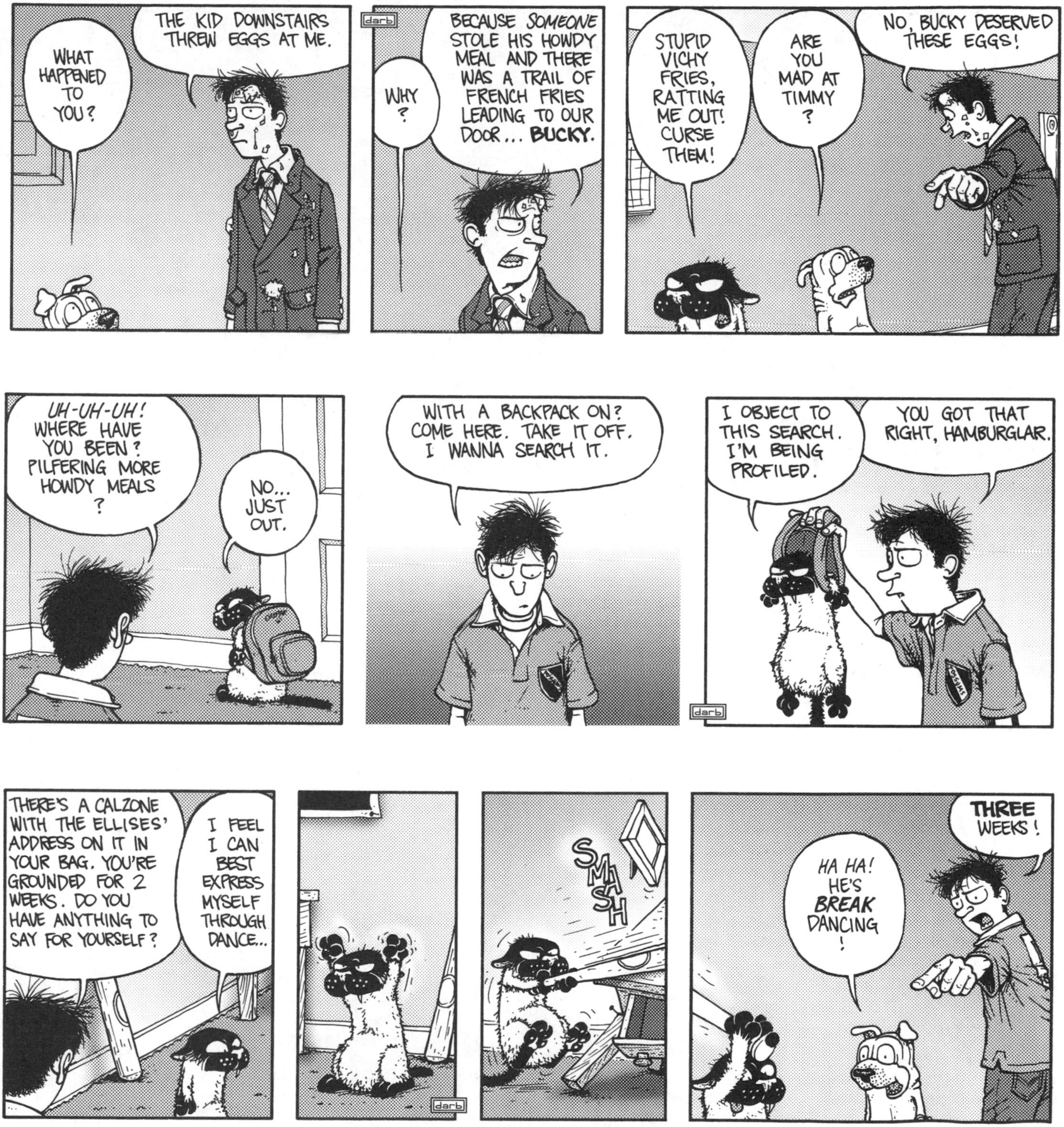
WHAT HAPPENED TO YOU?
THE KID DOWNSTAIRS THREW EGGS AT ME.
darb
WHY?
BECAUSE *SOMEONE* STOLE HIS HOWDY MEAL AND THERE WAS A TRAIL OF FRENCH FRIES LEADING TO OUR DOOR... **BUCKY**.
STUPID VICHY FRIES, RATTING ME OUT! CURSE THEM!
ARE YOU MAD AT TIMMY?
NO, BUCKY DESERVED THESE EGGS!
UH-UH-UH! WHERE HAVE YOU BEEN? PILFERING MORE HOWDY MEALS?
NO... JUST OUT.
WITH A BACKPACK ON? COME HERE. TAKE IT OFF. I WANNA SEARCH IT.
I OBJECT TO THIS SEARCH. I'M BEING PROFILED.
YOU GOT THAT RIGHT, HAMBURGLAR.
darb
THERE'S A CALZONE WITH THE ELLISES' ADDRESS ON IT IN YOUR BAG. YOU'RE GROUNDED FOR 2 WEEKS. DO YOU HAVE ANYTHING TO SAY FOR YOURSELF?
I FEEL I CAN BEST EXPRESS MYSELF THROUGH DANCE...
darb
SMASH
HA HA! HE'S ***BREAK*** DANCING!
THREE WEEKS!

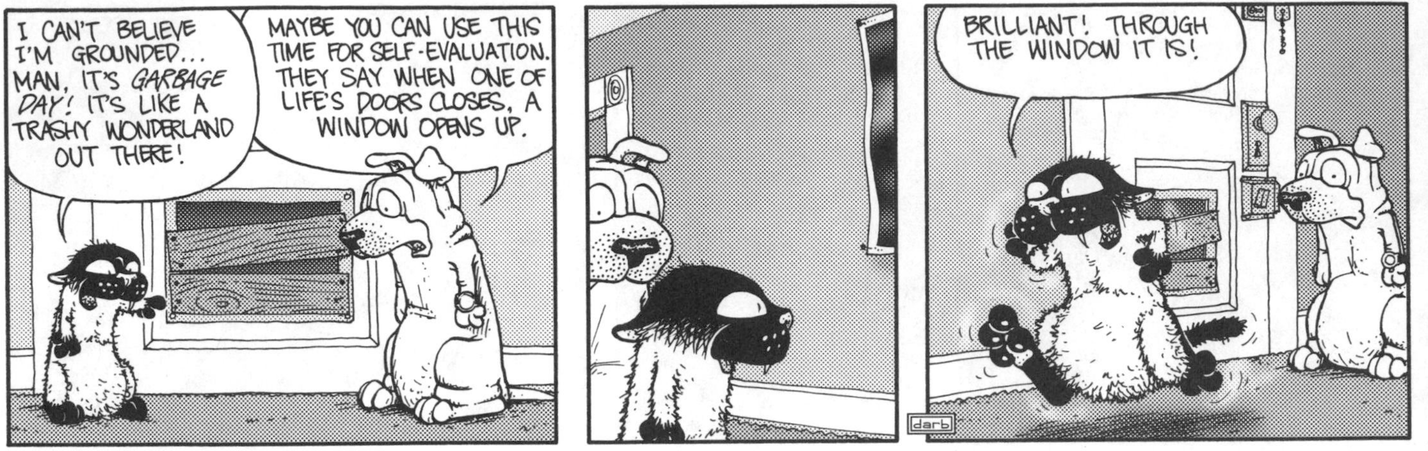
I CAN'T BELIEVE I'M GROUNDED... MAN, IT'S *GARBAGE DAY*! IT'S LIKE A TRASHY WONDERLAND OUT THERE!
MAYBE YOU CAN USE THIS TIME FOR SELF-EVALUATION. THEY SAY WHEN ONE OF LIFE'S DOORS CLOSES, A WINDOW OPENS UP.
BRILLIANT! THROUGH THE WINDOW IT IS!
darb

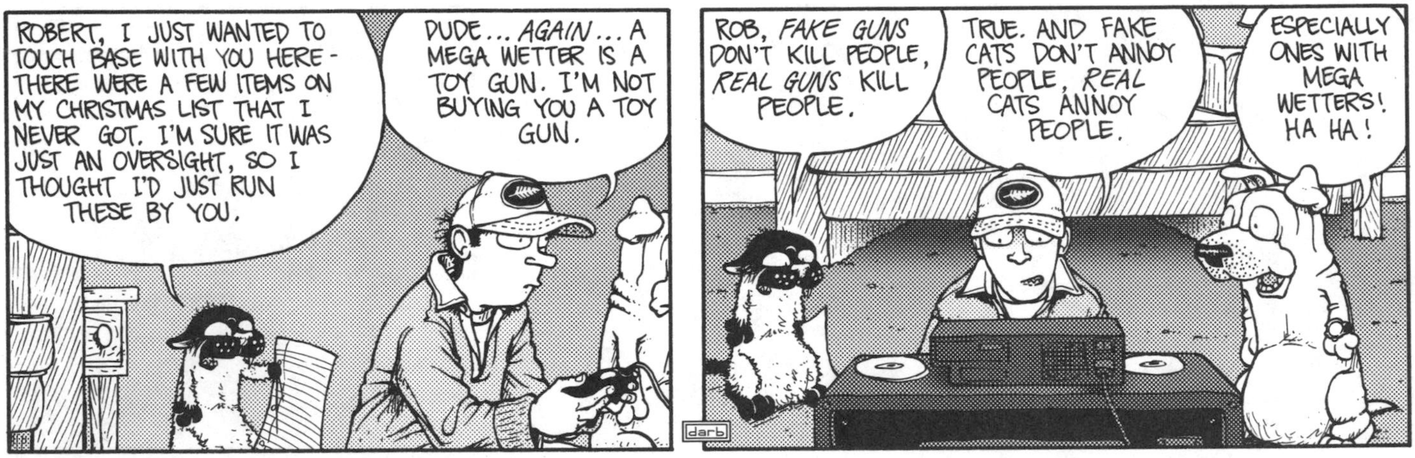
ROBERT, I JUST WANTED TO TOUCH BASE WITH YOU HERE - THERE WERE A FEW ITEMS ON MY CHRISTMAS LIST THAT I NEVER GOT. I'M SURE IT WAS JUST AN OVERSIGHT, SO I THOUGHT I'D JUST RUN THESE BY YOU.
DUDE... *AGAIN*... A MEGA WETTER IS A TOY GUN. I'M NOT BUYING YOU A TOY GUN.
darb
ROB, *FAKE GUNS* DON'T KILL PEOPLE, *REAL GUNS* KILL PEOPLE.
TRUE. AND FAKE CATS DON'T ANNOY PEOPLE, *REAL* CATS ANNOY PEOPLE.
ESPECIALLY ONES WITH MEGA WETTERS! HA HA!

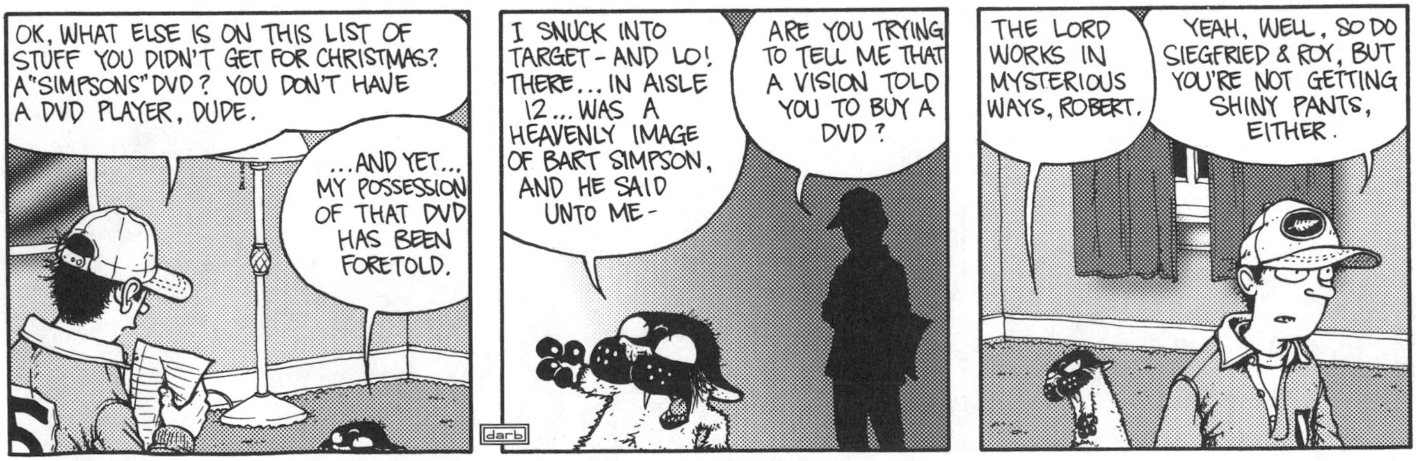
OK, WHAT ELSE IS ON THIS LIST OF STUFF YOU DIDN'T GET FOR CHRISTMAS? A "SIMPSONS" DVD? YOU DON'T HAVE A DVD PLAYER, DUDE.
...AND YET... MY POSSESSION OF THAT DVD HAS BEEN FORETOLD.
darb
I SNUCK INTO TARGET - AND LO! THERE... IN AISLE 12... WAS A HEAVENLY IMAGE OF BART SIMPSON, AND HE SAID UNTO ME-
ARE YOU TRYING TO TELL ME THAT A VISION TOLD YOU TO BUY A DVD?
THE LORD WORKS IN MYSTERIOUS WAYS, ROBERT.
YEAH, WELL, SO DO SIEGFRIED & ROY, BUT YOU'RE NOT GETTING SHINY PANTS, EITHER.

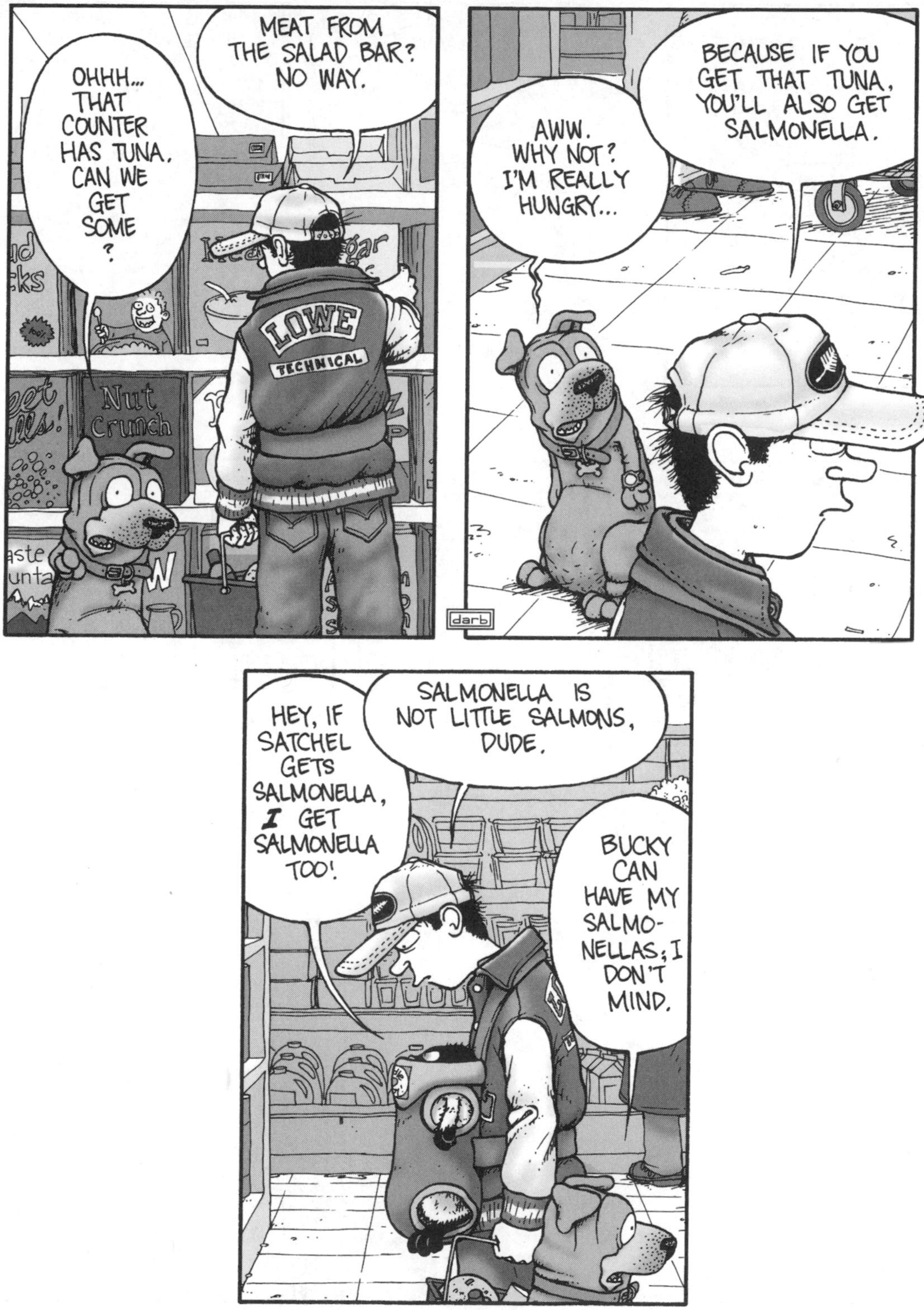
OHHH... THAT COUNTER HAS TUNA. CAN WE GET SOME ?
MEAT FROM THE SALAD BAR? NO WAY.
Nut Crunch
LOWE
TECHNICAL
AWW. WHY NOT? I'M REALLY HUNGRY...
BECAUSE IF YOU GET THAT TUNA, YOU'LL ALSO GET SALMONELLA.
darb
HEY, IF SATCHEL GETS SALMONELLA, *I* GET SALMONELLA TOO!
SALMONELLA IS NOT LITTLE SALMONS, DUDE.
BUCKY CAN HAVE MY SALMO-NELLAS; I DON'T MIND.

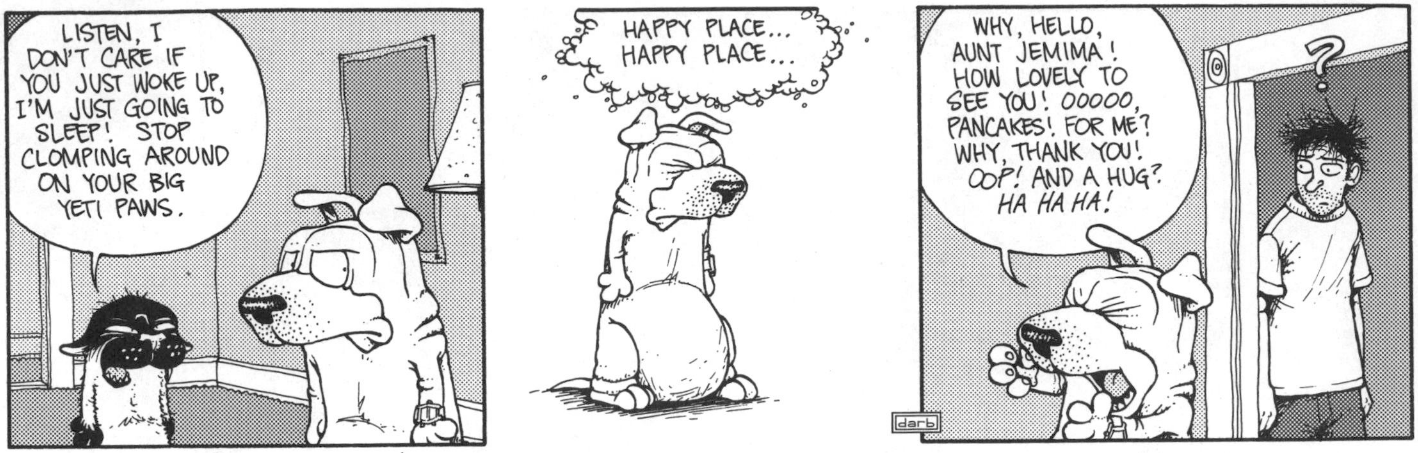
LISTEN, I DON'T CARE IF YOU JUST WOKE UP, I'M JUST GOING TO SLEEP! STOP CLOMPING AROUND ON YOUR BIG YETI PAWS.
HAPPY PLACE... HAPPY PLACE...
WHY, HELLO, AUNT JEMIMA! HOW LOVELY TO SEE YOU! OOOOO, PANCAKES! FOR ME? WHY, THANK YOU! OOP! AND A HUG? HA HA HA!
?
darb

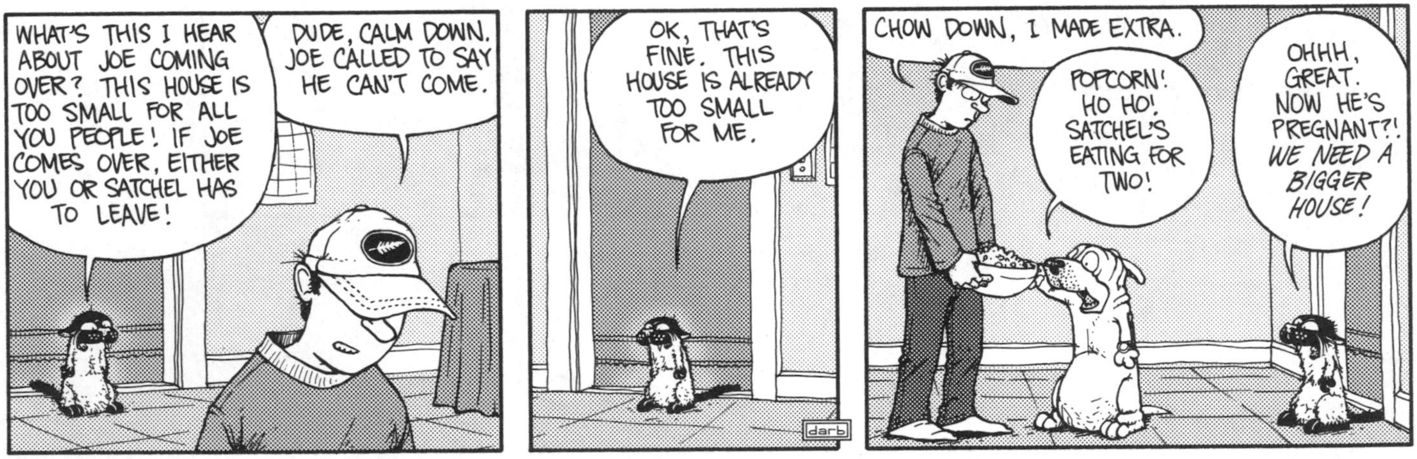
WHAT'S THIS I HEAR ABOUT JOE COMING OVER? THIS HOUSE IS TOO SMALL FOR ALL YOU PEOPLE! IF JOE COMES OVER, EITHER YOU OR SATCHEL HAS TO LEAVE!
DUDE, CALM DOWN. JOE CALLED TO SAY HE CAN'T COME.
OK, THAT'S FINE. THIS HOUSE IS ALREADY TOO SMALL FOR ME.
darb
CHOW DOWN, I MADE EXTRA.
POPCORN! HO HO! SATCHEL'S EATING FOR TWO!
OHHH, GREAT. NOW HE'S PREGNANT?! WE NEED A BIGGER HOUSE!

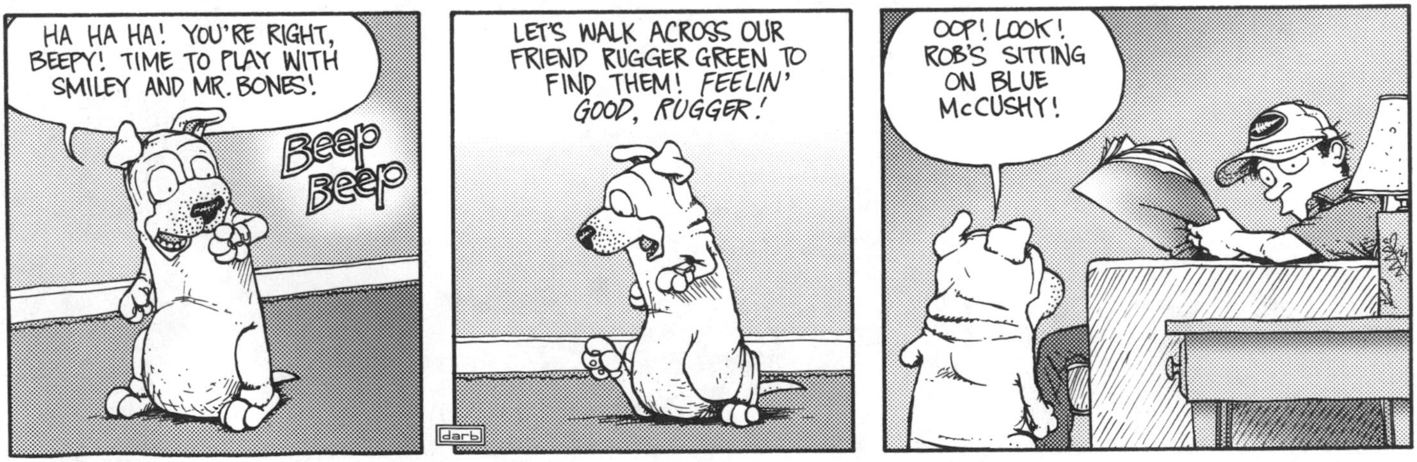
HA HA HA! YOU'RE RIGHT, BEEPY! TIME TO PLAY WITH SMILEY AND MR. BONES!
Beep Beep
LET'S WALK ACROSS OUR FRIEND RUGGER GREEN TO FIND THEM! FEELIN' GOOD, RUGGER!
darb
OOP! LOOK! ROB'S SITTING ON BLUE McCUSHY!

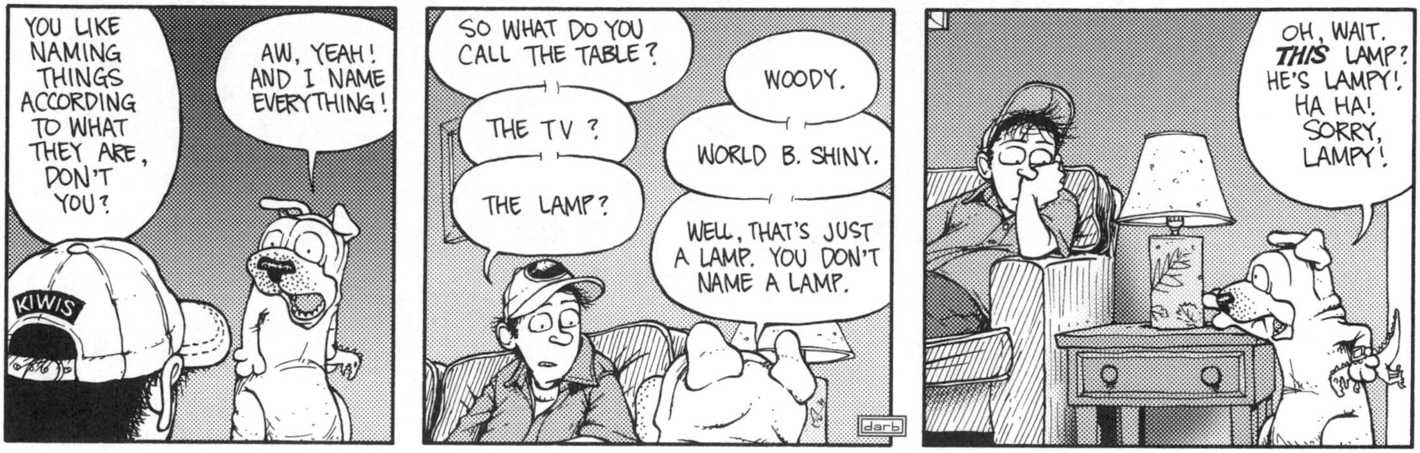
YOU LIKE NAMING THINGS ACCORDING TO WHAT THEY ARE, DON'T YOU?
KIWIS
AW, YEAH! AND I NAME EVERYTHING!
SO WHAT DO YOU CALL THE TABLE?
WOODY.
THE TV?
WORLD B. SHINY.
THE LAMP?
WELL, THAT'S JUST A LAMP. YOU DON'T NAME A LAMP.
darb
OH, WAIT. ***THIS*** LAMP? HE'S LAMPY! HA HA! SORRY, LAMPY!

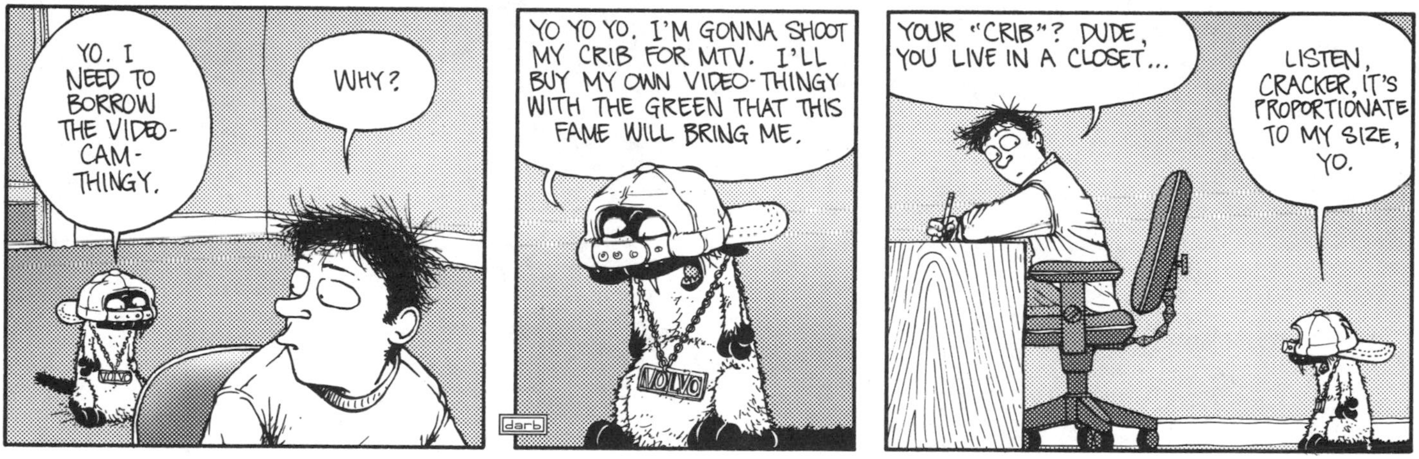
YO. I NEED TO BORROW THE VIDEO-CAM-THINGY.
WHY?
darb
YO YO YO. I'M GONNA SHOOT MY CRIB FOR MTV. I'LL BUY MY OWN VIDEO-THINGY WITH THE GREEN THAT THIS FAME WILL BRING ME.
VOLVO
YOUR "CRIB"? DUDE, YOU LIVE IN A CLOSET...
LISTEN, CRACKER, IT'S PROPORTIONATE TO MY SIZE, YO.

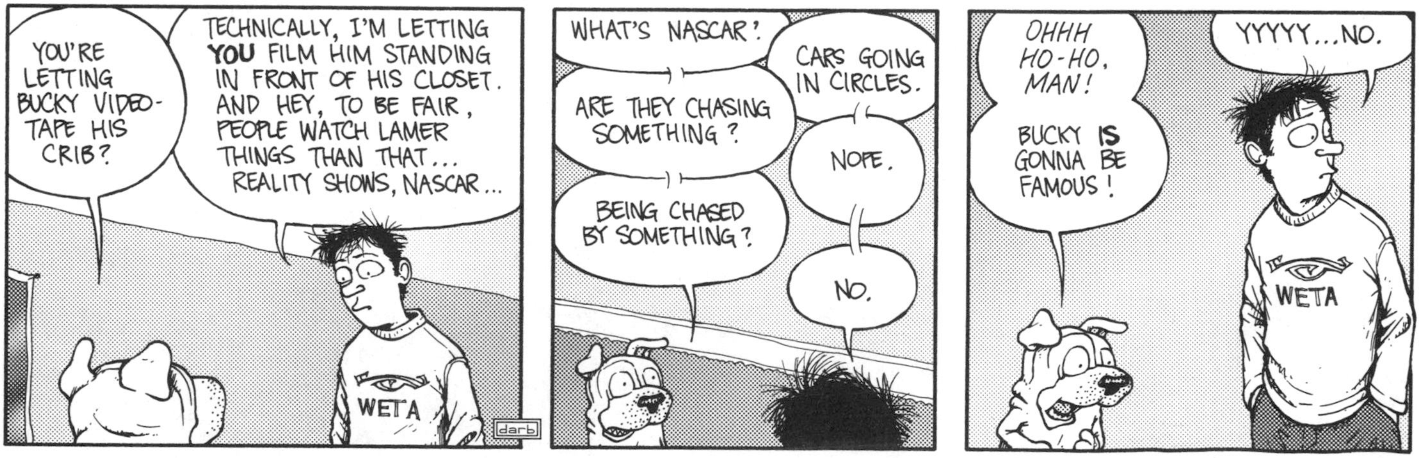
YOU'RE LETTING BUCKY VIDEO-TAPE HIS CRIB?
TECHNICALLY, I'M LETTING **YOU** FILM HIM STANDING IN FRONT OF HIS CLOSET. AND HEY, TO BE FAIR, PEOPLE WATCH LAMER THINGS THAN THAT... REALITY SHOWS, NASCAR...
WETA
darb
WHAT'S NASCAR?
CARS GOING IN CIRCLES.
ARE THEY CHASING SOMETHING?
NOPE.
BEING CHASED BY SOMETHING?
NO.
OHHH HO-HO, MAN!
BUCKY **IS** GONNA BE FAMOUS!
YYYYY...NO.
WETA

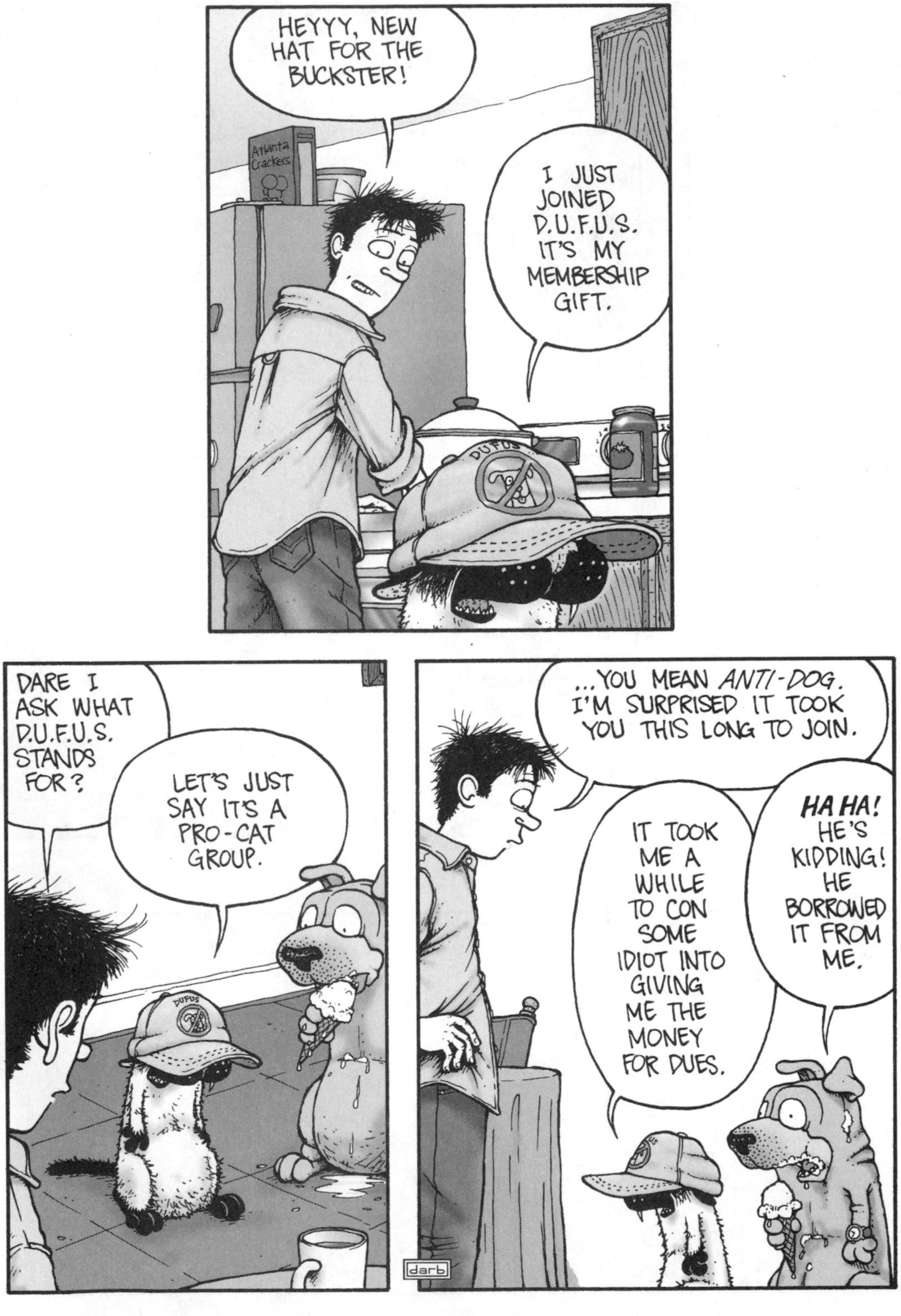
HEYYY, NEW HAT FOR THE BUCKSTER!
Atlanta Crackers
I JUST JOINED D.U.F.U.S. IT'S MY MEMBERSHIP GIFT.
DUFUS
DARE I ASK WHAT D.U.F.U.S. STANDS FOR?
LET'S JUST SAY IT'S A PRO-CAT GROUP.
DUFUS
...YOU MEAN ANTI-DOG. I'M SURPRISED IT TOOK YOU THIS LONG TO JOIN.
IT TOOK ME A WHILE TO CON SOME IDIOT INTO GIVING ME THE MONEY FOR DUES.
HA HA! HE'S KIDDING! HE BORROWED IT FROM ME.
darb

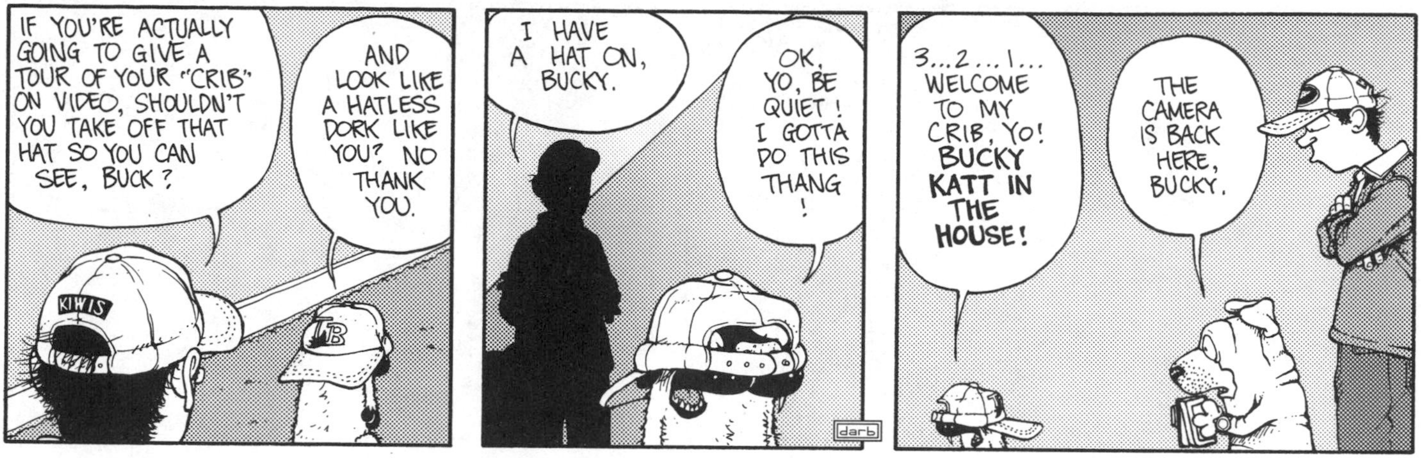
IF YOU'RE ACTUALLY GOING TO GIVE A TOUR OF YOUR "CRIB" ON VIDEO, SHOULDN'T YOU TAKE OFF THAT HAT SO YOU CAN SEE, BUCK?
AND LOOK LIKE A HATLESS DORK LIKE YOU? NO THANK YOU.
KIWIS
TB
I HAVE A HAT ON, BUCKY.
OK, YO, BE QUIET! I GOTTA DO THIS THANG!
3...2...1... WELCOME TO MY CRIB, YO! **BUCKY KATT IN THE HOUSE!**
THE CAMERA IS BACK HERE, BUCKY.
darb

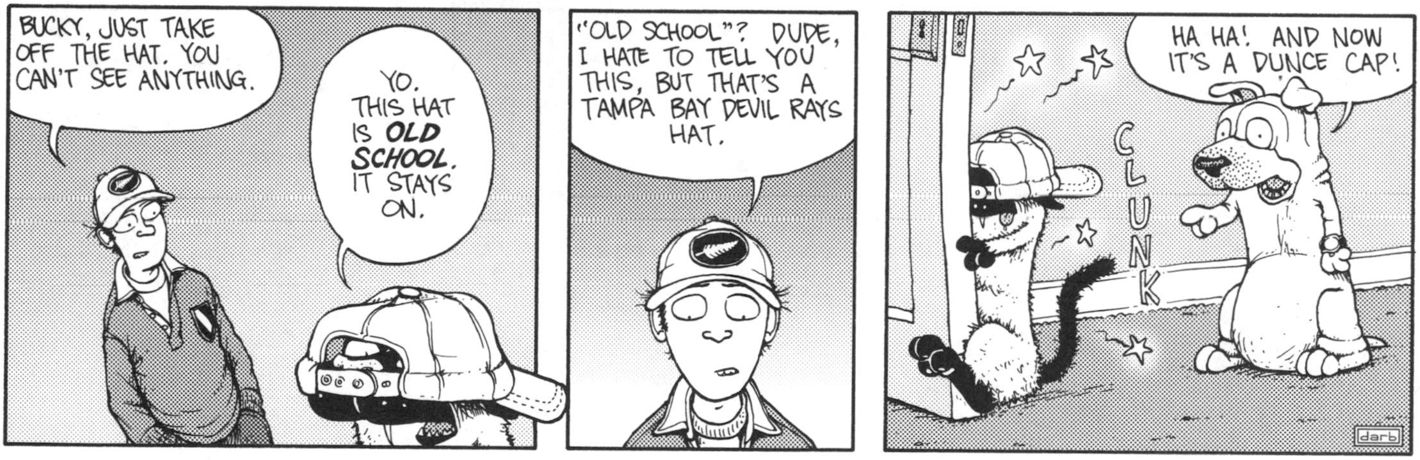
BUCKY, JUST TAKE OFF THE HAT. YOU CAN'T SEE ANYTHING.
YO. THIS HAT IS ***OLD SCHOOL.*** IT STAYS ON.
"OLD SCHOOL"? DUDE, I HATE TO TELL YOU THIS, BUT THAT'S A TAMPA BAY DEVIL RAYS HAT.
CLUNK
HA HA! AND NOW IT'S A DUNCE CAP!
darb

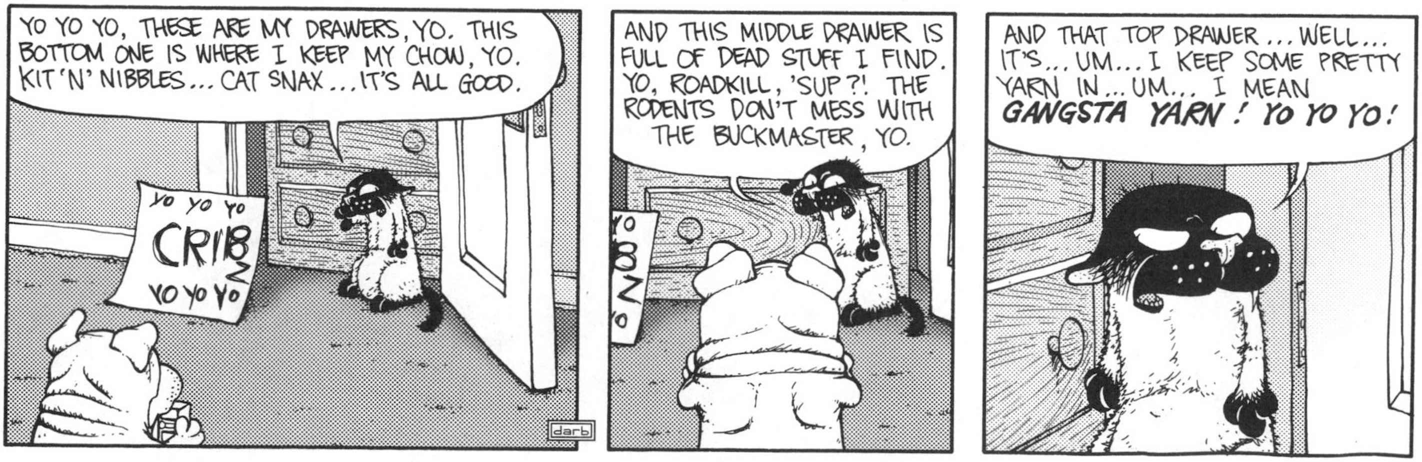
YO YO YO, THESE ARE MY DRAWERS, YO. THIS BOTTOM ONE IS WHERE I KEEP MY CHOW, YO. KIT 'N' NIBBLES... CAT SNAX... IT'S ALL GOOD.
YO YO YO
CRIBZ
YO YO YO
AND THIS MIDDLE DRAWER IS FULL OF DEAD STUFF I FIND. YO, ROADKILL, 'SUP?! THE RODENTS DON'T MESS WITH THE BUCKMASTER, YO.
AND THAT TOP DRAWER... WELL... IT'S... UM... I KEEP SOME PRETTY YARN IN... UM... I MEAN ***GANGSTA YARN! YO YO YO!***
darb

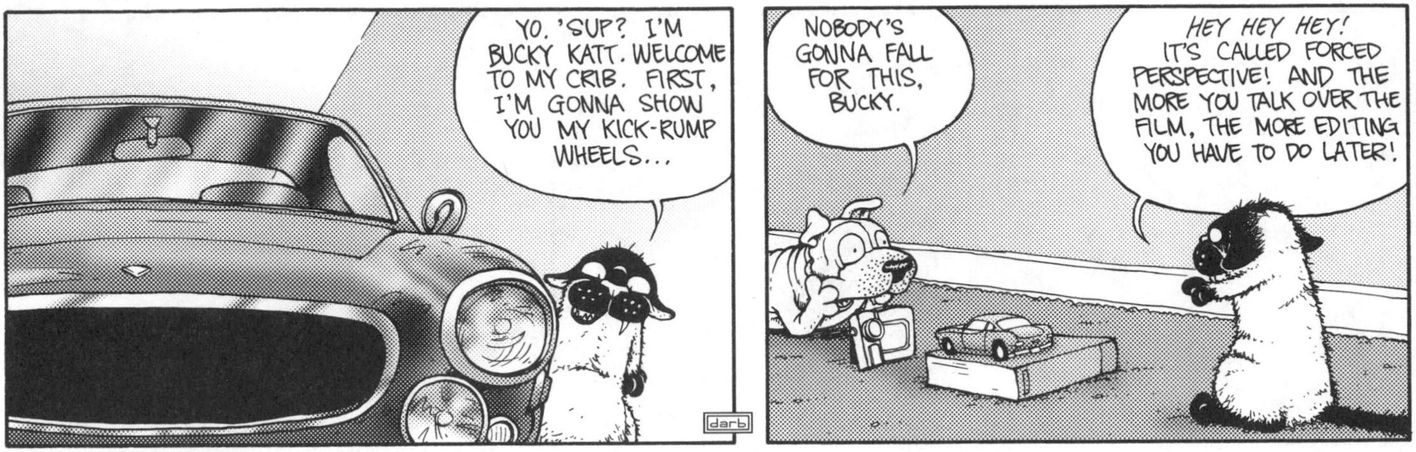
YO. 'SUP? I'M BUCKY KATT. WELCOME TO MY CRIB. FIRST, I'M GONNA SHOW YOU MY KICK-RUMP WHEELS...
NOBODY'S GONNA FALL FOR THIS, BUCKY.
HEY HEY HEY! IT'S CALLED FORCED PERSPECTIVE! AND THE MORE YOU TALK OVER THE FILM, THE MORE EDITING YOU HAVE TO DO LATER!
darb

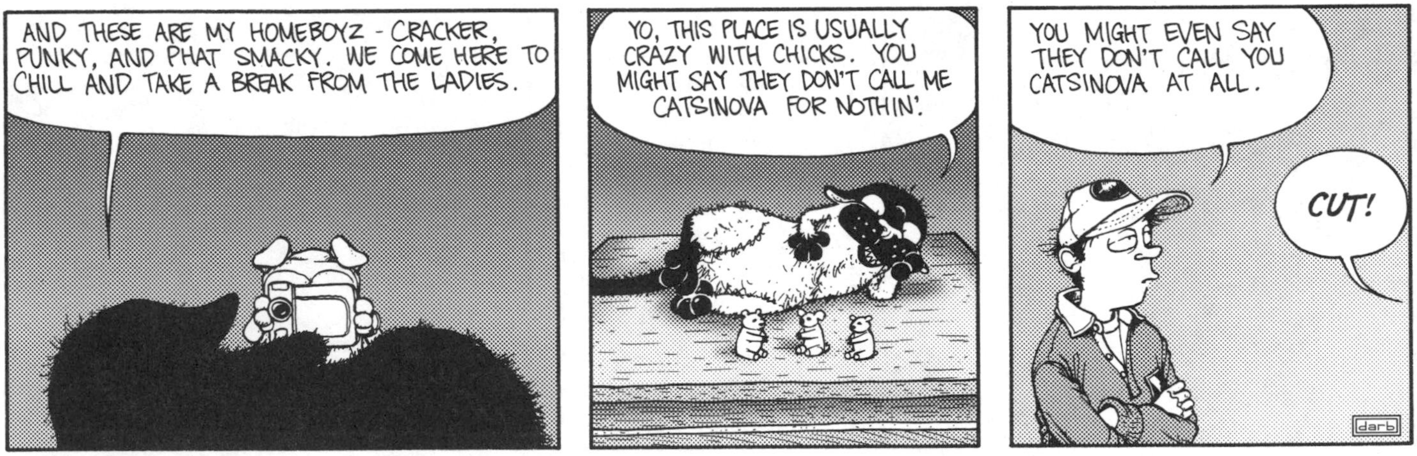
AND THESE ARE MY HOMEBOYZ - CRACKER, PUNKY, AND PHAT SMACKY. WE COME HERE TO CHILL AND TAKE A BREAK FROM THE LADIES.
YO, THIS PLACE IS USUALLY CRAZY WITH CHICKS. YOU MIGHT SAY THEY DON'T CALL ME CATSINOVA FOR NOTHIN'.
YOU MIGHT EVEN SAY THEY DON'T CALL YOU CATSINOVA AT ALL.
CUT!
darb

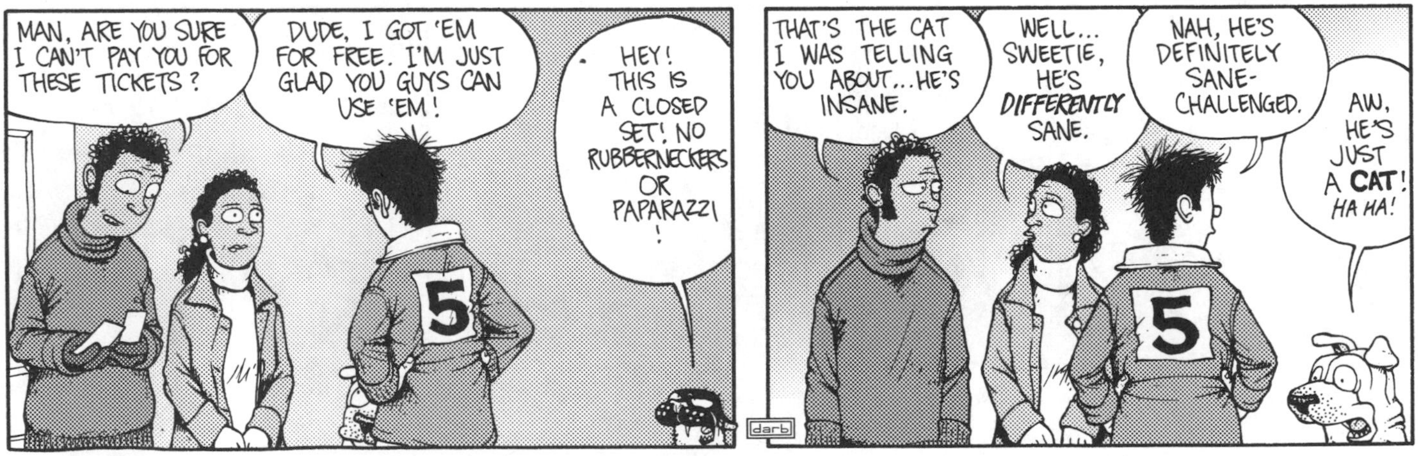
MAN, ARE YOU SURE I CAN'T PAY YOU FOR THESE TICKETS?
DUDE, I GOT 'EM FOR FREE. I'M JUST GLAD YOU GUYS CAN USE 'EM!
HEY! THIS IS A CLOSED SET! NO RUBBERNECKERS OR PAPARAZZI!
darb
THAT'S THE CAT I WAS TELLING YOU ABOUT... HE'S INSANE.
WELL... SWEETIE, HE'S **DIFFERENTLY** SANE.
NAH, HE'S DEFINITELY SANE-CHALLENGED.
AW, HE'S JUST A **CAT**! HA HA!
5

HA HA HA HA HA HA!
ARE YOU GUYS STILL MAKING FUN OF MY FRESHMAN YEARBOOK? PUT IT AWAY ALREADY!
Jim Rogers
s oregano, Mrs. Webster!"
Robert Wilco
"Dude, where's my retainer
darb
SO WERE YOU VOTED MOST LIKELY TO REMAIN CHICKLESS?
DUDE, I'M ABOUT TO BE VOTED MOST LIKELY TO KICK YOUR –
ASSUREDLY, THAT'S THE SKINNIEST LEATHER TIE I'VE EVER SEEN!

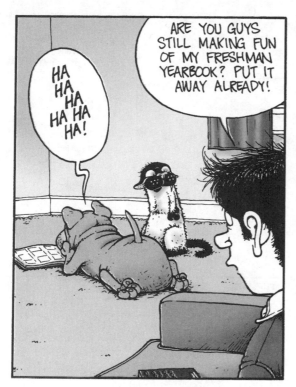

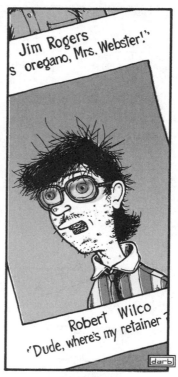

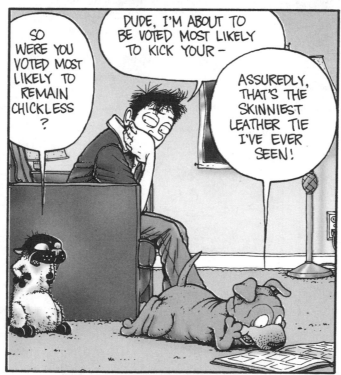

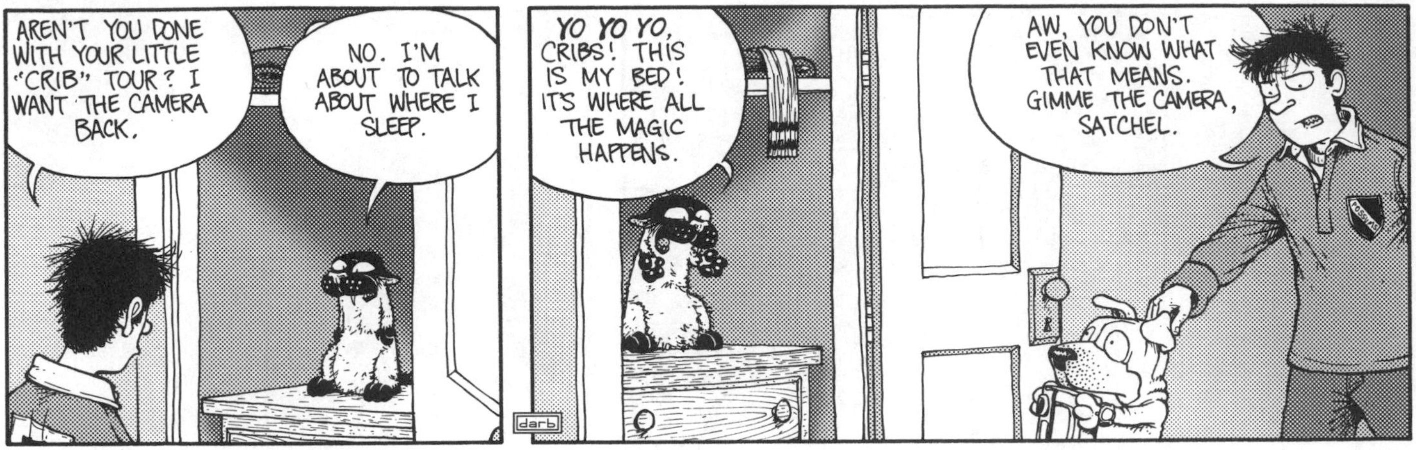
AREN'T YOU DONE WITH YOUR LITTLE "CRIB" TOUR? I WANT THE CAMERA BACK.
NO. I'M ABOUT TO TALK ABOUT WHERE I SLEEP.
YO YO YO, CRIBS! THIS IS MY BED! IT'S WHERE ALL THE MAGIC HAPPENS.
AW, YOU DON'T EVEN KNOW WHAT THAT MEANS. GIMME THE CAMERA, SATCHEL.

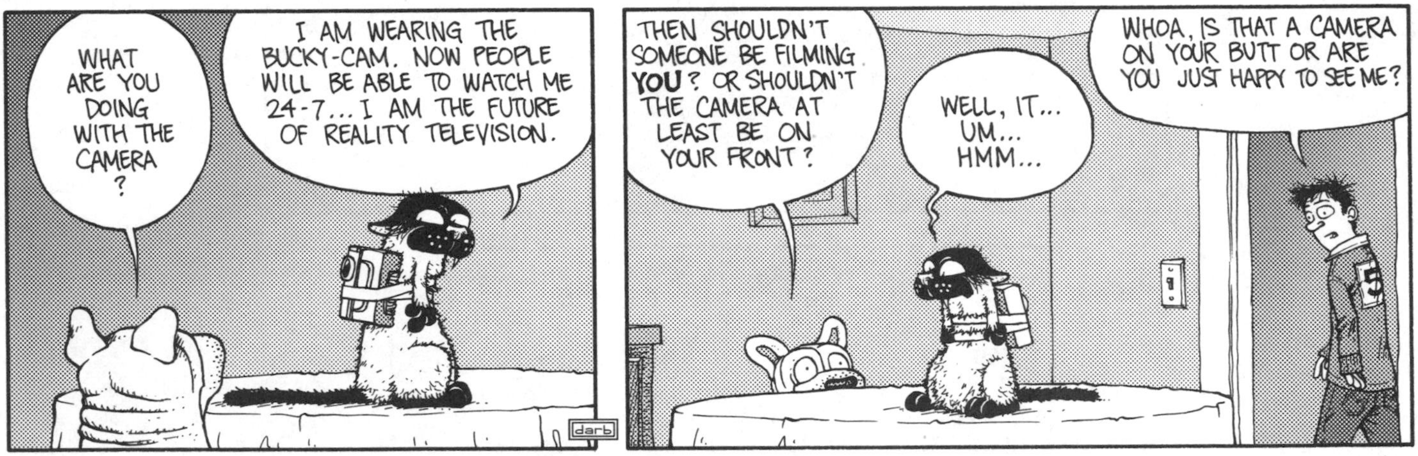
WHAT ARE YOU DOING WITH THE CAMERA ?
I AM WEARING THE BUCKY-CAM. NOW PEOPLE WILL BE ABLE TO WATCH ME 24-7... I AM THE FUTURE OF REALITY TELEVISION.
THEN SHOULDN'T SOMEONE BE FILMING YOU? OR SHOULDN'T THE CAMERA AT LEAST BE ON YOUR FRONT?
WELL, IT... UM... HMM...
WHOA, IS THAT A CAMERA ON YOUR BUTT OR ARE YOU JUST HAPPY TO SEE ME?

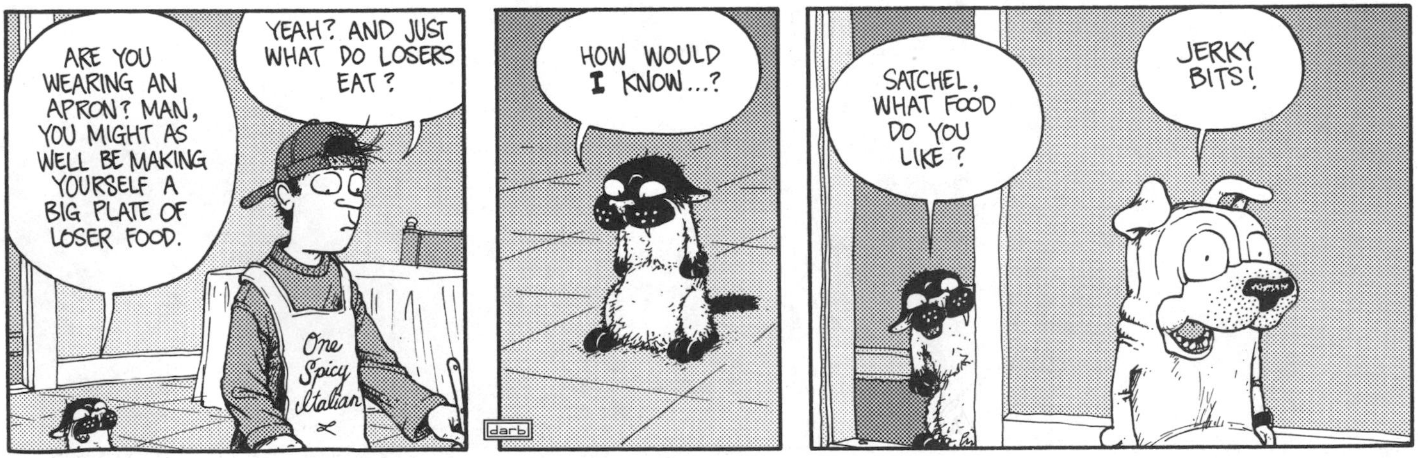
ARE YOU WEARING AN APRON? MAN, YOU MIGHT AS WELL BE MAKING YOURSELF A BIG PLATE OF LOSER FOOD.
YEAH? AND JUST WHAT DO LOSERS EAT?
One Spicy Italian
HOW WOULD I KNOW...?
SATCHEL, WHAT FOOD DO YOU LIKE?
JERKY BITS!

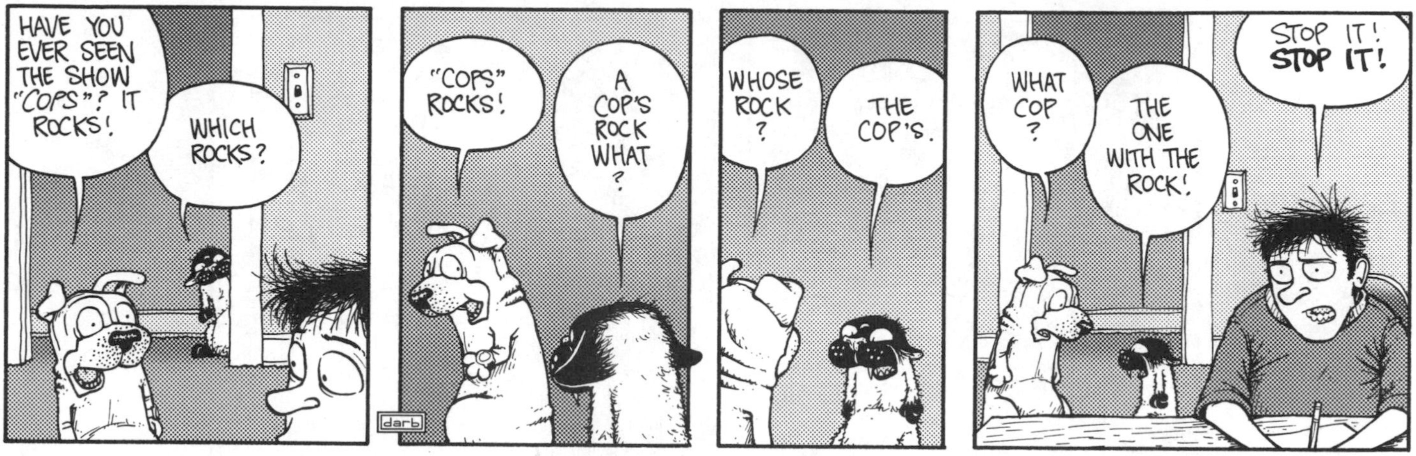
HAVE YOU EVER SEEN THE SHOW "COPS"? IT ROCKS!
WHICH ROCKS?
darb
"COPS" ROCKS!
A COP'S ROCK WHAT?
WHOSE ROCK?
THE COP'S.
WHAT COP?
THE ONE WITH THE ROCK!
STOP IT! **STOP IT!**

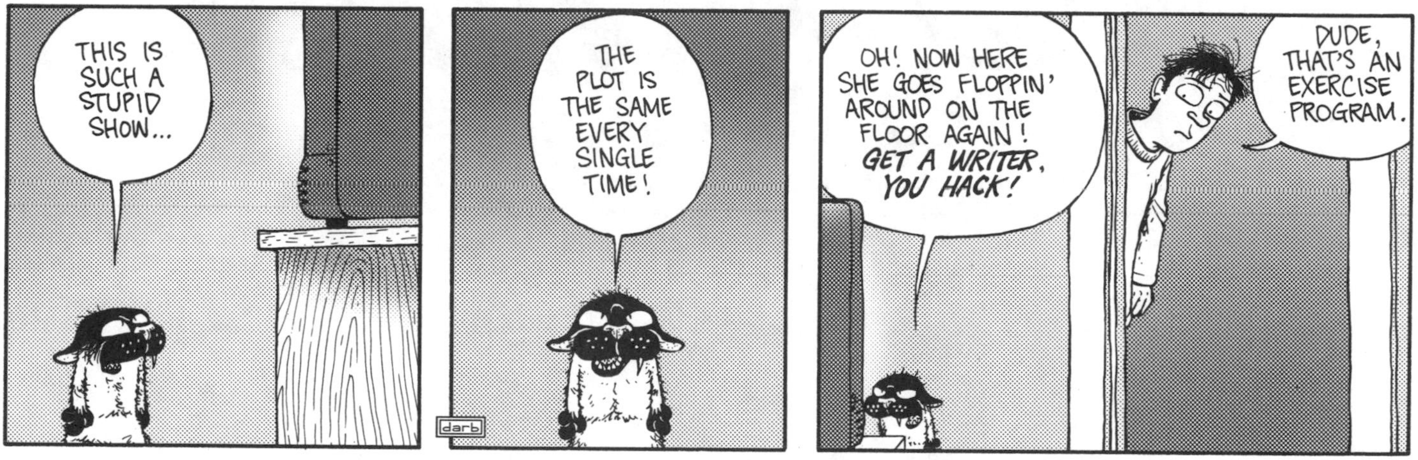
THIS IS SUCH A STUPID SHOW...
darb
THE PLOT IS THE SAME EVERY SINGLE TIME!
OH! NOW HERE SHE GOES FLOPPIN' AROUND ON THE FLOOR AGAIN! ***GET A WRITER, YOU HACK!***
DUDE, THAT'S AN EXERCISE PROGRAM.

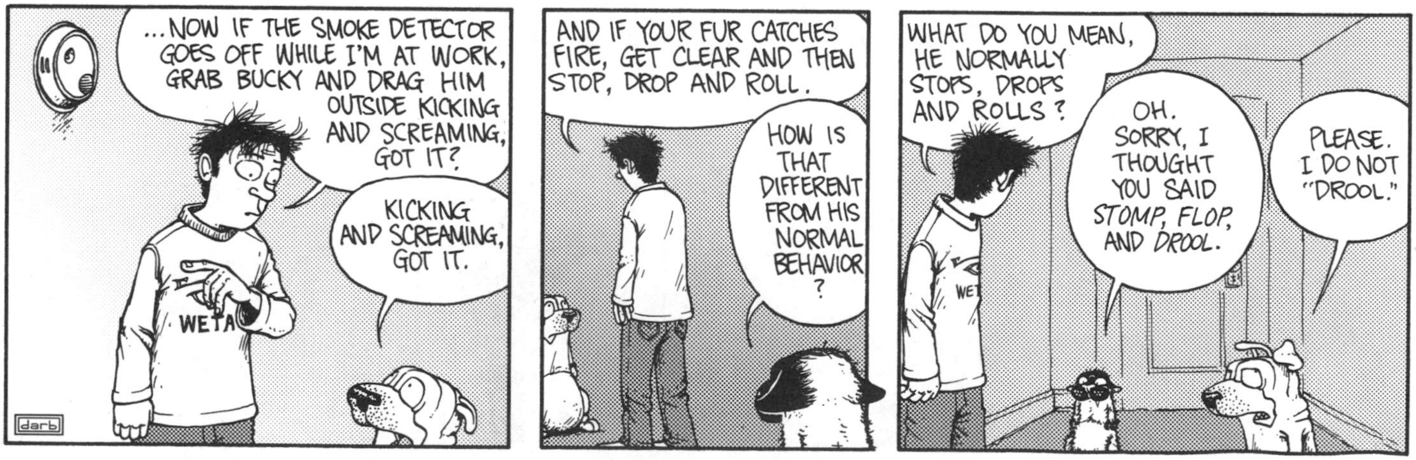
...NOW IF THE SMOKE DETECTOR GOES OFF WHILE I'M AT WORK, GRAB BUCKY AND DRAG HIM OUTSIDE KICKING AND SCREAMING, GOT IT?
KICKING AND SCREAMING, GOT IT.
WETA
darb
AND IF YOUR FUR CATCHES FIRE, GET CLEAR AND THEN STOP, DROP AND ROLL.
HOW IS THAT DIFFERENT FROM HIS NORMAL BEHAVIOR?
WHAT DO YOU MEAN, HE NORMALLY STOPS, DROPS AND ROLLS?
OH. SORRY, I THOUGHT YOU SAID *STOMP, FLOP,* AND *DROOL.*
PLEASE. I DO NOT "DROOL."

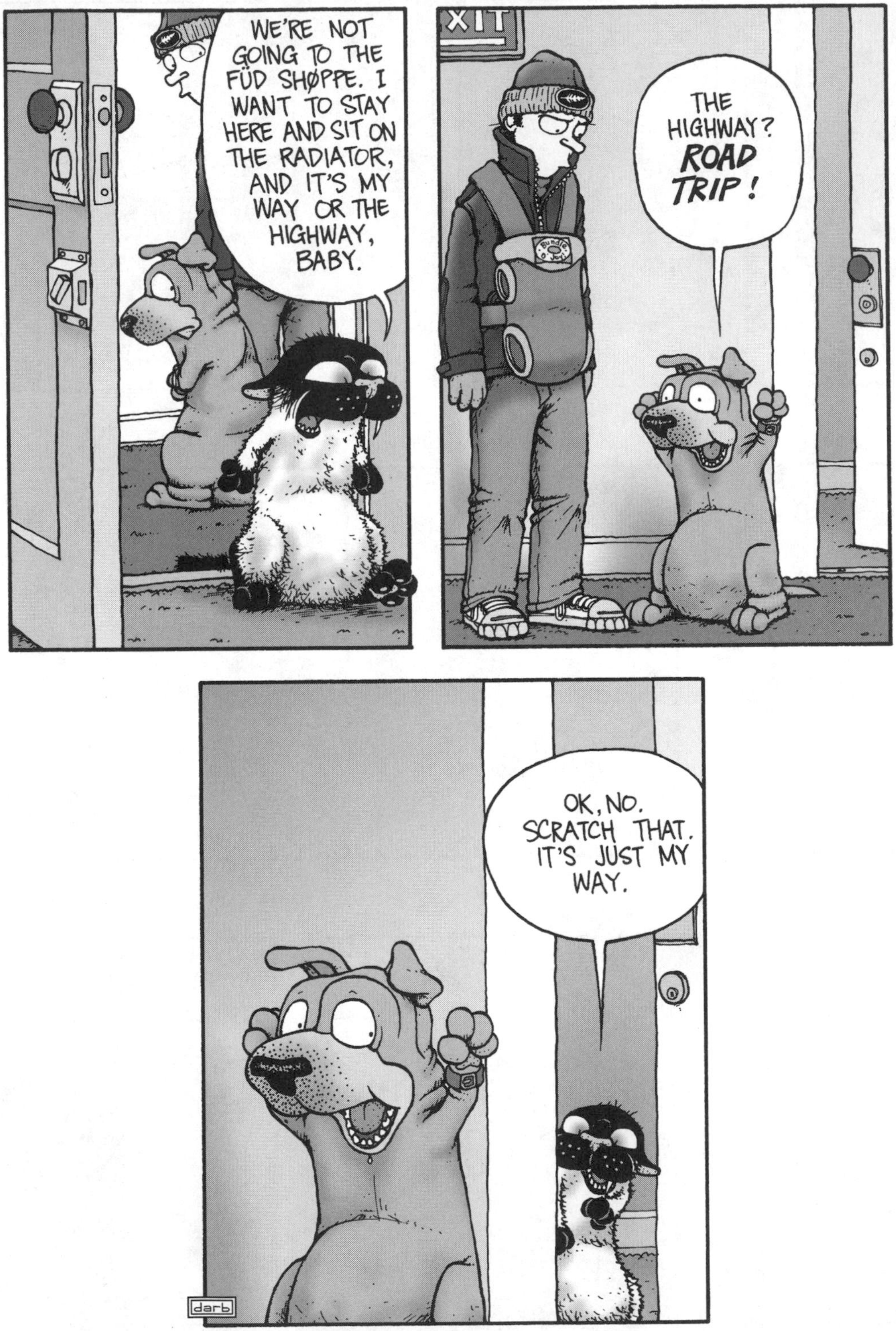
WE'RE NOT GOING TO THE FÜD SHØPPE. I WANT TO STAY HERE AND SIT ON THE RADIATOR, AND IT'S MY WAY OR THE HIGHWAY, BABY.
THE HIGHWAY? ROAD TRIP!
OK, NO. SCRATCH THAT. IT'S JUST MY WAY.
darb

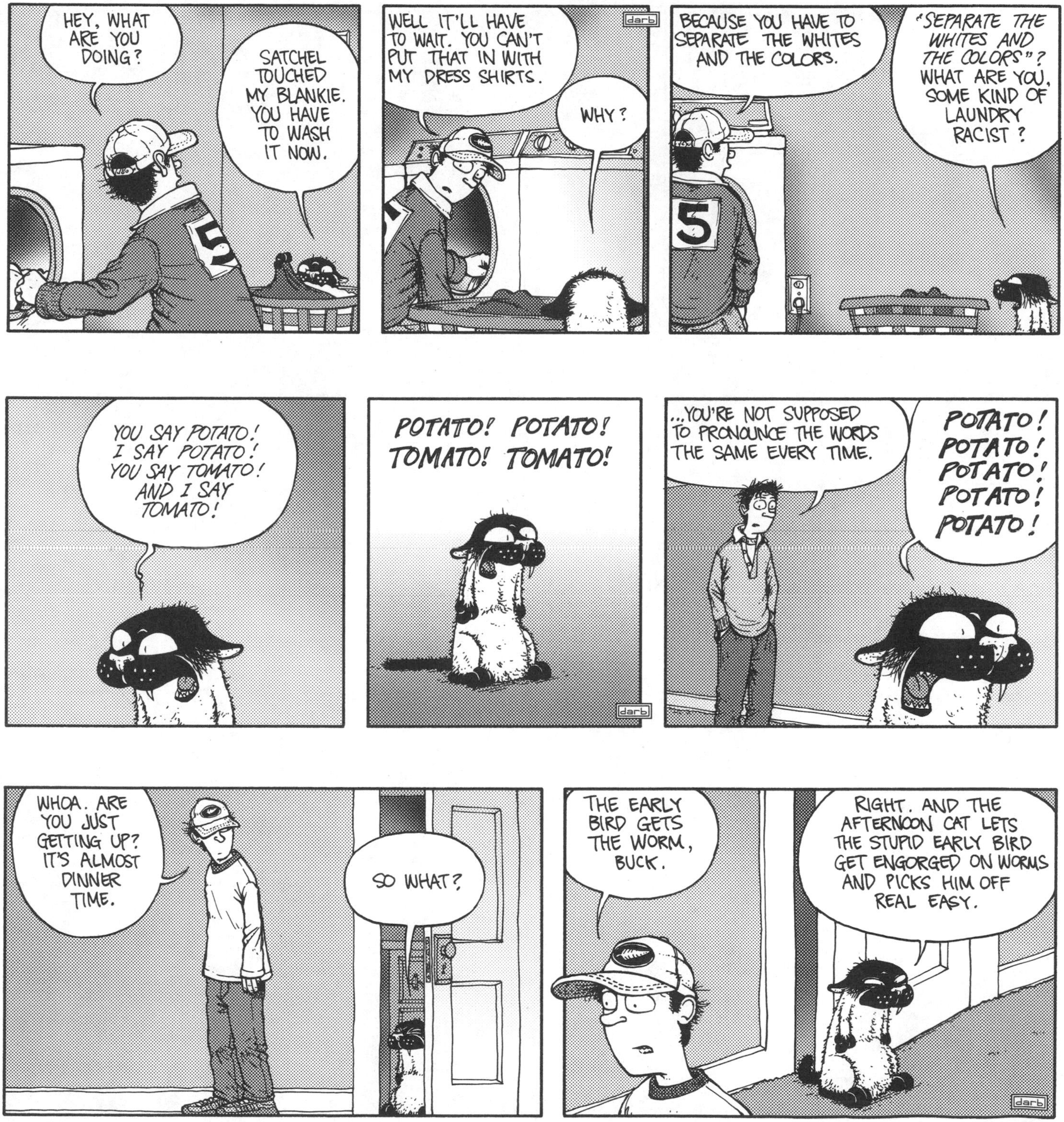
HEY, WHAT ARE YOU DOING?
SATCHEL TOUCHED MY BLANKIE. YOU HAVE TO WASH IT NOW.
darb
WELL IT'LL HAVE TO WAIT. YOU CAN'T PUT THAT IN WITH MY DRESS SHIRTS.
WHY?
BECAUSE YOU HAVE TO SEPARATE THE WHITES AND THE COLORS.
"SEPARATE THE WHITES AND THE COLORS"? WHAT ARE YOU, SOME KIND OF LAUNDRY RACIST?
YOU SAY POTATO! I SAY POTATO! YOU SAY TOMATO! AND I SAY TOMATO!
POTATO! POTATO! TOMATO! TOMATO!
darb
...YOU'RE NOT SUPPOSED TO PRONOUNCE THE WORDS THE SAME EVERY TIME.
POTATO! POTATO! POTATO! POTATO! POTATO!
WHOA. ARE YOU JUST GETTING UP? IT'S ALMOST DINNER TIME.
SO WHAT?
THE EARLY BIRD GETS THE WORM, BUCK.
RIGHT. AND THE AFTERNOON CAT LETS THE STUPID EARLY BIRD GET ENGORGED ON WORMS AND PICKS HIM OFF REAL EASY.
darb

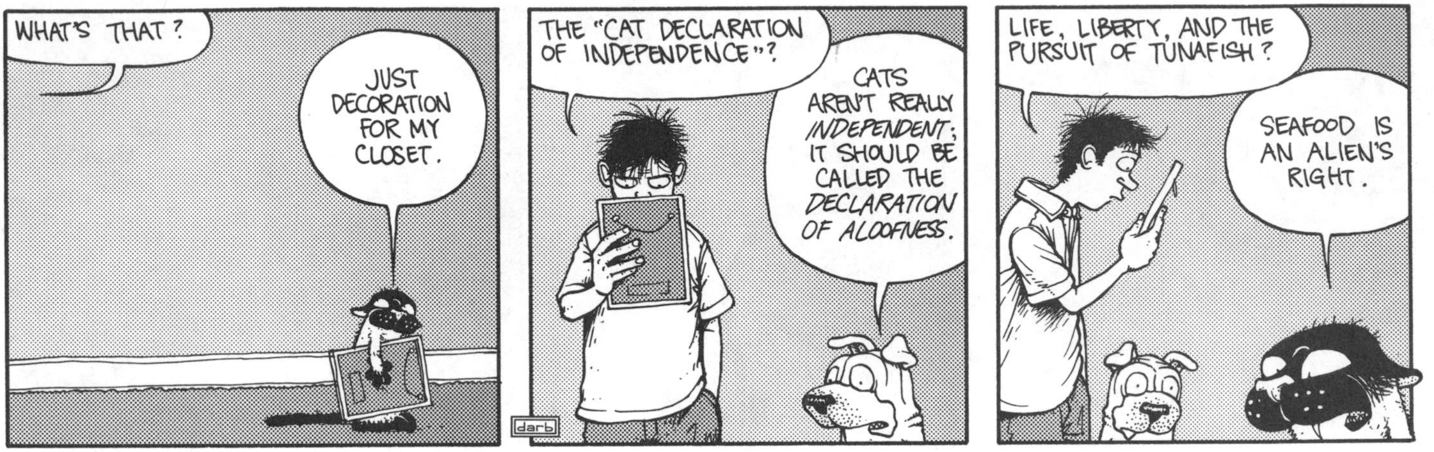
WHAT'S THAT?
JUST DECORATION FOR MY CLOSET.
THE "CAT DECLARATION OF INDEPENDENCE"?
CATS AREN'T REALLY *INDEPENDENT*; IT SHOULD BE CALLED THE *DECLARATION OF ALOOFNESS*.
LIFE, LIBERTY, AND THE PURSUIT OF TUNAFISH?
SEAFOOD IS AN ALIEN'S RIGHT.
darb

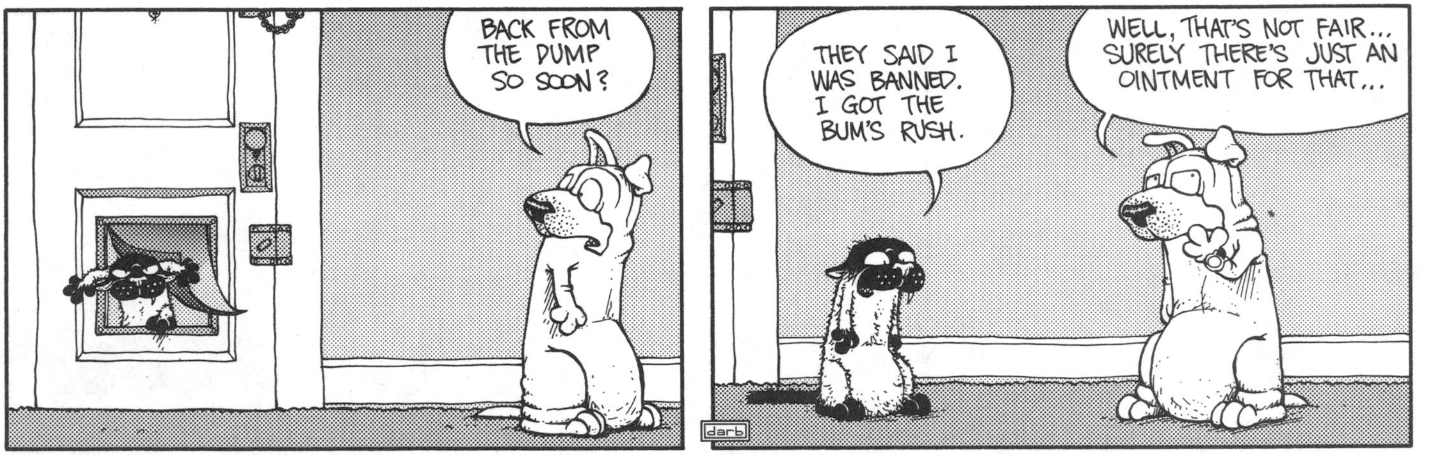
BACK FROM THE DUMP SO SOON?
THEY SAID I WAS BANNED. I GOT THE BUM'S RUSH.
WELL, THAT'S NOT FAIR... SURELY THERE'S JUST AN OINTMENT FOR THAT...
darb

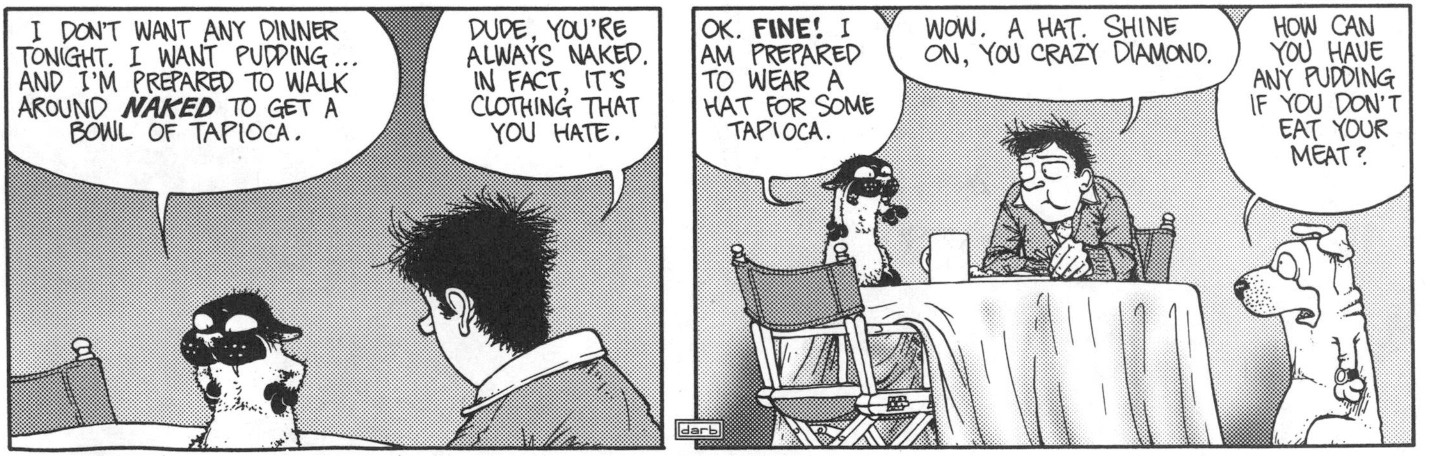
I DON'T WANT ANY DINNER TONIGHT. I WANT PUDDING... AND I'M PREPARED TO WALK AROUND ***NAKED*** TO GET A BOWL OF TAPIOCA.
DUDE, YOU'RE ALWAYS NAKED. IN FACT, IT'S CLOTHING THAT YOU HATE.
OK. **FINE!** I AM PREPARED TO WEAR A HAT FOR SOME TAPIOCA.
WOW. A HAT. SHINE ON, YOU CRAZY DIAMOND.
HOW CAN YOU HAVE ANY PUDDING IF YOU DON'T EAT YOUR MEAT?
darb

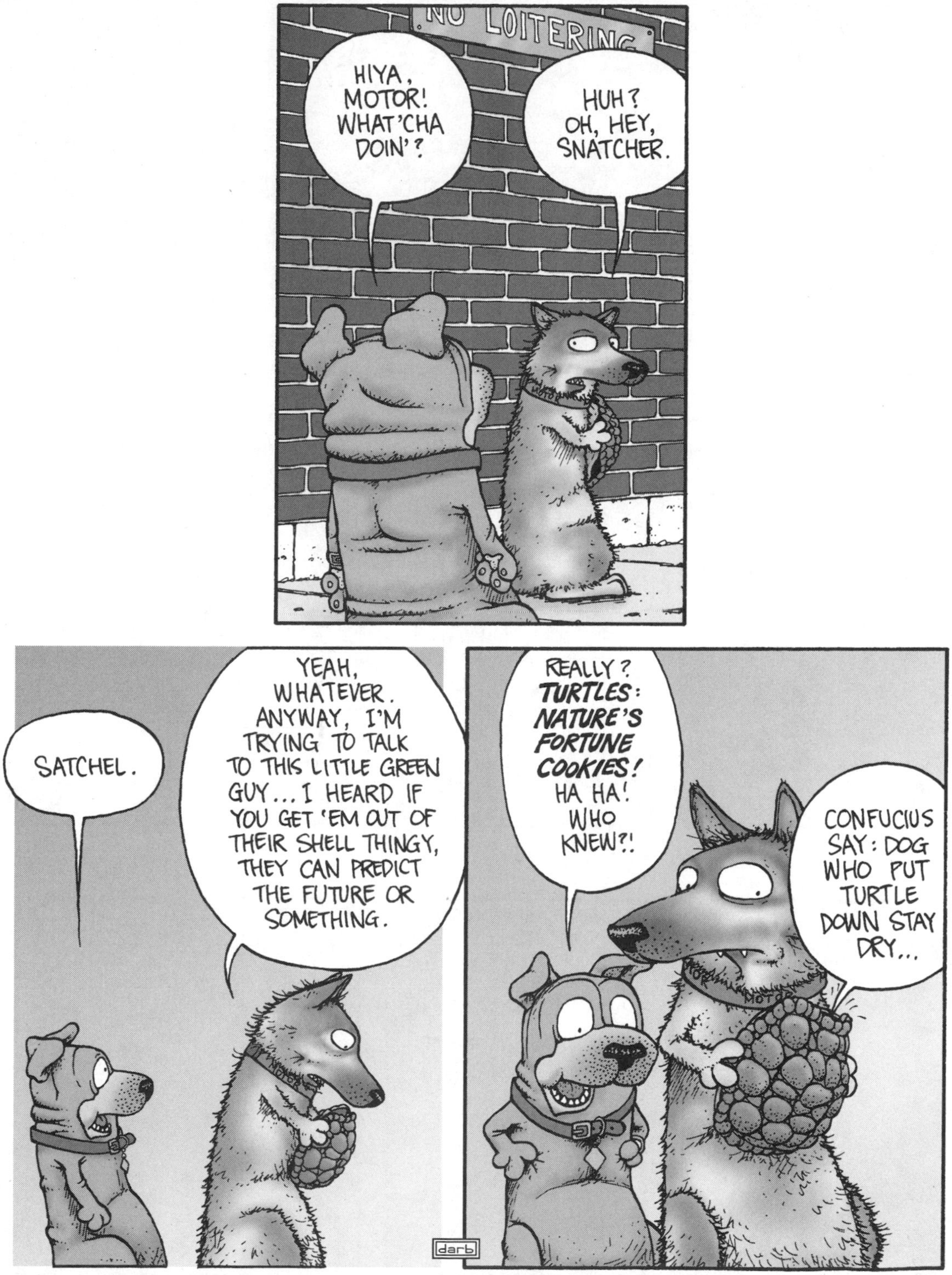
NO LOITERING
HIYA, MOTOR! WHAT'CHA DOIN'?
HUH? OH, HEY, SNATCHER.
SATCHEL.
YEAH, WHATEVER. ANYWAY, I'M TRYING TO TALK TO THIS LITTLE GREEN GUY... I HEARD IF YOU GET 'EM OUT OF THEIR SHELL THINGY, THEY CAN PREDICT THE FUTURE OR SOMETHING.
REALLY? TURTLES: NATURE'S FORTUNE COOKIES! HA HA! WHO KNEW?!
CONFUCIUS SAY: DOG WHO PUT TURTLE DOWN STAY DRY...
darb

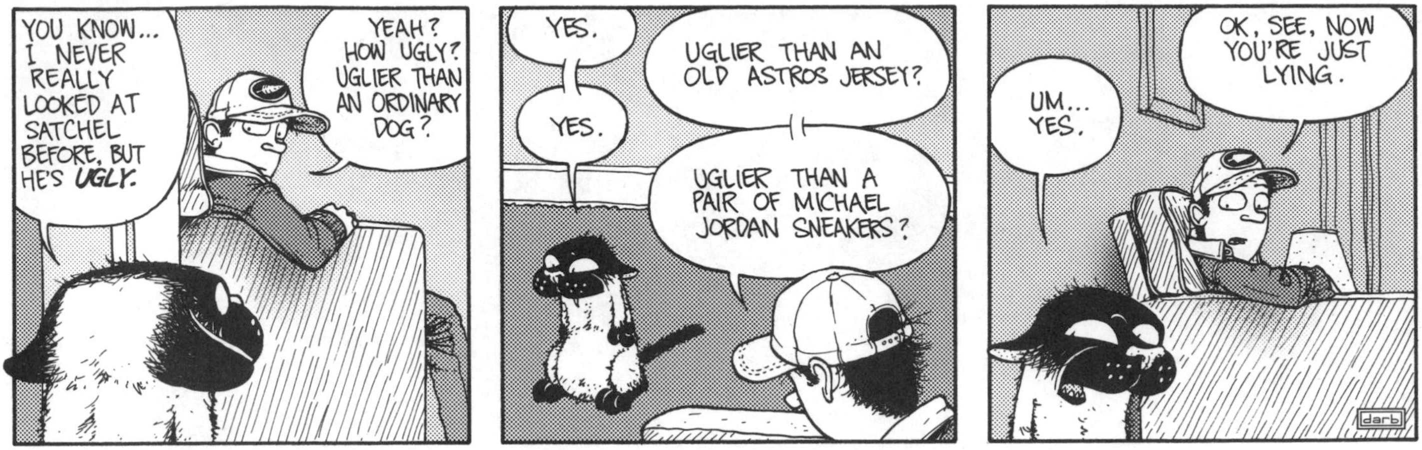
YOU KNOW... I NEVER REALLY LOOKED AT SATCHEL BEFORE, BUT HE'S UGLY.
YEAH? HOW UGLY? UGLIER THAN AN ORDINARY DOG?
YES.
YES.
UGLIER THAN AN OLD ASTROS JERSEY?
UGLIER THAN A PAIR OF MICHAEL JORDAN SNEAKERS?
UM... YES.
OK, SEE, NOW YOU'RE JUST LYING.
darb

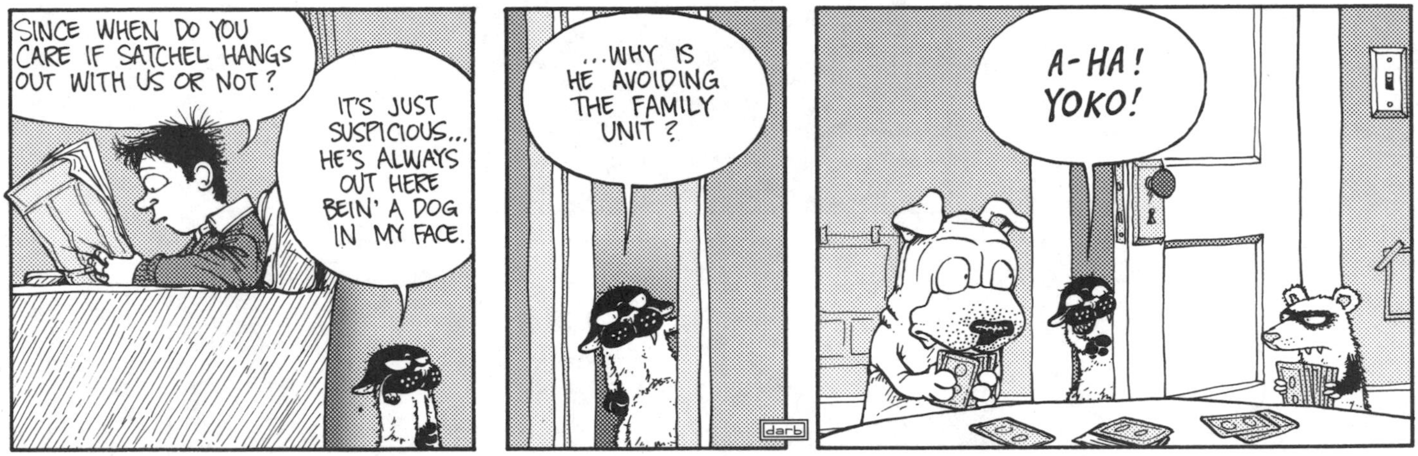
SINCE WHEN DO YOU CARE IF SATCHEL HANGS OUT WITH US OR NOT?
IT'S JUST SUSPICIOUS... HE'S ALWAYS OUT HERE BEIN' A DOG IN MY FACE.
...WHY IS HE AVOIDING THE FAMILY UNIT?
darb
A-HA! YOKO!

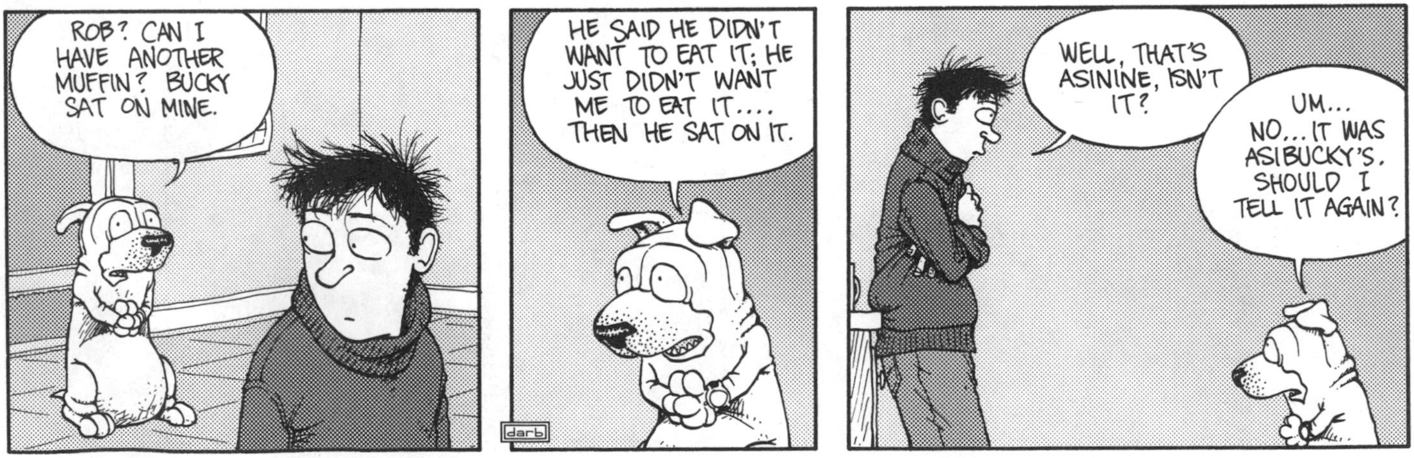
ROB? CAN I HAVE ANOTHER MUFFIN? BUCKY SAT ON MINE.
HE SAID HE DIDN'T WANT TO EAT IT; HE JUST DIDN'T WANT ME TO EAT IT.... THEN HE SAT ON IT.
darb
WELL, THAT'S ASININE, ISN'T IT?
UM... NO... IT WAS ASIBUCKY'S. SHOULD I TELL IT AGAIN?

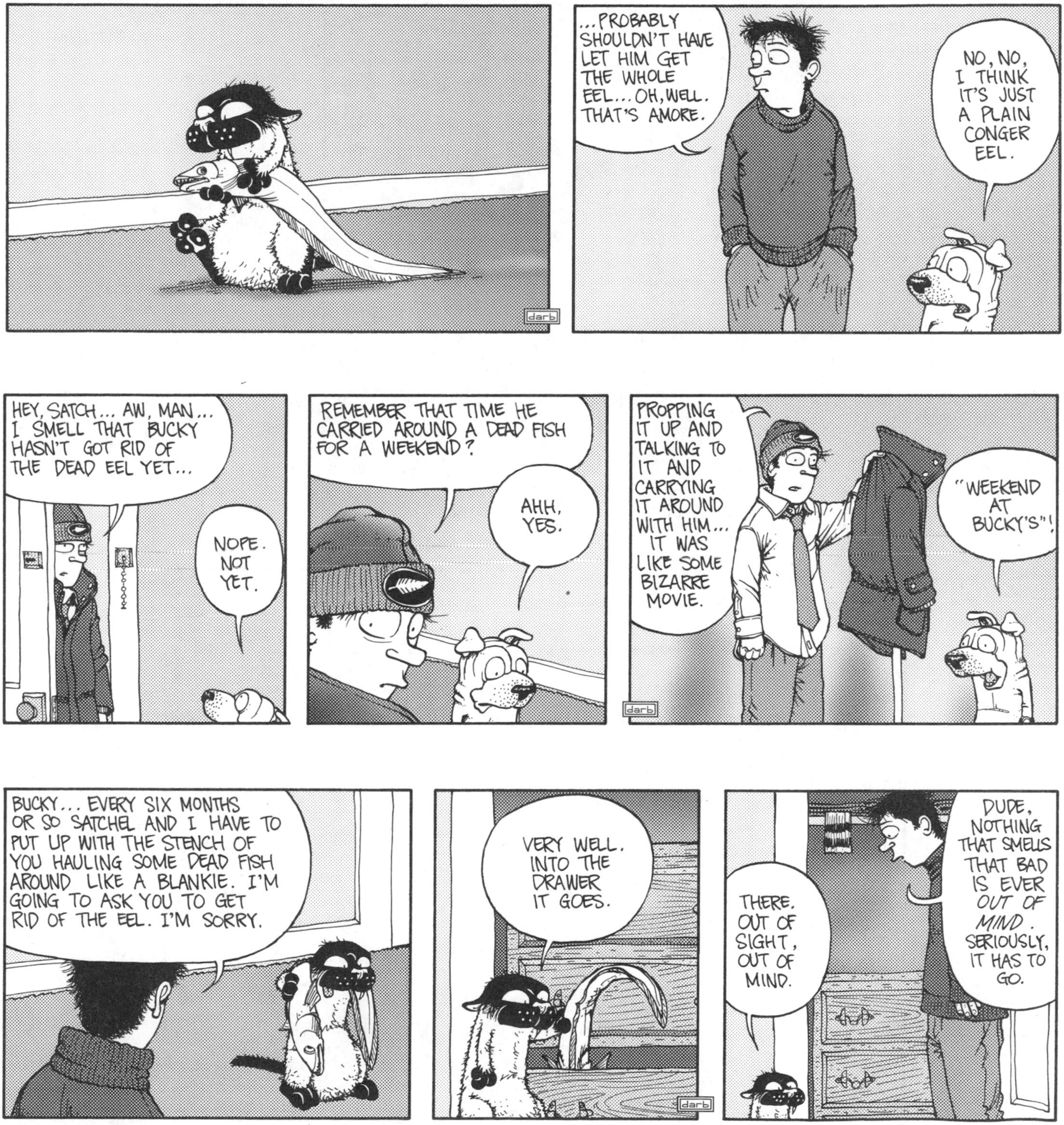
...PROBABLY SHOULDN'T HAVE LET HIM GET THE WHOLE EEL...OH, WELL. THAT'S AMORE.
NO, NO, I THINK IT'S JUST A PLAIN CONGER EEL.
HEY, SATCH... AW, MAN... I SMELL THAT BUCKY HASN'T GOT RID OF THE DEAD EEL YET...
NOPE. NOT YET.
REMEMBER THAT TIME HE CARRIED AROUND A DEAD FISH FOR A WEEKEND?
AHH, YES.
PROPPING IT UP AND TALKING TO IT AND CARRYING IT AROUND WITH HIM... IT WAS LIKE SOME BIZARRE MOVIE.
"WEEKEND AT BUCKY'S"!
BUCKY... EVERY SIX MONTHS OR SO SATCHEL AND I HAVE TO PUT UP WITH THE STENCH OF YOU HAULING SOME DEAD FISH AROUND LIKE A BLANKIE. I'M GOING TO ASK YOU TO GET RID OF THE EEL. I'M SORRY.
VERY WELL. INTO THE DRAWER IT GOES.
THERE. OUT OF SIGHT, OUT OF MIND.
DUDE, NOTHING THAT SMELLS THAT BAD IS EVER *OUT OF MIND*. SERIOUSLY, IT HAS TO GO.

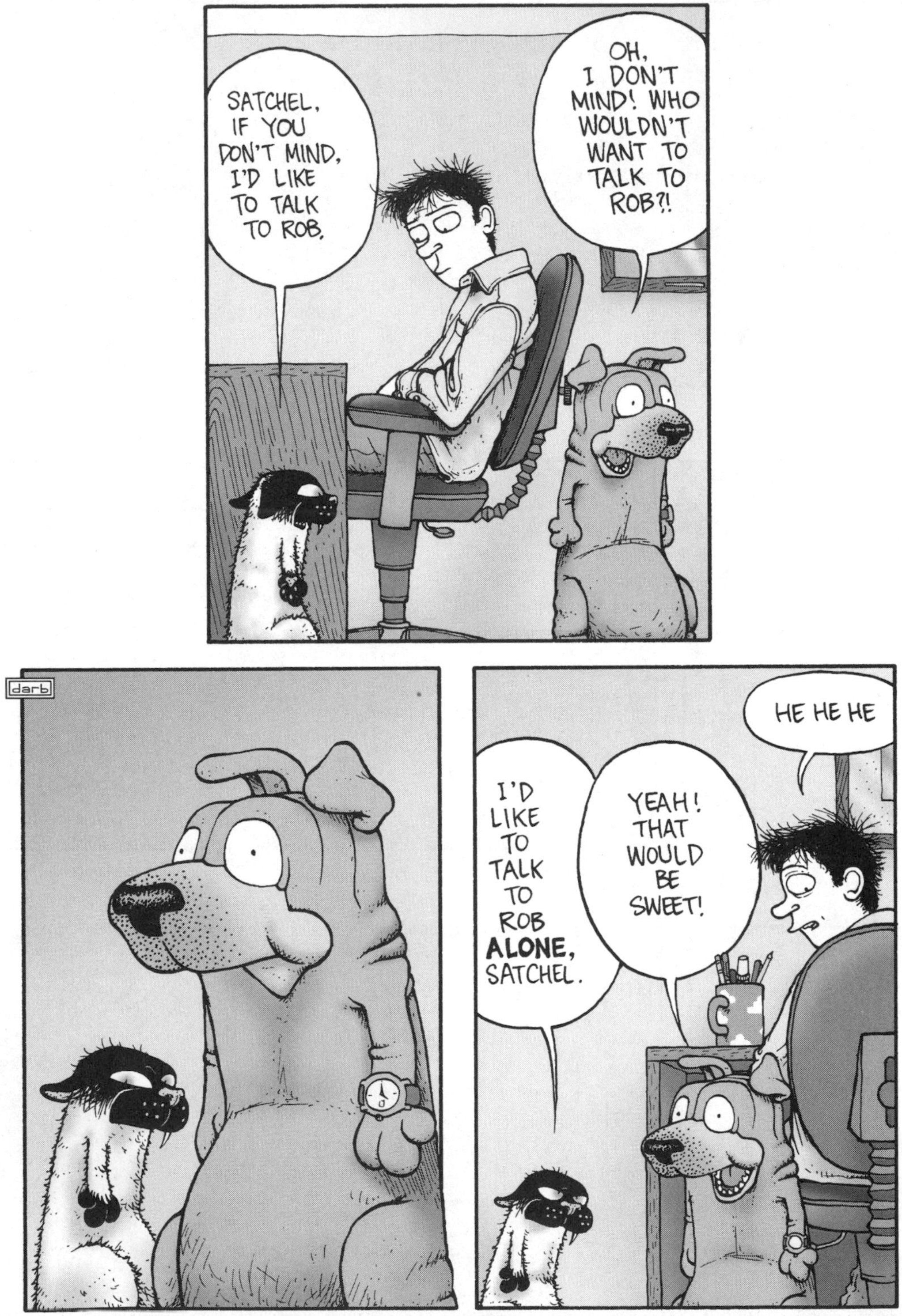
SATCHEL, IF YOU DON'T MIND, I'D LIKE TO TALK TO ROB.
OH, I DON'T MIND! WHO WOULDN'T WANT TO TALK TO ROB?!
darb
HE HE HE
I'D LIKE TO TALK TO ROB **ALONE,** SATCHEL.
YEAH! THAT WOULD BE SWEET!

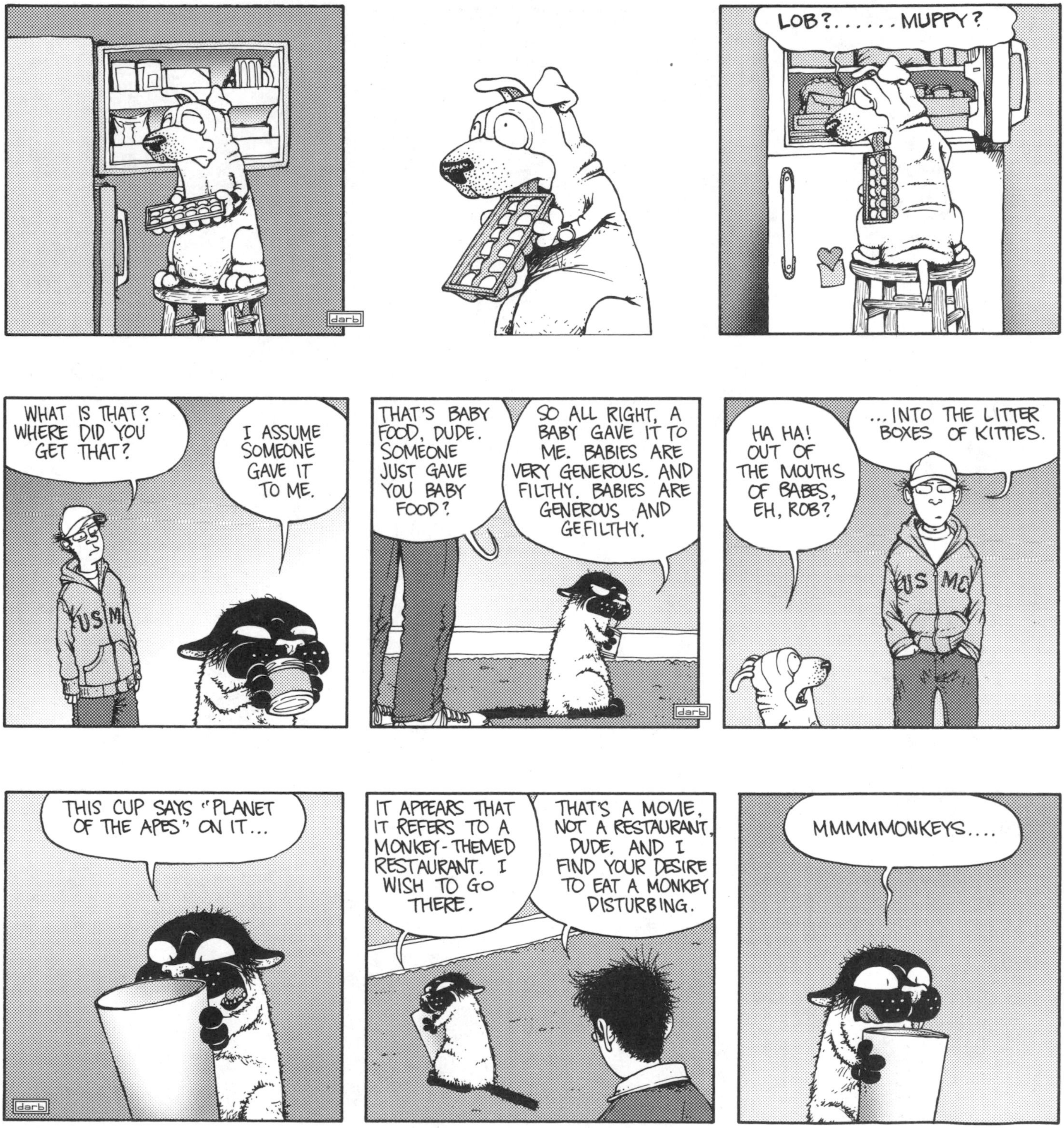
LOB?......MUPPY?
WHAT IS THAT? WHERE DID YOU GET THAT?
I ASSUME SOMEONE GAVE IT TO ME.
THAT'S BABY FOOD, DUDE. SOMEONE JUST GAVE YOU BABY FOOD?
SO ALL RIGHT, A BABY GAVE IT TO ME. BABIES ARE VERY GENEROUS. AND FILTHY. BABIES ARE GENEROUS AND GEFILTHY.
HA HA! OUT OF THE MOUTHS OF BABES, EH, ROB?
...INTO THE LITTER BOXES OF KITTIES.
THIS CUP SAYS "PLANET OF THE APES" ON IT...
IT APPEARS THAT IT REFERS TO A MONKEY-THEMED RESTAURANT. I WISH TO GO THERE.
THAT'S A MOVIE, NOT A RESTAURANT, DUDE. AND I FIND YOUR DESIRE TO EAT A MONKEY DISTURBING.
MMMMMONKEYS....

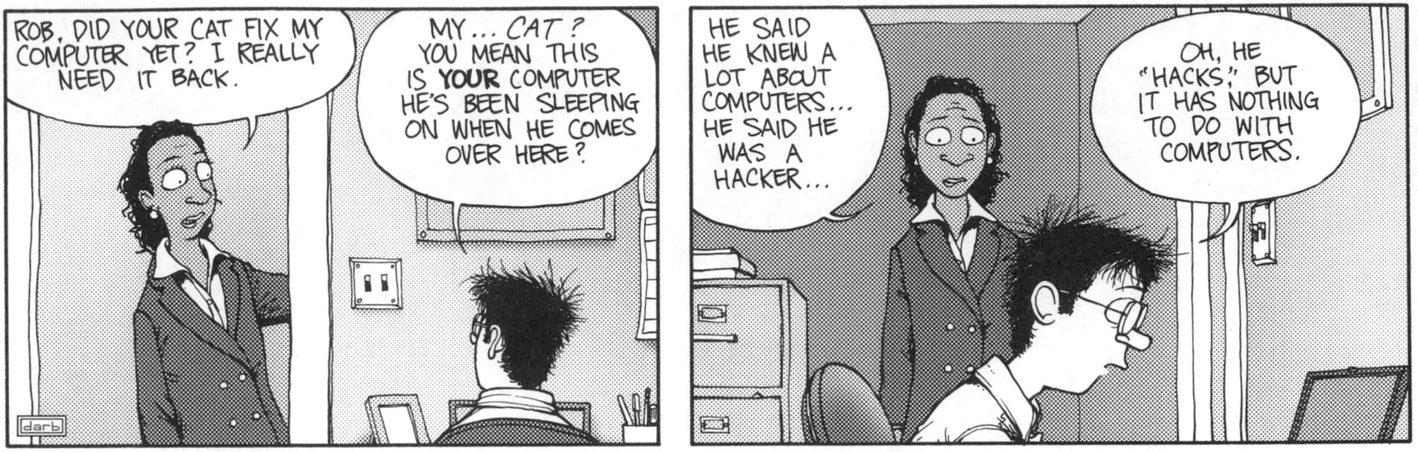
ROB, DID YOUR CAT FIX MY COMPUTER YET? I REALLY NEED IT BACK.
MY... *CAT?* YOU MEAN THIS IS **YOUR** COMPUTER HE'S BEEN SLEEPING ON WHEN HE COMES OVER HERE?
darb
HE SAID HE KNEW A LOT ABOUT COMPUTERS... HE SAID HE WAS A HACKER...
OH, HE "HACKS," BUT IT HAS NOTHING TO DO WITH COMPUTERS.

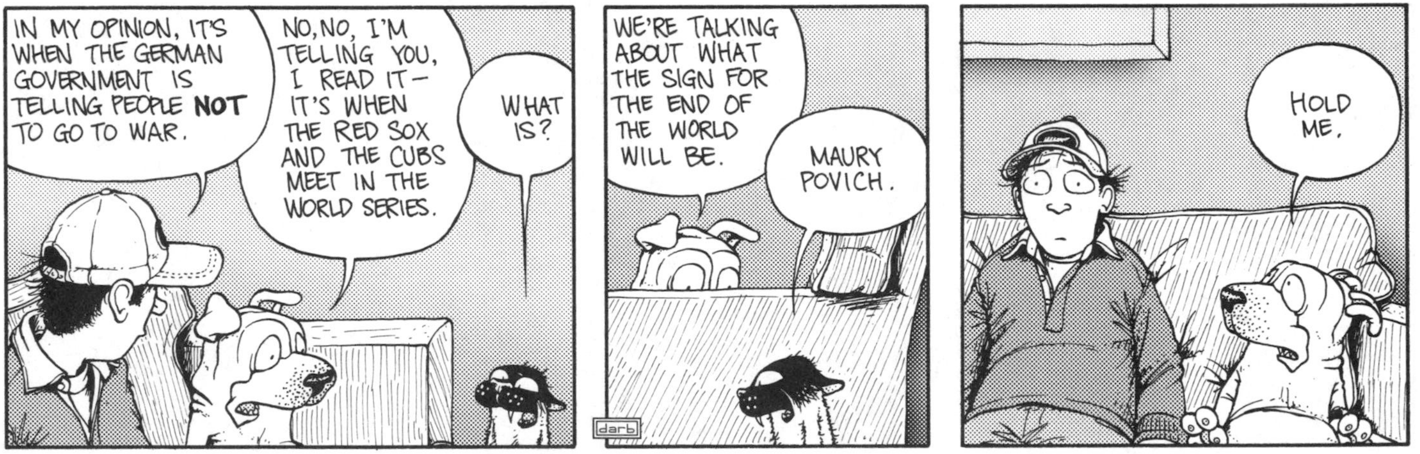
IN MY OPINION, IT'S WHEN THE GERMAN GOVERNMENT IS TELLING PEOPLE **NOT** TO GO TO WAR.
NO, NO, I'M TELLING YOU, I READ IT— IT'S WHEN THE RED SOX AND THE CUBS MEET IN THE WORLD SERIES.
WHAT IS?
WE'RE TALKING ABOUT WHAT THE SIGN FOR THE END OF THE WORLD WILL BE.
MAURY POVICH.
darb
HOLD ME.

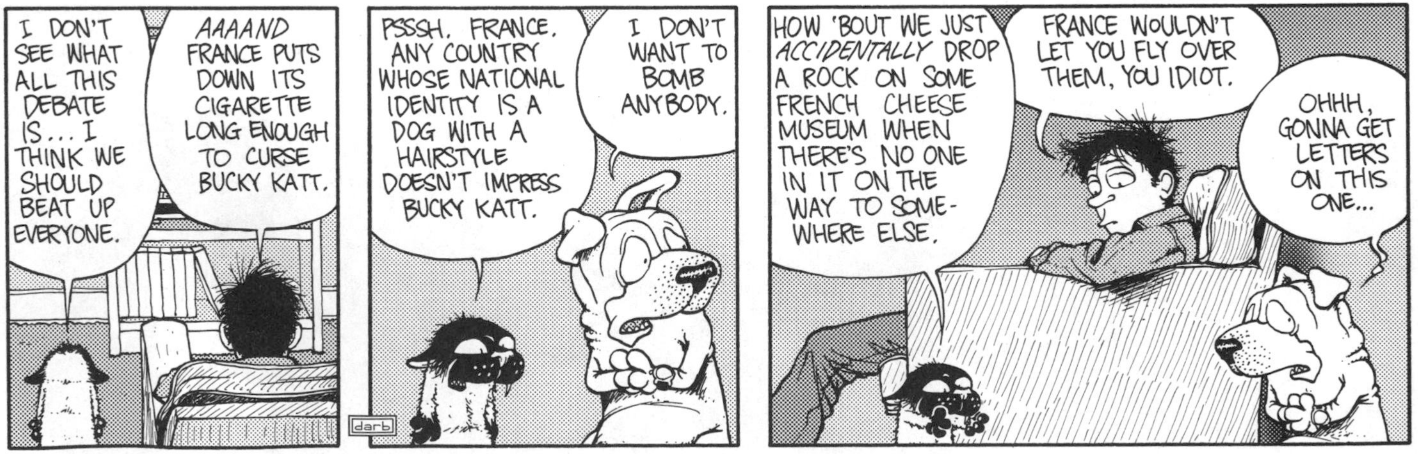
I DON'T SEE WHAT ALL THIS DEBATE IS... I THINK WE SHOULD BEAT UP EVERYONE.
AAAAND FRANCE PUTS DOWN ITS CIGARETTE LONG ENOUGH TO CURSE BUCKY KATT.
PSSSH. FRANCE. ANY COUNTRY WHOSE NATIONAL IDENTITY IS A DOG WITH A HAIRSTYLE DOESN'T IMPRESS BUCKY KATT.
I DON'T WANT TO BOMB ANYBODY.
darb
HOW 'BOUT WE JUST *ACCIDENTALLY* DROP A ROCK ON SOME FRENCH CHEESE MUSEUM WHEN THERE'S NO ONE IN IT ON THE WAY TO SOME-WHERE ELSE.
FRANCE WOULDN'T LET YOU FLY OVER THEM, YOU IDIOT.
OHHH, GONNA GET LETTERS ON THIS ONE...

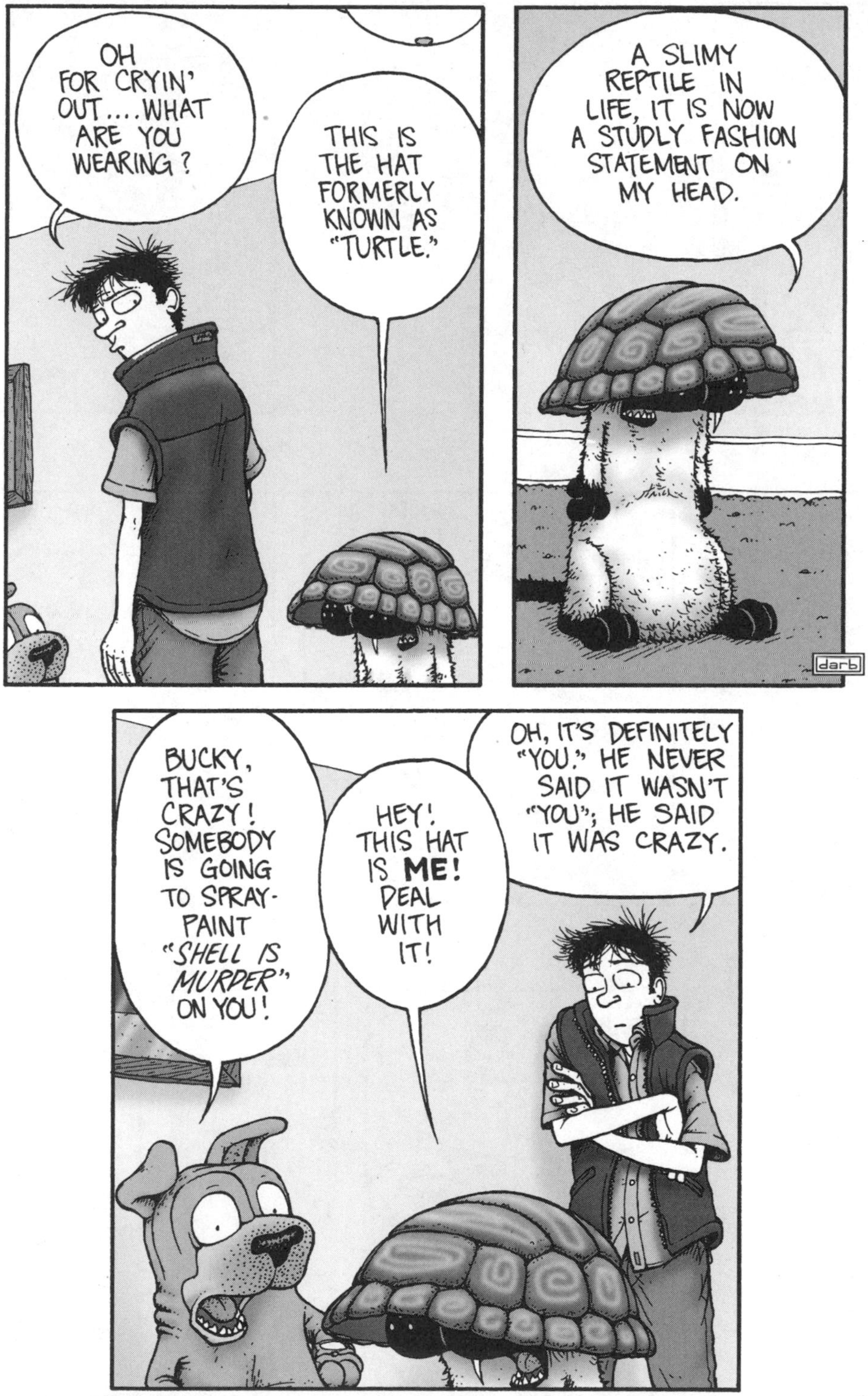
OH FOR CRYIN' OUT....WHAT ARE YOU WEARING?
THIS IS THE HAT FORMERLY KNOWN AS "TURTLE."
A SLIMY REPTILE IN LIFE, IT IS NOW A STUDLY FASHION STATEMENT ON MY HEAD.
darb
BUCKY, THAT'S CRAZY! SOMEBODY IS GOING TO SPRAY-PAINT "SHELL IS MURDER" ON YOU!
HEY! THIS HAT IS ME! DEAL WITH IT!
OH, IT'S DEFINITELY "YOU." HE NEVER SAID IT WASN'T "YOU"; HE SAID IT WAS CRAZY.

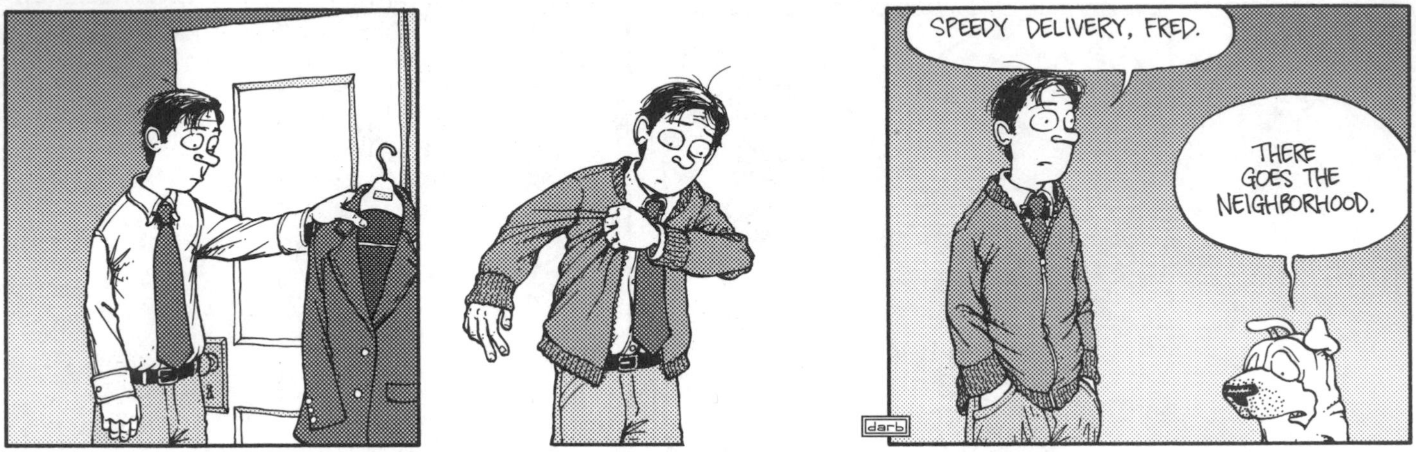
SPEEDY DELIVERY, FRED.
THERE GOES THE NEIGHBORHOOD.

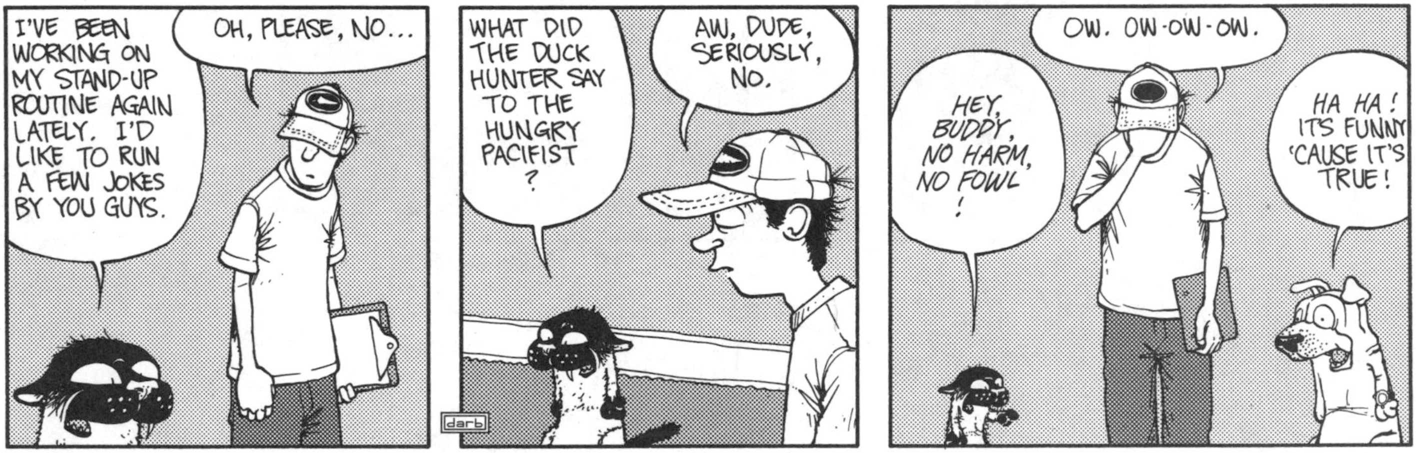
I'VE BEEN WORKING ON MY STAND-UP ROUTINE AGAIN LATELY. I'D LIKE TO RUN A FEW JOKES BY YOU GUYS.
OH, PLEASE, NO...
WHAT DID THE DUCK HUNTER SAY TO THE HUNGRY PACIFIST ?
AW, DUDE, SERIOUSLY, NO.
OW. OW-OW-OW.
HEY, BUDDY, NO HARM, NO FOWL !
HA HA! IT'S FUNNY 'CAUSE IT'S TRUE!

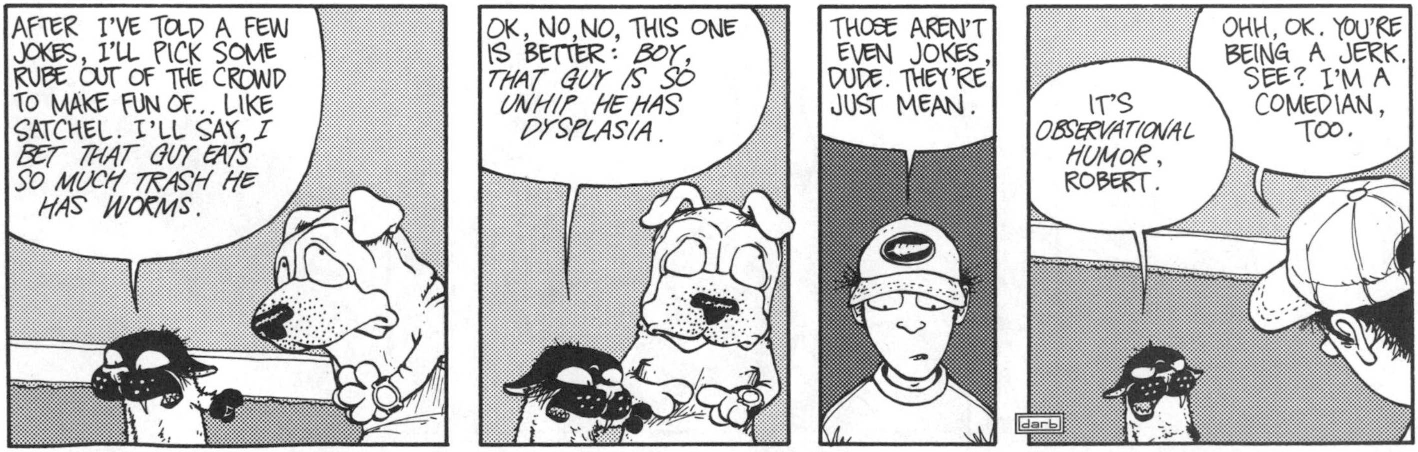
AFTER I'VE TOLD A FEW JOKES, I'LL PICK SOME RUBE OUT OF THE CROWD TO MAKE FUN OF... LIKE SATCHEL. I'LL SAY, *I BET THAT GUY EATS SO MUCH TRASH HE HAS WORMS*.
OK, NO, NO, THIS ONE IS BETTER: *BOY, THAT GUY IS SO UNHIP HE HAS DYSPLASIA*.
THOSE AREN'T EVEN JOKES, DUDE. THEY'RE JUST MEAN.
IT'S *OBSERVATIONAL HUMOR*, ROBERT.
OHH, OK. YOU'RE BEING A JERK. SEE? I'M A COMEDIAN, TOO.

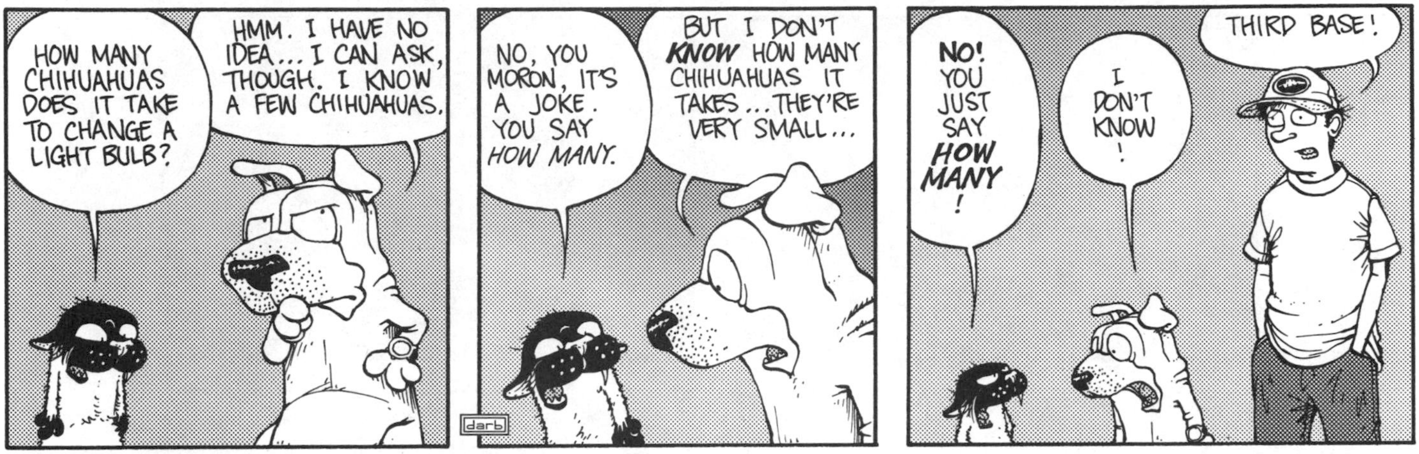
HOW MANY CHIHUAHUAS DOES IT TAKE TO CHANGE A LIGHT BULB?
HMM. I HAVE NO IDEA... I CAN ASK, THOUGH. I KNOW A FEW CHIHUAHUAS.
NO, YOU MORON, IT'S A JOKE. YOU SAY *HOW MANY.*
BUT I DON'T *KNOW* HOW MANY CHIHUAHUAS IT TAKES... THEY'RE VERY SMALL...
NO! YOU JUST SAY ***HOW MANY*** !
I DON'T KNOW !
THIRD BASE!
darb

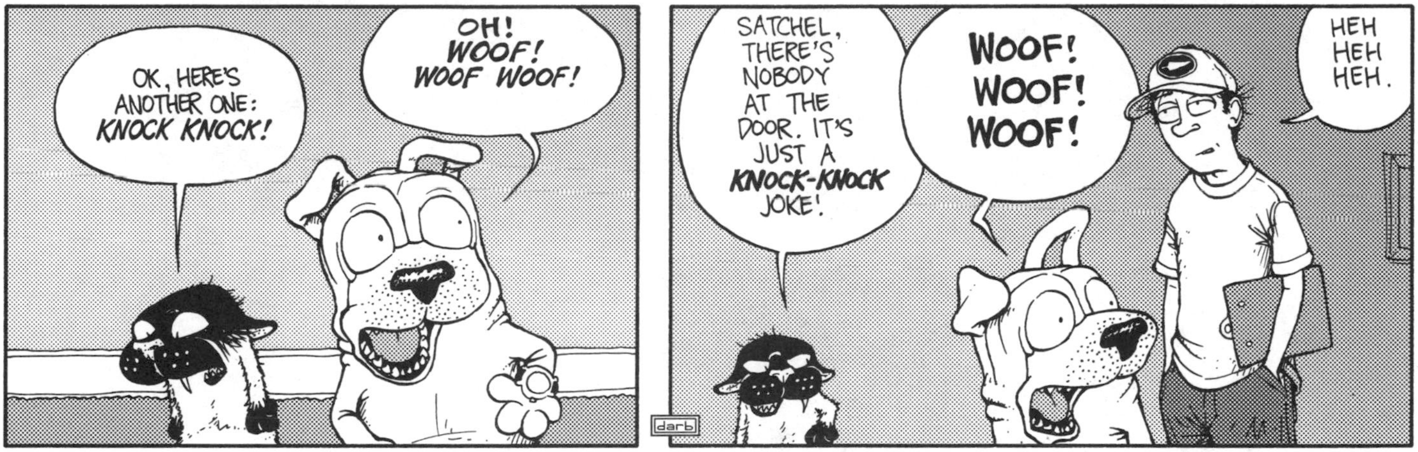
OK, HERE'S ANOTHER ONE: ***KNOCK KNOCK!***
OH! WOOF! WOOF WOOF!
SATCHEL, THERE'S NOBODY AT THE DOOR. IT'S JUST A ***KNOCK-KNOCK*** JOKE!
WOOF! WOOF! WOOF!
HEH HEH HEH.
darb

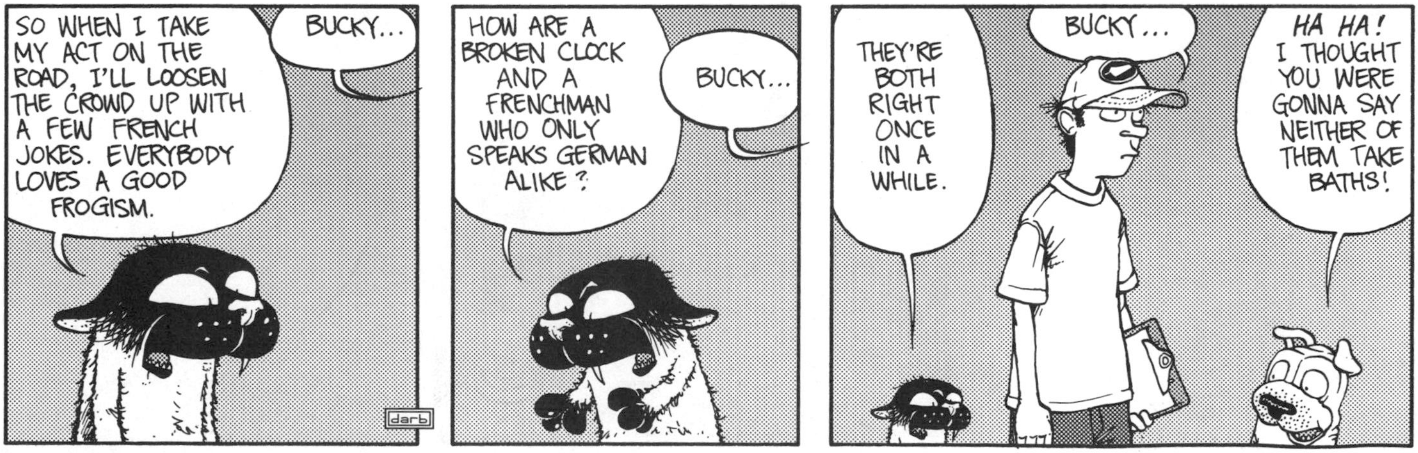
SO WHEN I TAKE MY ACT ON THE ROAD, I'LL LOOSEN THE CROWD UP WITH A FEW FRENCH JOKES. EVERYBODY LOVES A GOOD FROGISM.
BUCKY...
darb
HOW ARE A BROKEN CLOCK AND A FRENCHMAN WHO ONLY SPEAKS GERMAN ALIKE?
BUCKY...
THEY'RE BOTH RIGHT ONCE IN A WHILE.
BUCKY...
HA HA! I THOUGHT YOU WERE GONNA SAY NEITHER OF THEM TAKE BATHS!

AAAAAAEEEE!
darb

CRASH
TAKE YOUR STRING OUTSIDE!
HE'S GONNA SLEEP WELL TONIGHT! HA HA! AGAIN!

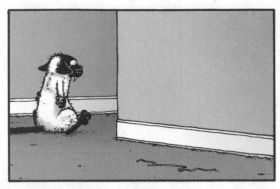

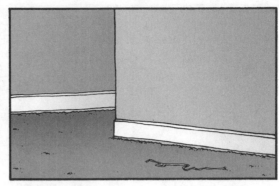

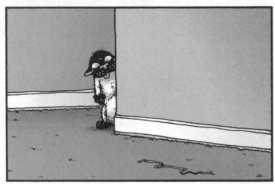

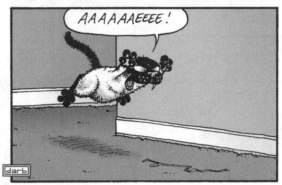

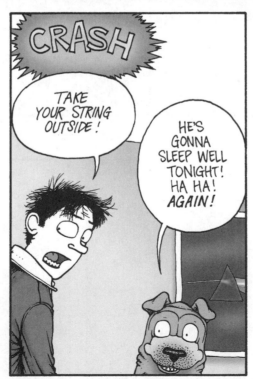

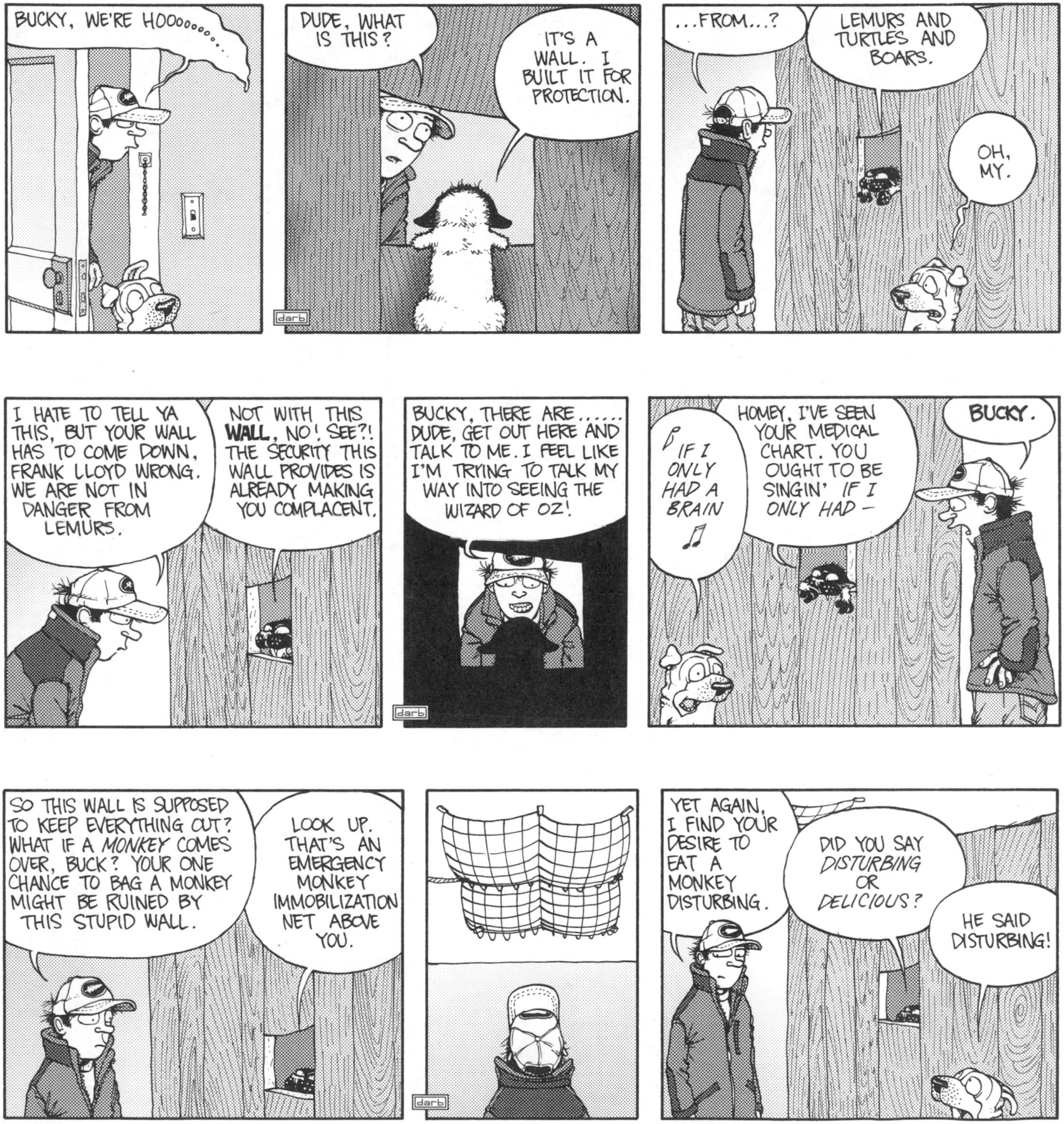
BUCKY, WE'RE HOOoooooo...
DUDE, WHAT IS THIS?
IT'S A WALL. I BUILT IT FOR PROTECTION.
...FROM...?
LEMURS AND TURTLES AND BOARS.
OH, MY.
darb
I HATE TO TELL YA THIS, BUT YOUR WALL HAS TO COME DOWN, FRANK LLOYD WRONG. WE ARE NOT IN DANGER FROM LEMURS.
NOT WITH THIS **WALL**, NO! SEE?! THE SECURITY THIS WALL PROVIDES IS ALREADY MAKING YOU COMPLACENT.
BUCKY, THERE ARE...... DUDE, GET OUT HERE AND TALK TO ME. I FEEL LIKE I'M TRYING TO TALK MY WAY INTO SEEING THE WIZARD OF OZ!
♪ *IF I ONLY HAD A BRAIN* ♫
HOMEY, I'VE SEEN YOUR MEDICAL CHART. YOU OUGHT TO BE SINGIN' *IF I ONLY HAD* —
BUCKY.
darb
SO THIS WALL IS SUPPOSED TO KEEP EVERYTHING OUT? WHAT IF A *MONKEY* COMES OVER, BUCK? YOUR ONE CHANCE TO BAG A MONKEY MIGHT BE RUINED BY THIS STUPID WALL.
LOOK UP. THAT'S AN EMERGENCY MONKEY IMMOBILIZATION NET ABOVE YOU.
YET AGAIN, I FIND YOUR DESIRE TO EAT A MONKEY DISTURBING.
DID YOU SAY *DISTURBING* OR *DELICIOUS*?
HE SAID DISTURBING!
darb

DID YOU REALIZE THAT YOUR WALL BLOCKS SATCHEL'S ROOM FROM THE FRONT DOOR BUT DOESN'T BLOCK YOURS?

WELL, I DIDN'T WANT TO BLOCK OFF MY **OWN** ROOM.

ONCE AGAIN, I WILL REMIND YOU OF THE GOLDEN RULE: *TREAT OTHERS AS YOU WOULD LIKE TO BE TREATED.*

AND ONCE AGAIN, I REMIND YOU THAT I AM NOT A GOLDEN RETRIEVER.

OK, THEN I GUESS YOUR CLOSET IS IN SATCHEL'S TERRITORY NOW.

NO, NO, SEE, IT... ...UM... UH-OH.

I CALL HIS BLANKIE!

ALL RIGHT! IF YOU'RE NOT GONNA LET ME INTO MY ROOM, I'M GONNA CLAIM YOUR CLOSET!

HEY! I'M WARNING YOU! STAY OUT OF MY CLOSET! THE EARTH SHALL TREMBLE AS I ADMINISTER PUNISHMENT TO THOSE WHO DEFY ME! HEY!

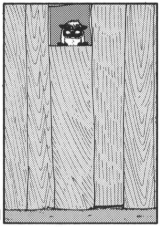

LIFT ME DOWN SO I CAN MAKE THE EARTH TREMBLE.

SAY PLEASE.

SATCHEL! GET OUT OF MY CLOSET!

NOT UNTIL YOU TEAR DOWN THAT WALL!

TELL YA WHAT... LET'S JUST SIT DOWN OVER A NICE CUP OF WARM MILK AND DISCUSS THIS...

WELL, I'D HAVE TO COME OUT OF THE CLOSET TO DO THAT.

WHOA. I'VE BEEN WAITIN' THREE YEARS FOR—

BUCKY...

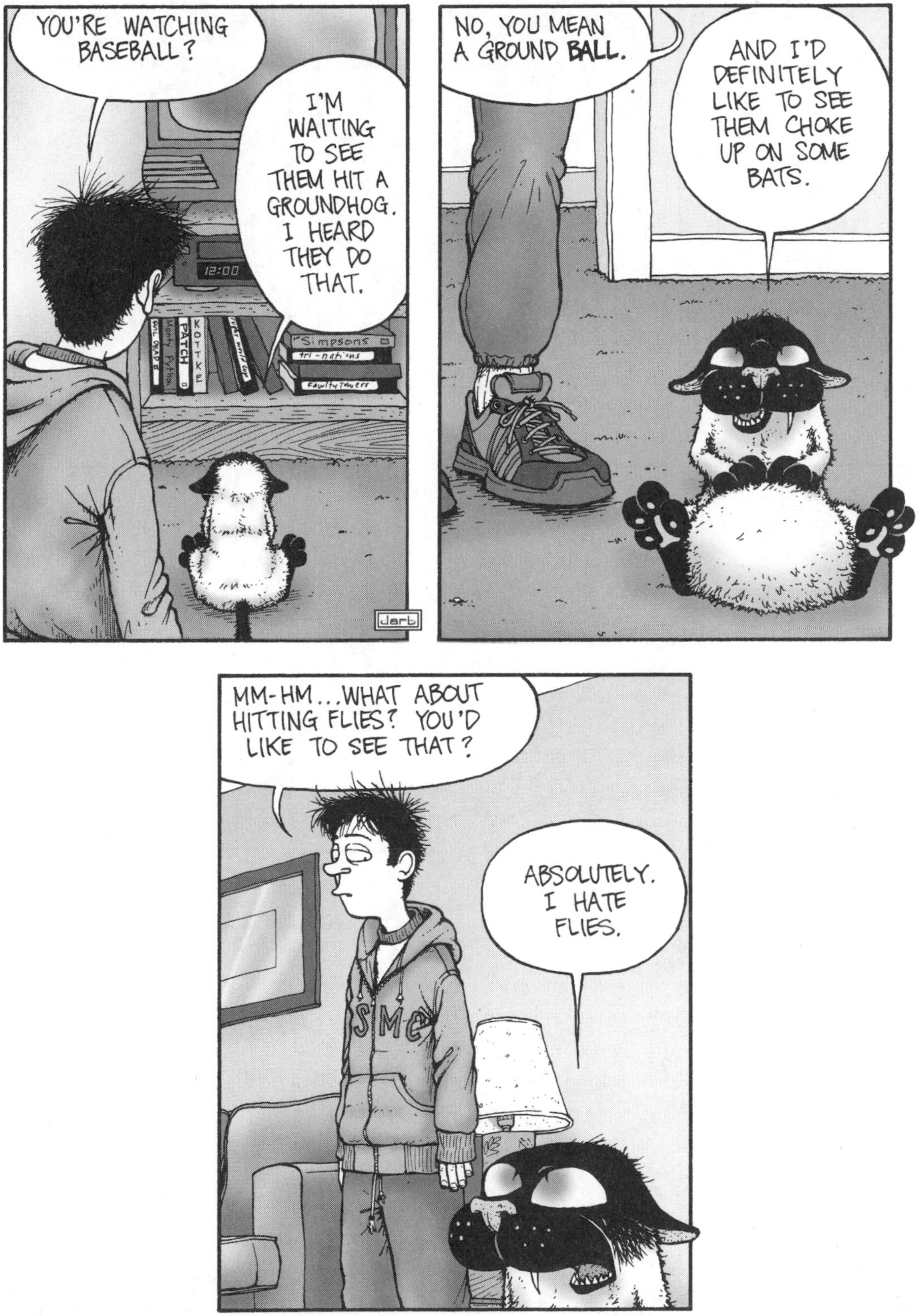
YOU'RE WATCHING BASEBALL?
I'M WAITING TO SEE THEM HIT A GROUNDHOG. I HEARD THEY DO THAT.
NO, YOU MEAN A GROUND **BALL**.
AND I'D DEFINITELY LIKE TO SEE THEM CHOKE UP ON SOME BATS.
MM-HM...WHAT ABOUT HITTING FLIES? YOU'D LIKE TO SEE THAT?
ABSOLUTELY. I HATE FLIES.

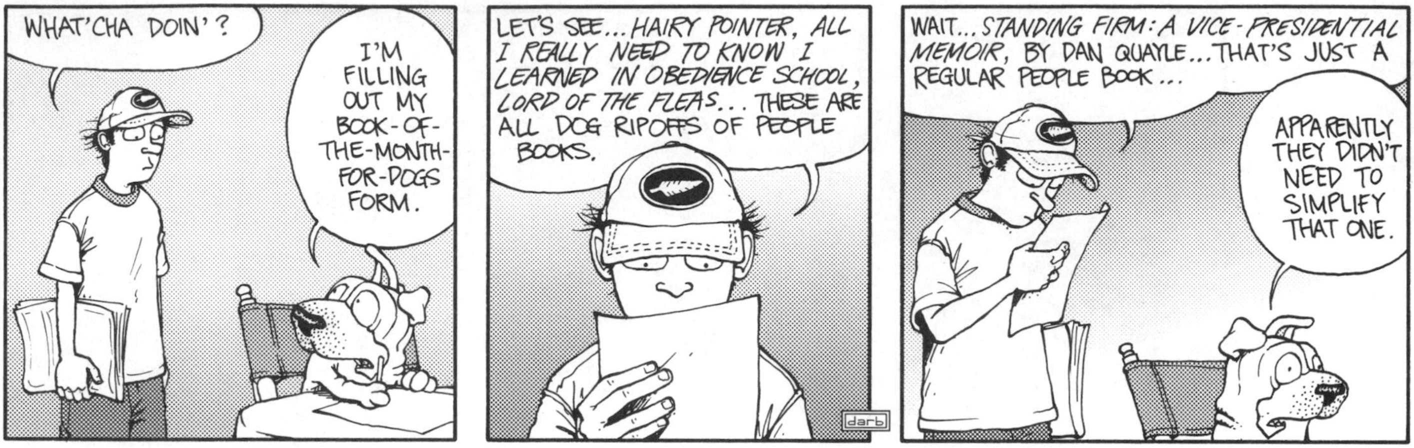
WHAT'CHA DOIN'?
I'M FILLING OUT MY BOOK-OF-THE-MONTH-FOR-DOGS FORM.
LET'S SEE... HAIRY POINTER, ALL I REALLY NEED TO KNOW I LEARNED IN OBEDIENCE SCHOOL, LORD OF THE FLEAS... THESE ARE ALL DOG RIPOFFS OF PEOPLE BOOKS.
darb
WAIT... STANDING FIRM: A VICE-PRESIDENTIAL MEMOIR, BY DAN QUAYLE... THAT'S JUST A REGULAR PEOPLE BOOK...
APPARENTLY THEY DIDN'T NEED TO SIMPLIFY THAT ONE.

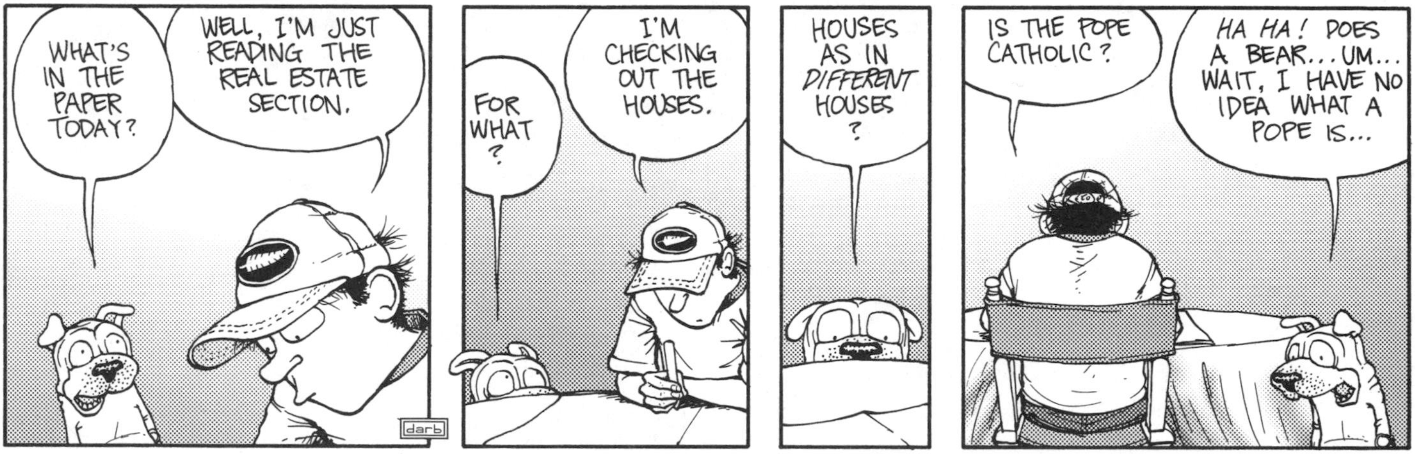
WHAT'S IN THE PAPER TODAY?
WELL, I'M JUST READING THE REAL ESTATE SECTION.
darb
FOR WHAT?
I'M CHECKING OUT THE HOUSES.
HOUSES AS IN DIFFERENT HOUSES?
IS THE POPE CATHOLIC?
HA HA! DOES A BEAR... UM... WAIT, I HAVE NO IDEA WHAT A POPE IS...

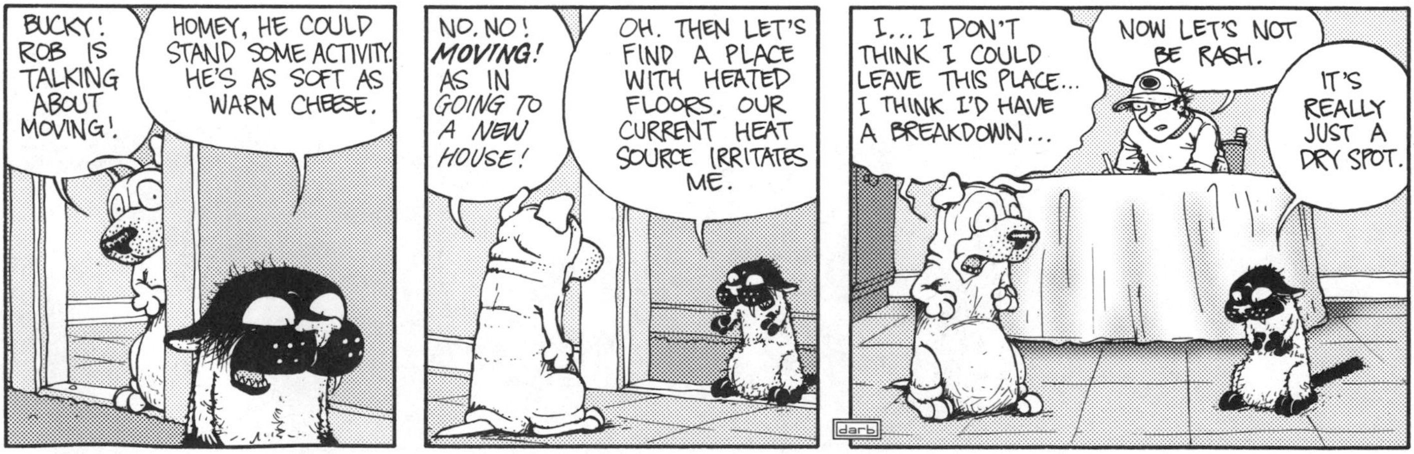
BUCKY! ROB IS TALKING ABOUT MOVING!
HOMEY, HE COULD STAND SOME ACTIVITY. HE'S AS SOFT AS WARM CHEESE.
NO, NO! MOVING! AS IN GOING TO A NEW HOUSE!
OH. THEN LET'S FIND A PLACE WITH HEATED FLOORS. OUR CURRENT HEAT SOURCE IRRITATES ME.
darb
I... I DON'T THINK I COULD LEAVE THIS PLACE... I THINK I'D HAVE A BREAKDOWN...
NOW LET'S NOT BE RASH.
IT'S REALLY JUST A DRY SPOT.

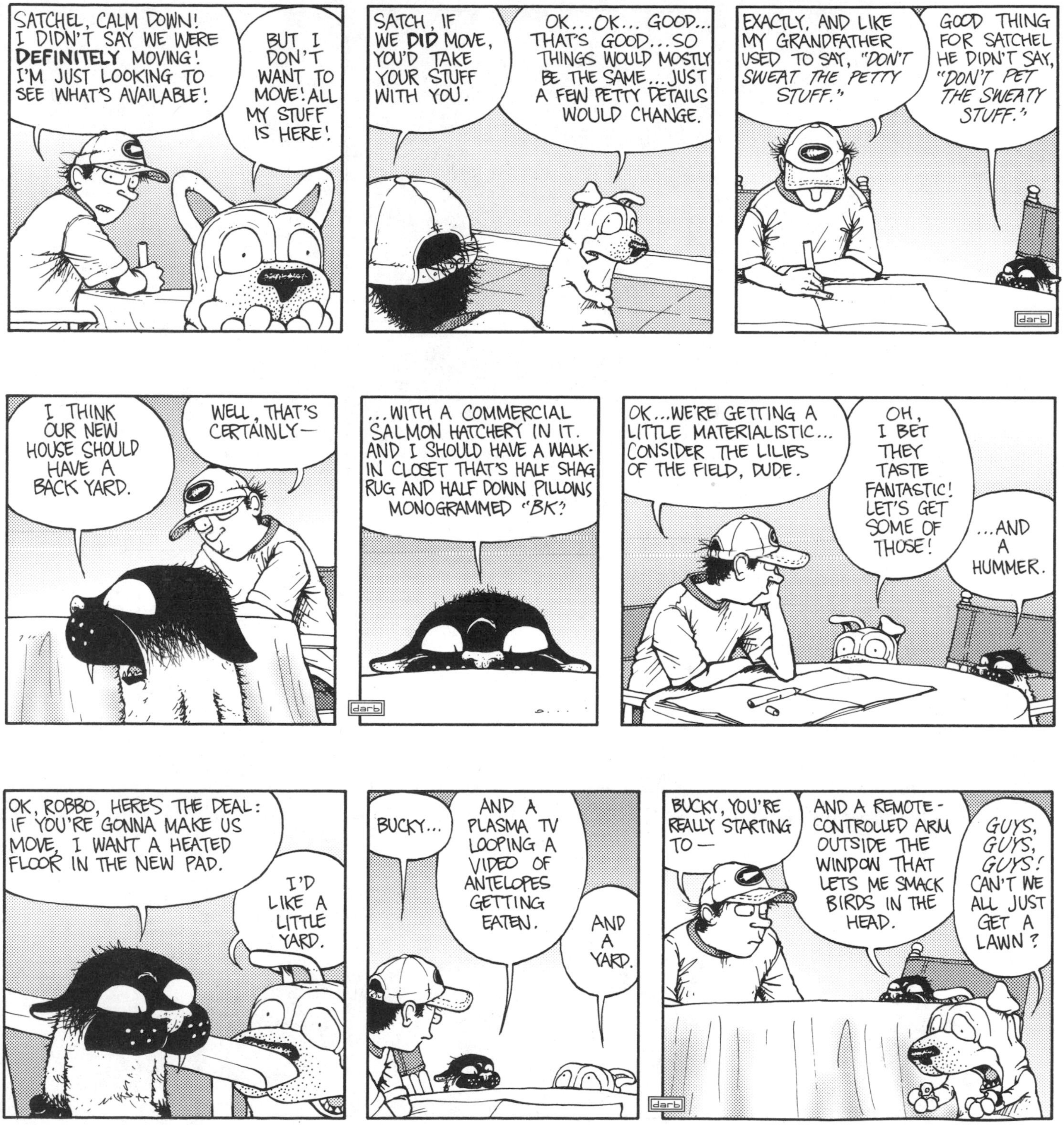
SATCHEL, CALM DOWN! I DIDN'T SAY WE WERE **DEFINITELY** MOVING! I'M JUST LOOKING TO SEE WHAT'S AVAILABLE!
BUT I DON'T WANT TO MOVE! ALL MY STUFF IS HERE!
SATCH, IF WE **DID** MOVE, YOU'D TAKE YOUR STUFF WITH YOU.
OK... OK... GOOD... THAT'S GOOD... SO THINGS WOULD MOSTLY BE THE SAME... JUST A FEW PETTY DETAILS WOULD CHANGE.
EXACTLY. AND LIKE MY GRANDFATHER USED TO SAY, *"DON'T SWEAT THE PETTY STUFF."*
GOOD THING FOR SATCHEL HE DIDN'T SAY, *"DON'T PET THE SWEATY STUFF."*
darb
I THINK OUR NEW HOUSE SHOULD HAVE A BACK YARD.
WELL, THAT'S CERTAINLY—
...WITH A COMMERCIAL SALMON HATCHERY IN IT. AND I SHOULD HAVE A WALK-IN CLOSET THAT'S HALF SHAG RUG AND HALF DOWN PILLOWS MONOGRAMMED *"BK"*
darb
OK... WE'RE GETTING A LITTLE MATERIALISTIC... CONSIDER THE LILIES OF THE FIELD, DUDE.
OH, I BET THEY TASTE FANTASTIC! LET'S GET SOME OF THOSE!
...AND A HUMMER.
OK, ROBBO, HERE'S THE DEAL: IF YOU'RE GONNA MAKE US MOVE, I WANT A HEATED FLOOR IN THE NEW PAD.
I'D LIKE A LITTLE YARD.
BUCKY...
AND A PLASMA TV LOOPING A VIDEO OF ANTELOPES GETTING EATEN.
AND A YARD.
darb
BUCKY, YOU'RE REALLY STARTING TO—
AND A REMOTE-CONTROLLED ARM OUTSIDE THE WINDOW THAT LETS ME SMACK BIRDS IN THE HEAD.
GUYS, GUYS, GUYS! CAN'T WE ALL JUST GET A LAWN?

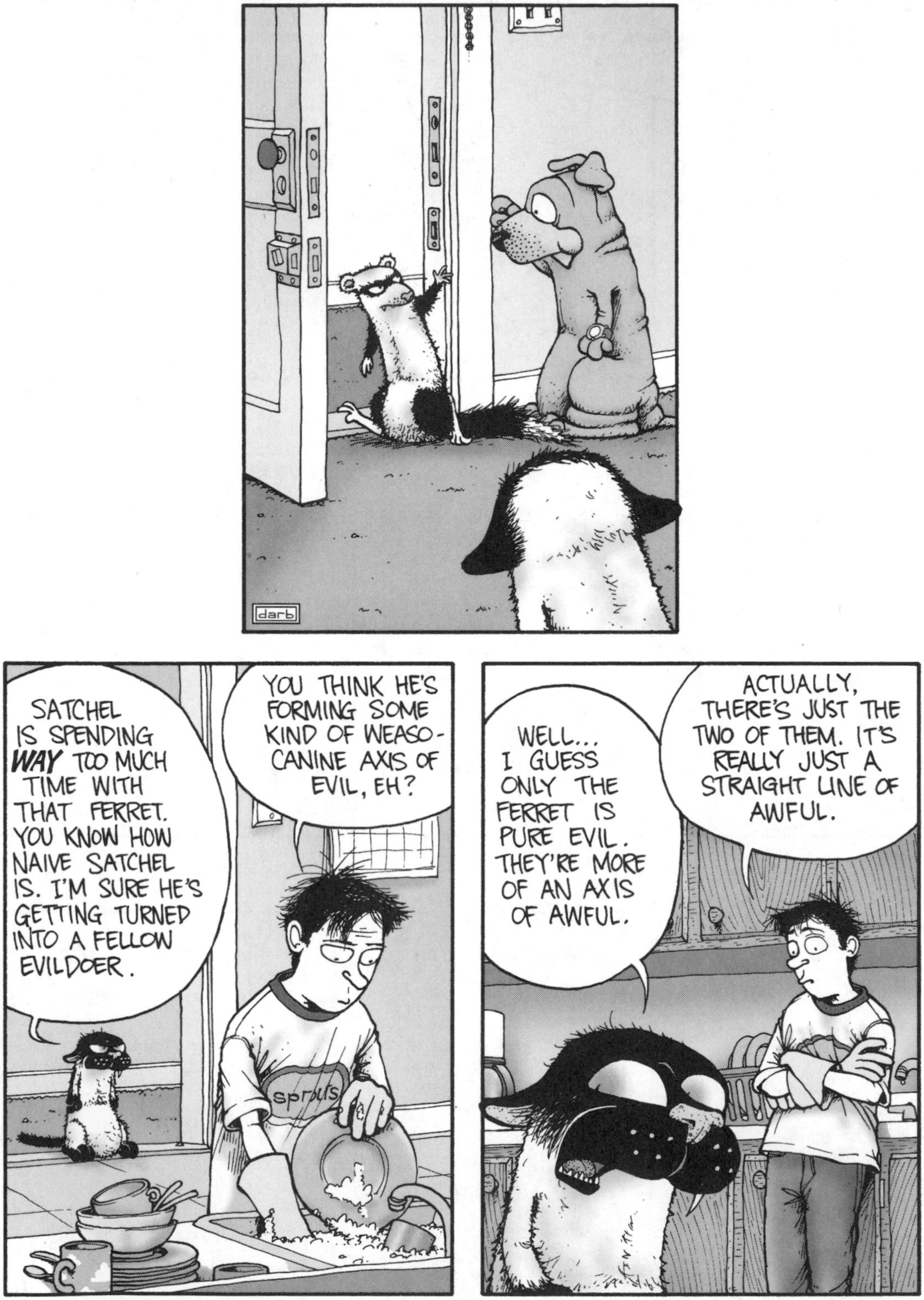
darb
SATCHEL IS SPENDING **WAY** TOO MUCH TIME WITH THAT FERRET. YOU KNOW HOW NAIVE SATCHEL IS. I'M SURE HE'S GETTING TURNED INTO A FELLOW EVILDOER.
YOU THINK HE'S FORMING SOME KIND OF WEASO-CANINE AXIS OF EVIL, EH?
WELL... I GUESS ONLY THE FERRET IS PURE EVIL. THEY'RE MORE OF AN AXIS OF AWFUL.
ACTUALLY, THERE'S JUST THE TWO OF THEM. IT'S REALLY JUST A STRAIGHT LINE OF AWFUL.

I NEED TO BORROW THIS CRYSTAL BALL.

THAT'S A PAPERWEIGHT, DUDE.

DOES IT SEE INTO THE FUTURE?

YEAH, PUT IT UP TO YOUR EYE.

CAN YOU SEE ME GRABBING THE BALL BACK? THAT'S THE FUTURE.

OH! IT WORKS!

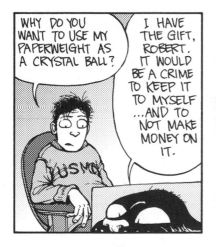

WHY DO YOU WANT TO USE MY PAPERWEIGHT AS A CRYSTAL BALL?

I HAVE THE GIFT, ROBERT. IT WOULD BE A CRIME TO KEEP IT TO MYSELF ...AND TO NOT MAKE MONEY ON IT.

MAKE MONEY HOW?

I'M STARTING SOMETHING OF A PSYCHIC HOTLINE.

MM-HM. SURE IT'S NOT MORE OF A PSYCHIC COLDLINE?

YOU'RE SAYING YOU HAVE THE GIFT OF TALKING TO THE DEAD?

TECHNIC- ALLY, I'M SAYING I CAN LIE TO ANYONE WITH A STRAIGHT FACE.

AS I SAY, I HAVE THE GIFT OF COMMUNICATING WITH THE AFTERLIFE. I MEAN, INITIALLY I HAD THE GIFT OF PREDICTING THE FUTURE, BUT I HAVE DECIDED THAT MY LIABILITY IS LOWER JUST TALKING TO PRETEND GHOSTS.

YOU'RE A FUZZY FRAUD.

OH...HOLD ON! I'M GETTING SOMETHING... YOUR BROTHER SAYS YOU NEED TO FIND A GIRLFRIEND...

MY BROTHER IS ALIVE, YOU IDIOT.

YEAH, I ASSUMED THAT WHEN HE CALLED. HE WANTS YOU TO CALL HIM BACK.

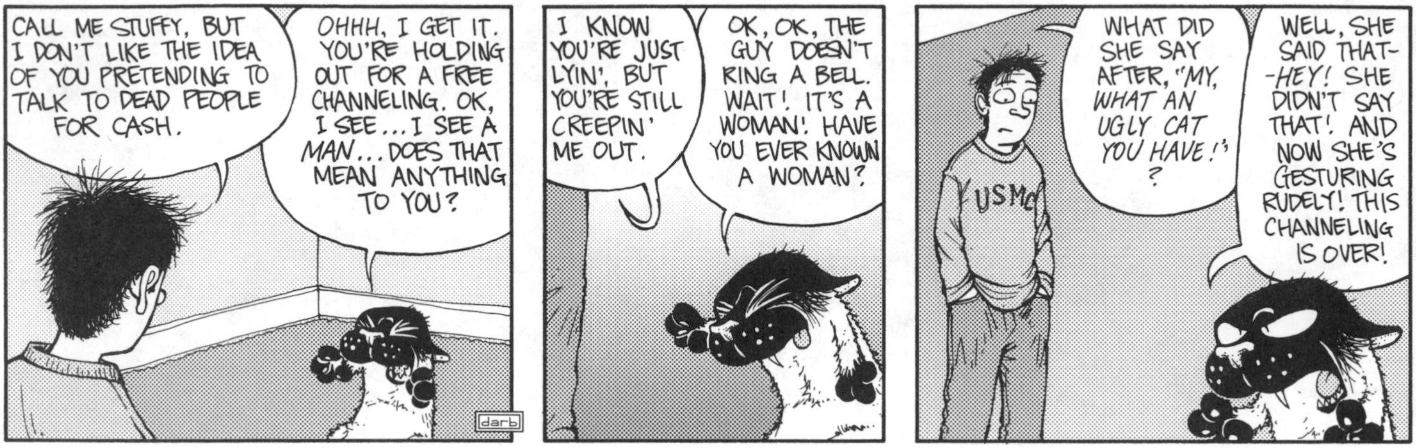
CALL ME STUFFY, BUT I DON'T LIKE THE IDEA OF YOU PRETENDING TO TALK TO DEAD PEOPLE FOR CASH.
OHHH, I GET IT. YOU'RE HOLDING OUT FOR A FREE CHANNELING. OK, I SEE... I SEE A MAN... DOES THAT MEAN ANYTHING TO YOU?
darb
I KNOW YOU'RE JUST LYIN', BUT YOU'RE STILL CREEPIN' ME OUT.
OK, OK, THE GUY DOESN'T RING A BELL. WAIT! IT'S A WOMAN! HAVE YOU EVER KNOWN A WOMAN?
WHAT DID SHE SAY AFTER, "MY, WHAT AN UGLY CAT YOU HAVE!"?
USMC
WELL, SHE SAID THAT- -HEY! SHE DIDN'T SAY THAT! AND NOW SHE'S GESTURING RUDELY! THIS CHANNELING IS OVER!

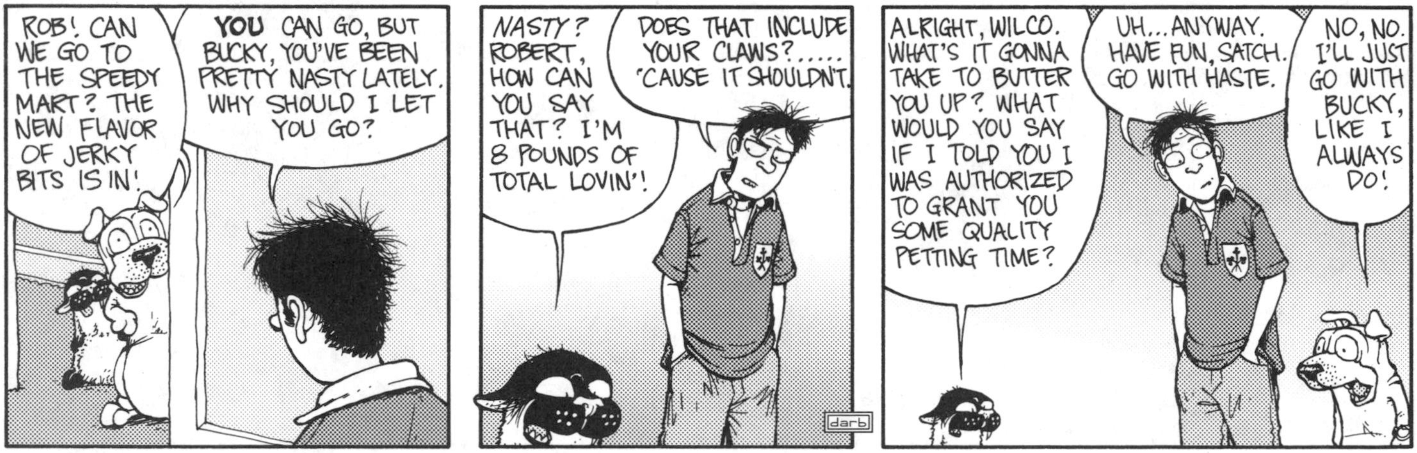
ROB! CAN WE GO TO THE SPEEDY MART? THE NEW FLAVOR OF JERKY BITS IS IN!
YOU CAN GO, BUT BUCKY, YOU'VE BEEN PRETTY NASTY LATELY. WHY SHOULD I LET YOU GO?
NASTY? ROBERT, HOW CAN YOU SAY THAT? I'M 8 POUNDS OF TOTAL LOVIN'!
DOES THAT INCLUDE YOUR CLAWS?..... 'CAUSE IT SHOULDN'T.
darb
ALRIGHT, WILCO. WHAT'S IT GONNA TAKE TO BUTTER YOU UP? WHAT WOULD YOU SAY IF I TOLD YOU I WAS AUTHORIZED TO GRANT YOU SOME QUALITY PETTING TIME?
UH... ANYWAY. HAVE FUN, SATCH. GO WITH HASTE.
NO, NO. I'LL JUST GO WITH BUCKY, LIKE I ALWAYS DO!

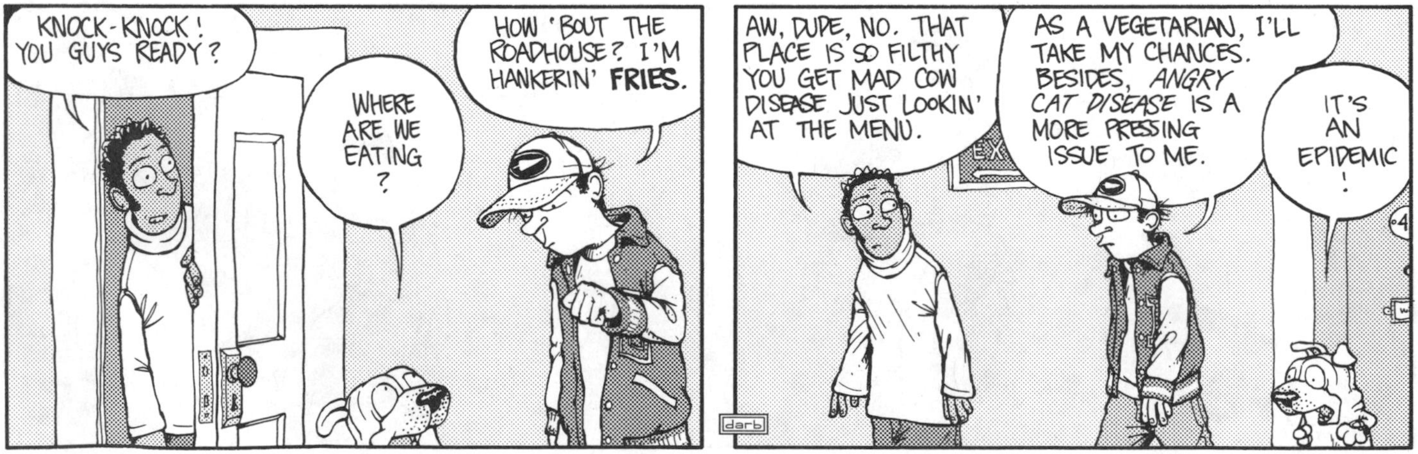
KNOCK-KNOCK! YOU GUYS READY?
WHERE ARE WE EATING?
HOW 'BOUT THE ROADHOUSE? I'M HANKERIN' FRIES.
darb
AW, DUDE, NO. THAT PLACE IS SO FILTHY YOU GET MAD COW DISEASE JUST LOOKIN' AT THE MENU.
AS A VEGETARIAN, I'LL TAKE MY CHANCES. BESIDES, ANGRY CAT DISEASE IS A MORE PRESSING ISSUE TO ME.
IT'S AN EPIDEMIC!

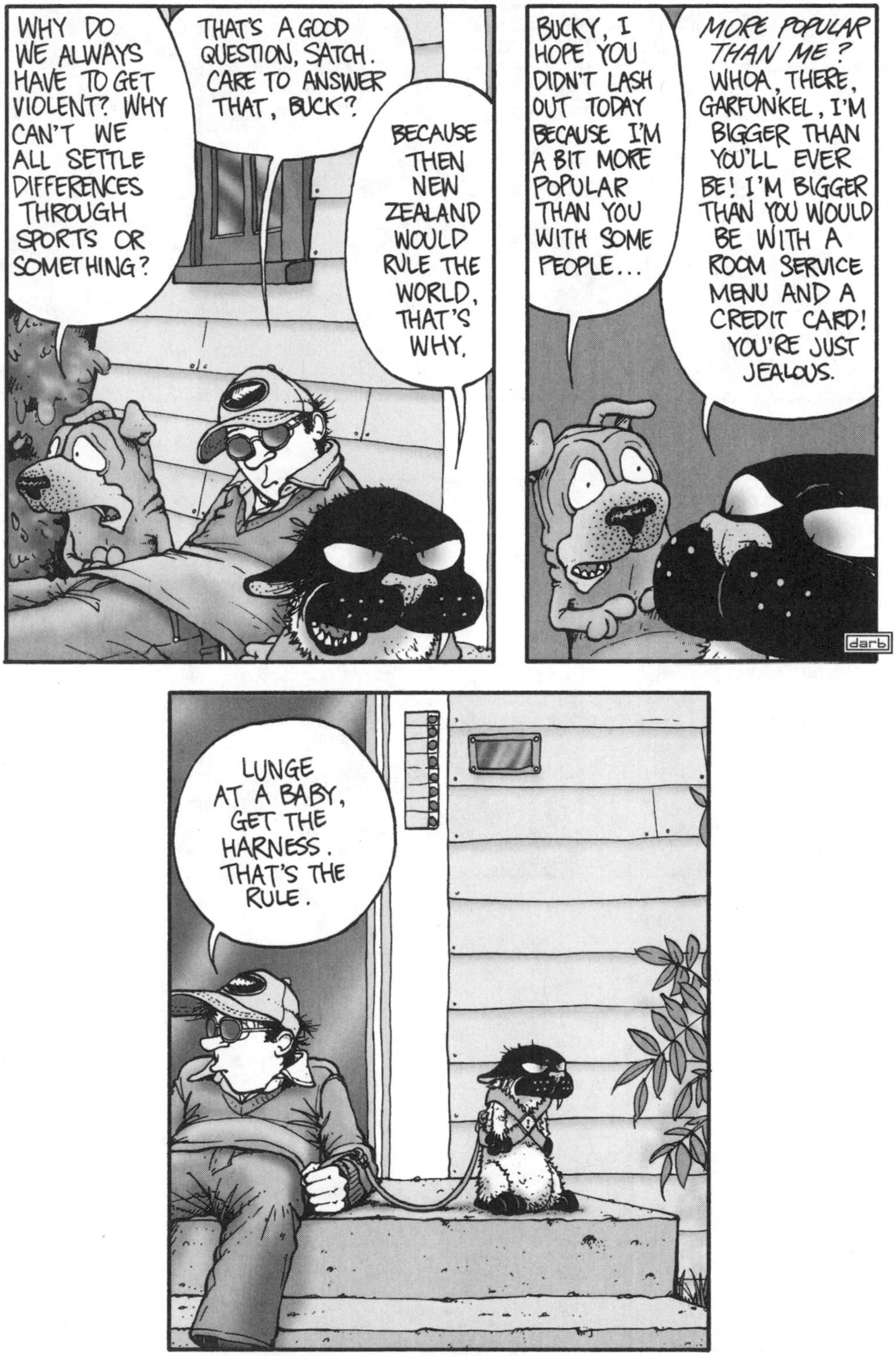
WHY DO WE ALWAYS HAVE TO GET VIOLENT? WHY CAN'T WE ALL SETTLE DIFFERENCES THROUGH SPORTS OR SOMETHING?
THAT'S A GOOD QUESTION, SATCH. CARE TO ANSWER THAT, BUCK?
BECAUSE THEN NEW ZEALAND WOULD RULE THE WORLD, THAT'S WHY.
BUCKY, I HOPE YOU DIDN'T LASH OUT TODAY BECAUSE I'M A BIT MORE POPULAR THAN YOU WITH SOME PEOPLE...
MORE POPULAR THAN ME? WHOA, THERE, GARFUNKEL, I'M BIGGER THAN YOU'LL EVER BE! I'M BIGGER THAN YOU WOULD BE WITH A ROOM SERVICE MENU AND A CREDIT CARD! YOU'RE JUST JEALOUS.
darb
LUNGE AT A BABY, GET THE HARNESS. THAT'S THE RULE.

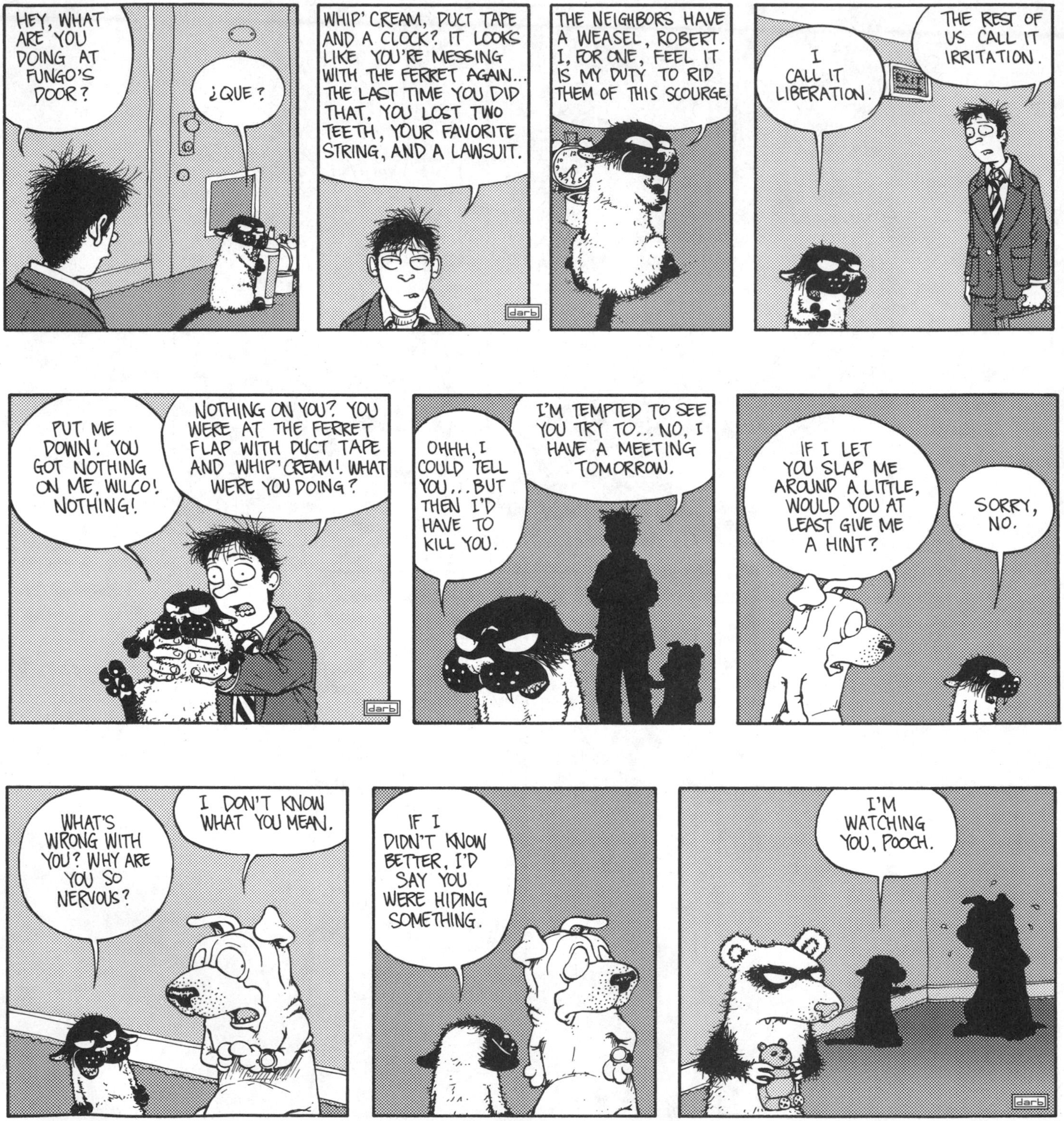
HEY, WHAT ARE YOU DOING AT FUNGO'S DOOR?
¿QUE?
WHIP' CREAM, DUCT TAPE AND A CLOCK? IT LOOKS LIKE YOU'RE MESSING WITH THE FERRET AGAIN... THE LAST TIME YOU DID THAT, YOU LOST TWO TEETH, YOUR FAVORITE STRING, AND A LAWSUIT.
THE NEIGHBORS HAVE A WEASEL, ROBERT. I, FOR ONE, FEEL IT IS MY DUTY TO RID THEM OF THIS SCOURGE.
I CALL IT LIBERATION.
THE REST OF US CALL IT IRRITATION.
EXIT
PUT ME DOWN! YOU GOT NOTHING ON ME, WILCO! NOTHING!
NOTHING ON YOU? YOU WERE AT THE FERRET FLAP WITH DUCT TAPE AND WHIP' CREAM! WHAT WERE YOU DOING?
OHHH, I COULD TELL YOU... BUT THEN I'D HAVE TO KILL YOU.
I'M TEMPTED TO SEE YOU TRY TO... NO, I HAVE A MEETING TOMORROW.
IF I LET YOU SLAP ME AROUND A LITTLE, WOULD YOU AT LEAST GIVE ME A HINT?
SORRY, NO.
WHAT'S WRONG WITH YOU? WHY ARE YOU SO NERVOUS?
I DON'T KNOW WHAT YOU MEAN.
IF I DIDN'T KNOW BETTER, I'D SAY YOU WERE HIDING SOMETHING.
I'M WATCHING YOU, POOCH.

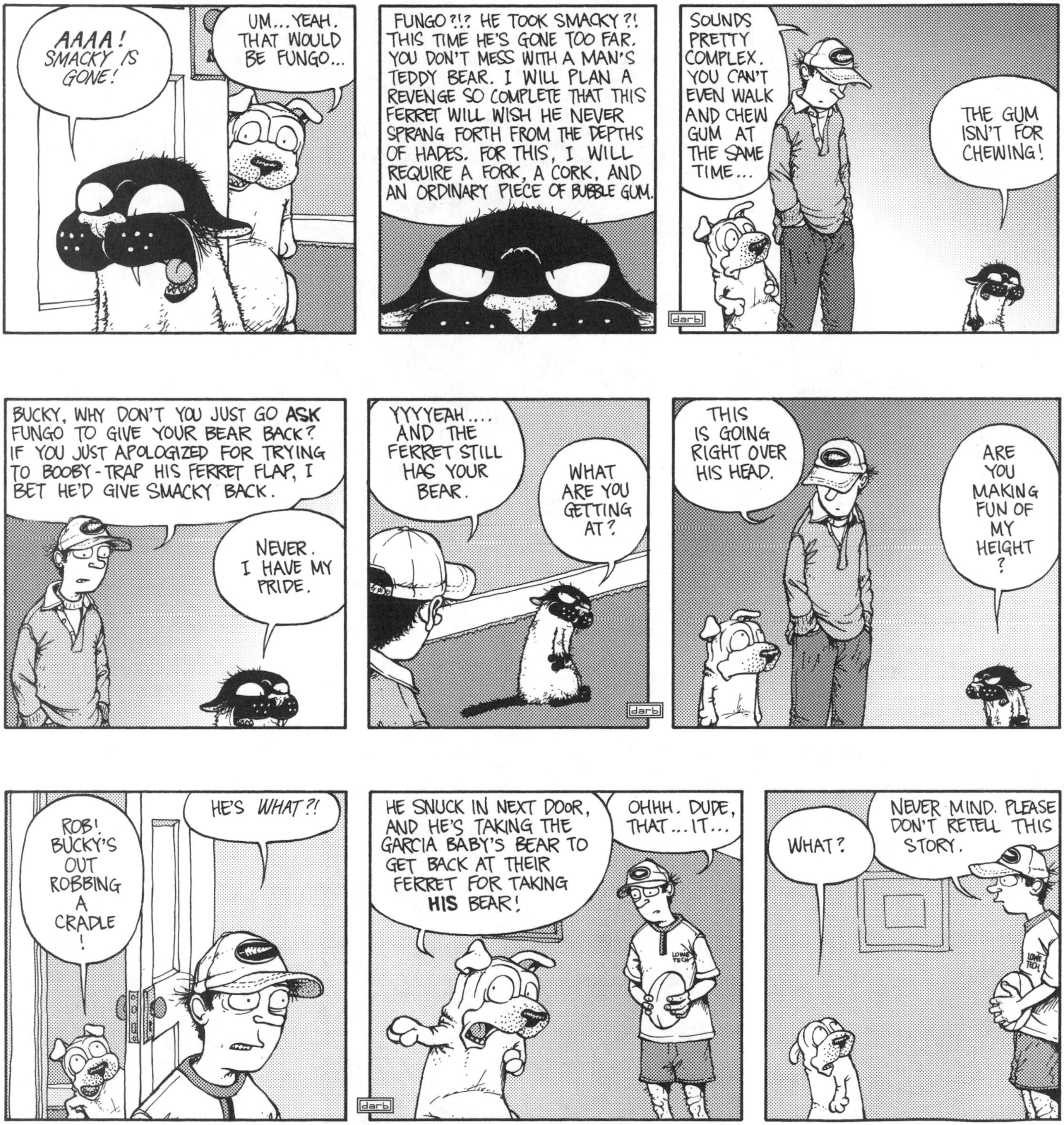
AAAA! SMACKY IS GONE!
UM... YEAH. THAT WOULD BE FUNGO...
FUNGO?!? HE TOOK SMACKY?! THIS TIME HE'S GONE TOO FAR. YOU DON'T MESS WITH A MAN'S TEDDY BEAR. I WILL PLAN A REVENGE SO COMPLETE THAT THIS FERRET WILL WISH HE NEVER SPRANG FORTH FROM THE DEPTHS OF HADES. FOR THIS, I WILL REQUIRE A FORK, A CORK, AND AN ORDINARY PIECE OF BUBBLE GUM.
SOUNDS PRETTY COMPLEX. YOU CAN'T EVEN WALK AND CHEW GUM AT THE SAME TIME...
THE GUM ISN'T FOR CHEWING!
BUCKY, WHY DON'T YOU JUST GO ASK FUNGO TO GIVE YOUR BEAR BACK? IF YOU JUST APOLOGIZED FOR TRYING TO BOOBY-TRAP HIS FERRET FLAP, I BET HE'D GIVE SMACKY BACK.
NEVER. I HAVE MY PRIDE.
YYYYEAH.... AND THE FERRET STILL HAS YOUR BEAR.
WHAT ARE YOU GETTING AT?
THIS IS GOING RIGHT OVER HIS HEAD.
ARE YOU MAKING FUN OF MY HEIGHT?
ROB! BUCKY'S OUT ROBBING A CRADLE!
HE'S WHAT?!
HE SNUCK IN NEXT DOOR, AND HE'S TAKING THE GARCIA BABY'S BEAR TO GET BACK AT THEIR FERRET FOR TAKING HIS BEAR!
OHHH. DUDE, THAT... IT...
WHAT?
NEVER MIND. PLEASE DON'T RETELL THIS STORY.

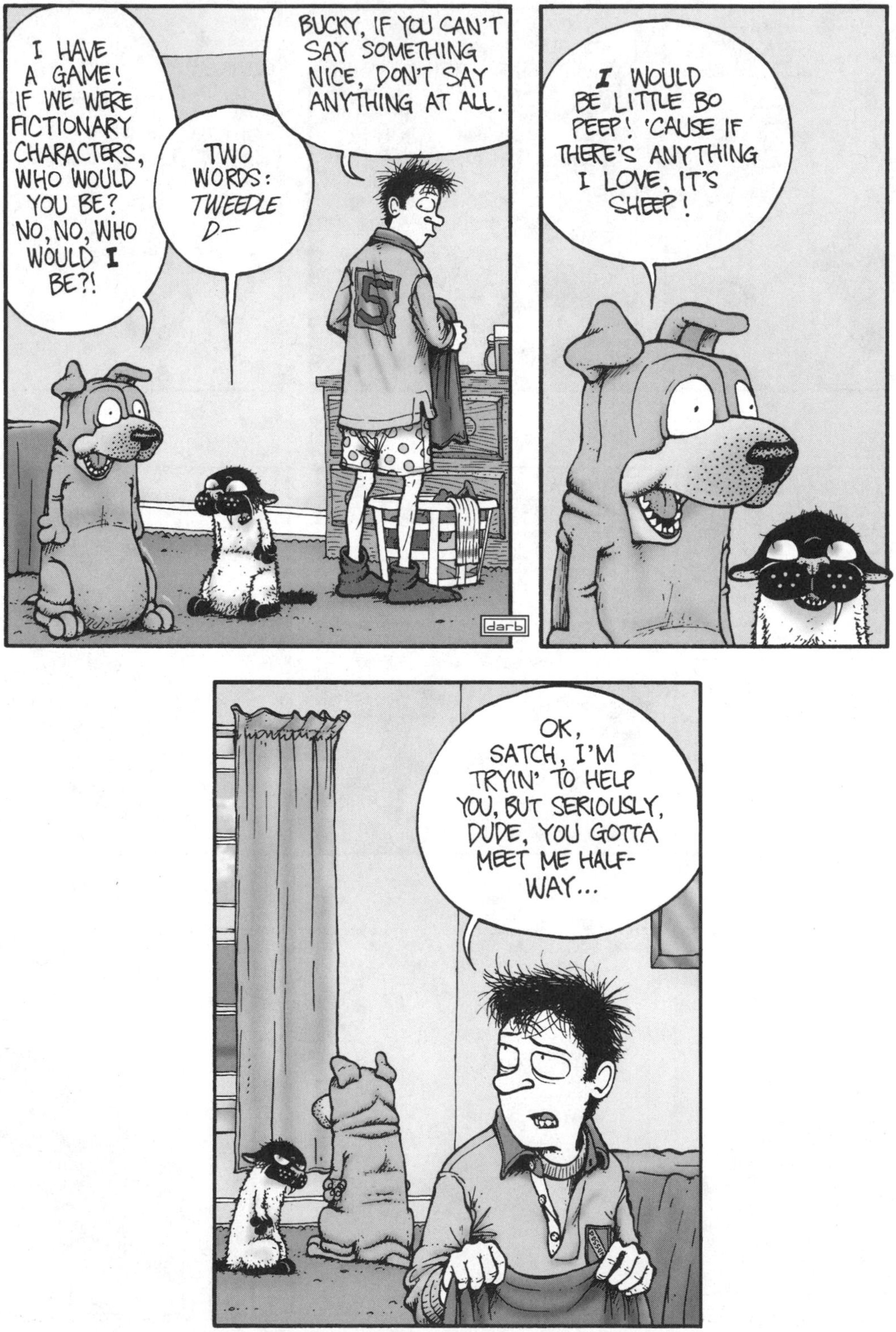
I HAVE A GAME! IF WE WERE FICTIONARY CHARACTERS, WHO WOULD YOU BE? NO, NO, WHO WOULD I BE?!
TWO WORDS: TWEEDLE D—
BUCKY, IF YOU CAN'T SAY SOMETHING NICE, DON'T SAY ANYTHING AT ALL.
darb
I WOULD BE LITTLE BO PEEP! 'CAUSE IF THERE'S ANYTHING I LOVE, IT'S SHEEP!
OK, SATCH, I'M TRYIN' TO HELP YOU, BUT SERIOUSLY, DUDE, YOU GOTTA MEET ME HALF-WAY...

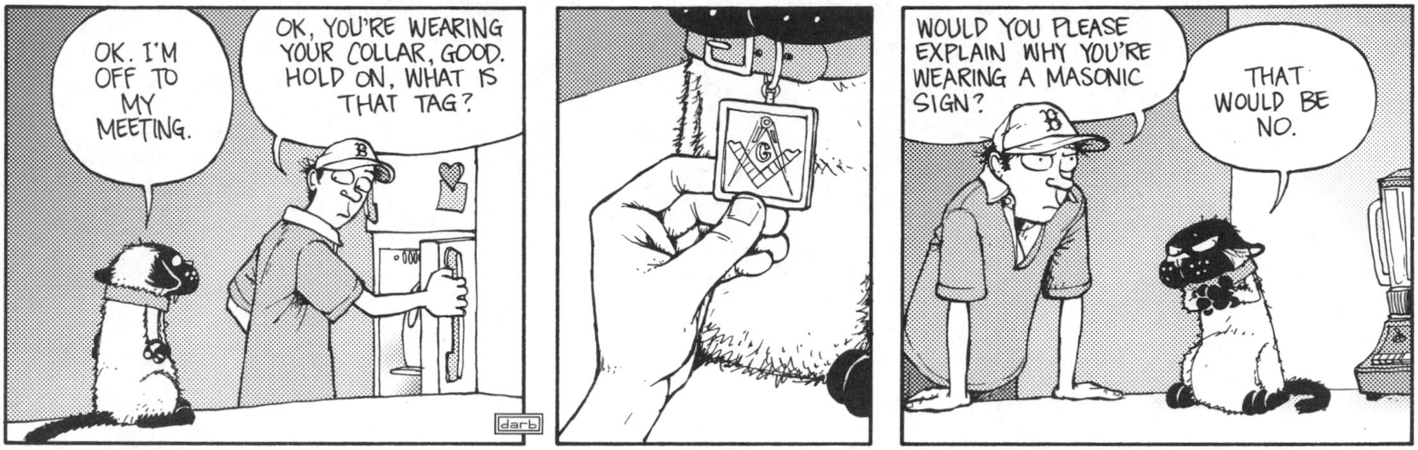
OK. I'M OFF TO MY MEETING.
OK, YOU'RE WEARING YOUR COLLAR, GOOD. HOLD ON, WHAT IS THAT TAG?
WOULD YOU PLEASE EXPLAIN WHY YOU'RE WEARING A MASONIC SIGN?
THAT WOULD BE NO.

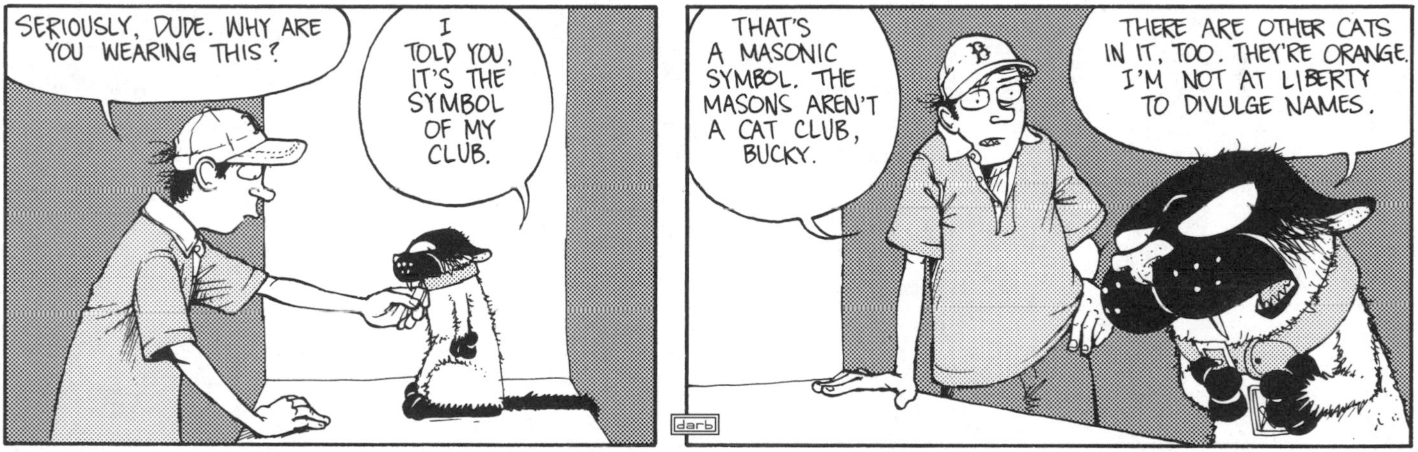
SERIOUSLY, DUDE. WHY ARE YOU WEARING THIS?
I TOLD YOU, IT'S THE SYMBOL OF MY CLUB.
THAT'S A MASONIC SYMBOL. THE MASONS AREN'T A CAT CLUB, BUCKY.
THERE ARE OTHER CATS IN IT, TOO. THEY'RE ORANGE. I'M NOT AT LIBERTY TO DIVULGE NAMES.

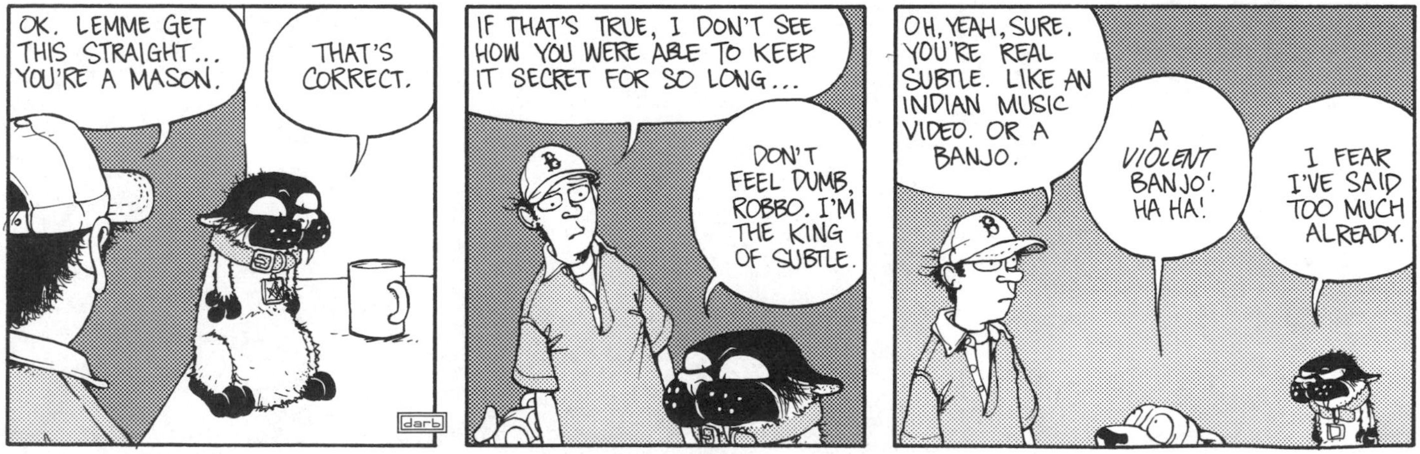
OK. LEMME GET THIS STRAIGHT... YOU'RE A MASON.
THAT'S CORRECT.
IF THAT'S TRUE, I DON'T SEE HOW YOU WERE ABLE TO KEEP IT SECRET FOR SO LONG...
DON'T FEEL DUMB, ROBBO. I'M THE KING OF SUBTLE.
OH, YEAH, SURE. YOU'RE REAL SUBTLE. LIKE AN INDIAN MUSIC VIDEO. OR A BANJO.
A VIOLENT BANJO! HA HA!
I FEAR I'VE SAID TOO MUCH ALREADY.

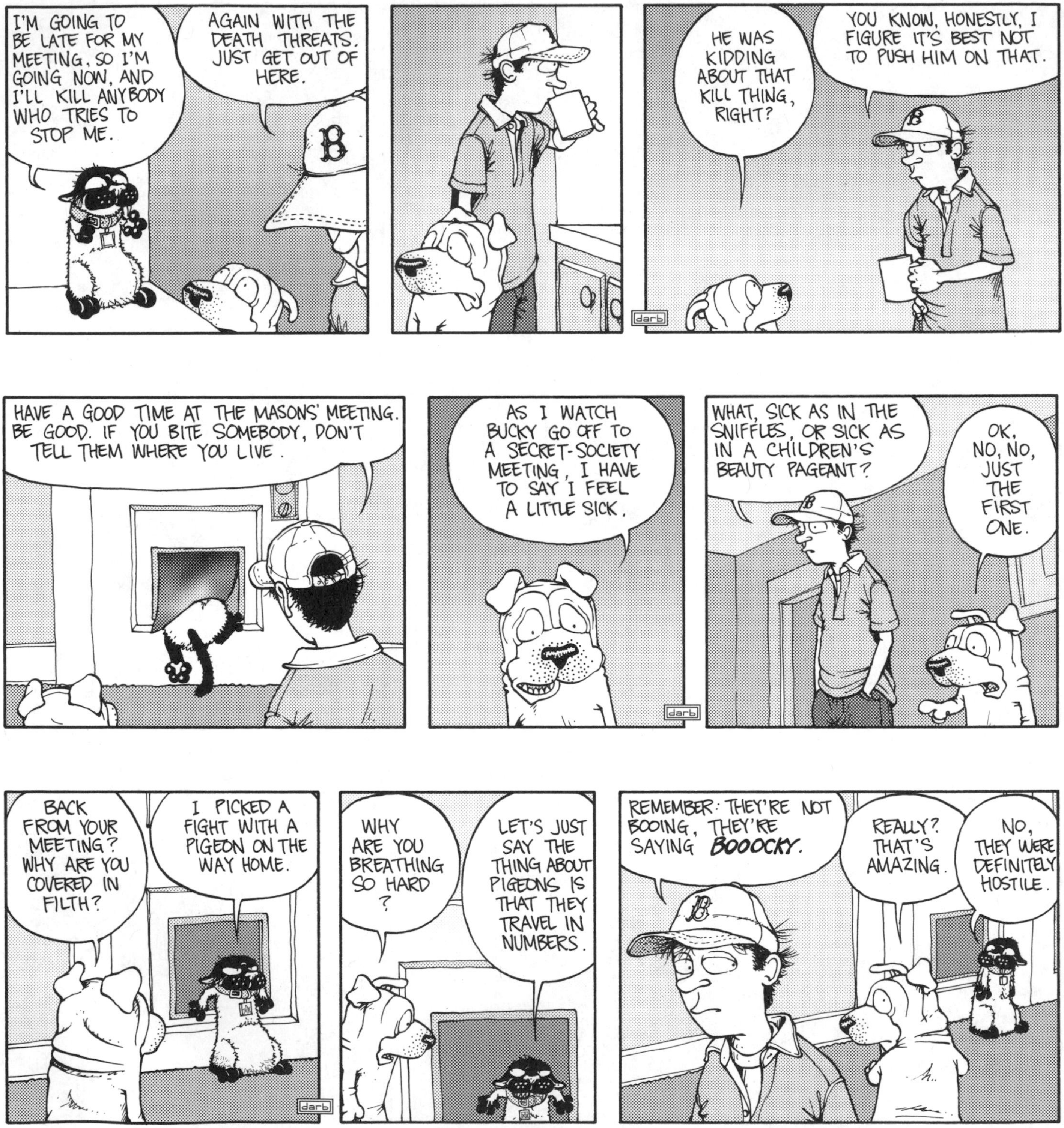
I'M GOING TO BE LATE FOR MY MEETING, SO I'M GOING NOW, AND I'LL KILL ANYBODY WHO TRIES TO STOP ME.
AGAIN WITH THE DEATH THREATS. JUST GET OUT OF HERE.
HE WAS KIDDING ABOUT THAT KILL THING, RIGHT?
YOU KNOW, HONESTLY, I FIGURE IT'S BEST NOT TO PUSH HIM ON THAT.
HAVE A GOOD TIME AT THE MASONS' MEETING. BE GOOD. IF YOU BITE SOMEBODY, DON'T TELL THEM WHERE YOU LIVE.
AS I WATCH BUCKY GO OFF TO A SECRET-SOCIETY MEETING, I HAVE TO SAY I FEEL A LITTLE SICK.
WHAT, SICK AS IN THE SNIFFLES, OR SICK AS IN A CHILDREN'S BEAUTY PAGEANT?
OK, NO, NO, JUST THE FIRST ONE.
BACK FROM YOUR MEETING? WHY ARE YOU COVERED IN FILTH?
I PICKED A FIGHT WITH A PIGEON ON THE WAY HOME.
WHY ARE YOU BREATHING SO HARD?
LET'S JUST SAY THE THING ABOUT PIGEONS IS THAT THEY TRAVEL IN NUMBERS.
REMEMBER: THEY'RE NOT BOOING, THEY'RE SAYING BOOOCKY.
REALLY? THAT'S AMAZING.
NO, THEY WERE DEFINITELY HOSTILE.

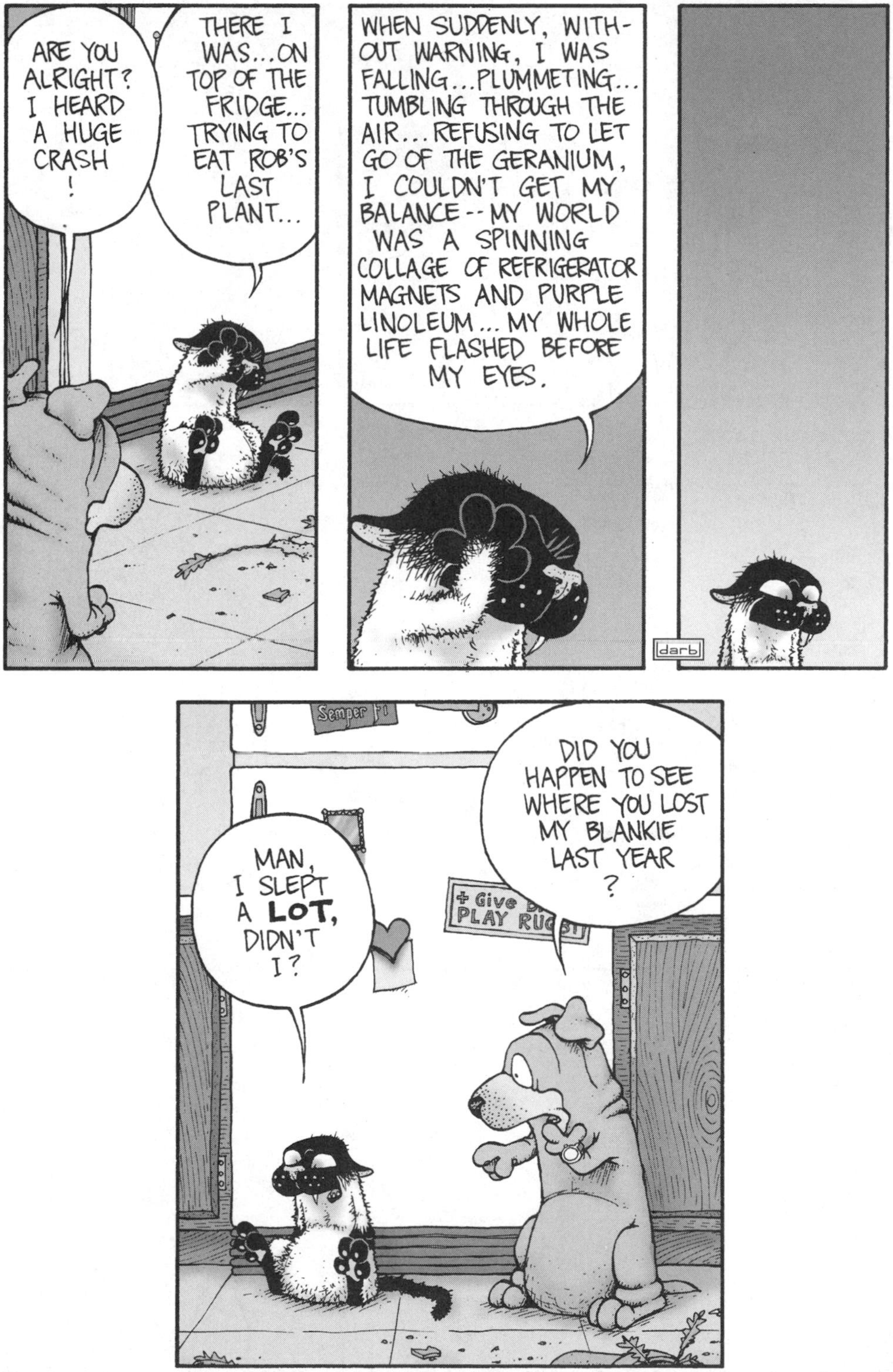

ARE YOU ALRIGHT? I HEARD A HUGE CRASH!
THERE I WAS...ON TOP OF THE FRIDGE... TRYING TO EAT ROB'S LAST PLANT...
WHEN SUDDENLY, WITH-OUT WARNING, I WAS FALLING...PLUMMETING... TUMBLING THROUGH THE AIR...REFUSING TO LET GO OF THE GERANIUM, I COULDN'T GET MY BALANCE--MY WORLD WAS A SPINNING COLLAGE OF REFRIGERATOR MAGNETS AND PURPLE LINOLEUM... MY WHOLE LIFE FLASHED BEFORE MY EYES.
darb
Semper Fi
MAN, I SLEPT A **LOT**, DIDN'T I?
DID YOU HAPPEN TO SEE WHERE YOU LOST MY BLANKIE LAST YEAR?

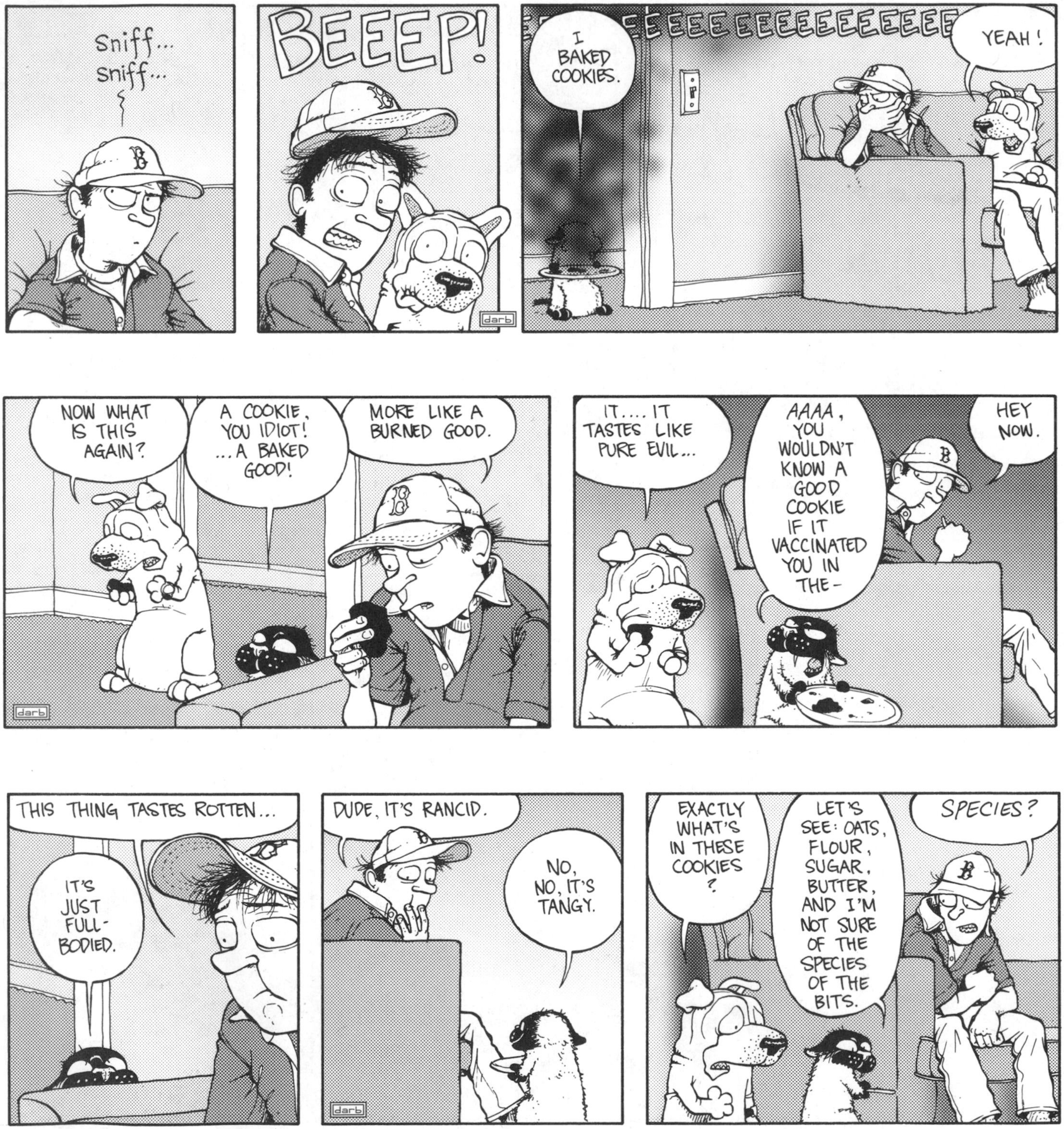
Sniff... sniff...
BEEEP!
EEEEEEEEEEEEEEEEE
I BAKED COOKIES.
YEAH!
NOW WHAT IS THIS AGAIN?
A COOKIE, YOU IDIOT! ...A BAKED GOOD!
MORE LIKE A BURNED GOOD.
IT.... IT TASTES LIKE PURE EVIL...
AAAA, YOU WOULDN'T KNOW A GOOD COOKIE IF IT VACCINATED YOU IN THE-
HEY NOW.
THIS THING TASTES ROTTEN...
IT'S JUST FULL-BODIED.
DUDE, IT'S RANCID.
NO, NO, IT'S TANGY.
EXACTLY WHAT'S IN THESE COOKIES?
LET'S SEE: OATS, FLOUR, SUGAR, BUTTER, AND I'M NOT SURE OF THE SPECIES OF THE BITS.
SPECIES?

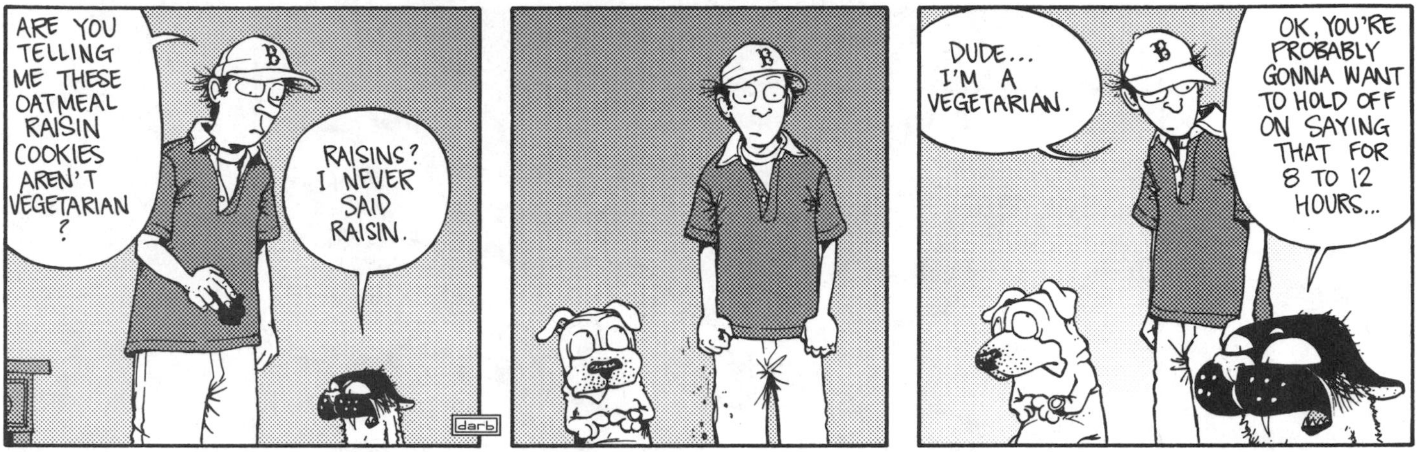
ARE YOU TELLING ME THESE OATMEAL RAISIN COOKIES AREN'T VEGETARIAN?
RAISINS? I NEVER SAID RAISIN.
darb
DUDE... I'M A VEGETARIAN.
OK, YOU'RE PROBABLY GONNA WANT TO HOLD OFF ON SAYING THAT FOR 8 TO 12 HOURS...

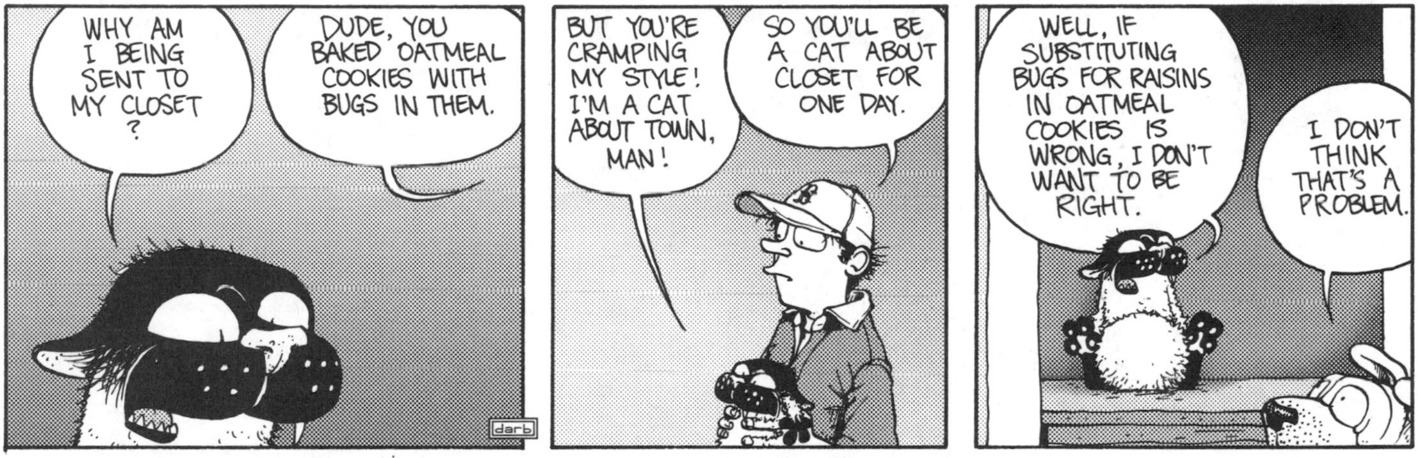
WHY AM I BEING SENT TO MY CLOSET?
DUDE, YOU BAKED OATMEAL COOKIES WITH BUGS IN THEM.
darb
BUT YOU'RE CRAMPING MY STYLE! I'M A CAT ABOUT TOWN, MAN!
SO YOU'LL BE A CAT ABOUT CLOSET FOR ONE DAY.
WELL, IF SUBSTITUTING BUGS FOR RAISINS IN OATMEAL COOKIES IS WRONG, I DON'T WANT TO BE RIGHT.
I DON'T THINK THAT'S A PROBLEM.

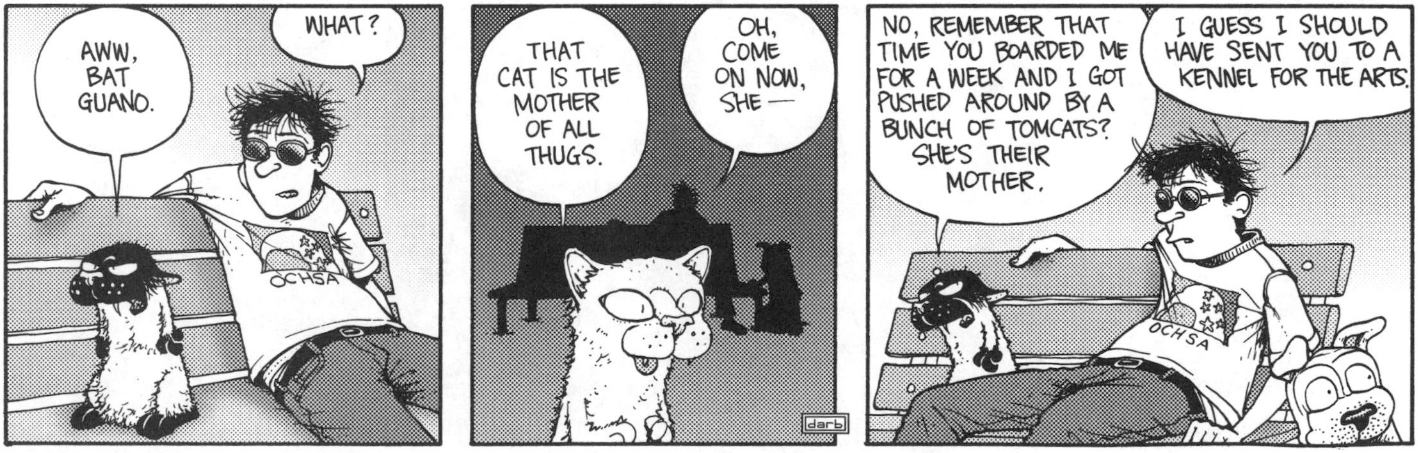
AWW, BAT GUANO.
WHAT?
OCHSA
THAT CAT IS THE MOTHER OF ALL THUGS.
OH, COME ON NOW, SHE—
darb
NO, REMEMBER THAT TIME YOU BOARDED ME FOR A WEEK AND I GOT PUSHED AROUND BY A BUNCH OF TOMCATS? SHE'S THEIR MOTHER.
I GUESS I SHOULD HAVE SENT YOU TO A KENNEL FOR THE ARTS.
OCHSA

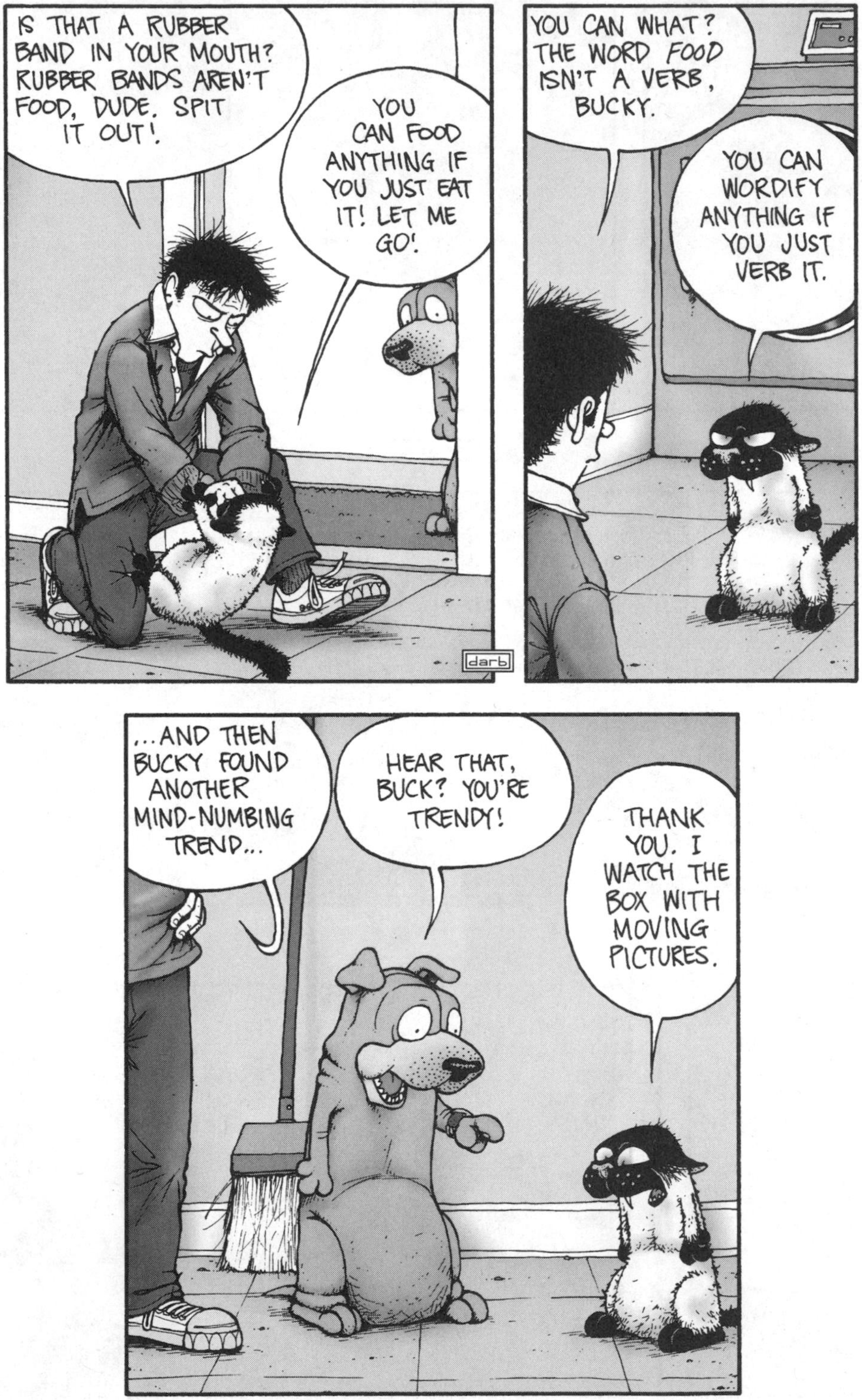
IS THAT A RUBBER BAND IN YOUR MOUTH? RUBBER BANDS AREN'T FOOD, DUDE. SPIT IT OUT!
YOU CAN FOOD ANYTHING IF YOU JUST EAT IT! LET ME GO!
darb
YOU CAN WHAT? THE WORD *FOOD* ISN'T A VERB, BUCKY.
YOU CAN WORDIFY ANYTHING IF YOU JUST VERB IT.
...AND THEN BUCKY FOUND ANOTHER MIND-NUMBING TREND...
HEAR THAT, BUCK? YOU'RE TRENDY!
THANK YOU. I WATCH THE BOX WITH MOVING PICTURES.

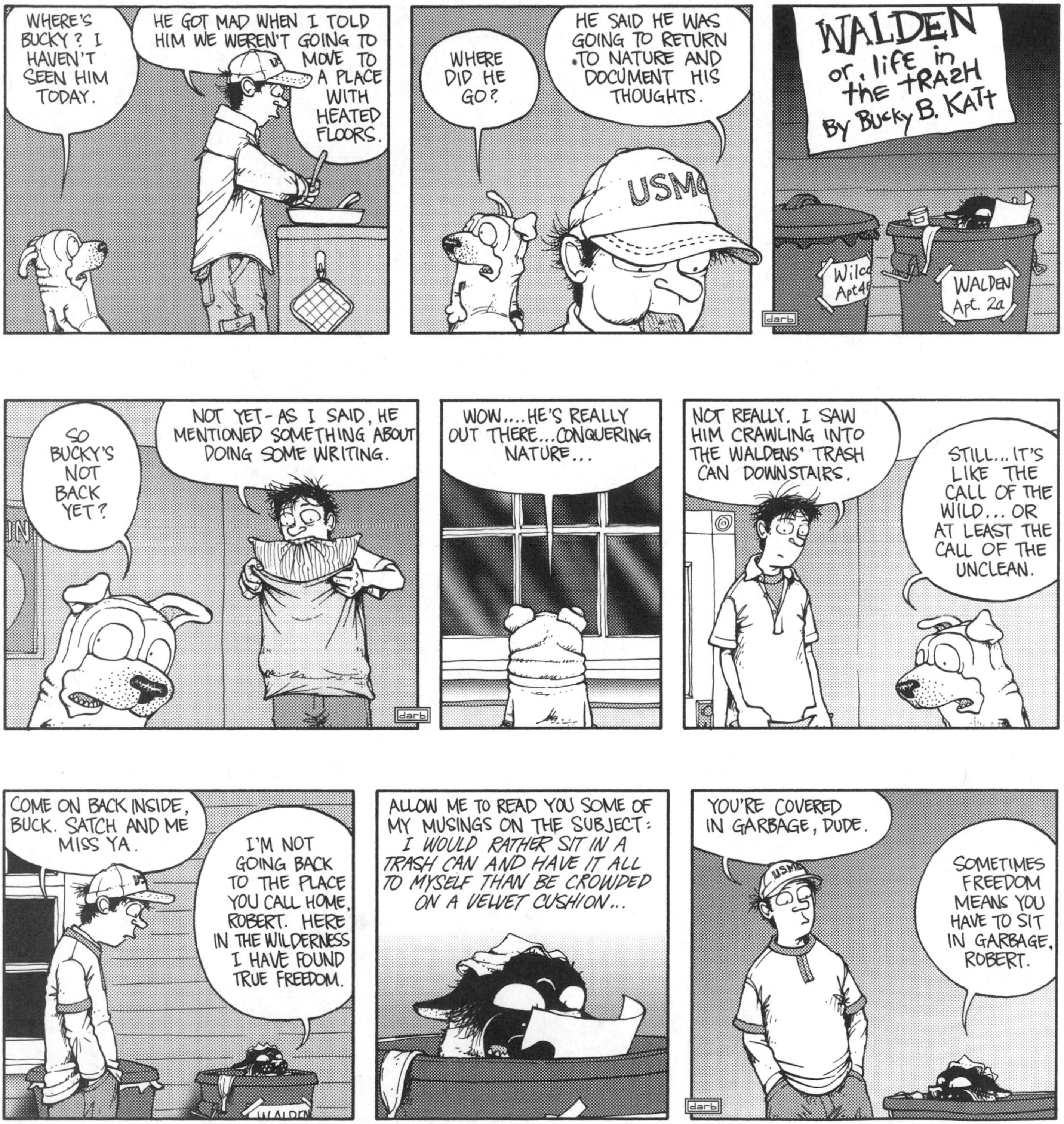
WHERE'S BUCKY? I HAVEN'T SEEN HIM TODAY.
HE GOT MAD WHEN I TOLD HIM WE WEREN'T GOING TO MOVE TO A PLACE WITH HEATED FLOORS.
WHERE DID HE GO?
HE SAID HE WAS GOING TO RETURN TO NATURE AND DOCUMENT HIS THOUGHTS.
USMC
WALDEN or, life in the TRASH By Bucky B. Katt
Wilco Apt4
WALDEN Apt. 2a
darb
SO BUCKY'S NOT BACK YET?
NOT YET- AS I SAID, HE MENTIONED SOMETHING ABOUT DOING SOME WRITING.
darb
WOW.... HE'S REALLY OUT THERE... CONQUERING NATURE...
NOT REALLY. I SAW HIM CRAWLING INTO THE WALDENS' TRASH CAN DOWNSTAIRS.
STILL... IT'S LIKE THE CALL OF THE WILD... OR AT LEAST THE CALL OF THE UNCLEAN.
COME ON BACK INSIDE, BUCK. SATCH AND ME MISS YA.
I'M NOT GOING BACK TO THE PLACE YOU CALL HOME, ROBERT. HERE IN THE WILDERNESS I HAVE FOUND TRUE FREEDOM.
ALLOW ME TO READ YOU SOME OF MY MUSINGS ON THE SUBJECT: *I WOULD RATHER SIT IN A TRASH CAN AND HAVE IT ALL TO MYSELF THAN BE CROWDED ON A VELVET CUSHION...*
YOU'RE COVERED IN GARBAGE, DUDE.
SOMETIMES FREEDOM MEANS YOU HAVE TO SIT IN GARBAGE, ROBERT.
darb

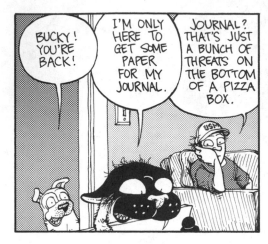

BUCKY! YOU'RE BACK!

I'M ONLY HERE TO GET SOME PAPER FOR MY JOURNAL.

JOURNAL? THAT'S JUST A BUNCH OF THREATS ON THE BOTTOM OF A PIZZA BOX.

IT'S NOT ALL THREATS. PARAGRAPH 42 EXPLORES MY THOUGHTS ABOUT THE MEANING OF LIFE.

"RATHER THAN LOVE, THAN MONEY, THAN FAME, GIVE ME TUNA?"

THERE'S A QUIET DIGNITY TO THAT, BUCKY.

VERY QUIET.

THE TIME I SPENT IN A TRASH CAN IN SOLITUDE HAS PAID OFF. MY PERSONAL OBSERVATIONS ON NATURE ARE READY TO BE READ.

KEEP IN MIND THIS IS JUST A ROUGH DRAFT.

EEW. IT FEELS LIKE MORE OF A SLIMY DRAFT.

AND THE NEXT THING THAT STRIKES ME IS THAT YOUR PERSONAL OBSERVATIONS ON NATURE SMELL LIKE ROTTEN MILK.

I'M HOPING THAT CAN BE REPLICATED THROUGH THE MIRACLE OF SCRATCH AND SNIFF.

I'M NOT SURPRISED YOU'RE MOCKING MY NATURE JOURNAL. GREAT MINDS LIKE MINE HAVE ALWAYS FACED OPPOSITION FROM PEA BRAINS. I BET YOU WOULDN'T MAKE FUN OF THOREAU!

THOREAU DIDN'T SIT IN A TRASH CAN FOR A WEEK.

CRAM IT.

WELL, THAT'S NOT VERY TRANSCENDENTAL.

I BELIEVE IT'S PRONOUNCED *THOR*-OH

80

MAN, WHERE HAVE YOU BEEN? GO GET ME MY BOWL, ROBBO.
... EXCUSE ME?
I SAID GET MY BOWL! HOW MANY TIMES DO I HAVE TO SAY IT? I AM BUCKY KATT! MASTER OF ALL I SURVEY!
CLICK
SURVEY THAT.
HA HA! GET HIS BOWL, DOOR!
darb

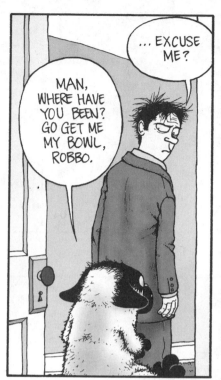

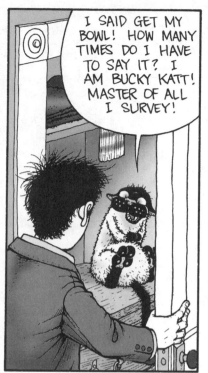

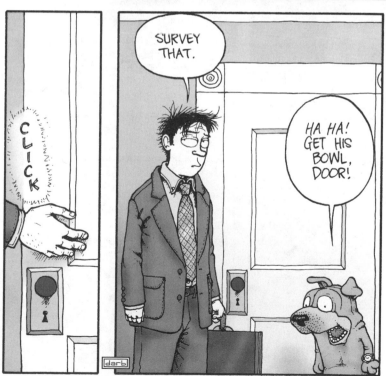

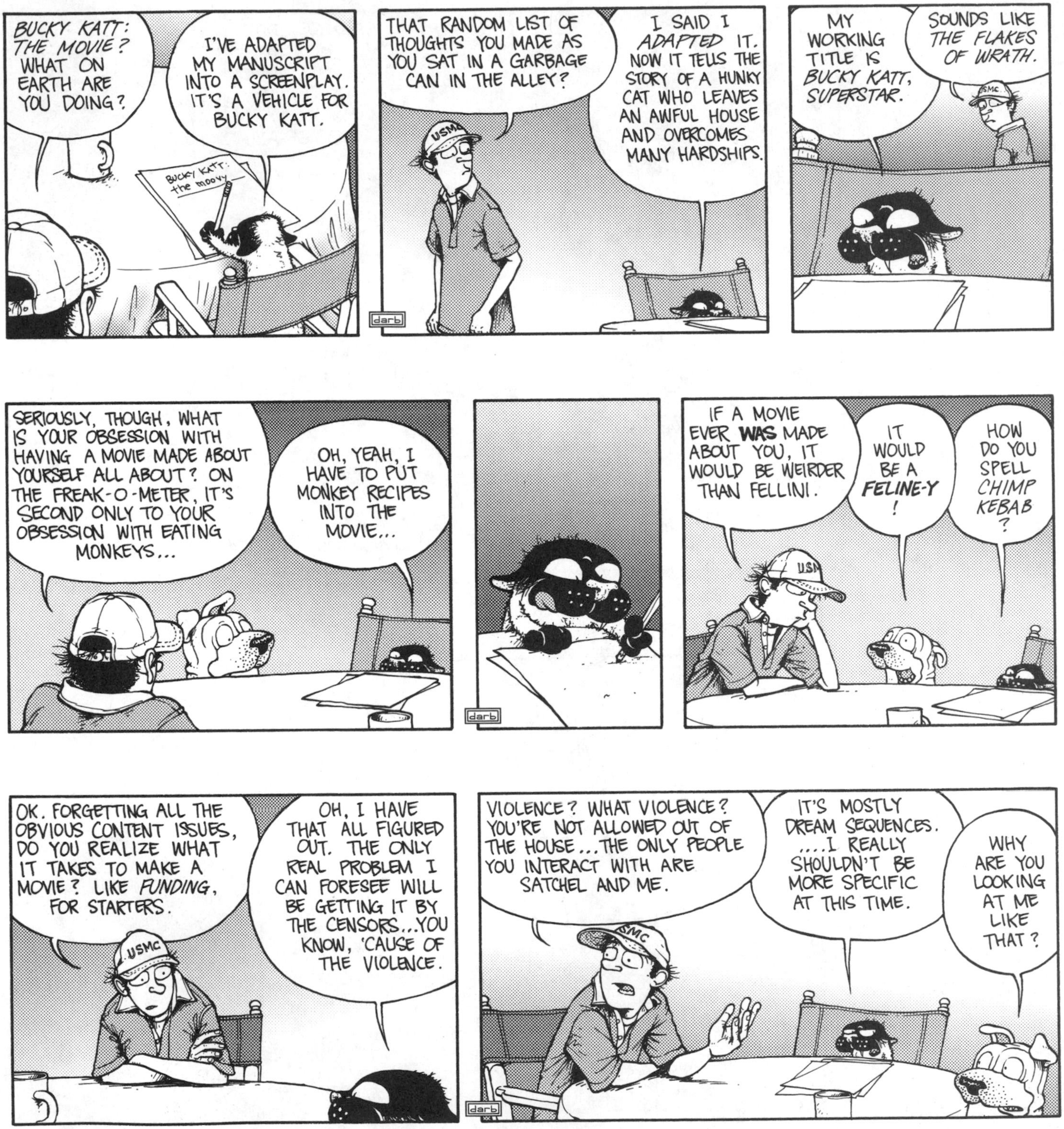
BUCKY KATT: THE MOVIE? WHAT ON EARTH ARE YOU DOING?
I'VE ADAPTED MY MANUSCRIPT INTO A SCREENPLAY. IT'S A VEHICLE FOR BUCKY KATT.
BUCKY KATT: the moovy
THAT RANDOM LIST OF THOUGHTS YOU MADE AS YOU SAT IN A GARBAGE CAN IN THE ALLEY?
I SAID I ADAPTED IT. NOW IT TELLS THE STORY OF A HUNKY CAT WHO LEAVES AN AWFUL HOUSE AND OVERCOMES MANY HARDSHIPS.
MY WORKING TITLE IS BUCKY KATT, SUPERSTAR.
SOUNDS LIKE THE FLAKES OF WRATH.
SERIOUSLY, THOUGH, WHAT IS YOUR OBSESSION WITH HAVING A MOVIE MADE ABOUT YOURSELF ALL ABOUT? ON THE FREAK-O-METER, IT'S SECOND ONLY TO YOUR OBSESSION WITH EATING MONKEYS...
OH, YEAH, I HAVE TO PUT MONKEY RECIPES INTO THE MOVIE...
IF A MOVIE EVER WAS MADE ABOUT YOU, IT WOULD BE WEIRDER THAN FELLINI.
IT WOULD BE A FELINE-Y!
HOW DO YOU SPELL CHIMP KEBAB?
OK. FORGETTING ALL THE OBVIOUS CONTENT ISSUES, DO YOU REALIZE WHAT IT TAKES TO MAKE A MOVIE? LIKE FUNDING, FOR STARTERS.
OH, I HAVE THAT ALL FIGURED OUT. THE ONLY REAL PROBLEM I CAN FORESEE WILL BE GETTING IT BY THE CENSORS...YOU KNOW, 'CAUSE OF THE VIOLENCE.
VIOLENCE? WHAT VIOLENCE? YOU'RE NOT ALLOWED OUT OF THE HOUSE...THE ONLY PEOPLE YOU INTERACT WITH ARE SATCHEL AND ME.
IT'S MOSTLY DREAM SEQUENCES. ....I REALLY SHOULDN'T BE MORE SPECIFIC AT THIS TIME.
WHY ARE YOU LOOKING AT ME LIKE THAT?

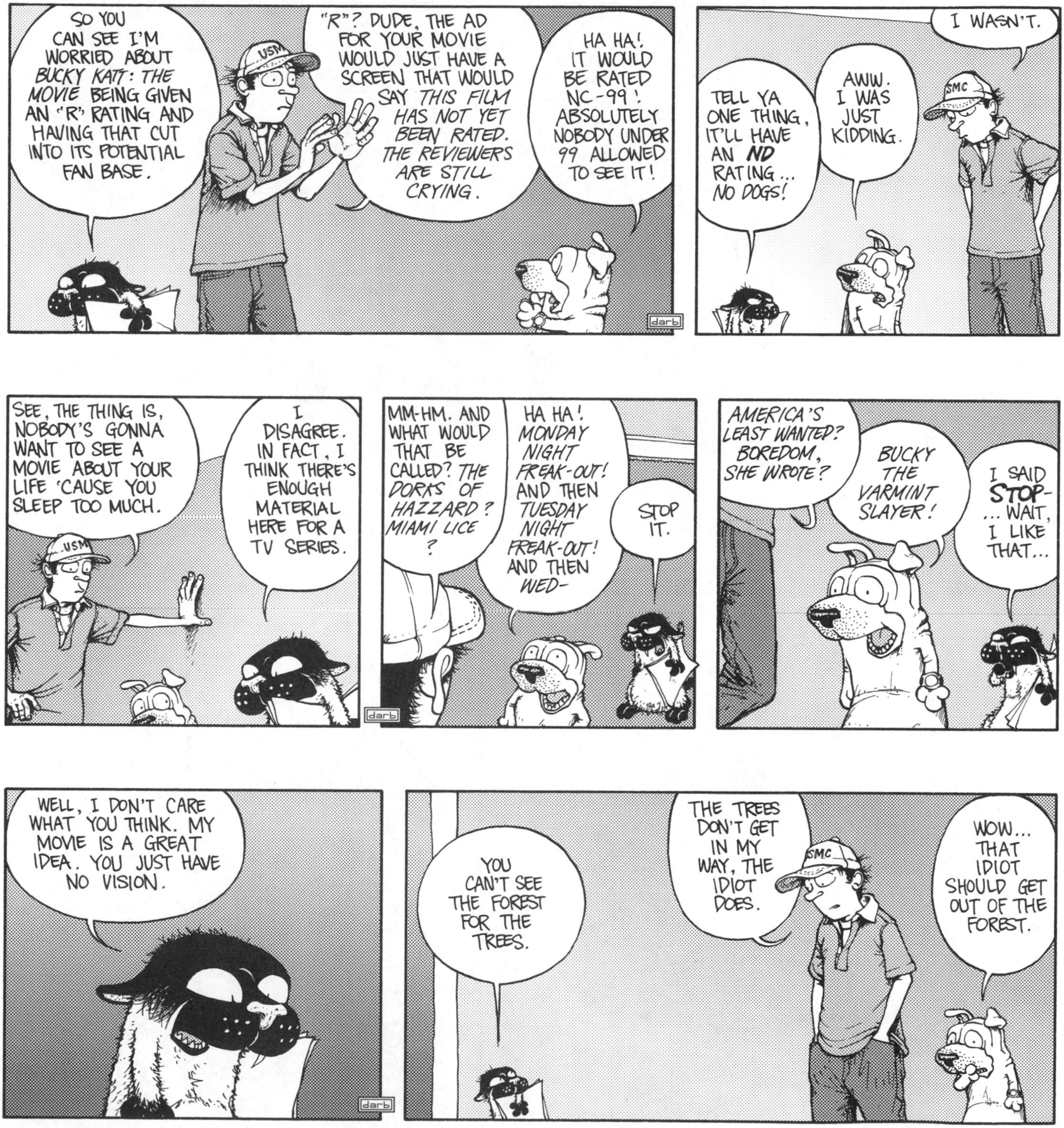
SO YOU CAN SEE I'M WORRIED ABOUT BUCKY KATT: THE MOVIE BEING GIVEN AN "R" RATING AND HAVING THAT CUT INTO ITS POTENTIAL FAN BASE.
"R"? DUDE, THE AD FOR YOUR MOVIE WOULD JUST HAVE A SCREEN THAT WOULD SAY THIS FILM HAS NOT YET BEEN RATED. THE REVIEWERS ARE STILL CRYING.
HA HA! IT WOULD BE RATED NC-99! ABSOLUTELY NOBODY UNDER 99 ALLOWED TO SEE IT!
TELL YA ONE THING, IT'LL HAVE AN ND RATING... NO DOGS!
AWW. I WAS JUST KIDDING.
I WASN'T.
SEE, THE THING IS, NOBODY'S GONNA WANT TO SEE A MOVIE ABOUT YOUR LIFE 'CAUSE YOU SLEEP TOO MUCH.
I DISAGREE. IN FACT, I THINK THERE'S ENOUGH MATERIAL HERE FOR A TV SERIES.
MM-HM. AND WHAT WOULD THAT BE CALLED? THE DORKS OF HAZZARD? MIAMI LICE?
HA HA! MONDAY NIGHT FREAK-OUT! AND THEN TUESDAY NIGHT FREAK-OUT! AND THEN WED-
STOP IT.
AMERICA'S LEAST WANTED? BOREDOM, SHE WROTE?
BUCKY THE VARMINT SLAYER!
I SAID STOP-... WAIT, I LIKE THAT...
WELL, I DON'T CARE WHAT YOU THINK. MY MOVIE IS A GREAT IDEA. YOU JUST HAVE NO VISION.
YOU CAN'T SEE THE FOREST FOR THE TREES.
THE TREES DON'T GET IN MY WAY, THE IDIOT DOES.
WOW... THAT IDIOT SHOULD GET OUT OF THE FOREST.

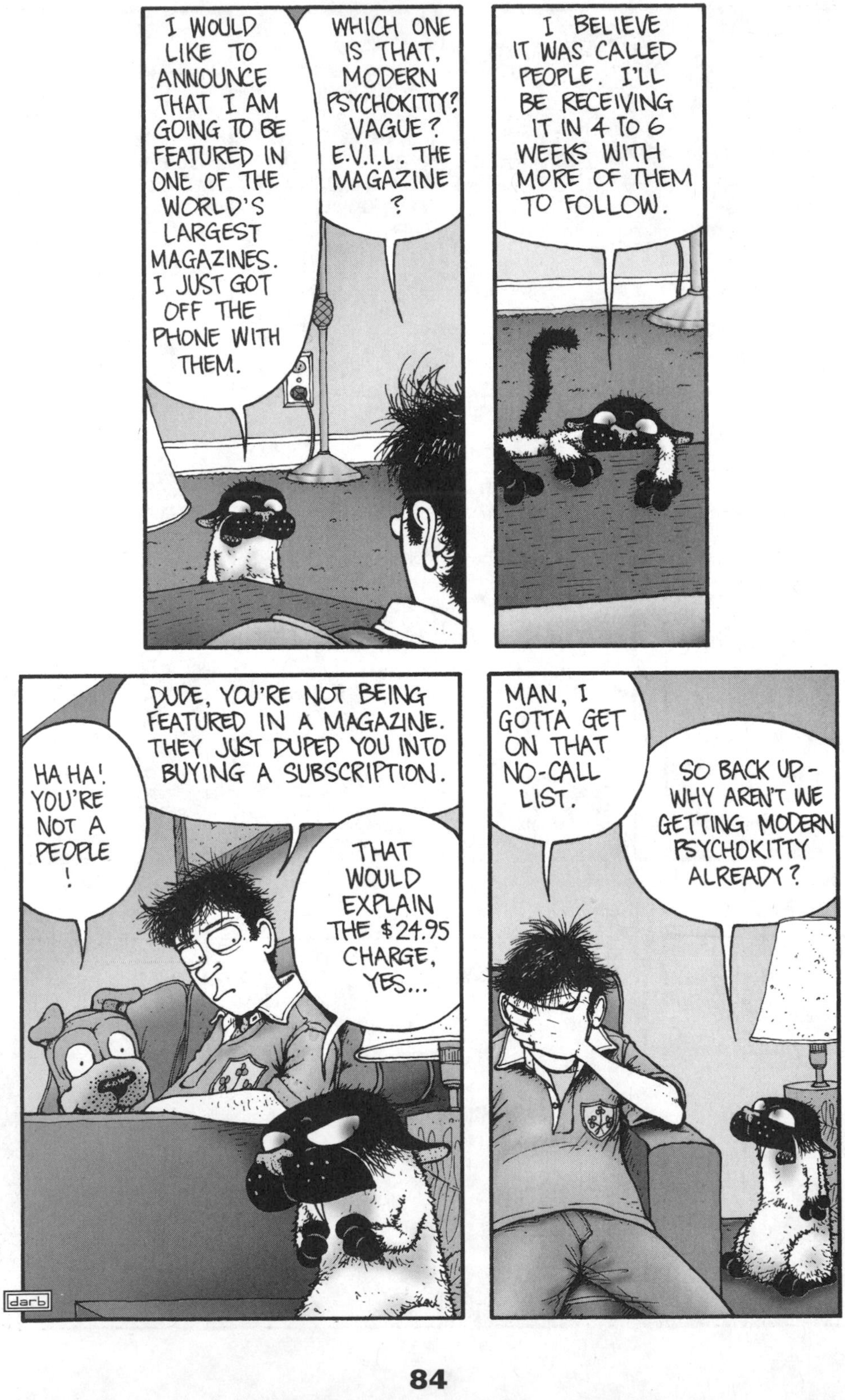
I WOULD LIKE TO ANNOUNCE THAT I AM GOING TO BE FEATURED IN ONE OF THE WORLD'S LARGEST MAGAZINES. I JUST GOT OFF THE PHONE WITH THEM.
WHICH ONE IS THAT. MODERN PSYCHOKITTY? VAGUE? E.V.I.L. THE MAGAZINE?
I BELIEVE IT WAS CALLED PEOPLE. I'LL BE RECEIVING IT IN 4 TO 6 WEEKS WITH MORE OF THEM TO FOLLOW.
DUDE, YOU'RE NOT BEING FEATURED IN A MAGAZINE. THEY JUST DUPED YOU INTO BUYING A SUBSCRIPTION.
HA HA! YOU'RE NOT A PEOPLE!
THAT WOULD EXPLAIN THE $24.95 CHARGE, YES...
MAN, I GOTTA GET ON THAT NO-CALL LIST.
SO BACK UP - WHY AREN'T WE GETTING MODERN PSYCHOKITTY ALREADY?
darb

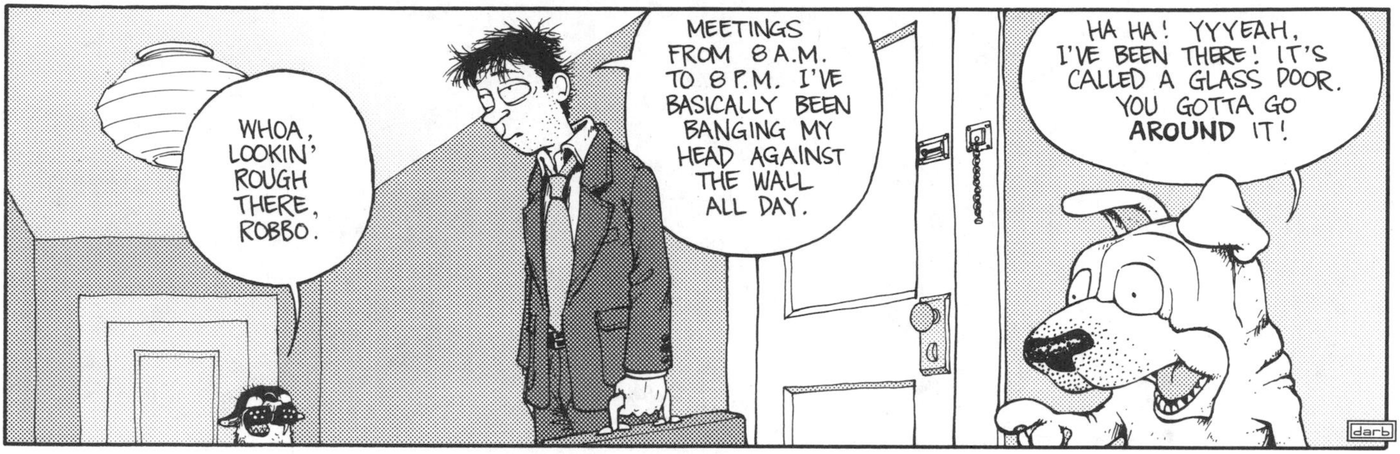
WHOA, LOOKIN' ROUGH THERE, ROBBO.
MEETINGS FROM 8 A.M. TO 8 P.M. I'VE BASICALLY BEEN BANGING MY HEAD AGAINST THE WALL ALL DAY.
HA HA! YYYEAH, I'VE BEEN THERE! IT'S CALLED A GLASS DOOR. YOU GOTTA GO **AROUND** IT!
darb

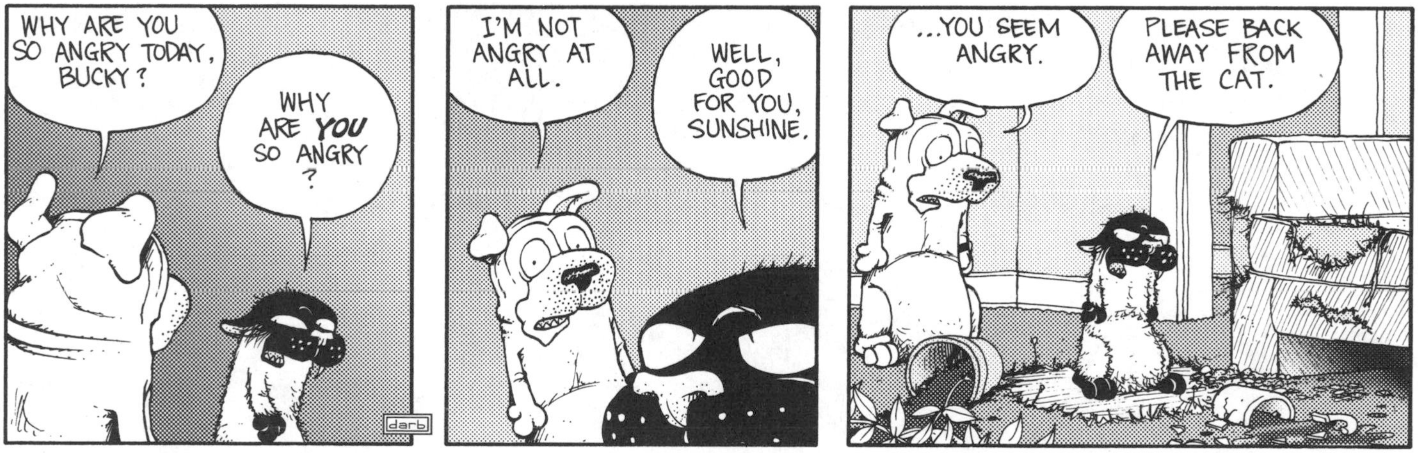
WHY ARE YOU SO ANGRY TODAY, BUCKY?
WHY ARE ***YOU*** SO ANGRY?
darb
I'M NOT ANGRY AT ALL.
WELL, GOOD FOR YOU, SUNSHINE.
...YOU SEEM ANGRY.
PLEASE BACK AWAY FROM THE CAT.

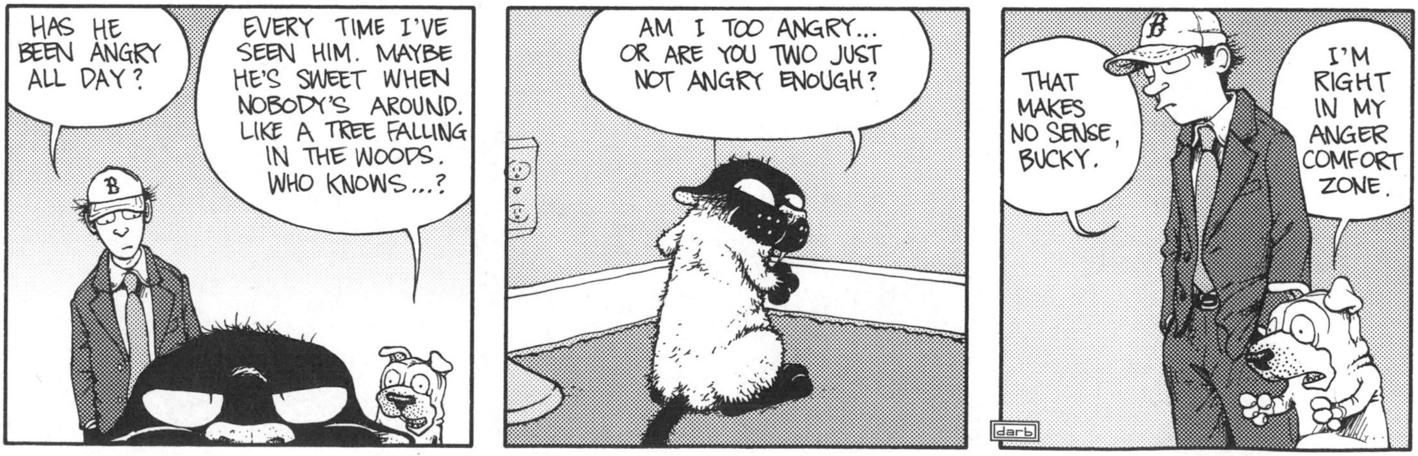
HAS HE BEEN ANGRY ALL DAY?
EVERY TIME I'VE SEEN HIM. MAYBE HE'S SWEET WHEN NOBODY'S AROUND. LIKE A TREE FALLING IN THE WOODS. WHO KNOWS...?
AM I TOO ANGRY... OR ARE YOU TWO JUST NOT ANGRY ENOUGH?
THAT MAKES NO SENSE, BUCKY.
I'M RIGHT IN MY ANGER COMFORT ZONE.
darb

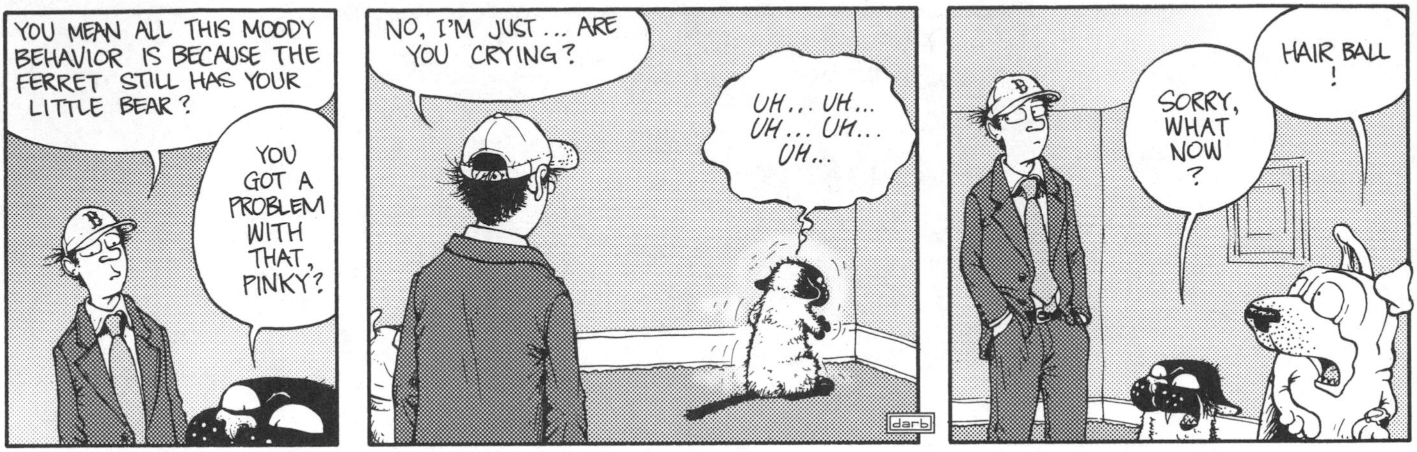
YOU MEAN ALL THIS MOODY BEHAVIOR IS BECAUSE THE FERRET STILL HAS YOUR LITTLE BEAR?
YOU GOT A PROBLEM WITH THAT, PINKY?
NO, I'M JUST... ARE YOU CRYING?
UH... UH... UH... UH... UH...
darb
SORRY, WHAT NOW?
HAIR BALL!

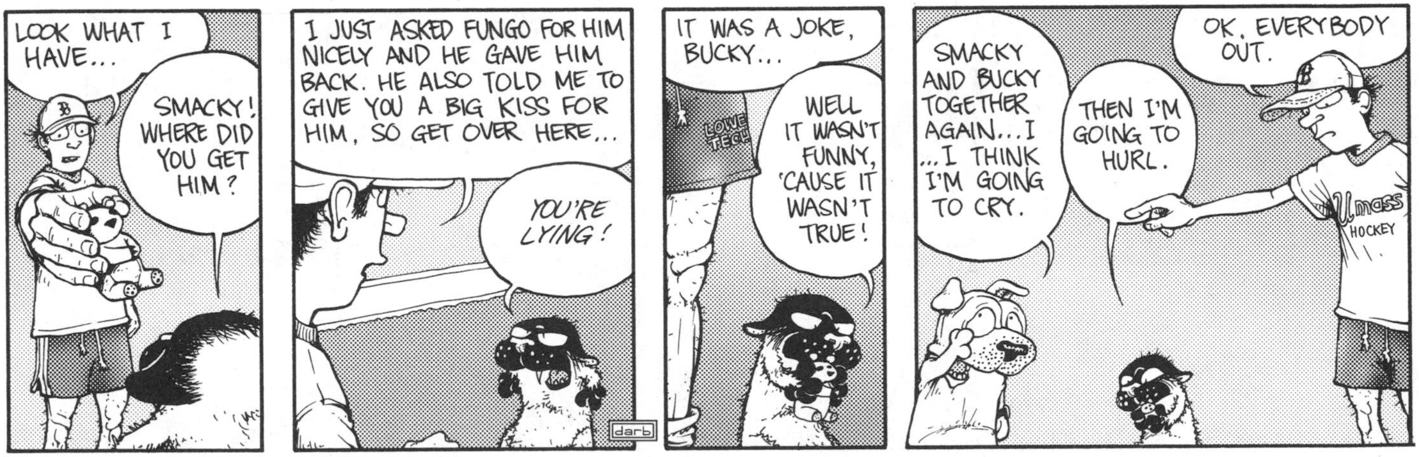
LOOK WHAT I HAVE...
SMACKY! WHERE DID YOU GET HIM?
I JUST ASKED FUNGO FOR HIM NICELY AND HE GAVE HIM BACK. HE ALSO TOLD ME TO GIVE YOU A BIG KISS FOR HIM, SO GET OVER HERE...
YOU'RE LYING!
darb
IT WAS A JOKE, BUCKY...
LOWE TECH
WELL IT WASN'T FUNNY, 'CAUSE IT WASN'T TRUE!
SMACKY AND BUCKY TOGETHER AGAIN... I ...I THINK I'M GOING TO CRY.
THEN I'M GOING TO HURL.
OK, EVERYBODY OUT.
UMass HOCKEY

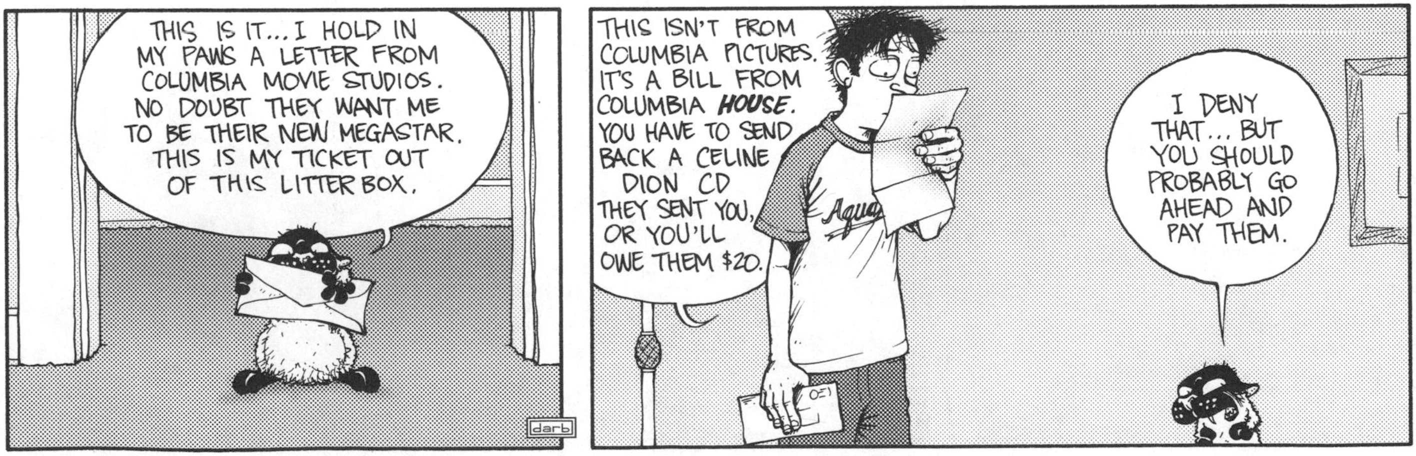
THIS IS IT... I HOLD IN MY PAWS A LETTER FROM COLUMBIA MOVIE STUDIOS. NO DOUBT THEY WANT ME TO BE THEIR NEW MEGASTAR. THIS IS MY TICKET OUT OF THIS LITTER BOX.
darb
THIS ISN'T FROM COLUMBIA PICTURES. IT'S A BILL FROM COLUMBIA HOUSE. YOU HAVE TO SEND BACK A CELINE DION CD THEY SENT YOU, OR YOU'LL OWE THEM $20.
I DENY THAT... BUT YOU SHOULD PROBABLY GO AHEAD AND PAY THEM.

WHAT IS THAT ?
JUST A LITTLE SIGN FOR OUTSIDE OF THE NEIGHBORS' HOUSE.
thiss FERRET AtE MY BABY !!
DUDE, YOU CAN'T PUT THAT SIGN UP.... IT'S NOT TRUE.
PERHAPS. BUT I ASK YOU - IS PUTTING UP A FAKE SIGN WRONG ?
YEAH, IT'S ILLEGAL.
WELL, IF LYING ABOUT SOMEONE YOU DON'T LIKE TO GET THEM EVICTED FROM THEIR HOUSE IS WRONG, I DON'T WANT TO BE RIGHT.
OH. OK, WELL, YOU'RE SAFE, THEN.
darb

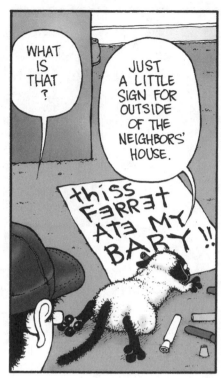

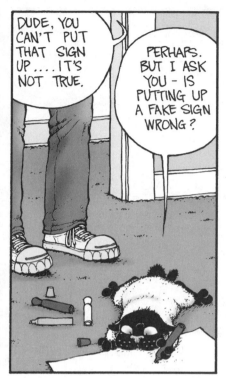

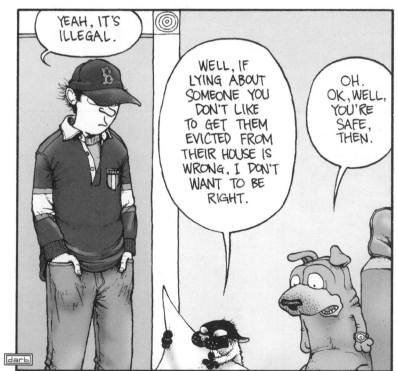

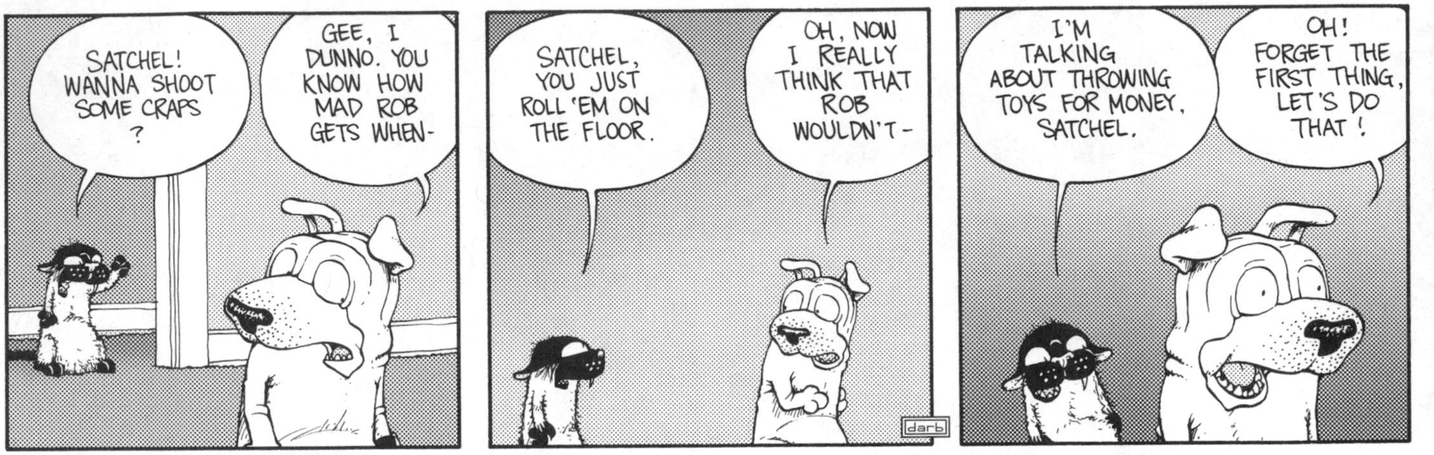
SATCHEL! WANNA SHOOT SOME CRAPS ?
GEE, I DUNNO. YOU KNOW HOW MAD ROB GETS WHEN-
SATCHEL, YOU JUST ROLL 'EM ON THE FLOOR.
OH, NOW I REALLY THINK THAT ROB WOULDN'T-
I'M TALKING ABOUT THROWING TOYS FOR MONEY, SATCHEL.
OH! FORGET THE FIRST THING, LET'S DO THAT!
darb

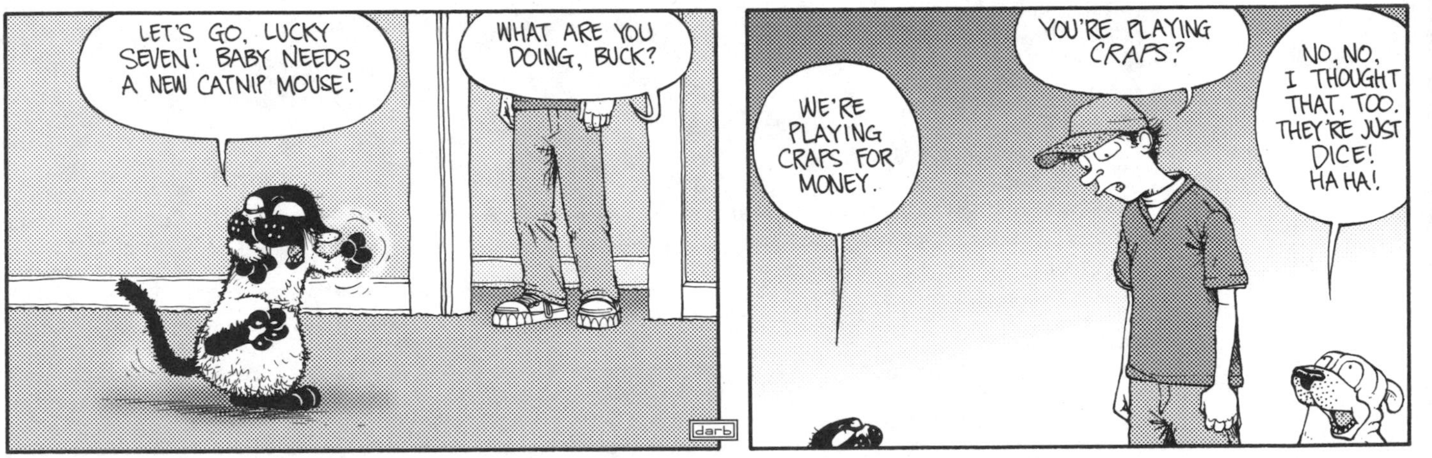
LET'S GO, LUCKY SEVEN! BABY NEEDS A NEW CATNIP MOUSE!
WHAT ARE YOU DOING, BUCK?
darb
WE'RE PLAYING CRAPS FOR MONEY.
YOU'RE PLAYING CRAPS?
NO, NO, I THOUGHT THAT, TOO. THEY'RE JUST DICE! HA HA!

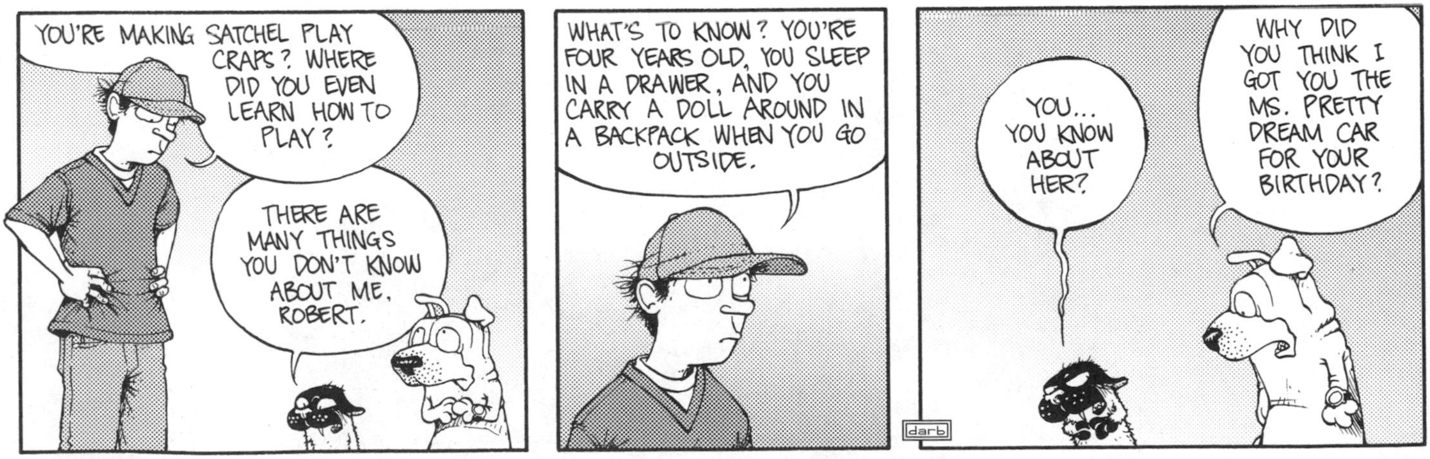
YOU'RE MAKING SATCHEL PLAY CRAPS? WHERE DID YOU EVEN LEARN HOW TO PLAY?
THERE ARE MANY THINGS YOU DON'T KNOW ABOUT ME, ROBERT.
WHAT'S TO KNOW? YOU'RE FOUR YEARS OLD, YOU SLEEP IN A DRAWER, AND YOU CARRY A DOLL AROUND IN A BACKPACK WHEN YOU GO OUTSIDE.
darb
YOU... YOU KNOW ABOUT HER?
WHY DID YOU THINK I GOT YOU THE MS. PRETTY DREAM CAR FOR YOUR BIRTHDAY?

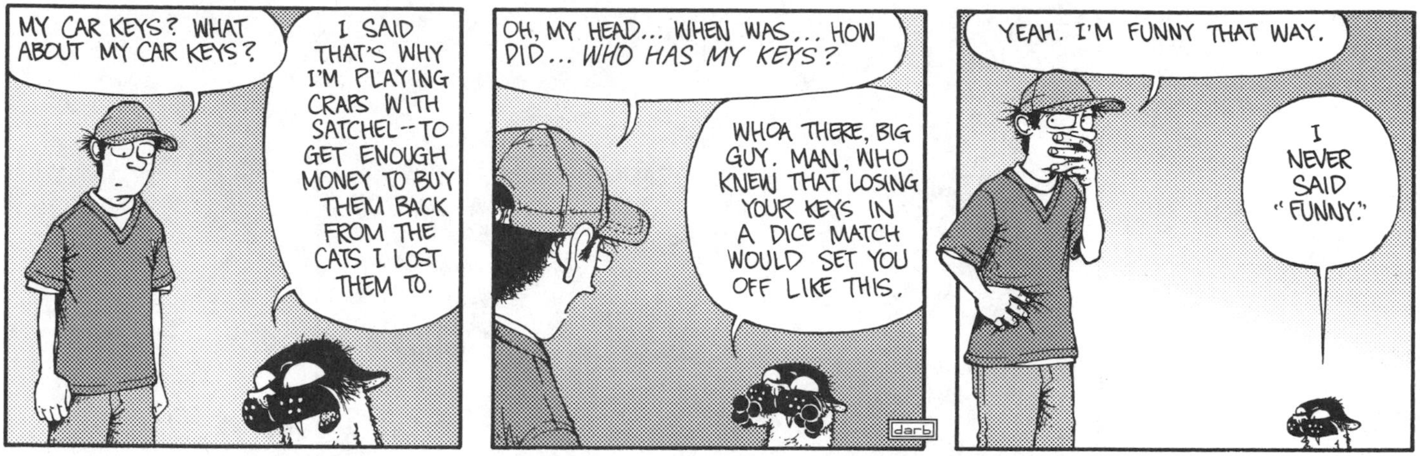
MY CAR KEYS? WHAT ABOUT MY CAR KEYS?
I SAID THAT'S WHY I'M PLAYING CRAPS WITH SATCHEL--TO GET ENOUGH MONEY TO BUY THEM BACK FROM THE CATS I LOST THEM TO.
OH, MY HEAD... WHEN WAS... HOW DID... *WHO HAS MY KEYS?*
WHOA THERE, BIG GUY. MAN, WHO KNEW THAT LOSING YOUR KEYS IN A DICE MATCH WOULD SET YOU OFF LIKE THIS.
darb
YEAH. I'M FUNNY THAT WAY.
I NEVER SAID "FUNNY."

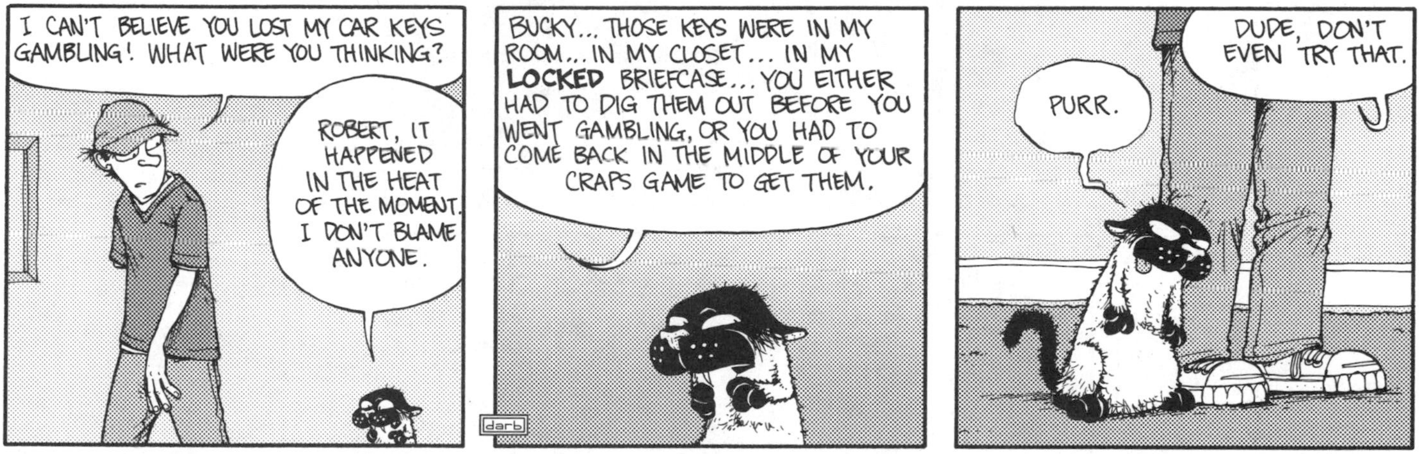
I CAN'T BELIEVE YOU LOST MY CAR KEYS GAMBLING! WHAT WERE YOU THINKING?
ROBERT, IT HAPPENED IN THE HEAT OF THE MOMENT. I DON'T BLAME ANYONE.
BUCKY... THOSE KEYS WERE IN MY ROOM... IN MY CLOSET... IN MY **LOCKED** BRIEFCASE... YOU EITHER HAD TO DIG THEM OUT BEFORE YOU WENT GAMBLING, OR YOU HAD TO COME BACK IN THE MIDDLE OF YOUR CRAPS GAME TO GET THEM.
darb
PURR.
DUDE, DON'T EVEN TRY THAT.

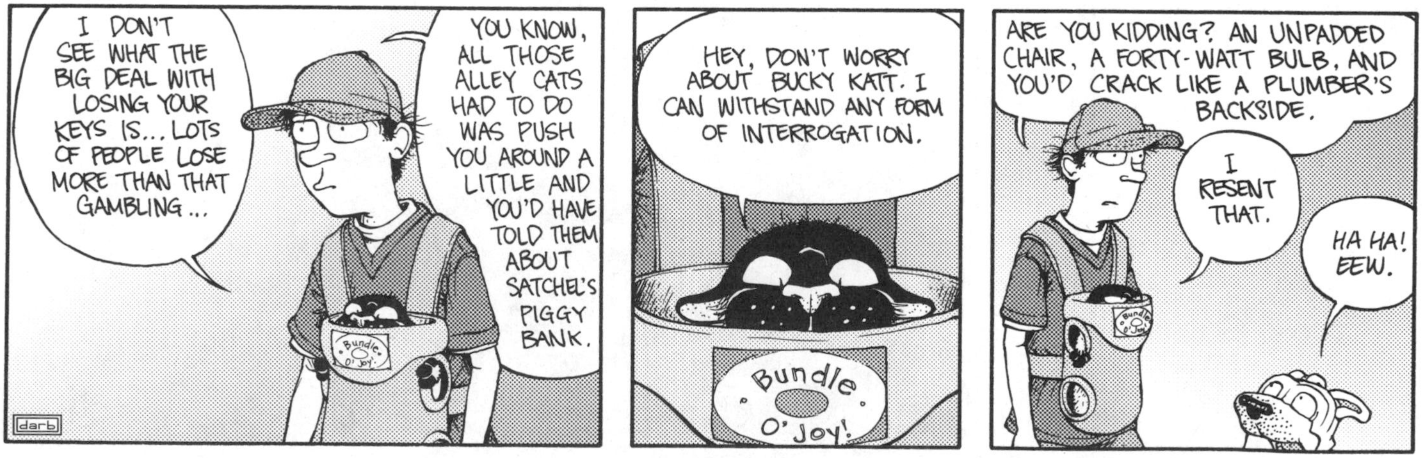
I DON'T SEE WHAT THE BIG DEAL WITH LOSING YOUR KEYS IS... LOTS OF PEOPLE LOSE MORE THAN THAT GAMBLING...
YOU KNOW, ALL THOSE ALLEY CATS HAD TO DO WAS PUSH YOU AROUND A LITTLE AND YOU'D HAVE TOLD THEM ABOUT SATCHEL'S PIGGY BANK.
Bundle O' Joy!
darb
HEY, DON'T WORRY ABOUT BUCKY KATT. I CAN WITHSTAND ANY FORM OF INTERROGATION.
Bundle O' Joy!
ARE YOU KIDDING? AN UNPADDED CHAIR, A FORTY-WATT BULB, AND YOU'D CRACK LIKE A PLUMBER'S BACKSIDE.
I RESENT THAT.
HA HA! EEW.
Bundle O' Joy

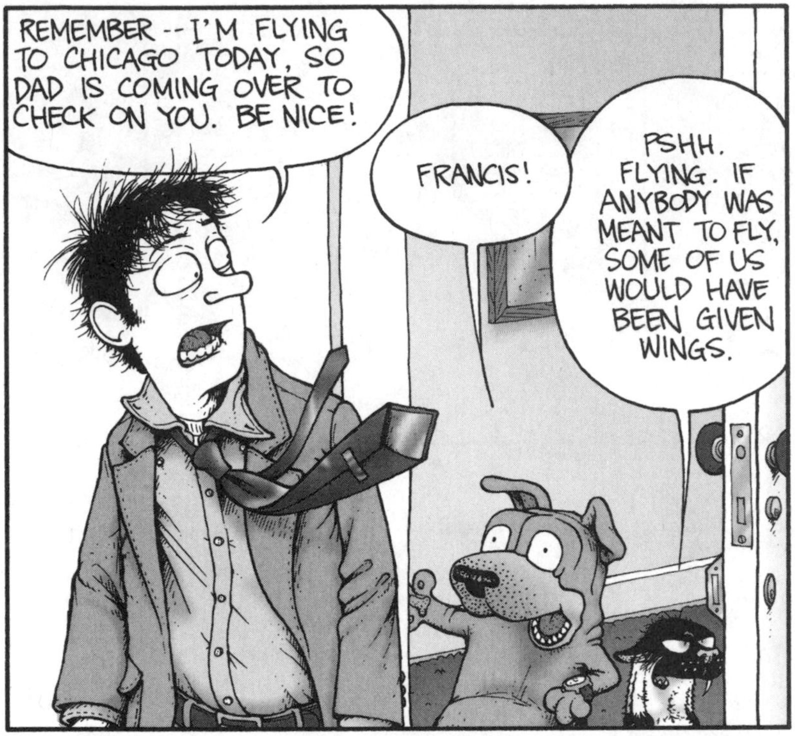
REMEMBER -- I'M FLYING TO CHICAGO TODAY, SO DAD IS COMING OVER TO CHECK ON YOU. BE NICE!
FRANCIS!
PSHH. FLYING. IF ANYBODY WAS MEANT TO FLY, SOME OF US WOULD HAVE BEEN GIVEN WINGS.

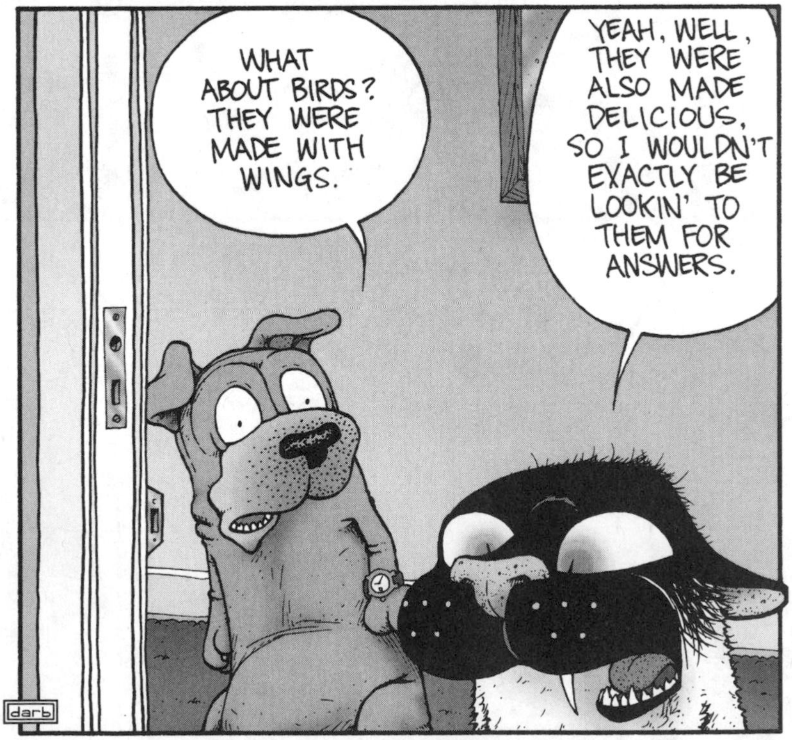
WHAT ABOUT BIRDS? THEY WERE MADE WITH WINGS.
YEAH, WELL, THEY WERE ALSO MADE DELICIOUS, SO I WOULDN'T EXACTLY BE LOOKIN' TO THEM FOR ANSWERS.
darb

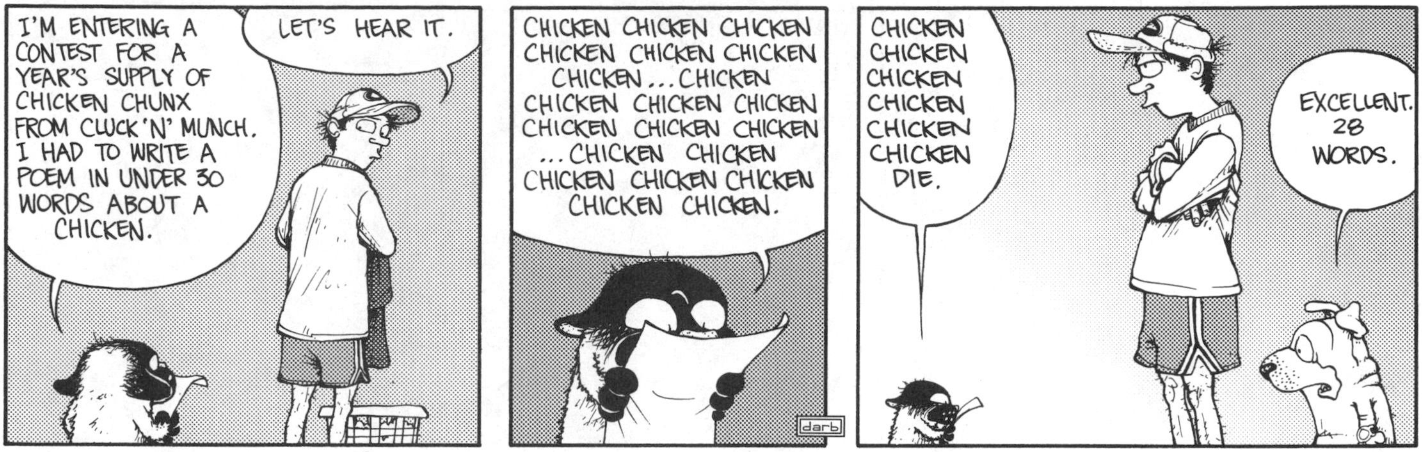
I'M ENTERING A CONTEST FOR A YEAR'S SUPPLY OF CHICKEN CHUNX FROM CLUCK 'N' MUNCH. I HAD TO WRITE A POEM IN UNDER 30 WORDS ABOUT A CHICKEN.
LET'S HEAR IT.
CHICKEN CHICKEN CHICKEN CHICKEN CHICKEN CHICKEN CHICKEN... CHICKEN CHICKEN CHICKEN CHICKEN CHICKEN CHICKEN CHICKEN ...CHICKEN CHICKEN CHICKEN CHICKEN CHICKEN CHICKEN CHICKEN.
darb
CHICKEN CHICKEN CHICKEN CHICKEN CHICKEN CHICKEN DIE.
EXCELLENT. 28 WORDS.

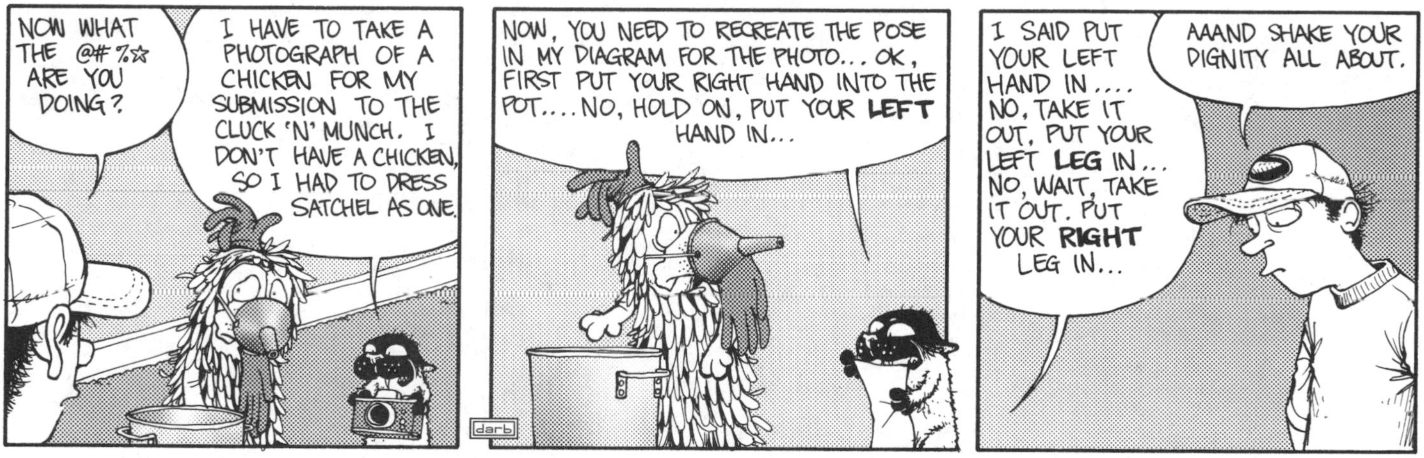
NOW WHAT THE @#%☆ ARE YOU DOING?
I HAVE TO TAKE A PHOTOGRAPH OF A CHICKEN FOR MY SUBMISSION TO THE CLUCK 'N' MUNCH. I DON'T HAVE A CHICKEN, SO I HAD TO DRESS SATCHEL AS ONE.
darb
NOW, YOU NEED TO RECREATE THE POSE IN MY DIAGRAM FOR THE PHOTO... OK, FIRST PUT YOUR RIGHT HAND INTO THE POT.... NO, HOLD ON, PUT YOUR **LEFT** HAND IN...
I SAID PUT YOUR LEFT HAND IN.... NO, TAKE IT OUT, PUT YOUR LEFT **LEG** IN... NO, WAIT, TAKE IT OUT. PUT YOUR **RIGHT** LEG IN...
AAAND SHAKE YOUR DIGNITY ALL ABOUT.

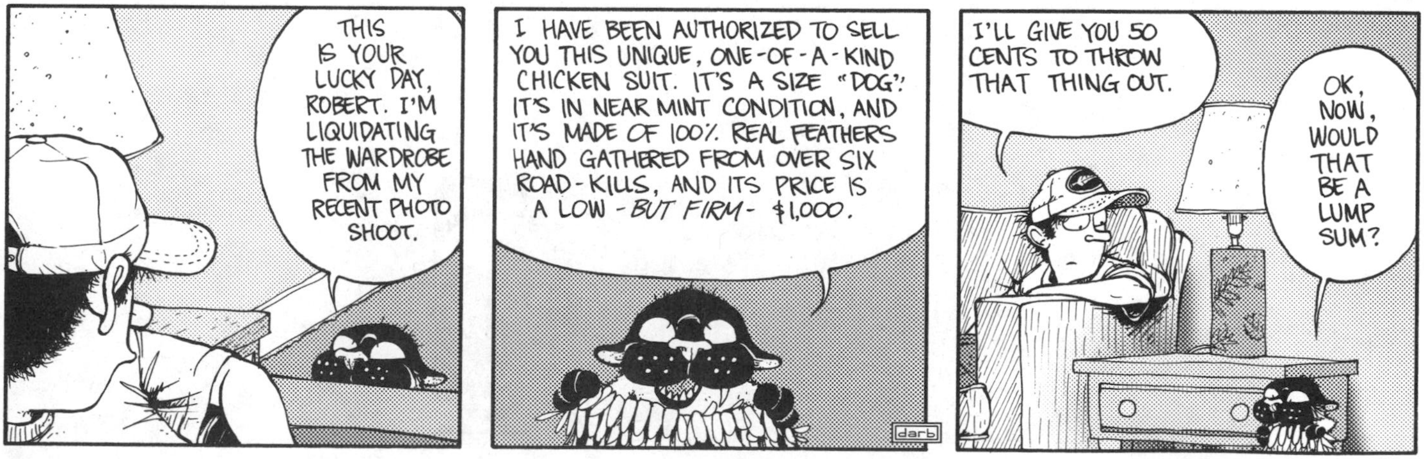
THIS IS YOUR LUCKY DAY, ROBERT. I'M LIQUIDATING THE WARDROBE FROM MY RECENT PHOTO SHOOT.
I HAVE BEEN AUTHORIZED TO SELL YOU THIS UNIQUE, ONE-OF-A-KIND CHICKEN SUIT. IT'S A SIZE "DOG". IT'S IN NEAR MINT CONDITION, AND IT'S MADE OF 100% REAL FEATHERS HAND GATHERED FROM OVER SIX ROAD-KILLS, AND ITS PRICE IS A LOW *- BUT FIRM -* $1,000.
darb
I'LL GIVE YOU 50 CENTS TO THROW THAT THING OUT.
OK, NOW, WOULD THAT BE A LUMP SUM?

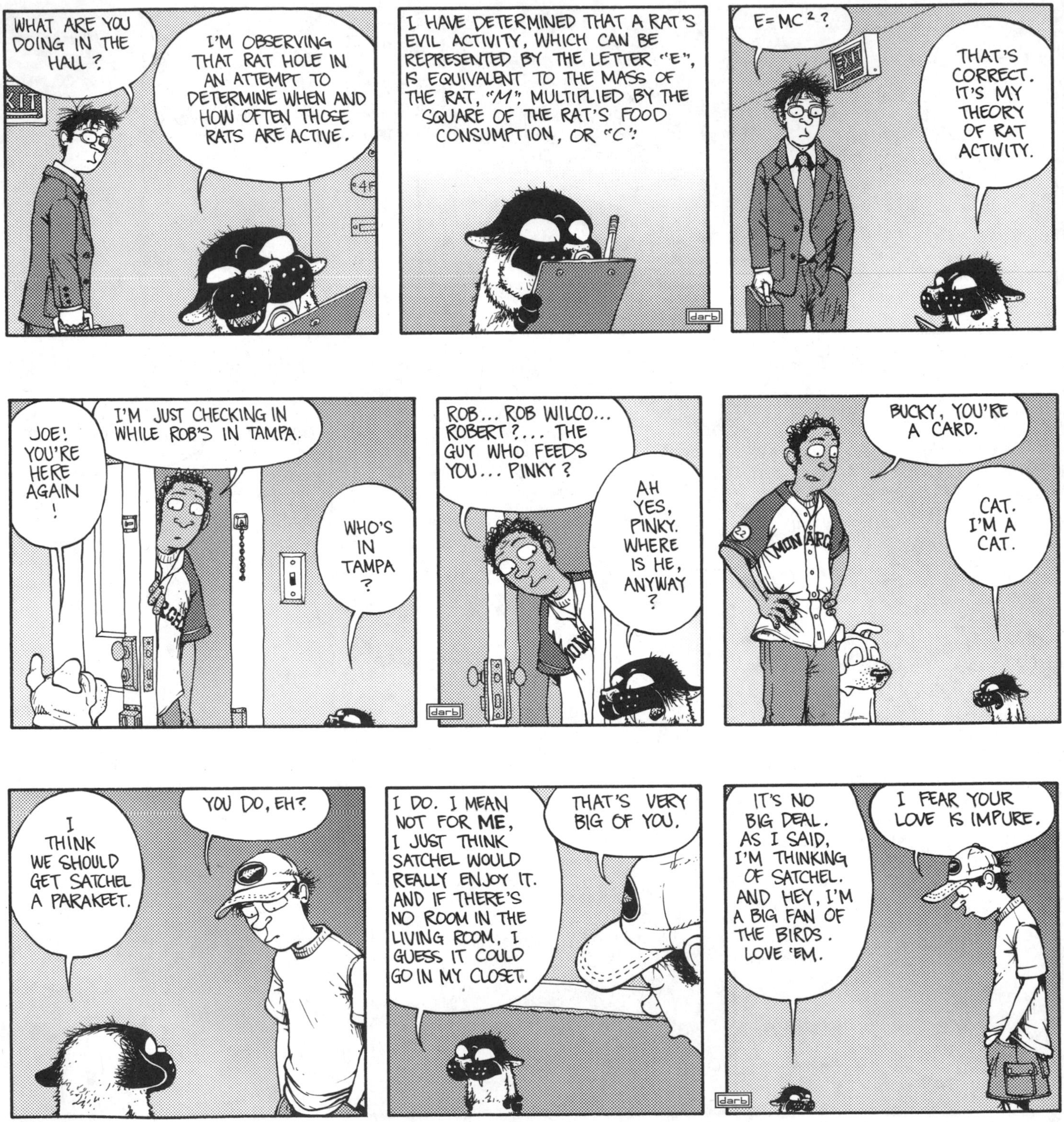
WHAT ARE YOU DOING IN THE HALL?
I'M OBSERVING THAT RAT HOLE IN AN ATTEMPT TO DETERMINE WHEN AND HOW OFTEN THOSE RATS ARE ACTIVE.
I HAVE DETERMINED THAT A RAT'S EVIL ACTIVITY, WHICH CAN BE REPRESENTED BY THE LETTER "E", IS EQUIVALENT TO THE MASS OF THE RAT, "M", MULTIPLIED BY THE SQUARE OF THE RAT'S FOOD CONSUMPTION, OR "C".
E=MC²?
THAT'S CORRECT. IT'S MY THEORY OF RAT ACTIVITY.
darb
JOE! YOU'RE HERE AGAIN!
I'M JUST CHECKING IN WHILE ROB'S IN TAMPA.
WHO'S IN TAMPA?
ROB... ROB WILCO... ROBERT?... THE GUY WHO FEEDS YOU... PINKY?
AH YES, PINKY. WHERE IS HE, ANYWAY?
BUCKY, YOU'RE A CARD.
CAT. I'M A CAT.
darb
I THINK WE SHOULD GET SATCHEL A PARAKEET.
YOU DO, EH?
I DO. I MEAN NOT FOR ME, I JUST THINK SATCHEL WOULD REALLY ENJOY IT. AND IF THERE'S NO ROOM IN THE LIVING ROOM, I GUESS IT COULD GO IN MY CLOSET.
THAT'S VERY BIG OF YOU.
IT'S NO BIG DEAL. AS I SAID, I'M THINKING OF SATCHEL. AND HEY, I'M A BIG FAN OF THE BIRDS. LOVE 'EM.
I FEAR YOUR LOVE IS IMPURE.
darb

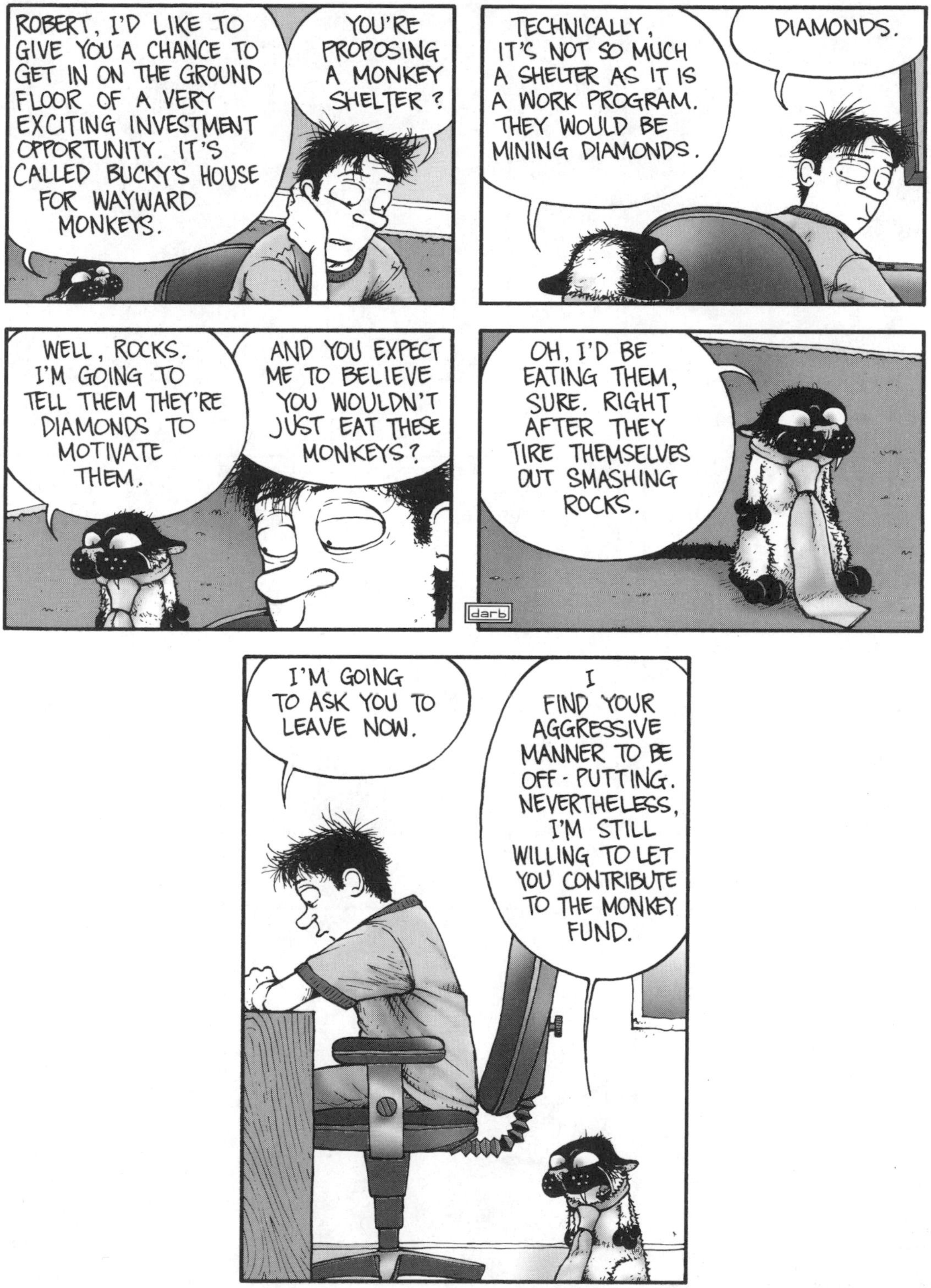
ROBERT, I'D LIKE TO GIVE YOU A CHANCE TO GET IN ON THE GROUND FLOOR OF A VERY EXCITING INVESTMENT OPPORTUNITY. IT'S CALLED BUCKY'S HOUSE FOR WAYWARD MONKEYS.
YOU'RE PROPOSING A MONKEY SHELTER?
TECHNICALLY, IT'S NOT SO MUCH A SHELTER AS IT IS A WORK PROGRAM. THEY WOULD BE MINING DIAMONDS.
DIAMONDS.
WELL, ROCKS. I'M GOING TO TELL THEM THEY'RE DIAMONDS TO MOTIVATE THEM.
AND YOU EXPECT ME TO BELIEVE YOU WOULDN'T JUST EAT THESE MONKEYS?
OH, I'D BE EATING THEM, SURE. RIGHT AFTER THEY TIRE THEMSELVES OUT SMASHING ROCKS.
darb
I'M GOING TO ASK YOU TO LEAVE NOW.
I FIND YOUR AGGRESSIVE MANNER TO BE OFF-PUTTING. NEVERTHELESS, I'M STILL WILLING TO LET YOU CONTRIBUTE TO THE MONKEY FUND.

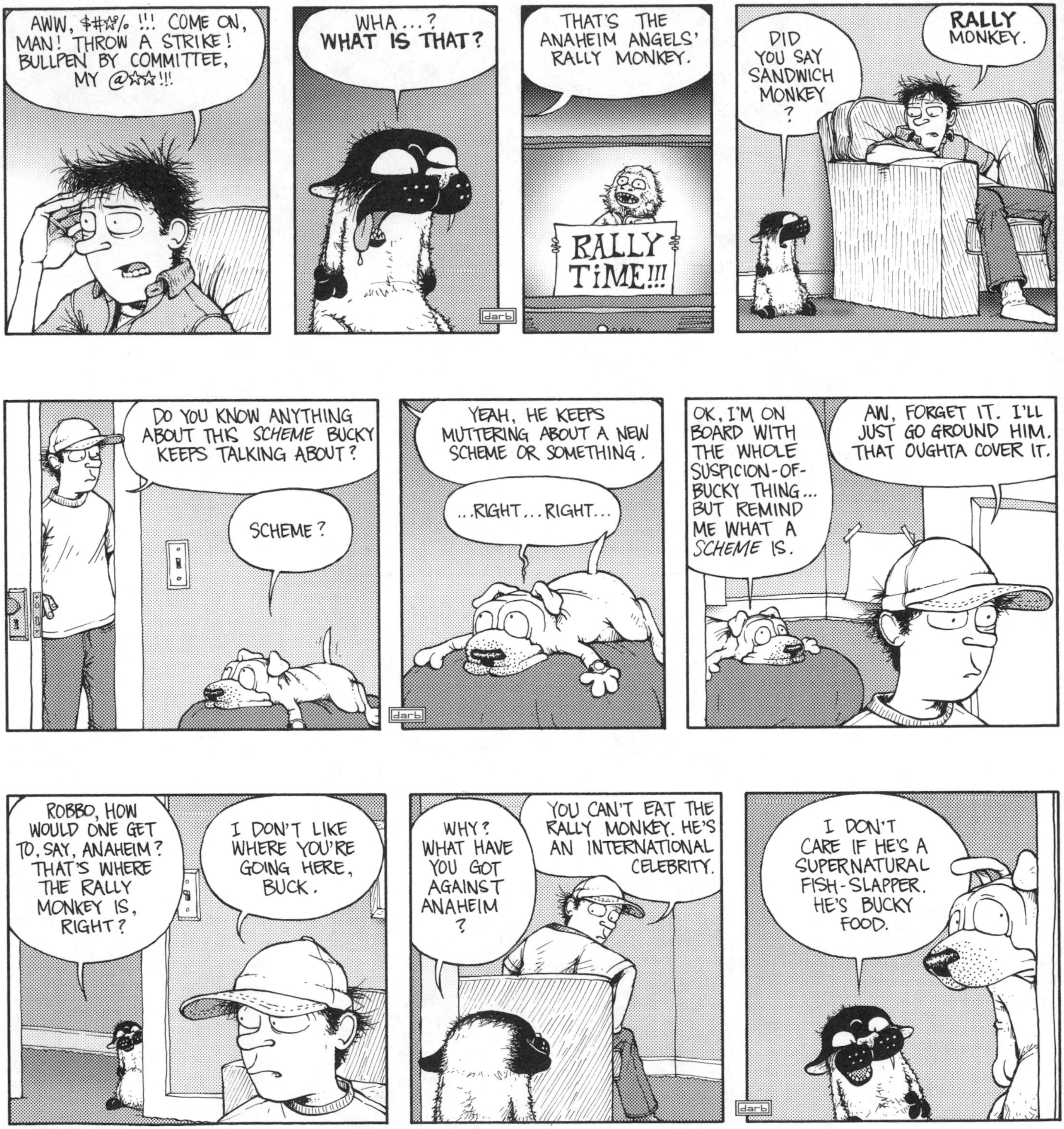
AWW, $#☆% !!! COME ON, MAN! THROW A STRIKE! BULLPEN BY COMMITTEE, MY @☆☆!!!
WHA...? WHAT IS THAT?
THAT'S THE ANAHEIM ANGELS' RALLY MONKEY.
RALLY TIME!!!
DID YOU SAY SANDWICH MONKEY?
RALLY MONKEY.
darb
DO YOU KNOW ANYTHING ABOUT THIS SCHEME BUCKY KEEPS TALKING ABOUT?
SCHEME?
YEAH, HE KEEPS MUTTERING ABOUT A NEW SCHEME OR SOMETHING.
...RIGHT...RIGHT...
OK, I'M ON BOARD WITH THE WHOLE SUSPICION-OF-BUCKY THING... BUT REMIND ME WHAT A SCHEME IS.
AW, FORGET IT. I'LL JUST GO GROUND HIM. THAT OUGHTA COVER IT.
darb
ROBBO, HOW WOULD ONE GET TO, SAY, ANAHEIM? THAT'S WHERE THE RALLY MONKEY IS, RIGHT?
I DON'T LIKE WHERE YOU'RE GOING HERE, BUCK.
WHY? WHAT HAVE YOU GOT AGAINST ANAHEIM?
YOU CAN'T EAT THE RALLY MONKEY. HE'S AN INTERNATIONAL CELEBRITY.
I DON'T CARE IF HE'S A SUPERNATURAL FISH-SLAPPER. HE'S BUCKY FOOD.
darb

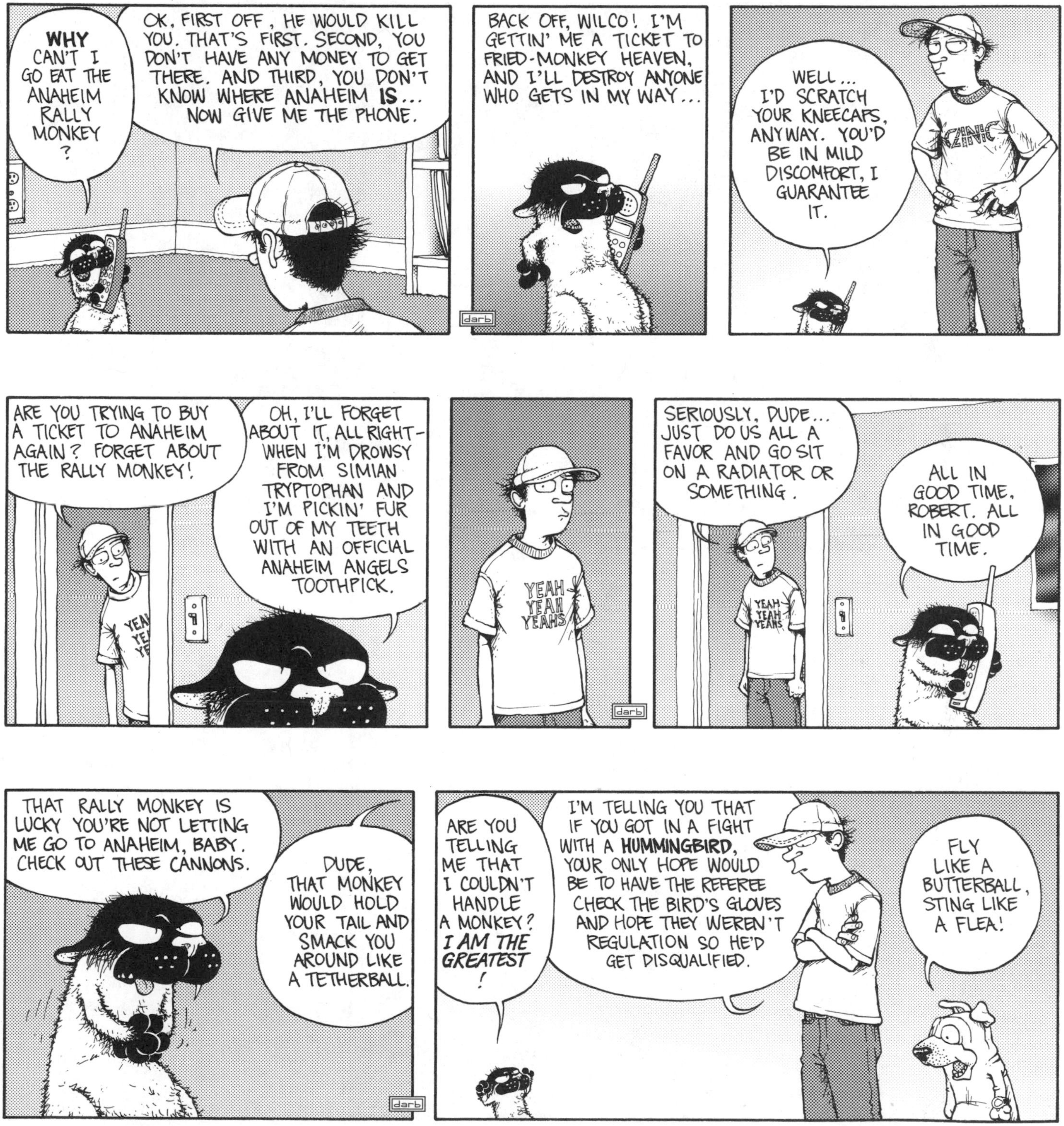
WHY CAN'T I GO EAT THE ANAHEIM RALLY MONKEY ?
OK. FIRST OFF, HE WOULD KILL YOU. THAT'S FIRST. SECOND, YOU DON'T HAVE ANY MONEY TO GET THERE. AND THIRD, YOU DON'T KNOW WHERE ANAHEIM IS... NOW GIVE ME THE PHONE.
BACK OFF, WILCO! I'M GETTIN' ME A TICKET TO FRIED-MONKEY HEAVEN, AND I'LL DESTROY ANYONE WHO GETS IN MY WAY...
WELL... I'D SCRATCH YOUR KNEECAPS, ANYWAY. YOU'D BE IN MILD DISCOMFORT, I GUARANTEE IT.
darb
ARE YOU TRYING TO BUY A TICKET TO ANAHEIM AGAIN? FORGET ABOUT THE RALLY MONKEY!
OH, I'LL FORGET ABOUT IT, ALL RIGHT- WHEN I'M DROWSY FROM SIMIAN TRYPTOPHAN AND I'M PICKIN' FUR OUT OF MY TEETH WITH AN OFFICIAL ANAHEIM ANGELS TOOTHPICK.
YEAH YEAH YEAHS
SERIOUSLY, DUDE... JUST DO US ALL A FAVOR AND GO SIT ON A RADIATOR OR SOMETHING.
ALL IN GOOD TIME, ROBERT. ALL IN GOOD TIME.
darb
THAT RALLY MONKEY IS LUCKY YOU'RE NOT LETTING ME GO TO ANAHEIM, BABY. CHECK OUT THESE CANNONS.
DUDE, THAT MONKEY WOULD HOLD YOUR TAIL AND SMACK YOU AROUND LIKE A TETHERBALL.
ARE YOU TELLING ME THAT I COULDN'T HANDLE A MONKEY? I AM THE GREATEST!
I'M TELLING YOU THAT IF YOU GOT IN A FIGHT WITH A HUMMINGBIRD, YOUR ONLY HOPE WOULD BE TO HAVE THE REFEREE CHECK THE BIRD'S GLOVES AND HOPE THEY WEREN'T REGULATION SO HE'D GET DISQUALIFIED.
FLY LIKE A BUTTERBALL, STING LIKE A FLEA!
darb

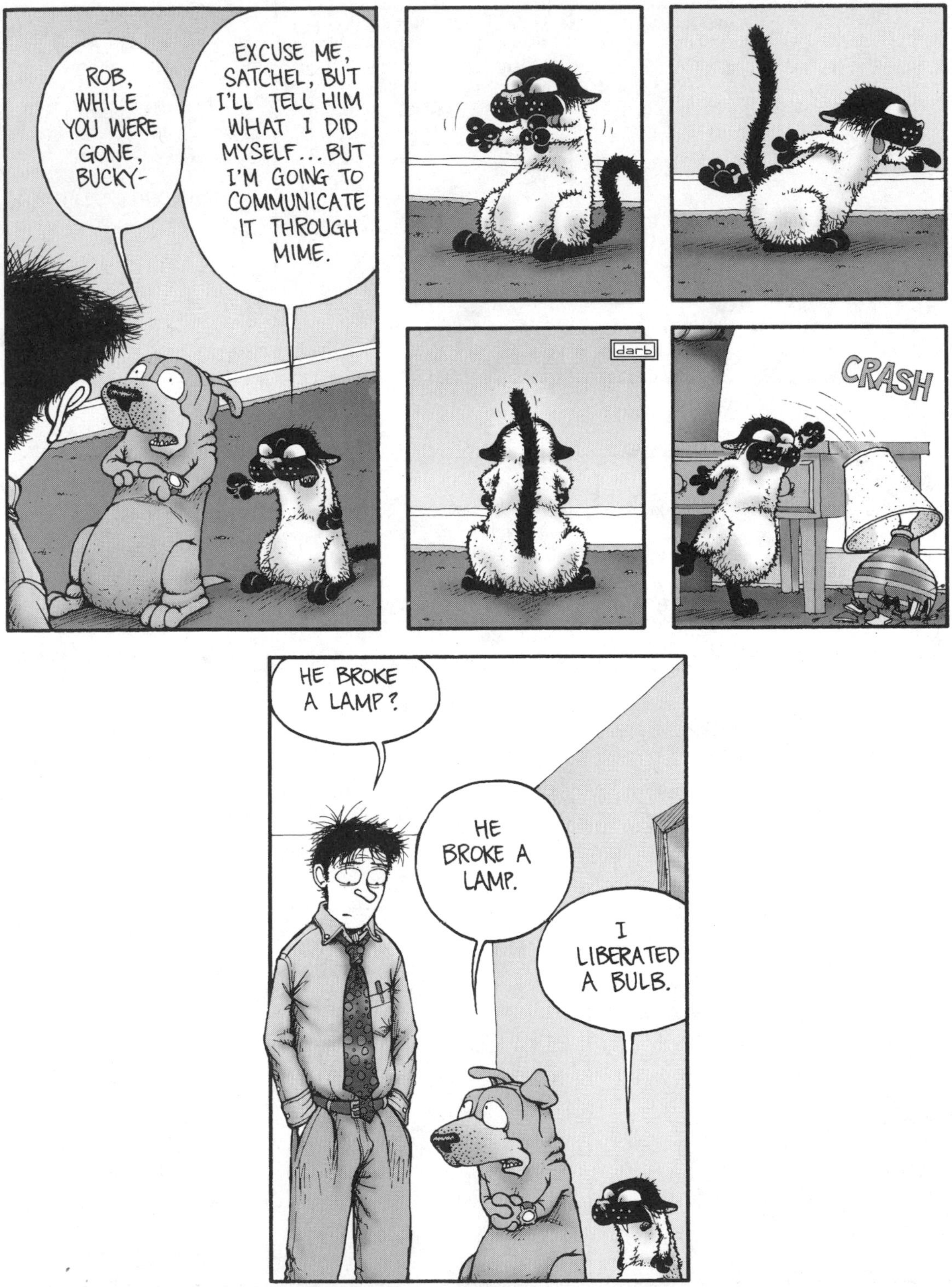
ROB, WHILE YOU WERE GONE, BUCKY-
EXCUSE ME, SATCHEL, BUT I'LL TELL HIM WHAT I DID MYSELF... BUT I'M GOING TO COMMUNICATE IT THROUGH MIME.
darb
CRASH
HE BROKE A LAMP?
HE BROKE A LAMP.
I LIBERATED A BULB.

YOU HAVE BEEN THROUGH A TERRIBLE ORDEAL...
HELLO, MRS. PAPAGUS. YES, WE'VE BEEN TO THE VET.
4F
NO, NO... AN *EMOTIONAL* ORDEAL. ONE OF YOU IS HAVING *RELATIONSHIP* PROBLEMS.
darb
SHE'S A MEDIUM.
HOW DID SHE KNOW THAT ?
SHE LOOKS A LOT BIGGER THAN THAT.
WHY SO BLUE, BUDDY ?
GIRLS.
DID YOU SAY *GIRLS* ?
DIDN'T I? THAT'S WHAT I TRIED TO SAY.
DO DOGS HAVE THOSE PROBLEMS?
APPARENTLY!
darb
DO YOU WANT TO TALK ABOUT IT WITH ME?
ROB, THIS IS A **GIRL** PROBLEM. YOU DON'T KNOW ANYTHING ABOUT GIRLS.
WHY DOES EVERYONE ALWAYS ASSUME I KNOW NOTHING ABOUT WOMEN?!
I MEAN, APART FROM THE FACT THAT THEY DON'T CALL HERE AND I NEVER GO ON DATES.
I WAS GONNA SAY.
darb

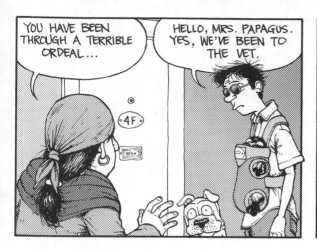

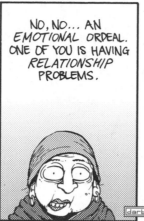

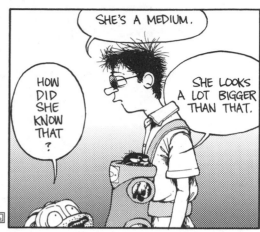

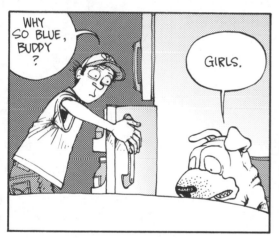

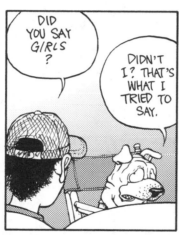

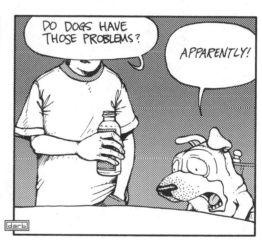

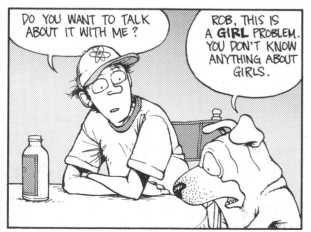

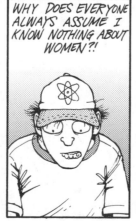

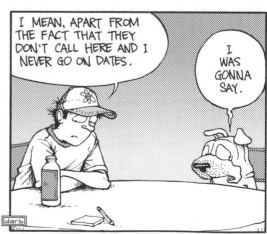

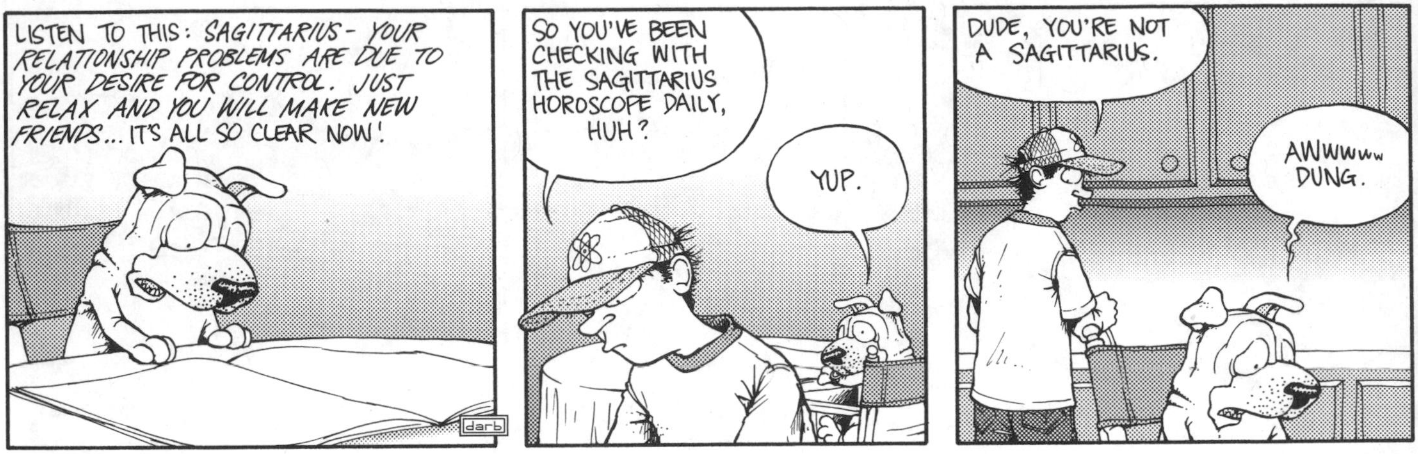
LISTEN TO THIS: SAGITTARIUS - YOUR RELATIONSHIP PROBLEMS ARE DUE TO YOUR DESIRE FOR CONTROL. JUST RELAX AND YOU WILL MAKE NEW FRIENDS... IT'S ALL SO CLEAR NOW!
SO YOU'VE BEEN CHECKING WITH THE SAGITTARIUS HOROSCOPE DAILY, HUH?
YUP.
DUDE, YOU'RE NOT A SAGITTARIUS.
AWWWWW DUNG.

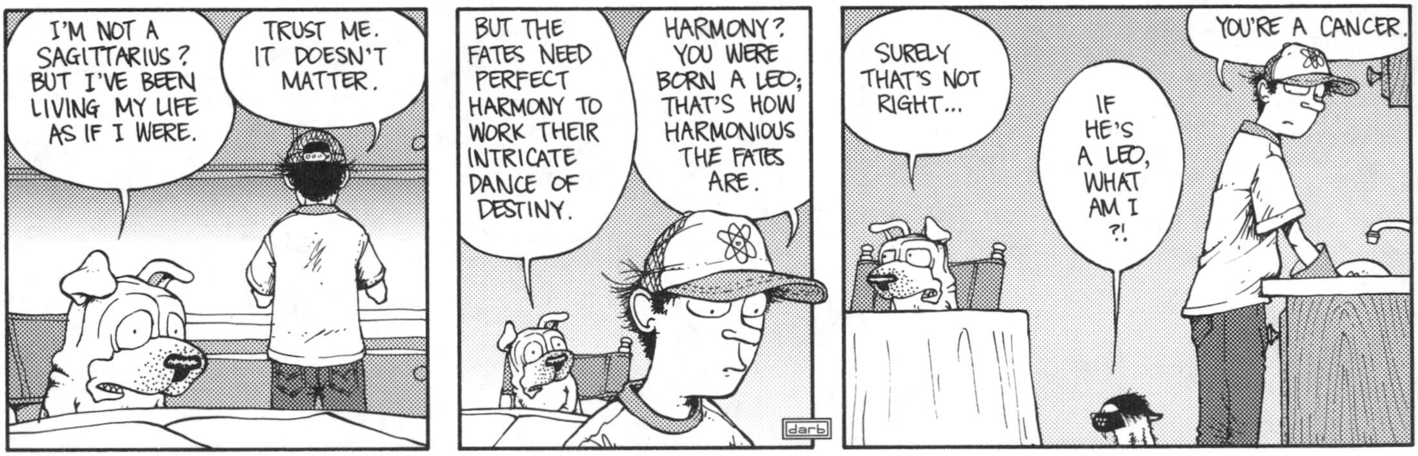
I'M NOT A SAGITTARIUS? BUT I'VE BEEN LIVING MY LIFE AS IF I WERE.
TRUST ME. IT DOESN'T MATTER.
BUT THE FATES NEED PERFECT HARMONY TO WORK THEIR INTRICATE DANCE OF DESTINY.
HARMONY? YOU WERE BORN A LEO; THAT'S HOW HARMONIOUS THE FATES ARE.
SURELY THAT'S NOT RIGHT...
YOU'RE A CANCER.
IF HE'S A LEO, WHAT AM I ?!

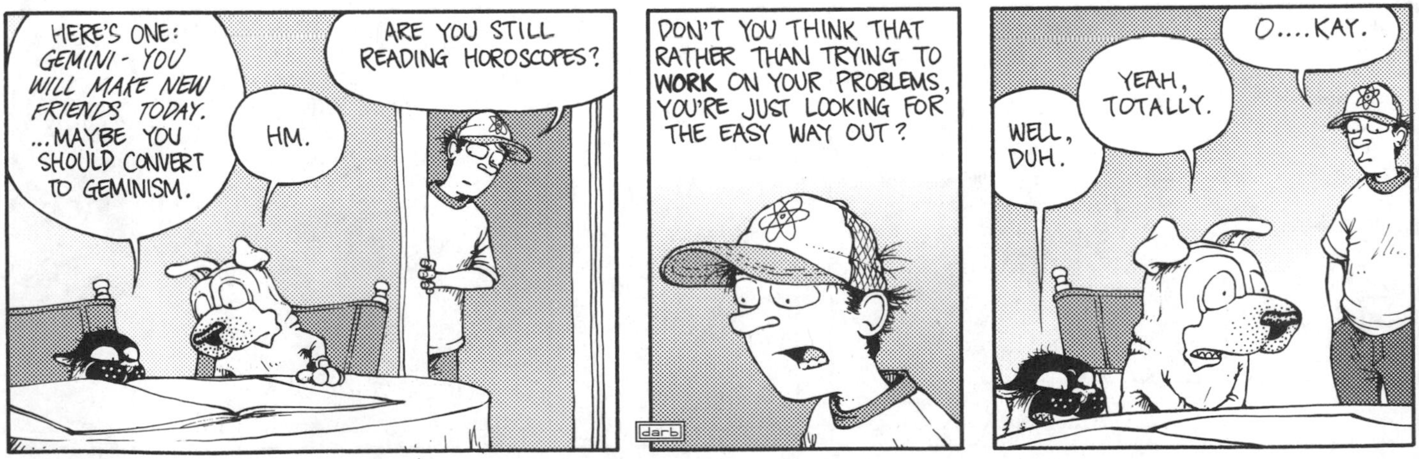
HERE'S ONE: GEMINI - YOU WILL MAKE NEW FRIENDS TODAY. ...MAYBE YOU SHOULD CONVERT TO GEMINISM.
HM.
ARE YOU STILL READING HOROSCOPES?
DON'T YOU THINK THAT RATHER THAN TRYING TO WORK ON YOUR PROBLEMS, YOU'RE JUST LOOKING FOR THE EASY WAY OUT?
O....KAY.
YEAH, TOTALLY.
WELL, DUH.

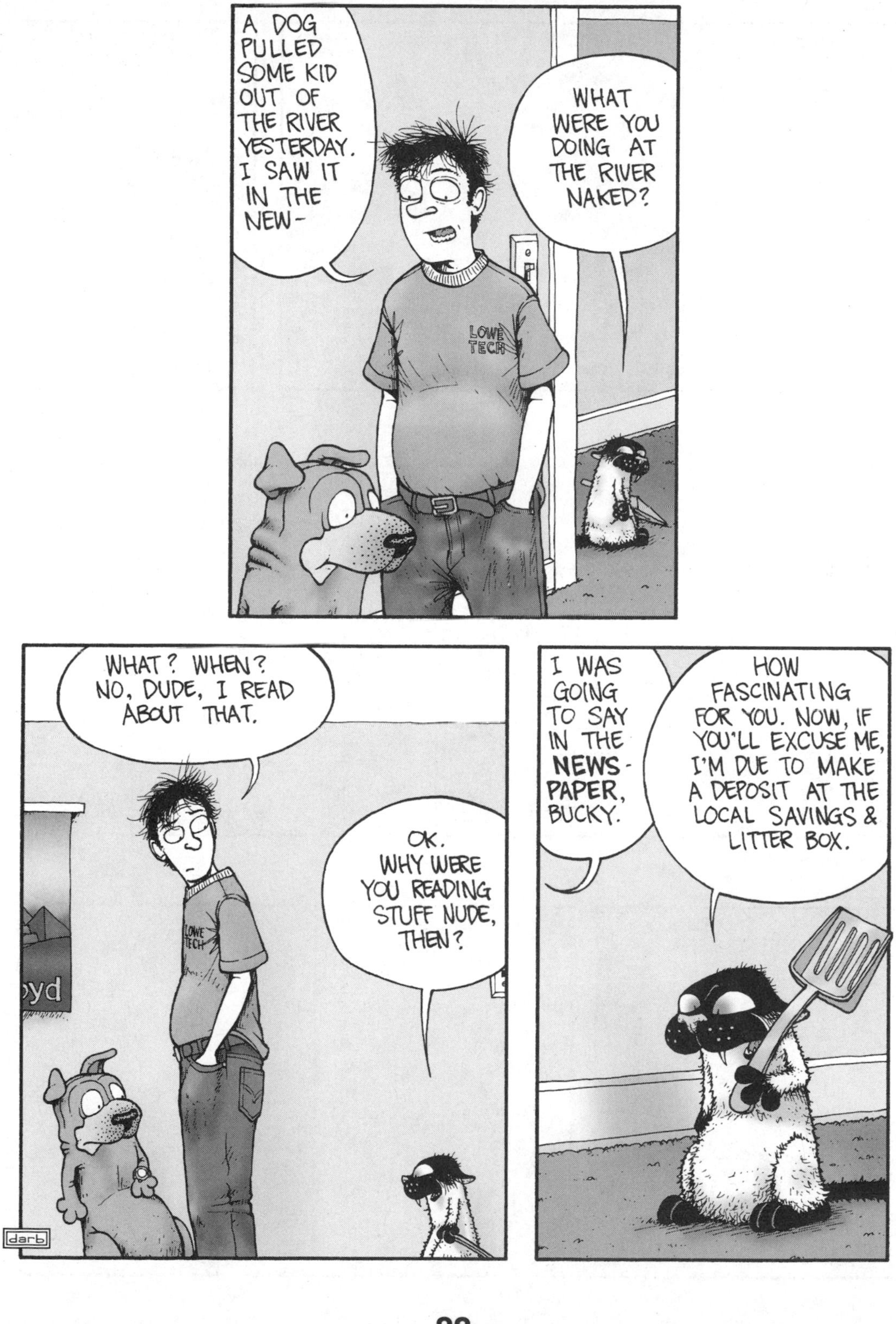
A DOG PULLED SOME KID OUT OF THE RIVER YESTERDAY. I SAW IT IN THE NEW-
WHAT WERE YOU DOING AT THE RIVER NAKED?
LOWE TECH
WHAT? WHEN? NO, DUDE, I READ ABOUT THAT.
OK. WHY WERE YOU READING STUFF NUDE, THEN?
darb
I WAS GOING TO SAY IN THE **NEWS-PAPER**, BUCKY.
HOW FASCINATING FOR YOU. NOW, IF YOU'LL EXCUSE ME, I'M DUE TO MAKE A DEPOSIT AT THE LOCAL SAVINGS & LITTER BOX.

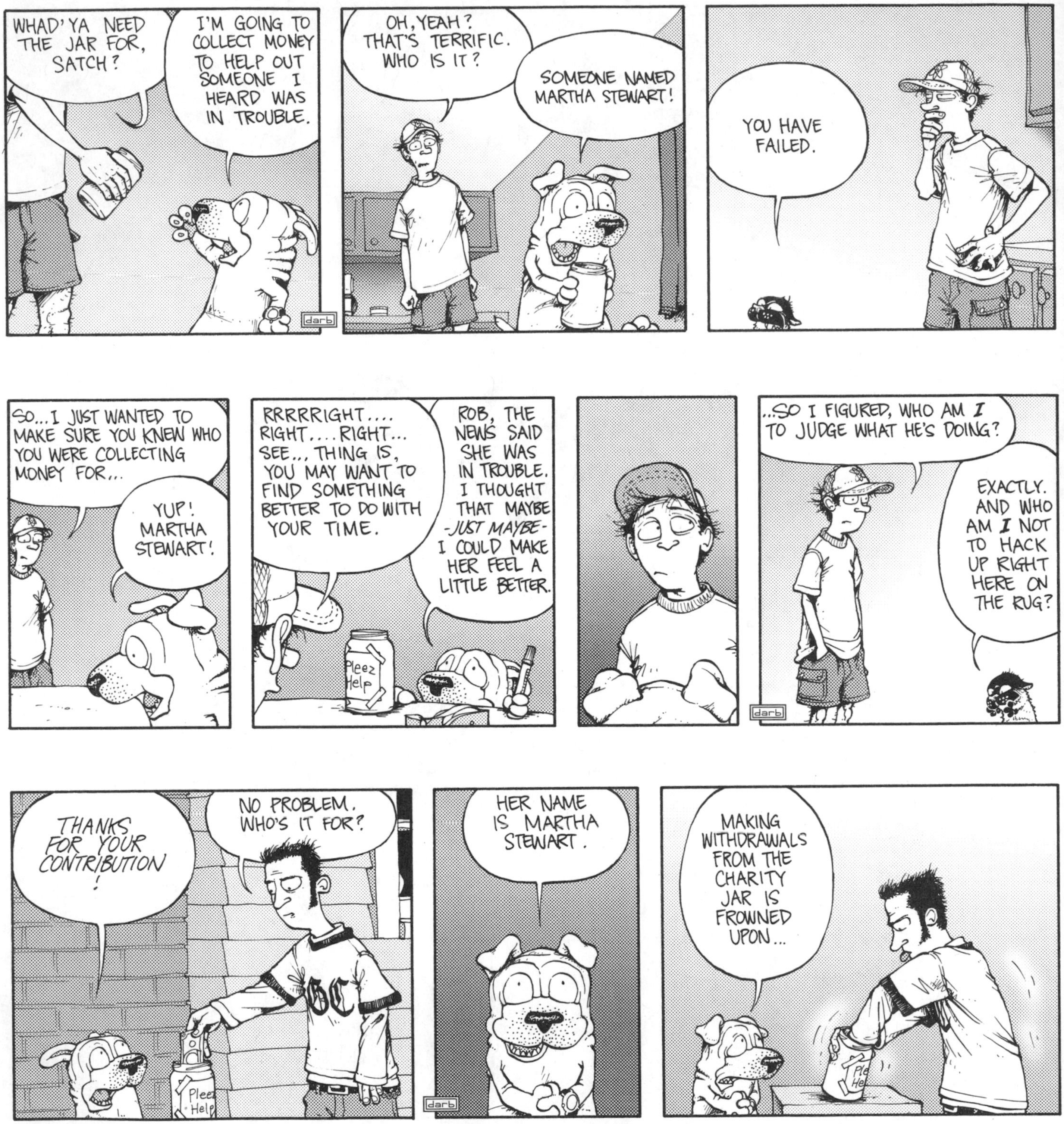
WHAD'YA NEED THE JAR FOR, SATCH?
I'M GOING TO COLLECT MONEY TO HELP OUT SOMEONE I HEARD WAS IN TROUBLE.
OH, YEAH? THAT'S TERRIFIC. WHO IS IT?
SOMEONE NAMED MARTHA STEWART!
YOU HAVE FAILED.
SO... I JUST WANTED TO MAKE SURE YOU KNEW WHO YOU WERE COLLECTING MONEY FOR...
YUP! MARTHA STEWART!
RRRRRIGHT.... RIGHT.... RIGHT... SEE.., THING IS, YOU MAY WANT TO FIND SOMETHING BETTER TO DO WITH YOUR TIME.
ROB, THE NEWS SAID SHE WAS IN TROUBLE. I THOUGHT THAT MAYBE -JUST MAYBE- I COULD MAKE HER FEEL A LITTLE BETTER.
Pleez Help
..SO I FIGURED, WHO AM I TO JUDGE WHAT HE'S DOING?
EXACTLY. AND WHO AM I NOT TO HACK UP RIGHT HERE ON THE RUG?
THANKS FOR YOUR CONTRIBUTION!
NO PROBLEM. WHO'S IT FOR?
Pleez Help
HER NAME IS MARTHA STEWART.
MAKING WITHDRAWALS FROM THE CHARITY JAR IS FROWNED UPON...

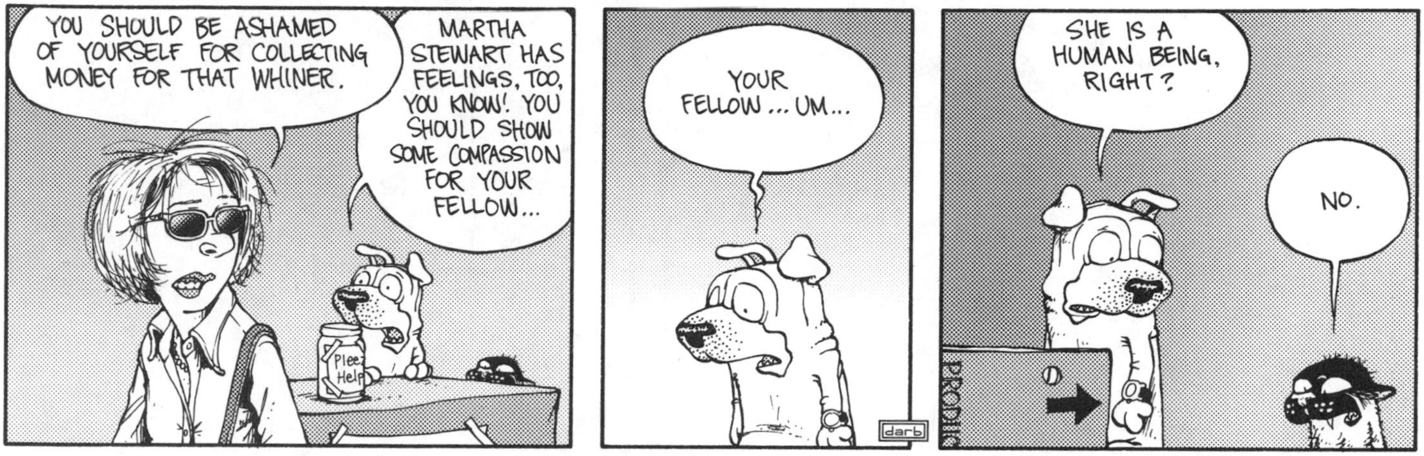
YOU SHOULD BE ASHAMED OF YOURSELF FOR COLLECTING MONEY FOR THAT WHINER.
MARTHA STEWART HAS FEELINGS, TOO, YOU KNOW! YOU SHOULD SHOW SOME COMPASSION FOR YOUR FELLOW...
YOUR FELLOW... UM...
SHE IS A HUMAN BEING, RIGHT?
NO.

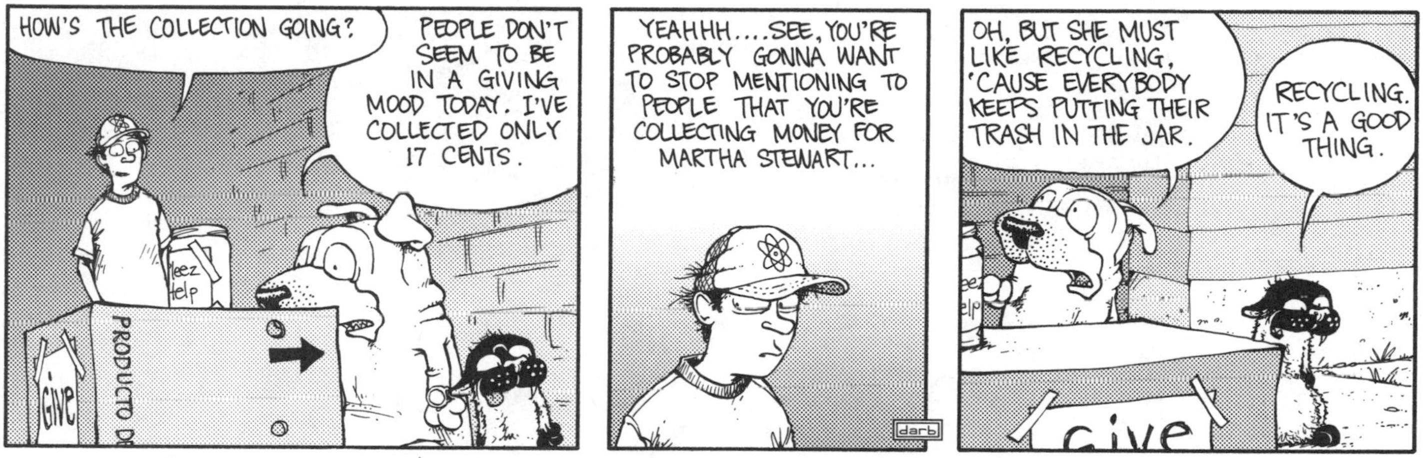
HOW'S THE COLLECTION GOING?
PEOPLE DON'T SEEM TO BE IN A GIVING MOOD TODAY. I'VE COLLECTED ONLY 17 CENTS.
YEAHHH.... SEE, YOU'RE PROBABLY GONNA WANT TO STOP MENTIONING TO PEOPLE THAT YOU'RE COLLECTING MONEY FOR MARTHA STEWART...
OH, BUT SHE MUST LIKE RECYCLING, 'CAUSE EVERYBODY KEEPS PUTTING THEIR TRASH IN THE JAR.
RECYCLING. IT'S A GOOD THING.

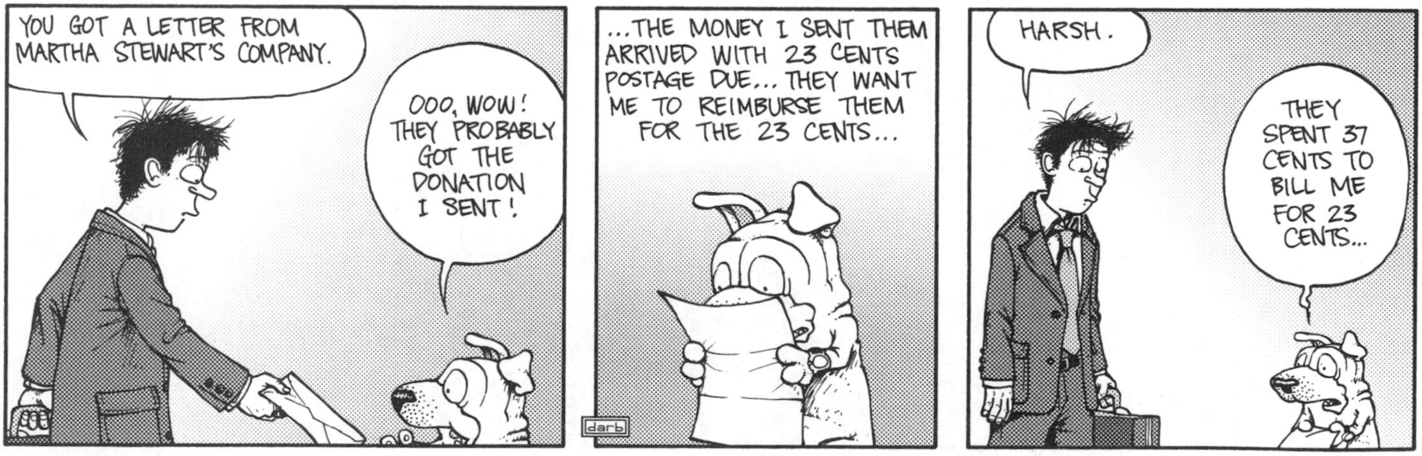
YOU GOT A LETTER FROM MARTHA STEWART'S COMPANY.
OOO, WOW! THEY PROBABLY GOT THE DONATION I SENT!
...THE MONEY I SENT THEM ARRIVED WITH 23 CENTS POSTAGE DUE... THEY WANT ME TO REIMBURSE THEM FOR THE 23 CENTS...
HARSH.
THEY SPENT 37 CENTS TO BILL ME FOR 23 CENTS...

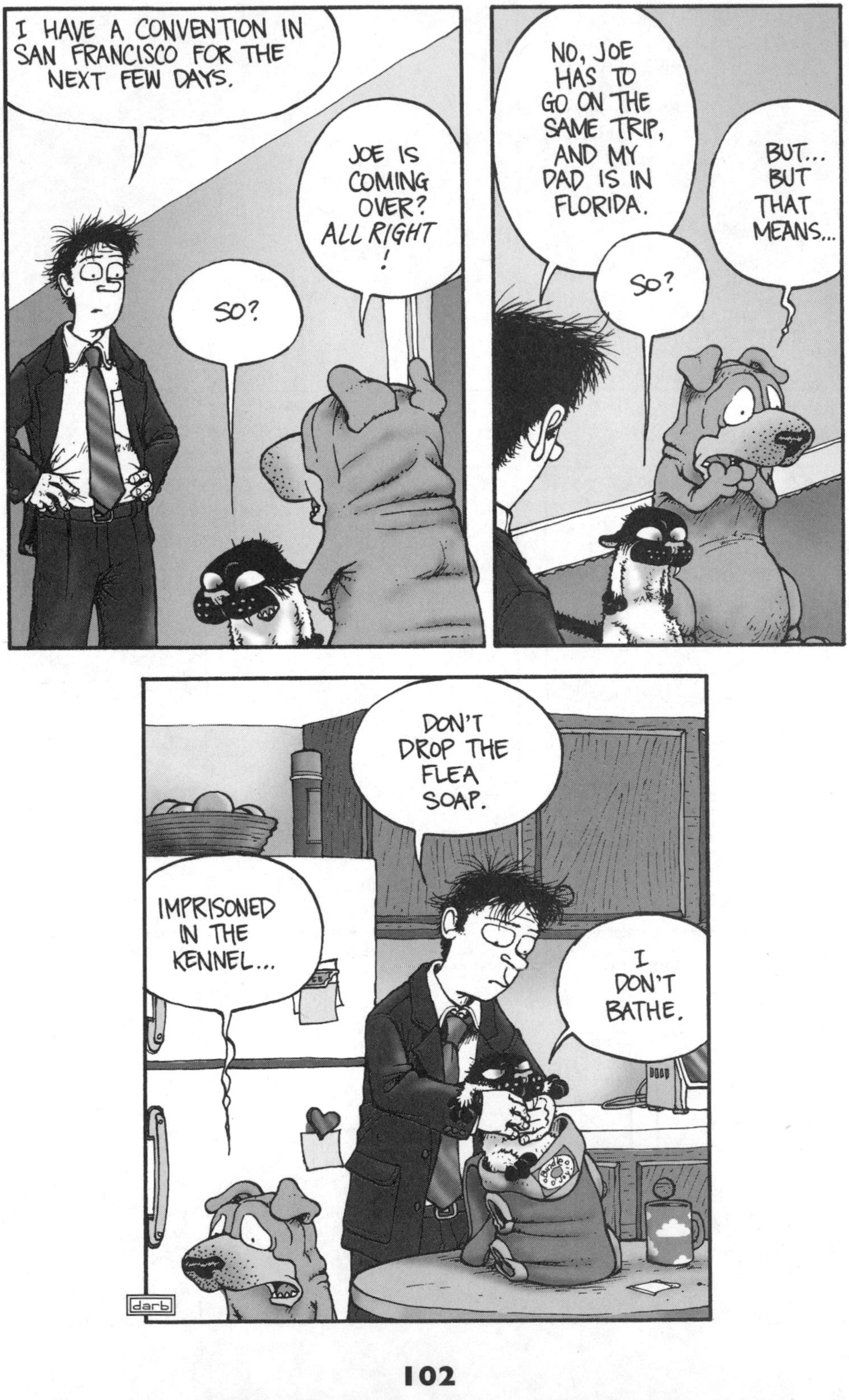
I HAVE A CONVENTION IN SAN FRANCISCO FOR THE NEXT FEW DAYS.
SO?
JOE IS COMING OVER? ALL RIGHT!
NO, JOE HAS TO GO ON THE SAME TRIP, AND MY DAD IS IN FLORIDA.
SO?
BUT... BUT THAT MEANS...
DON'T DROP THE FLEA SOAP.
IMPRISONED IN THE KENNEL...
I DON'T BATHE.
darb

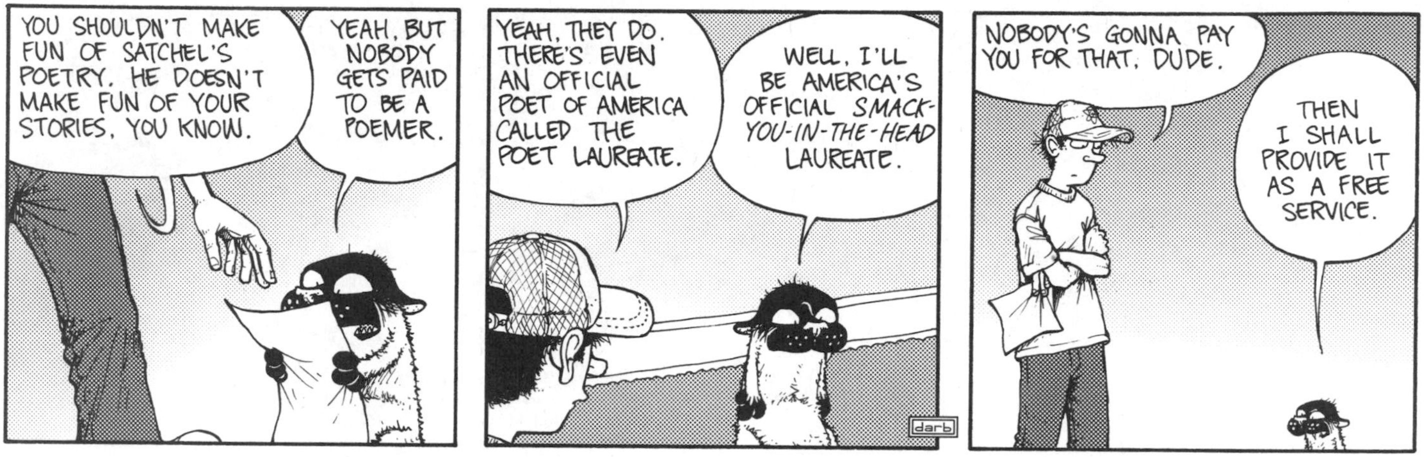
YOU SHOULDN'T MAKE FUN OF SATCHEL'S POETRY. HE DOESN'T MAKE FUN OF YOUR STORIES, YOU KNOW.
YEAH, BUT NOBODY GETS PAID TO BE A POEMER.
YEAH, THEY DO. THERE'S EVEN AN OFFICIAL POET OF AMERICA CALLED THE POET LAUREATE.
WELL, I'LL BE AMERICA'S OFFICIAL *SMACK-YOU-IN-THE-HEAD* LAUREATE.
darb
NOBODY'S GONNA PAY YOU FOR THAT, DUDE.
THEN I SHALL PROVIDE IT AS A FREE SERVICE.

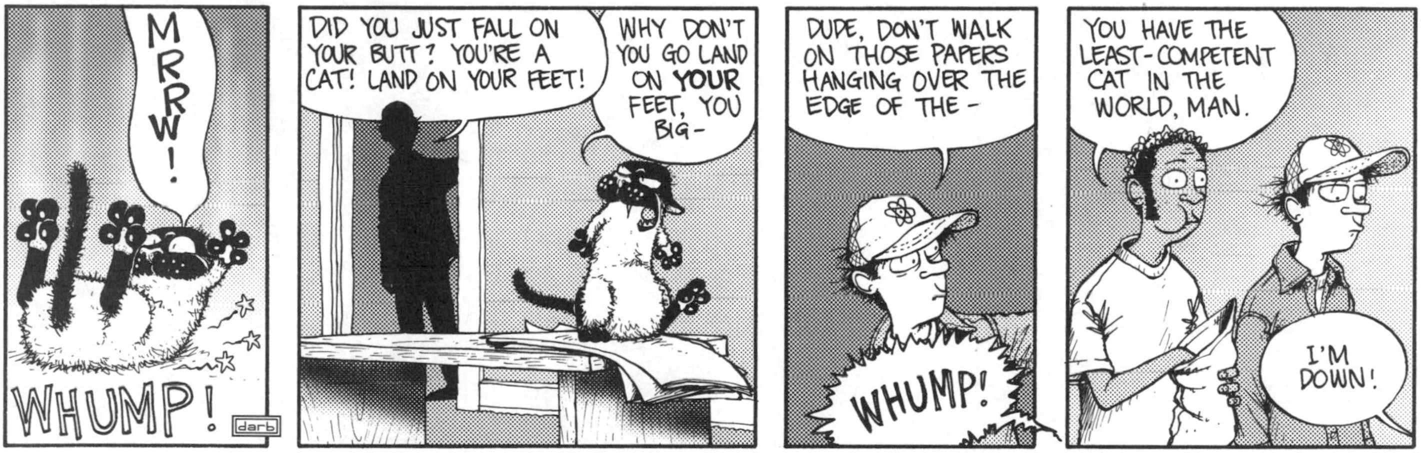
MRRW!
WHUMP!
darb
DID YOU JUST FALL ON YOUR BUTT? YOU'RE A CAT! LAND ON YOUR FEET!
WHY DON'T YOU GO LAND ON **YOUR** FEET, YOU BIG-
DUDE, DON'T WALK ON THOSE PAPERS HANGING OVER THE EDGE OF THE-
WHUMP!
YOU HAVE THE LEAST-COMPETENT CAT IN THE WORLD, MAN.
I'M DOWN!

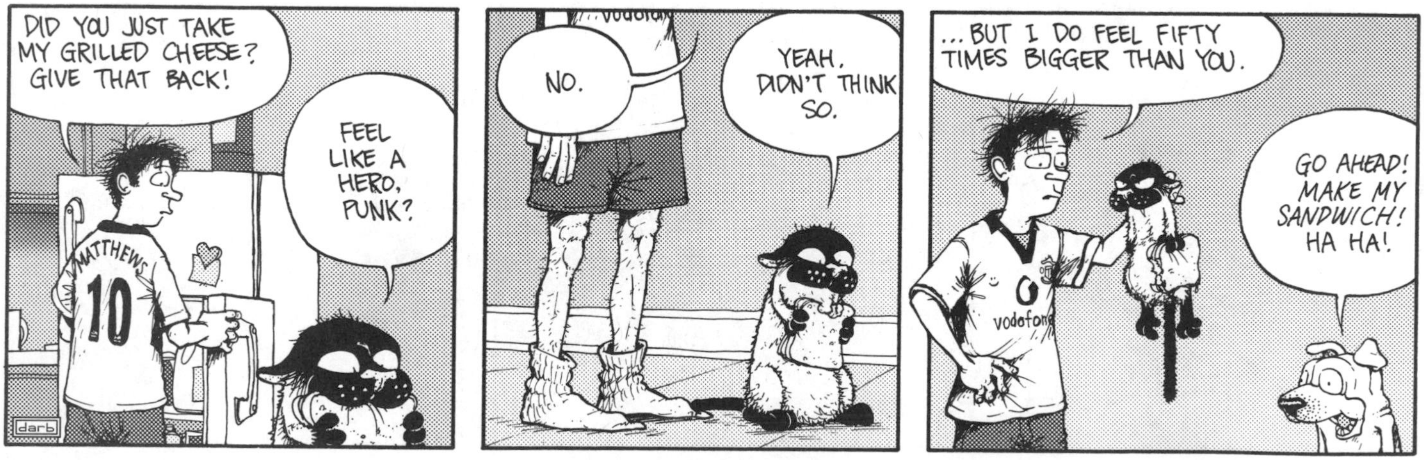
DID YOU JUST TAKE MY GRILLED CHEESE? GIVE THAT BACK!
FEEL LIKE A HERO, PUNK?
darb
NO.
YEAH, DIDN'T THINK SO.
...BUT I DO FEEL FIFTY TIMES BIGGER THAN YOU.
GO AHEAD! MAKE MY SANDWICH! HA HA!

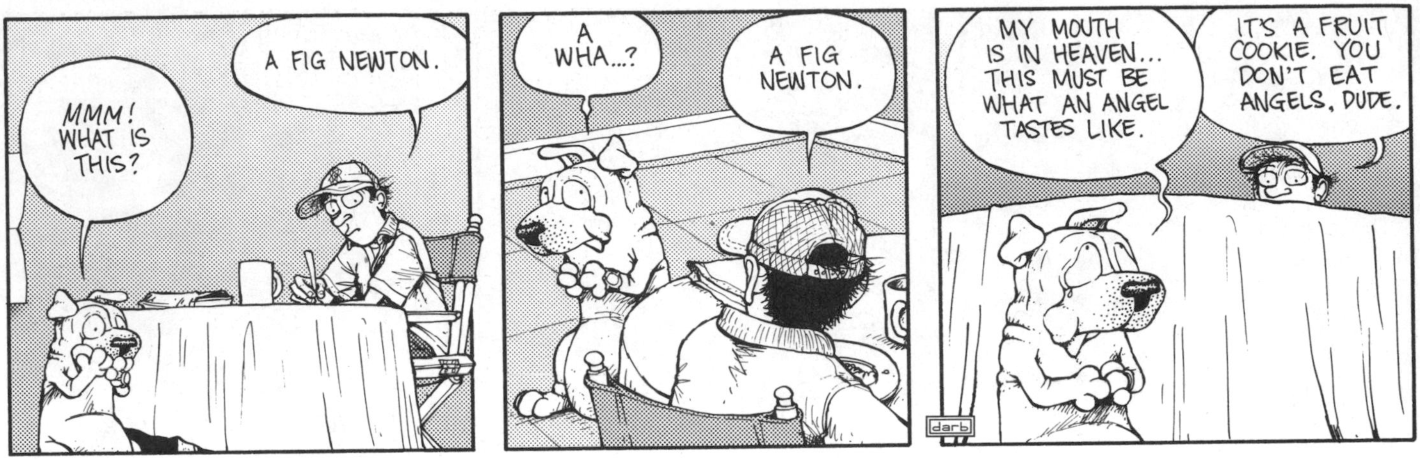
MMM! WHAT IS THIS?
A FIG NEWTON.
A WHA...?
A FIG NEWTON.
MY MOUTH IS IN HEAVEN... THIS MUST BE WHAT AN ANGEL TASTES LIKE.
IT'S A FRUIT COOKIE. YOU DON'T EAT ANGELS, DUDE.
darb

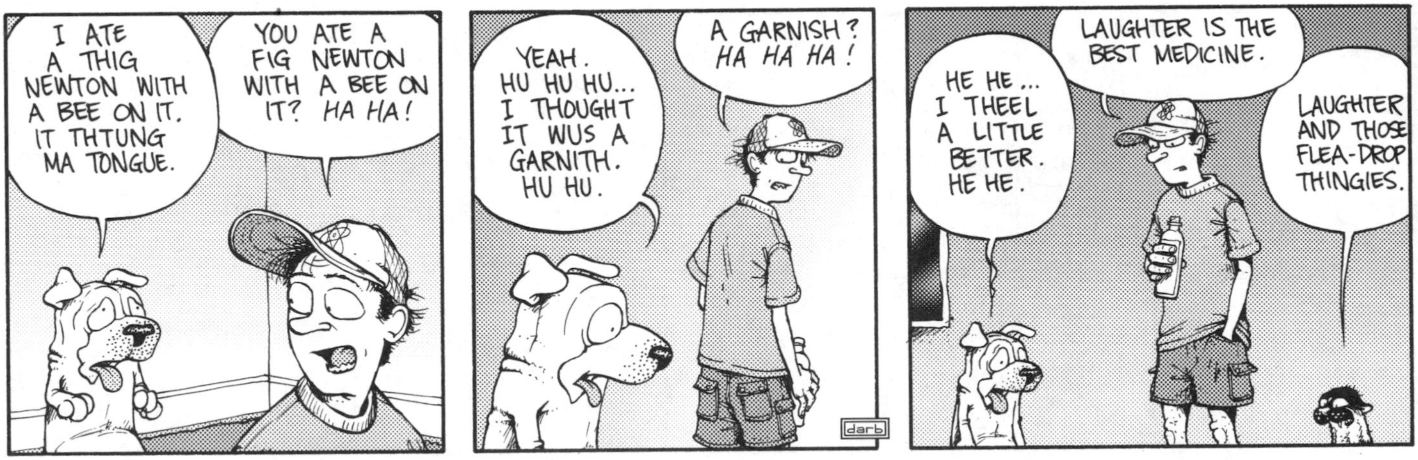
I ATE A THIG NEWTON WITH A BEE ON IT. IT THTUNG MA TONGUE.
YOU ATE A FIG NEWTON WITH A BEE ON IT? HA HA!
YEAH. HU HU HU... I THOUGHT IT WUS A GARNITH. HU HU.
A GARNISH? HA HA HA!
darb
HE HE... I THEEL A LITTLE BETTER. HE HE.
LAUGHTER IS THE BEST MEDICINE.
LAUGHTER AND THOSE FLEA-DROP THINGIES.

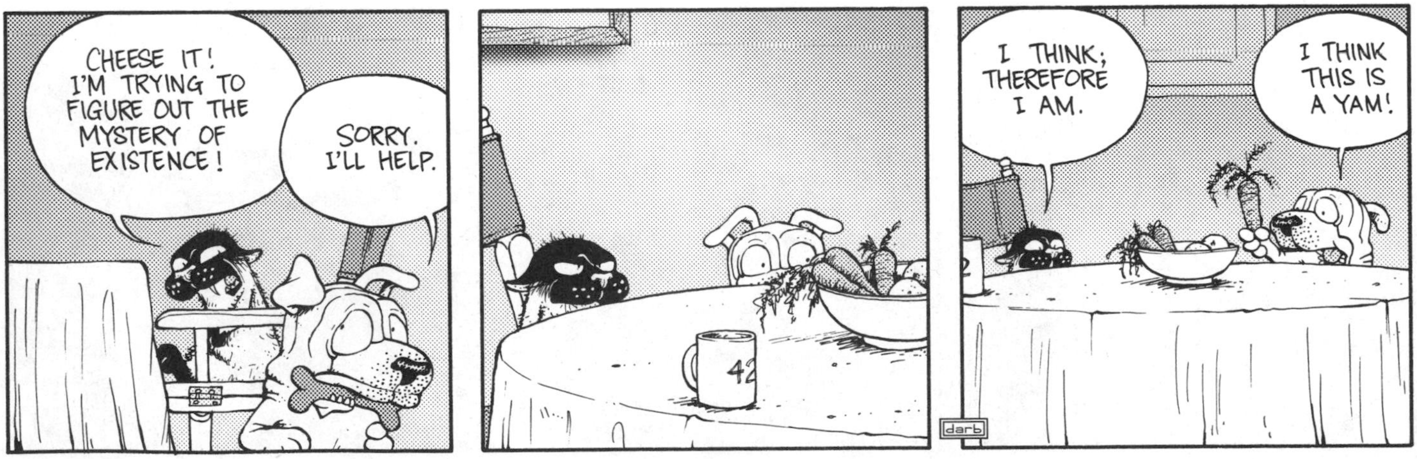
CHEESE IT! I'M TRYING TO FIGURE OUT THE MYSTERY OF EXISTENCE!
SORRY. I'LL HELP.
42
I THINK; THEREFORE I AM.
I THINK THIS IS A YAM!
darb

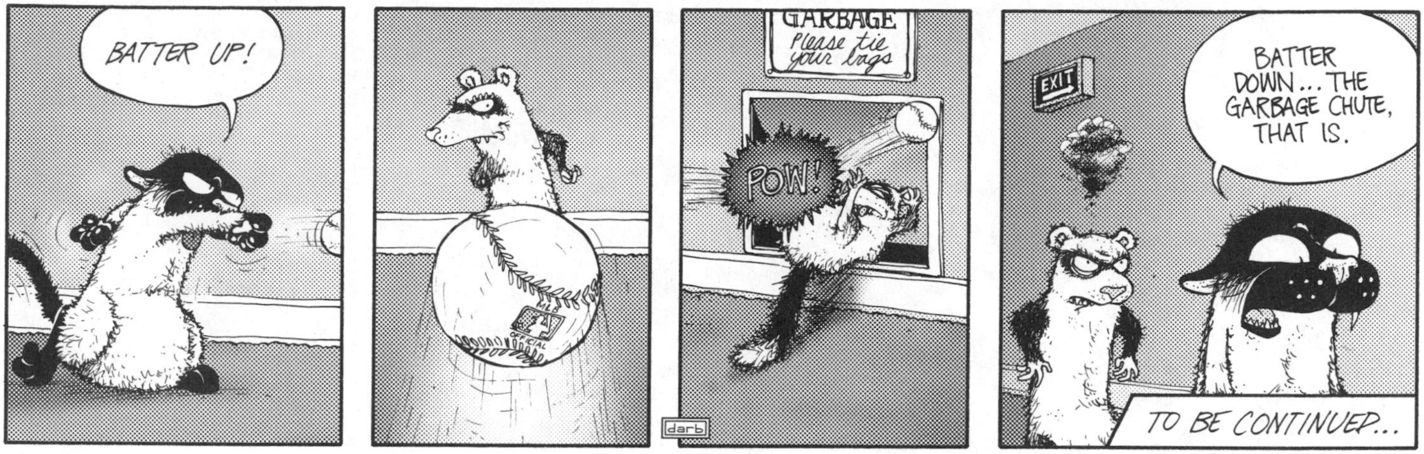
BATTER UP!
GARBAGE Please tie your bags
POW!
EXIT
BATTER DOWN... THE GARBAGE CHUTE, THAT IS.
TO BE CONTINUED...

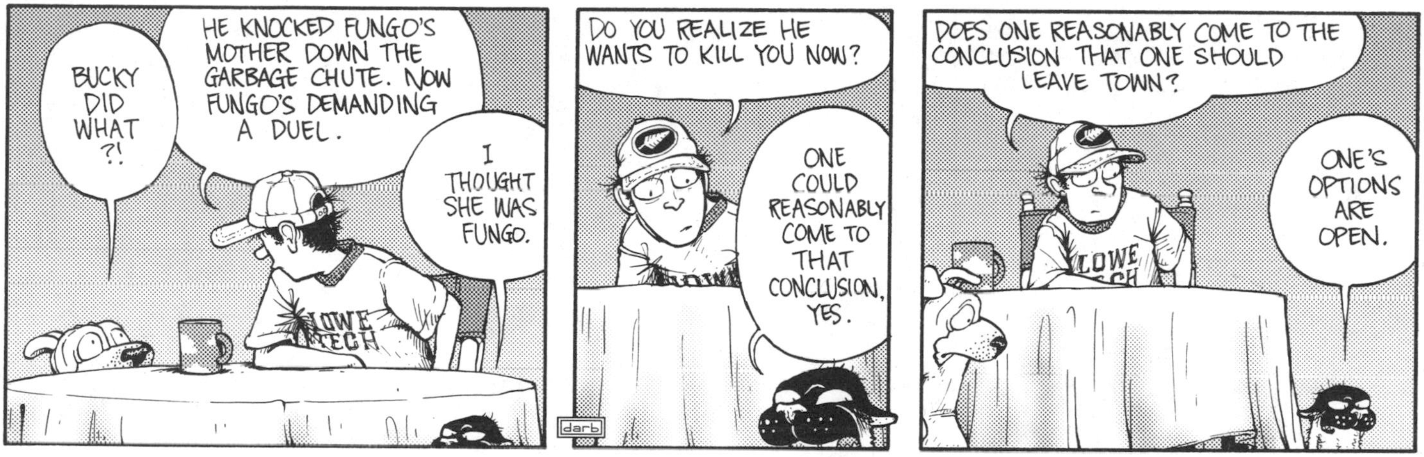
HE KNOCKED FUNGO'S MOTHER DOWN THE GARBAGE CHUTE. NOW FUNGO'S DEMANDING A DUEL.
BUCKY DID WHAT ?!
I THOUGHT SHE WAS FUNGO.
DO YOU REALIZE HE WANTS TO KILL YOU NOW?
ONE COULD REASONABLY COME TO THAT CONCLUSION, YES.
DOES ONE REASONABLY COME TO THE CONCLUSION THAT ONE SHOULD LEAVE TOWN?
ONE'S OPTIONS ARE OPEN.

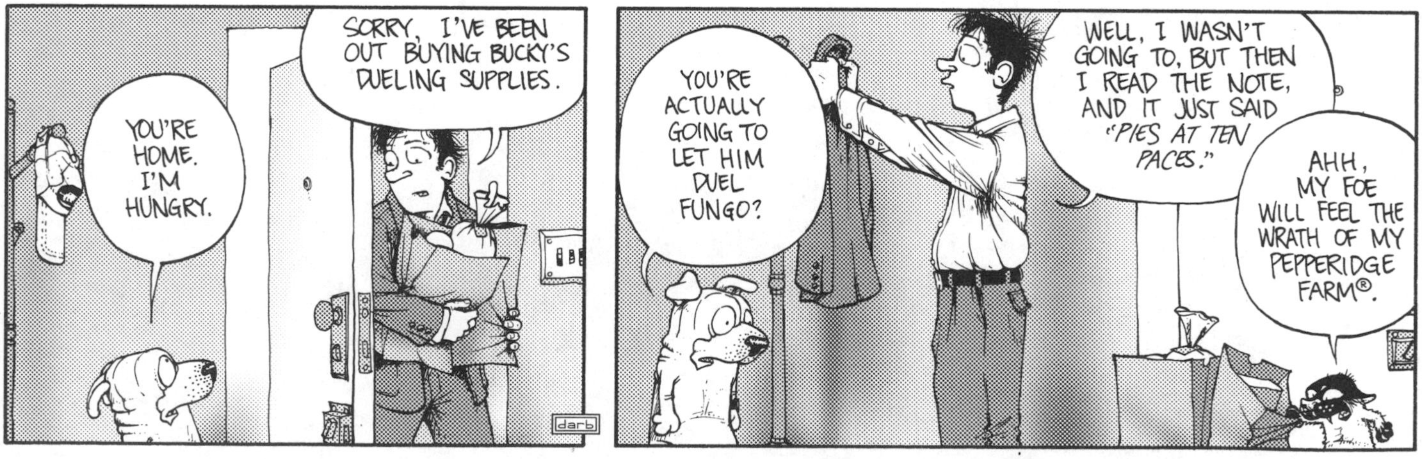
YOU'RE HOME. I'M HUNGRY.
SORRY, I'VE BEEN OUT BUYING BUCKY'S DUELING SUPPLIES.
YOU'RE ACTUALLY GOING TO LET HIM DUEL FUNGO?
WELL, I WASN'T GOING TO, BUT THEN I READ THE NOTE, AND IT JUST SAID "PIES AT TEN PACES."
AHH, MY FOE WILL FEEL THE WRATH OF MY PEPPERIDGE FARM®.

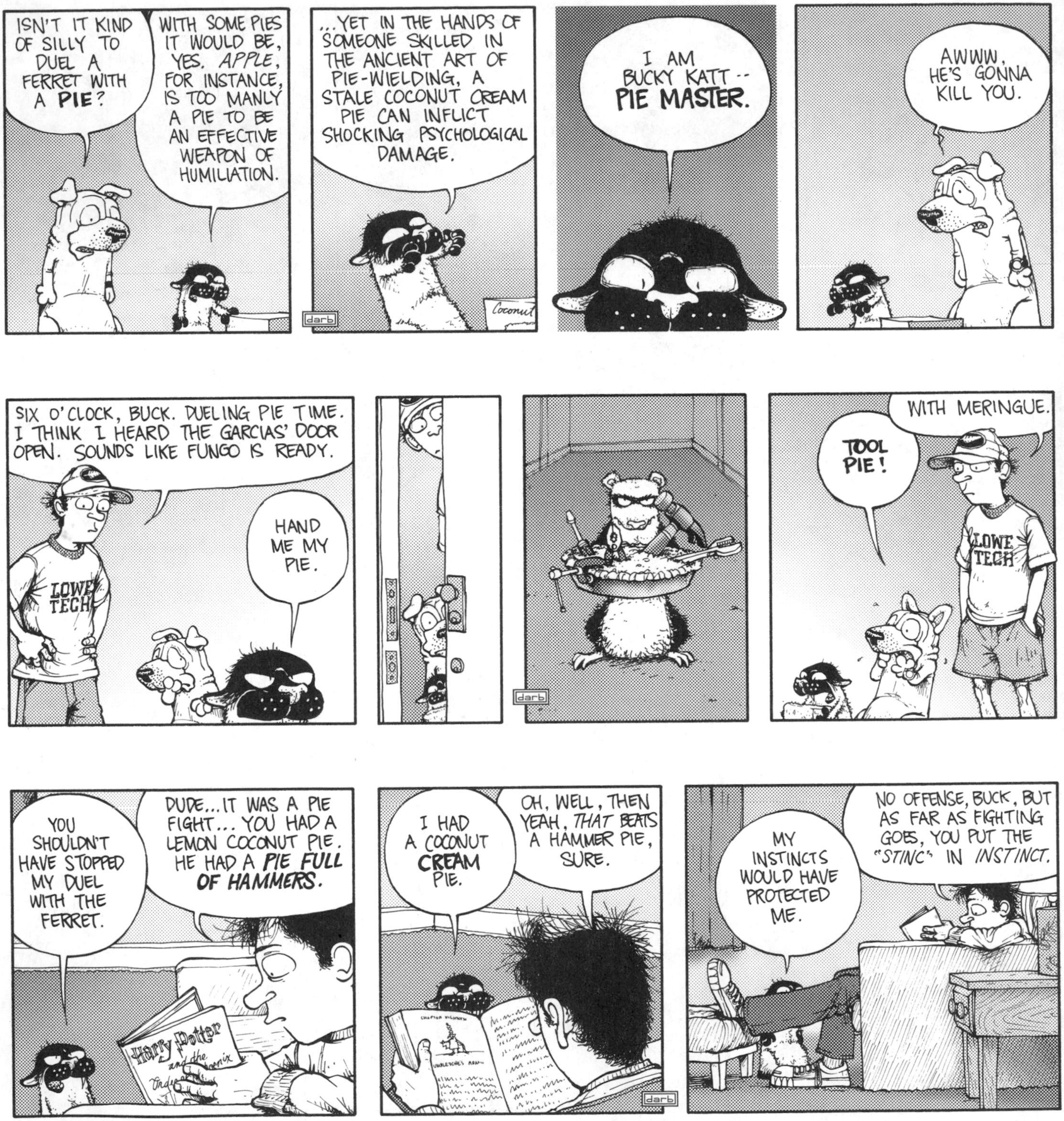
ISN'T IT KIND OF SILLY TO DUEL A FERRET WITH A **PIE**?
WITH SOME PIES IT WOULD BE, YES. *APPLE*, FOR INSTANCE, IS TOO MANLY A PIE TO BE AN EFFECTIVE WEAPON OF HUMILIATION.
...YET IN THE HANDS OF SOMEONE SKILLED IN THE ANCIENT ART OF PIE-WIELDING, A STALE COCONUT CREAM PIE CAN INFLICT SHOCKING PSYCHOLOGICAL DAMAGE.
darb
Coconut
I AM BUCKY KATT -- **PIE MASTER.**
AWWW, HE'S GONNA KILL YOU.
SIX O'CLOCK, BUCK. DUELING PIE TIME. I THINK I HEARD THE GARCIAS' DOOR OPEN. SOUNDS LIKE FUNGO IS READY.
LOWE TECH
HAND ME MY PIE.
darb
WITH MERINGUE.
TOOL PIE!
LOWE TECH
YOU SHOULDN'T HAVE STOPPED MY DUEL WITH THE FERRET.
DUDE...IT WAS A PIE FIGHT... YOU HAD A LEMON COCONUT PIE. HE HAD A ***PIE FULL OF HAMMERS***.
Harry Potter and the
I HAD A COCONUT **CREAM** PIE.
OH, WELL, THEN YEAH, *THAT* BEATS A HAMMER PIE, SURE.
darb
MY INSTINCTS WOULD HAVE PROTECTED ME.
NO OFFENSE, BUCK, BUT AS FAR AS FIGHTING GOES, YOU PUT THE "*STINC*" IN *INSTINCT*.

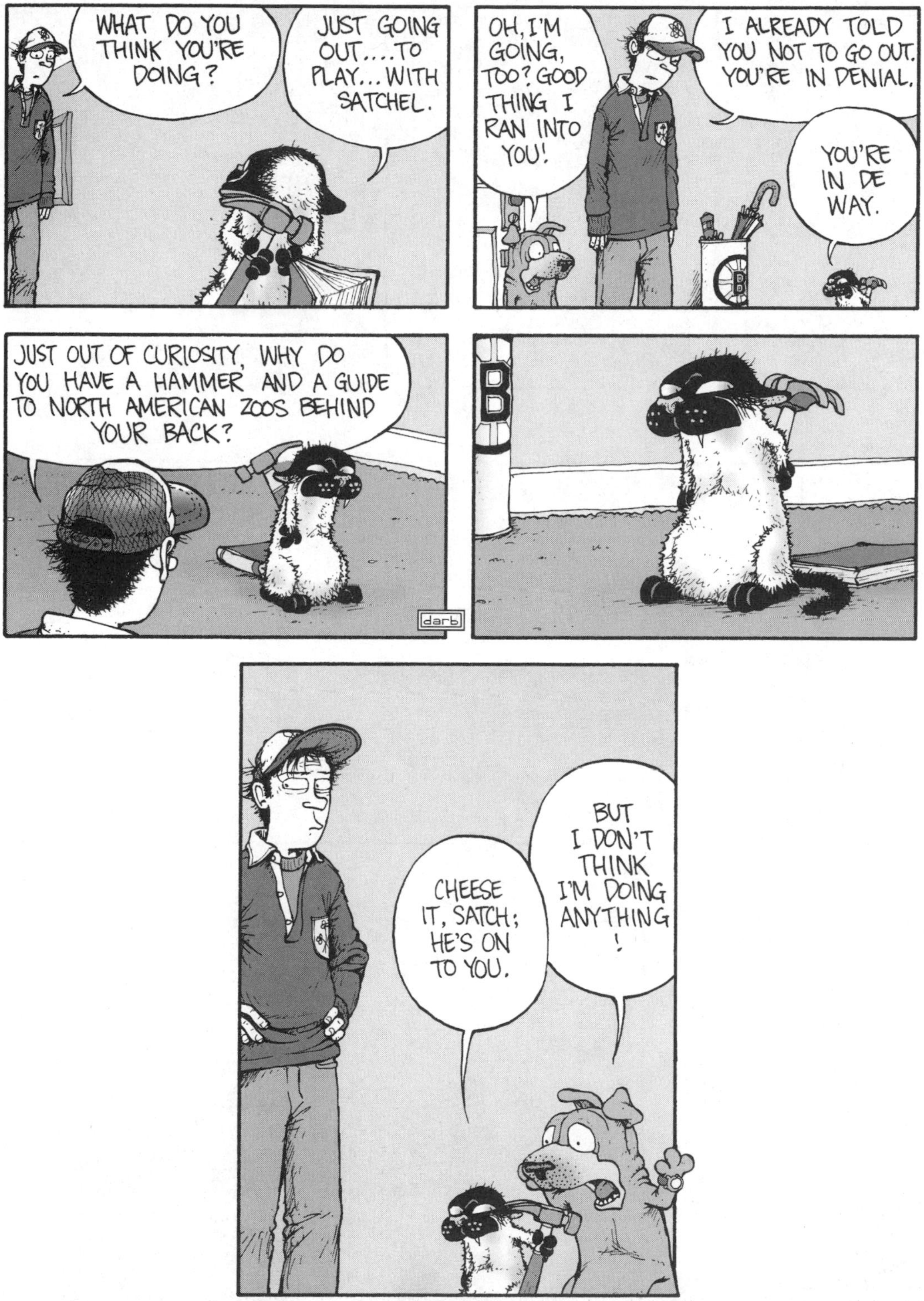
WHAT DO YOU THINK YOU'RE DOING?
JUST GOING OUT....TO PLAY...WITH SATCHEL.
OH, I'M GOING, TOO? GOOD THING I RAN INTO YOU!
I ALREADY TOLD YOU NOT TO GO OUT. YOU'RE IN DENIAL.
YOU'RE IN DE WAY.
JUST OUT OF CURIOSITY, WHY DO YOU HAVE A HAMMER AND A GUIDE TO NORTH AMERICAN ZOOS BEHIND YOUR BACK?
darb
B
BUT I DON'T THINK I'M DOING ANYTHING!
CHEESE IT, SATCH; HE'S ON TO YOU.

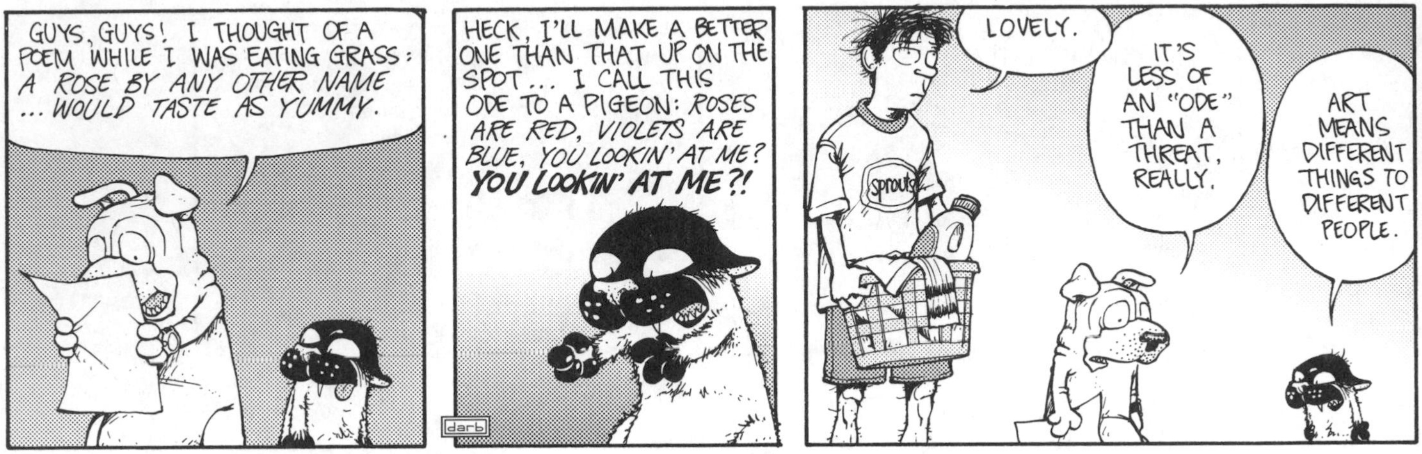
GUYS, GUYS! I THOUGHT OF A POEM WHILE I WAS EATING GRASS: *A ROSE BY ANY OTHER NAME ... WOULD TASTE AS YUMMY.*
HECK, I'LL MAKE A BETTER ONE THAN THAT UP ON THE SPOT... I CALL THIS ODE TO A PIGEON: *ROSES ARE RED, VIOLETS ARE BLUE, YOU LOOKIN' AT ME?* ***YOU LOOKIN' AT ME?!***
LOVELY.
IT'S LESS OF AN "ODE" THAN A THREAT, REALLY.
ART MEANS DIFFERENT THINGS TO DIFFERENT PEOPLE.

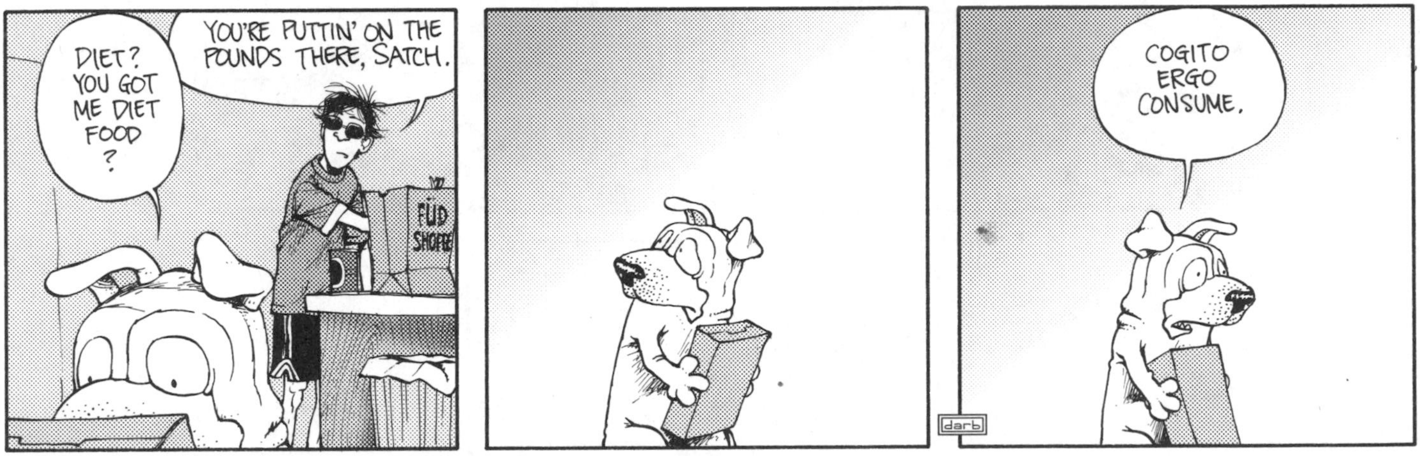
YOU'RE PUTTIN' ON THE POUNDS THERE, SATCH.
DIET? YOU GOT ME DIET FOOD?
COGITO ERGO CONSUME.

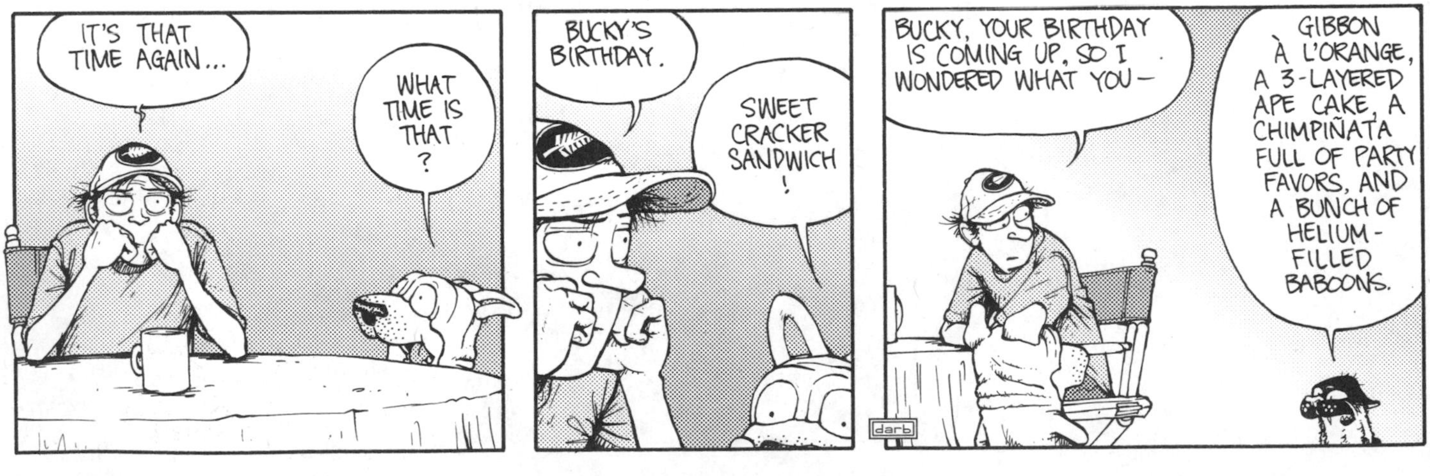
IT'S THAT TIME AGAIN...
WHAT TIME IS THAT?
BUCKY'S BIRTHDAY.
SWEET CRACKER SANDWICH!
BUCKY, YOUR BIRTHDAY IS COMING UP, SO I WONDERED WHAT YOU—
GIBBON À L'ORANGE, A 3-LAYERED APE CAKE, A CHIMPIÑATA FULL OF PARTY FAVORS, AND A BUNCH OF HELIUM-FILLED BABOONS.

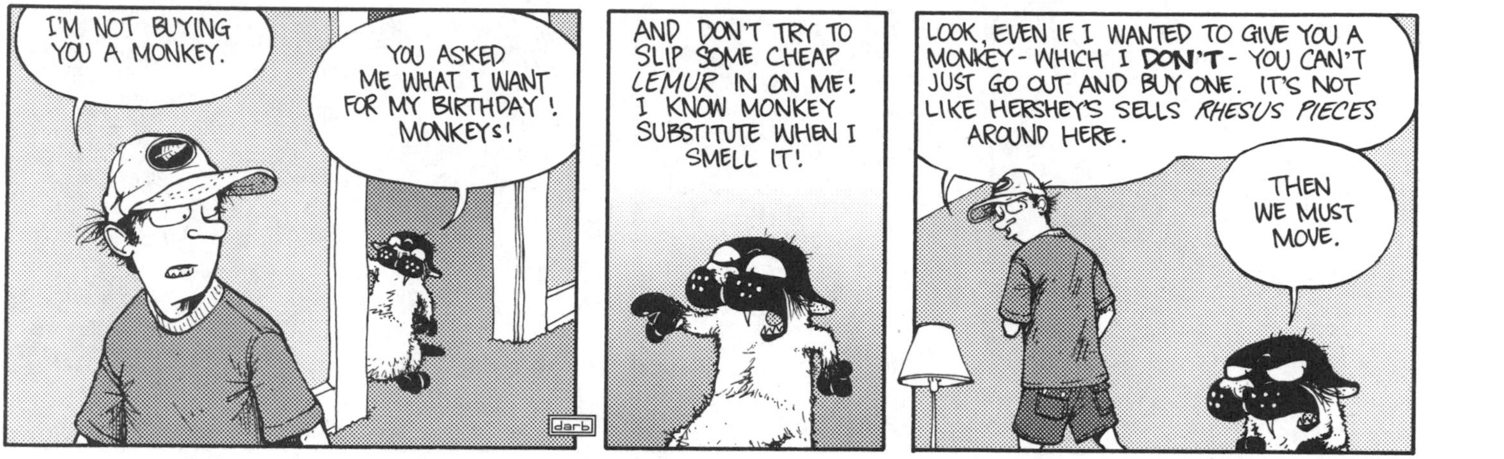
I'M NOT BUYING YOU A MONKEY.
YOU ASKED ME WHAT I WANT FOR MY BIRTHDAY! MONKEYS!
AND DON'T TRY TO SLIP SOME CHEAP *LEMUR* IN ON ME! I KNOW MONKEY SUBSTITUTE WHEN I SMELL IT!
LOOK, EVEN IF I WANTED TO GIVE YOU A MONKEY - WHICH I **DON'T** - YOU CAN'T JUST GO OUT AND BUY ONE. IT'S NOT LIKE HERSHEY'S SELLS *RHESUS PIECES* AROUND HERE.
THEN WE MUST MOVE.
darb

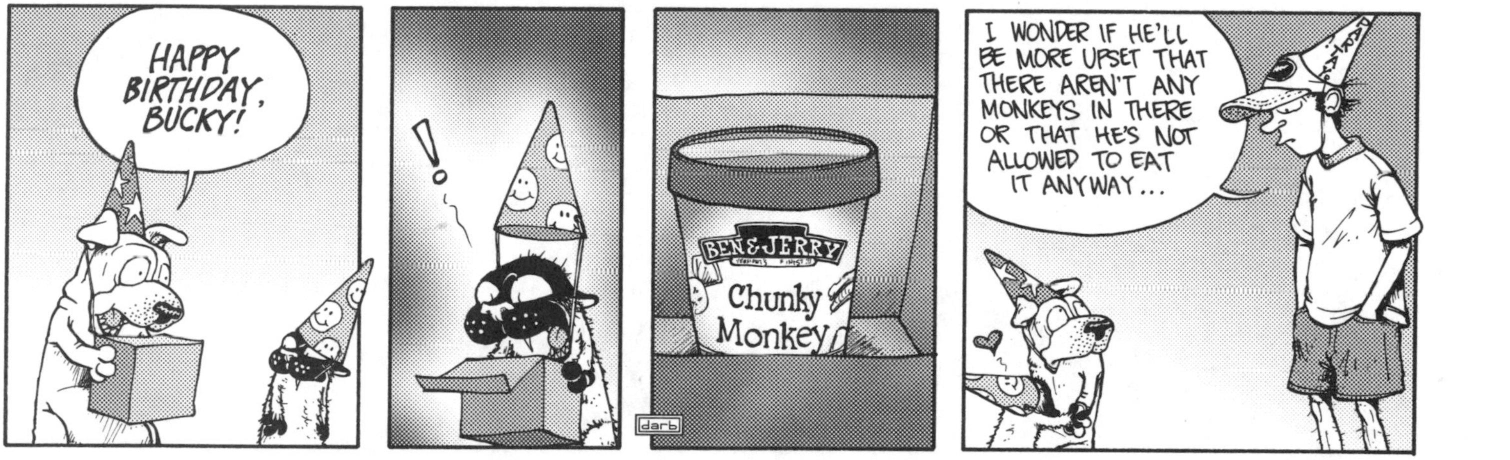
HAPPY BIRTHDAY, BUCKY!
!
BEN&JERRY
Chunky Monkey
I WONDER IF HE'LL BE MORE UPSET THAT THERE AREN'T ANY MONKEYS IN THERE OR THAT HE'S NOT ALLOWED TO EAT IT ANYWAY...
darb

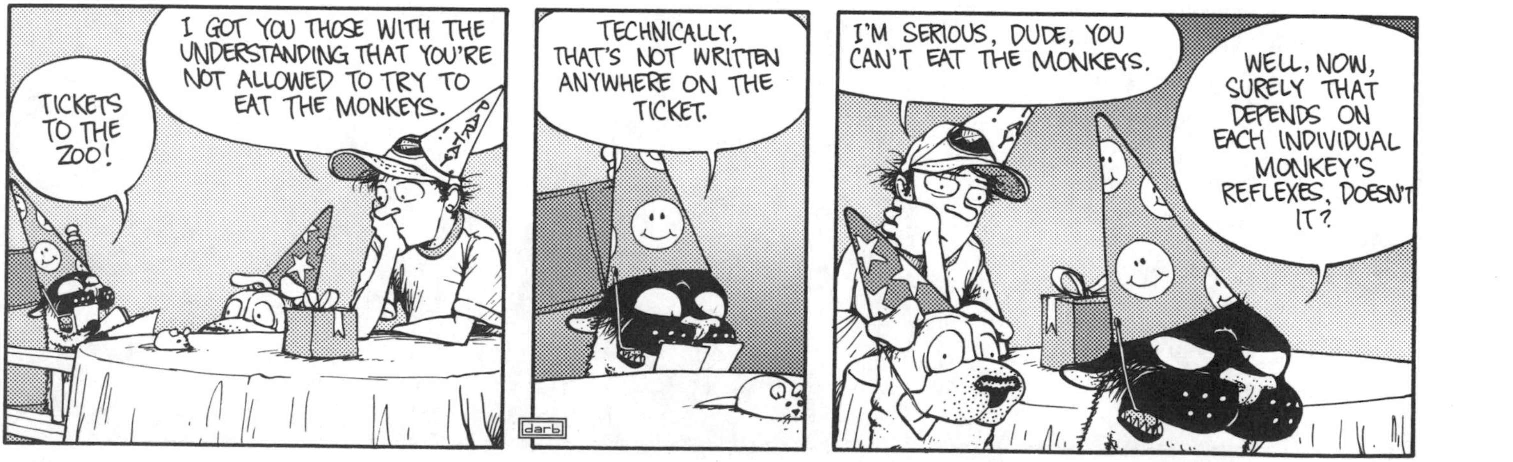
TICKETS TO THE ZOO!
I GOT YOU THOSE WITH THE UNDERSTANDING THAT YOU'RE NOT ALLOWED TO TRY TO EAT THE MONKEYS.
TECHNICALLY, THAT'S NOT WRITTEN ANYWHERE ON THE TICKET.
I'M SERIOUS, DUDE, YOU CAN'T EAT THE MONKEYS.
WELL, NOW, SURELY THAT DEPENDS ON EACH INDIVIDUAL MONKEY'S REFLEXES, DOESN'T IT?
darb

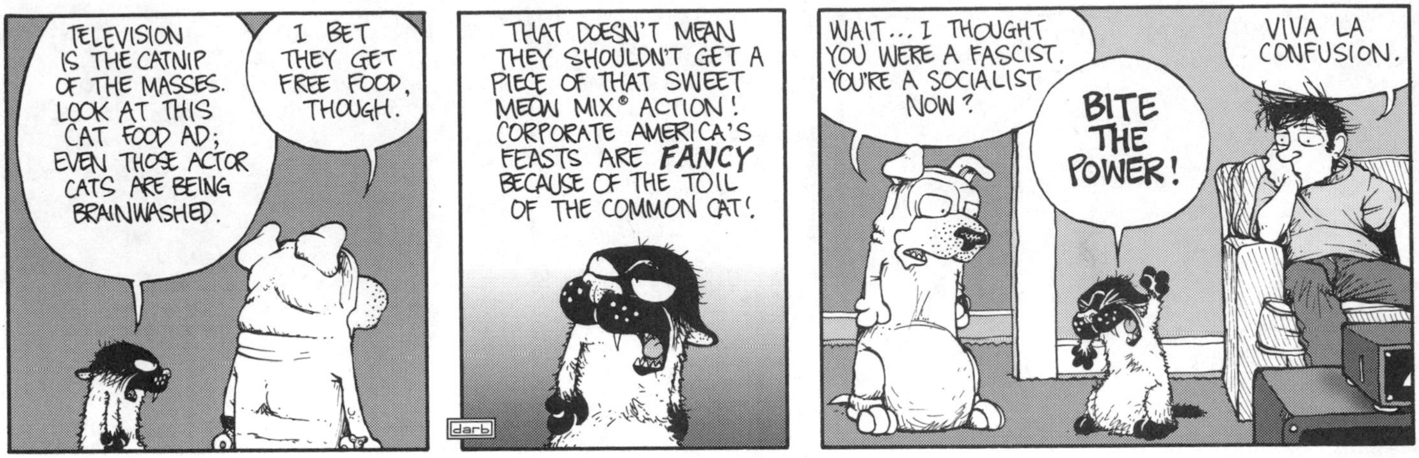
TELEVISION IS THE CATNIP OF THE MASSES. LOOK AT THIS CAT FOOD AD; EVEN THOSE ACTOR CATS ARE BEING BRAINWASHED.
I BET THEY GET FREE FOOD, THOUGH.
THAT DOESN'T MEAN THEY SHOULDN'T GET A PIECE OF THAT SWEET MEOW MIX® ACTION! CORPORATE AMERICA'S FEASTS ARE FANCY BECAUSE OF THE TOIL OF THE COMMON CAT!
darb
WAIT... I THOUGHT YOU WERE A FASCIST. YOU'RE A SOCIALIST NOW?
BITE THE POWER!
VIVA LA CONFUSION.

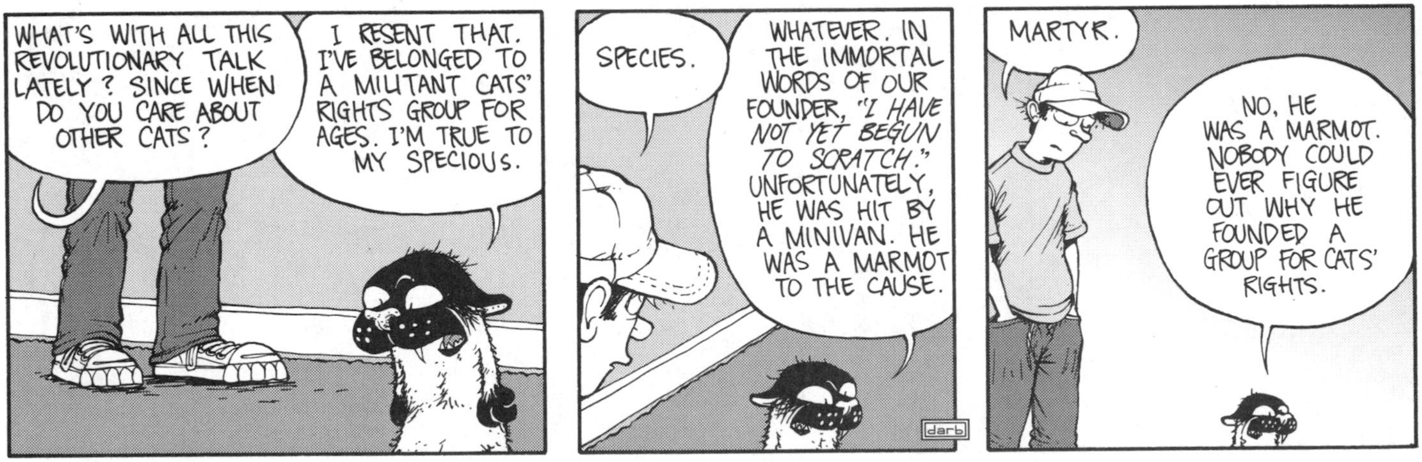
WHAT'S WITH ALL THIS REVOLUTIONARY TALK LATELY? SINCE WHEN DO YOU CARE ABOUT OTHER CATS?
I RESENT THAT. I'VE BELONGED TO A MILITANT CATS' RIGHTS GROUP FOR AGES. I'M TRUE TO MY SPECIOUS.
SPECIES.
WHATEVER. IN THE IMMORTAL WORDS OF OUR FOUNDER, "I HAVE NOT YET BEGUN TO SCRATCH." UNFORTUNATELY, HE WAS HIT BY A MINIVAN. HE WAS A MARMOT TO THE CAUSE.
darb
MARTYR.
NO, HE WAS A MARMOT. NOBODY COULD EVER FIGURE OUT WHY HE FOUNDED A GROUP FOR CATS' RIGHTS.

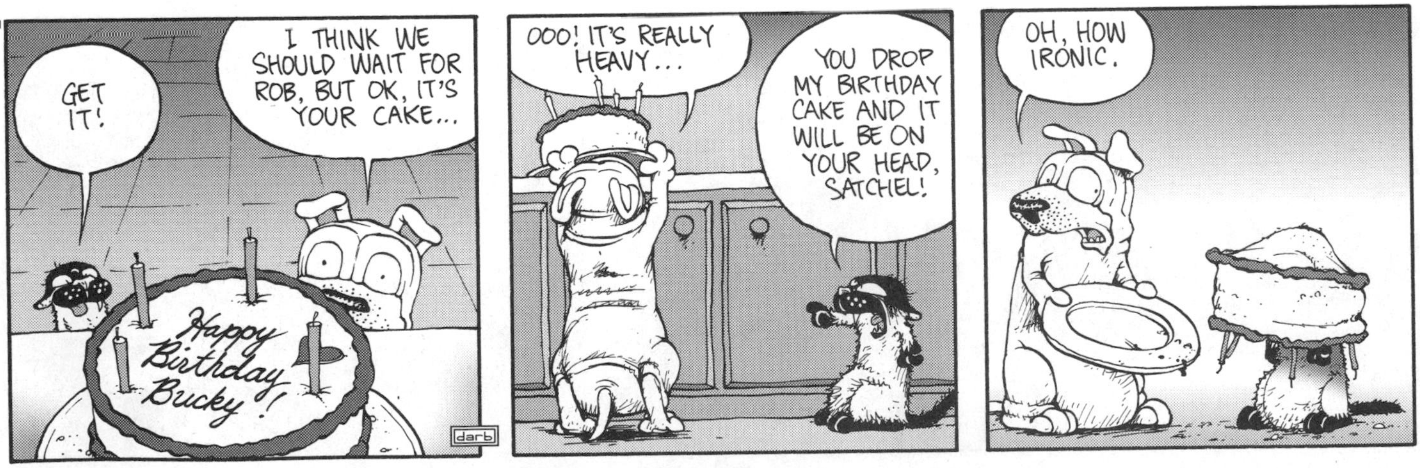
GET IT!
I THINK WE SHOULD WAIT FOR ROB, BUT OK, IT'S YOUR CAKE...
Happy Birthday Bucky!
darb
OOO! IT'S REALLY HEAVY...
YOU DROP MY BIRTHDAY CAKE AND IT WILL BE ON YOUR HEAD, SATCHEL!
OH, HOW IRONIC.

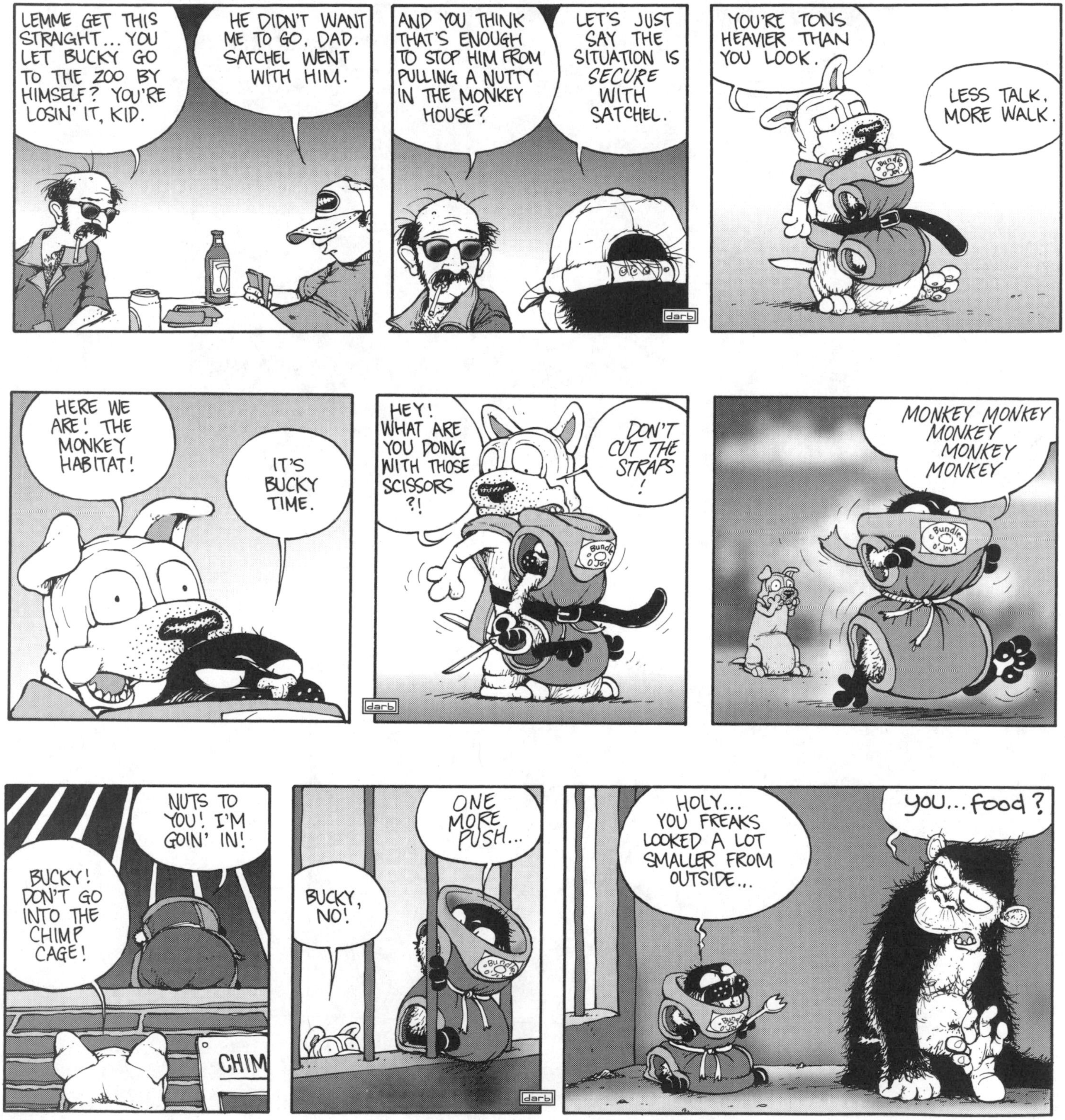
LEMME GET THIS STRAIGHT... YOU LET BUCKY GO TO THE ZOO BY HIMSELF? YOU'RE LOSIN' IT, KID.
HE DIDN'T WANT ME TO GO, DAD. SATCHEL WENT WITH HIM.
AND YOU THINK THAT'S ENOUGH TO STOP HIM FROM PULLING A NUTTY IN THE MONKEY HOUSE?
LET'S JUST SAY THE SITUATION IS *SECURE* WITH SATCHEL.
darb
YOU'RE TONS HEAVIER THAN YOU LOOK.
LESS TALK. MORE WALK.
Bundle O'Joy
HERE WE ARE! THE MONKEY HABITAT!
IT'S BUCKY TIME.
darb
HEY! WHAT ARE YOU DOING WITH THOSE SCISSORS?!
DON'T CUT THE STRAPS!
Bundle O'Joy
MONKEY MONKEY MONKEY MONKEY MONKEY
Bundle O'Joy
NUTS TO YOU! I'M GOIN' IN!
BUCKY! DON'T GO INTO THE CHIMP CAGE!
CHIM
ONE MORE PUSH...
BUCKY, NO!
darb
HOLY... YOU FREAKS LOOKED A LOT SMALLER FROM OUTSIDE...
you... food?

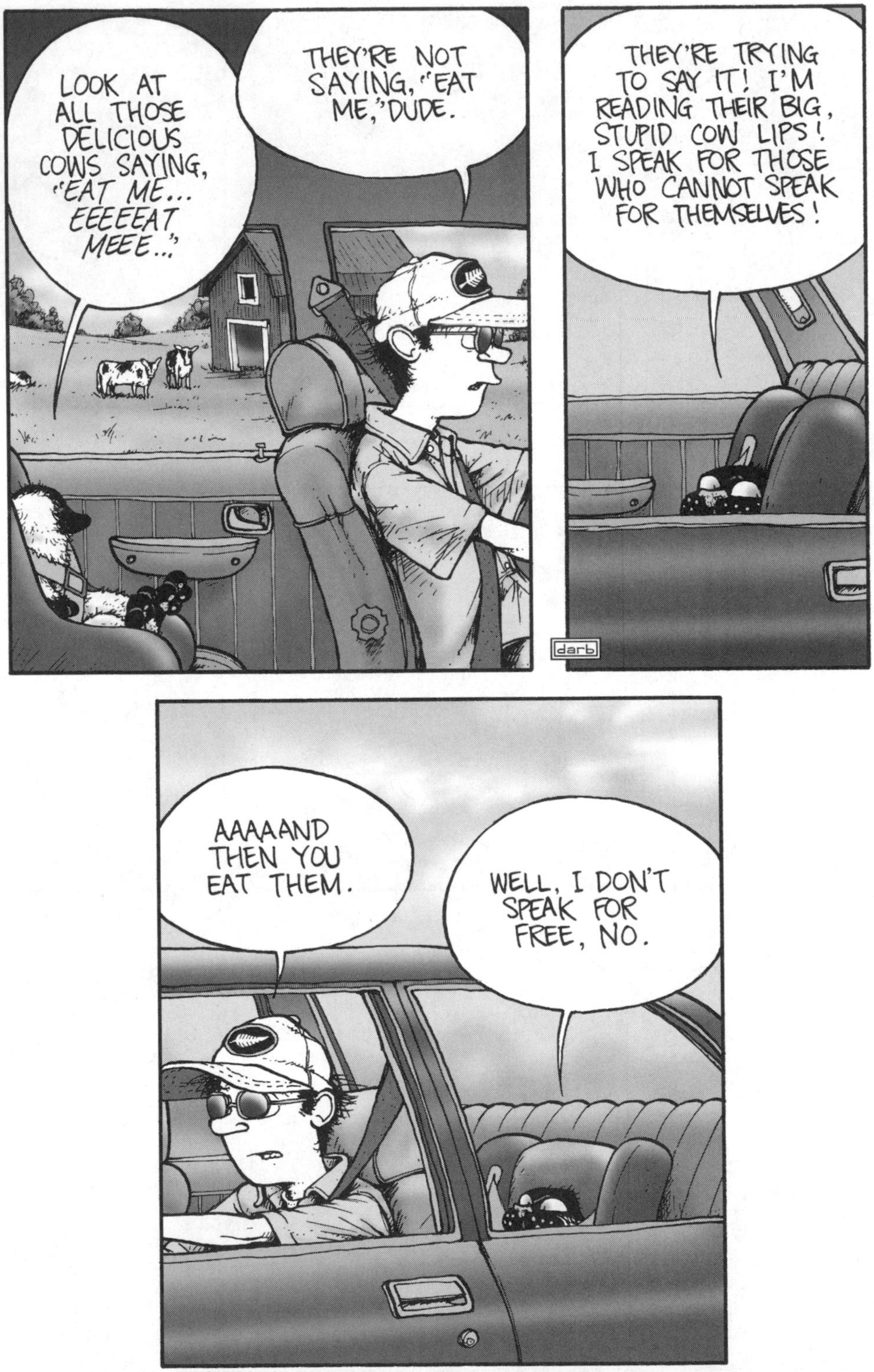
LOOK AT ALL THOSE DELICIOUS COWS SAYING, "EAT ME... EEEEEAT MEEE..."
THEY'RE NOT SAYING, "EAT ME," DUDE.
THEY'RE TRYING TO SAY IT! I'M READING THEIR BIG, STUPID COW LIPS! I SPEAK FOR THOSE WHO CANNOT SPEAK FOR THEMSELVES!
darb
AAAAAND THEN YOU EAT THEM.
WELL, I DON'T SPEAK FOR FREE, NO.

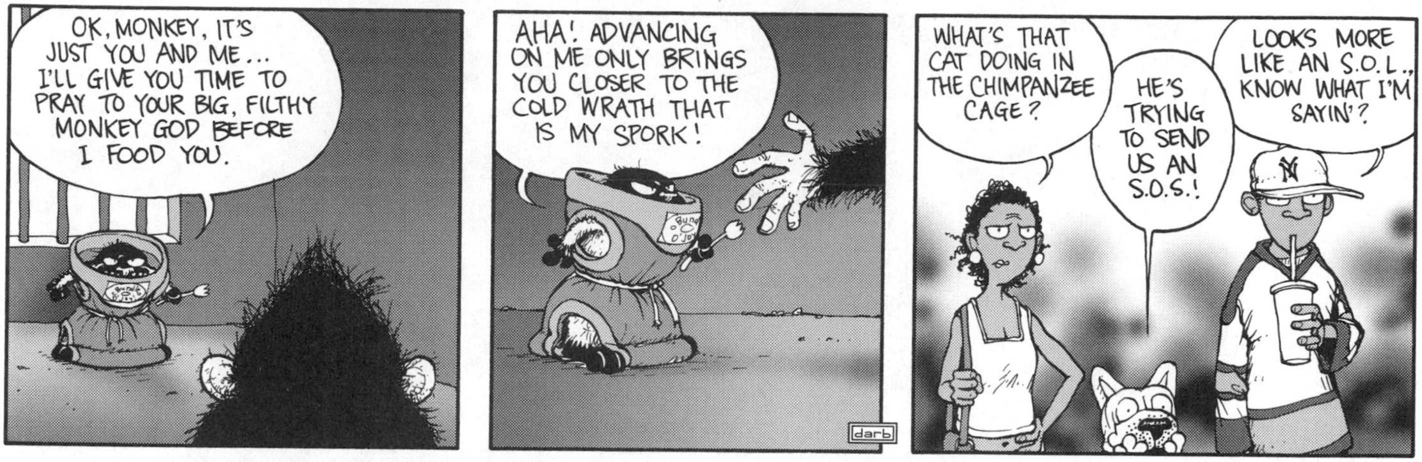
OK, MONKEY, IT'S JUST YOU AND ME... I'LL GIVE YOU TIME TO PRAY TO YOUR BIG, FILTHY MONKEY GOD BEFORE I FOOD YOU.
AHA! ADVANCING ON ME ONLY BRINGS YOU CLOSER TO THE COLD WRATH THAT IS MY SPORK!
WHAT'S THAT CAT DOING IN THE CHIMPANZEE CAGE?
HE'S TRYING TO SEND US AN S.O.S.!
LOOKS MORE LIKE AN S.O.L., KNOW WHAT I'M SAYIN'?

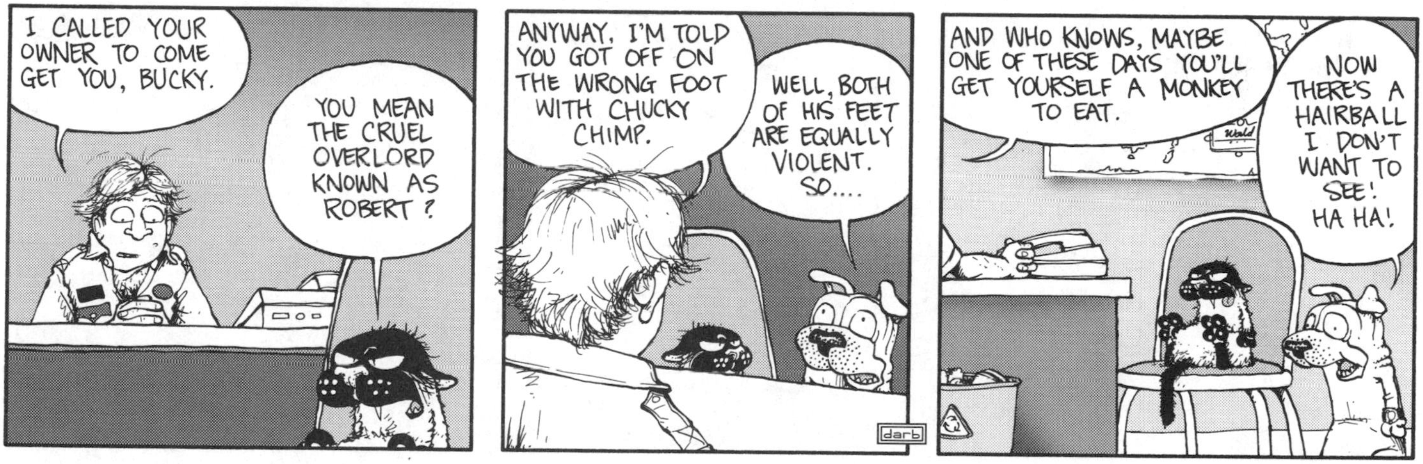
I CALLED YOUR OWNER TO COME GET YOU, BUCKY.
YOU MEAN THE CRUEL OVERLORD KNOWN AS ROBERT?
ANYWAY, I'M TOLD YOU GOT OFF ON THE WRONG FOOT WITH CHUCKY CHIMP.
WELL, BOTH OF HIS FEET ARE EQUALLY VIOLENT. SO....
AND WHO KNOWS, MAYBE ONE OF THESE DAYS YOU'LL GET YOURSELF A MONKEY TO EAT.
NOW THERE'S A HAIRBALL I DON'T WANT TO SEE! HA HA!

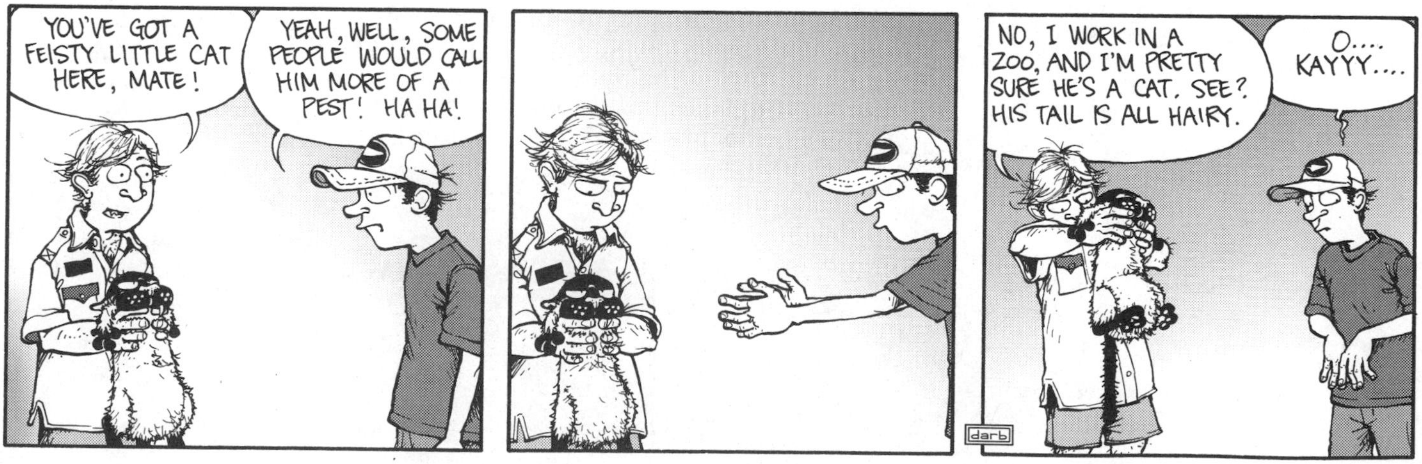
YOU'VE GOT A FEISTY LITTLE CAT HERE, MATE!
YEAH, WELL, SOME PEOPLE WOULD CALL HIM MORE OF A PEST! HA HA!
NO, I WORK IN A ZOO, AND I'M PRETTY SURE HE'S A CAT. SEE? HIS TAIL IS ALL HAIRY.
O.... KAYYY....

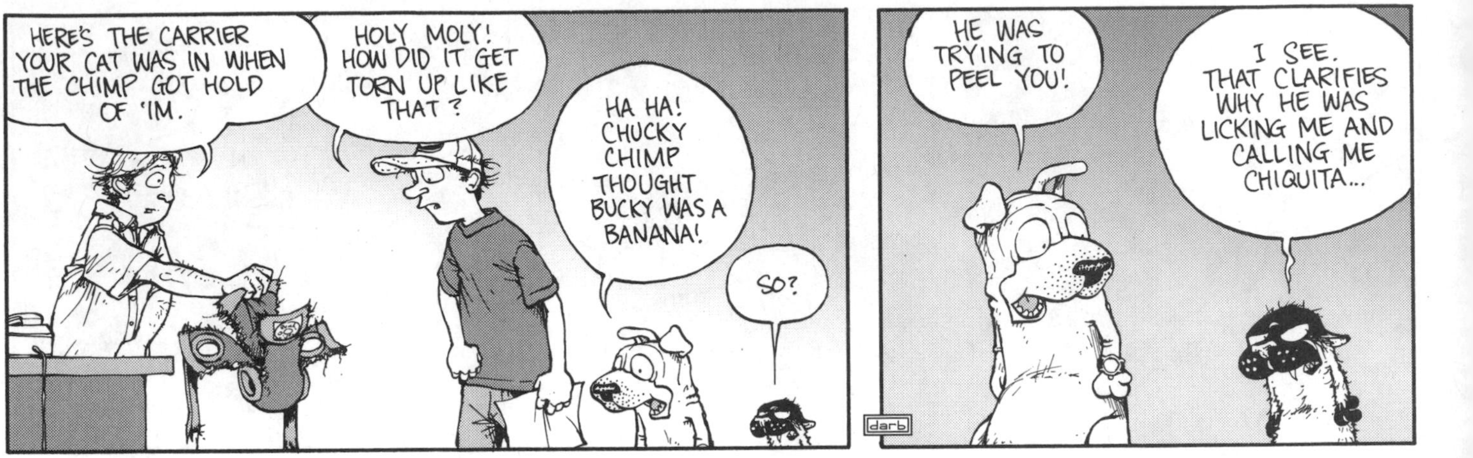
HERE'S THE CARRIER YOUR CAT WAS IN WHEN THE CHIMP GOT HOLD OF 'IM.
HOLY MOLY! HOW DID IT GET TORN UP LIKE THAT?
HA HA! CHUCKY CHIMP THOUGHT BUCKY WAS A BANANA!
SO?
HE WAS TRYING TO PEEL YOU!
I SEE. THAT CLARIFIES WHY HE WAS LICKING ME AND CALLING ME CHIQUITA...
darb

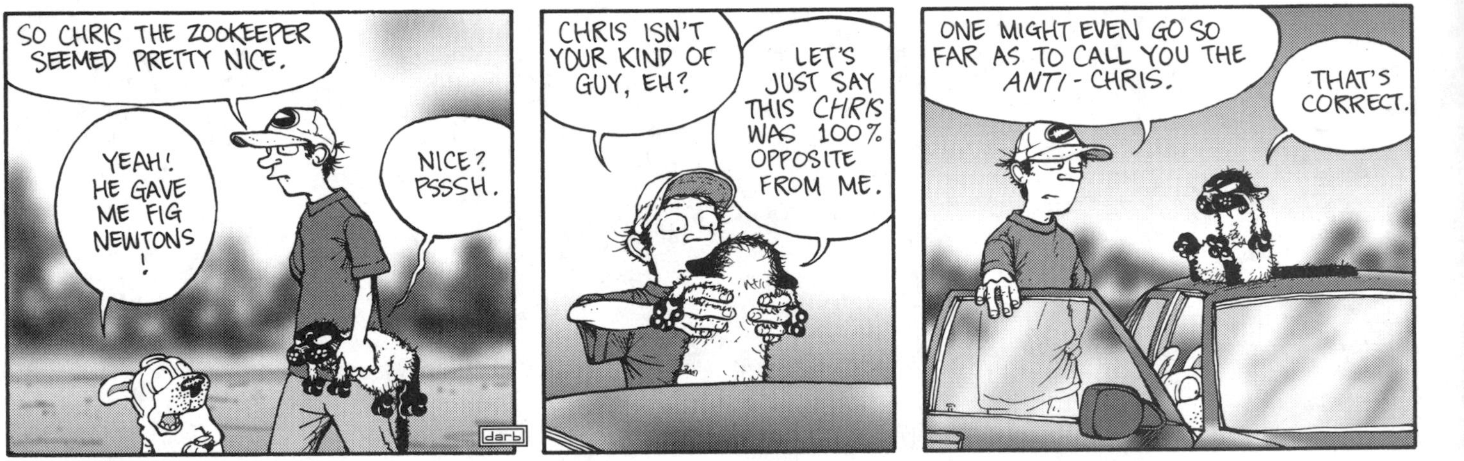
SO CHRIS THE ZOOKEEPER SEEMED PRETTY NICE.
YEAH! HE GAVE ME FIG NEWTONS!
NICE? PSSSH.
darb
CHRIS ISN'T YOUR KIND OF GUY, EH?
LET'S JUST SAY THIS CHRIS WAS 100% OPPOSITE FROM ME.
ONE MIGHT EVEN GO SO FAR AS TO CALL YOU THE ANTI-CHRIS.
THAT'S CORRECT.

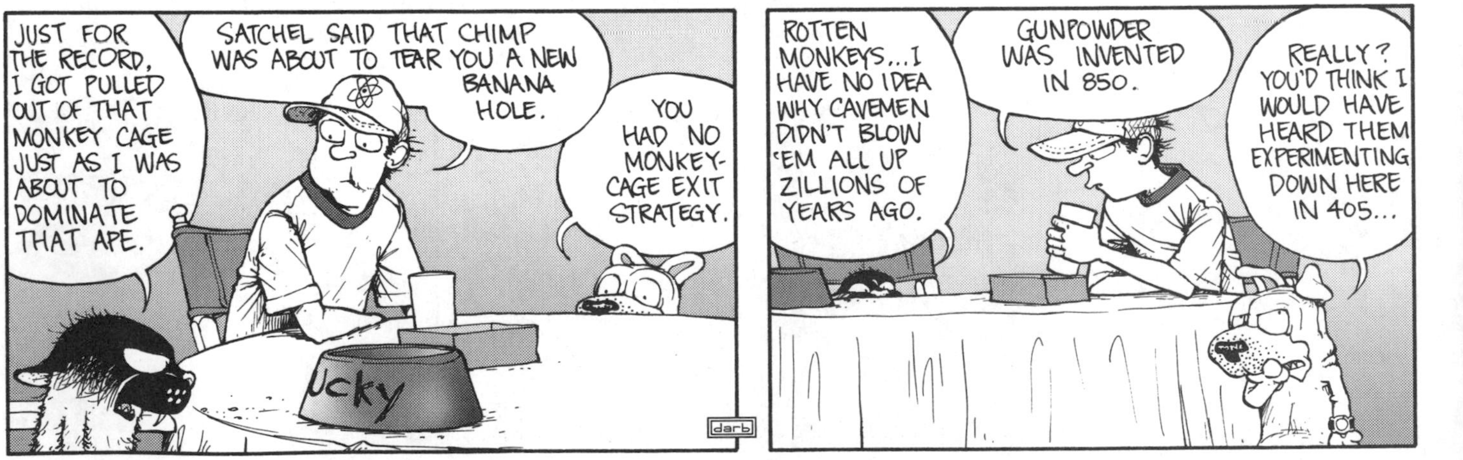
JUST FOR THE RECORD, I GOT PULLED OUT OF THAT MONKEY CAGE JUST AS I WAS ABOUT TO DOMINATE THAT APE.
SATCHEL SAID THAT CHIMP WAS ABOUT TO TEAR YOU A NEW BANANA HOLE.
YOU HAD NO MONKEY-CAGE EXIT STRATEGY.
UCKY
darb
ROTTEN MONKEYS... I HAVE NO IDEA WHY CAVEMEN DIDN'T BLOW 'EM ALL UP ZILLIONS OF YEARS AGO.
GUNPOWDER WAS INVENTED IN 850.
REALLY? YOU'D THINK I WOULD HAVE HEARD THEM EXPERIMENTING DOWN HERE IN 405...

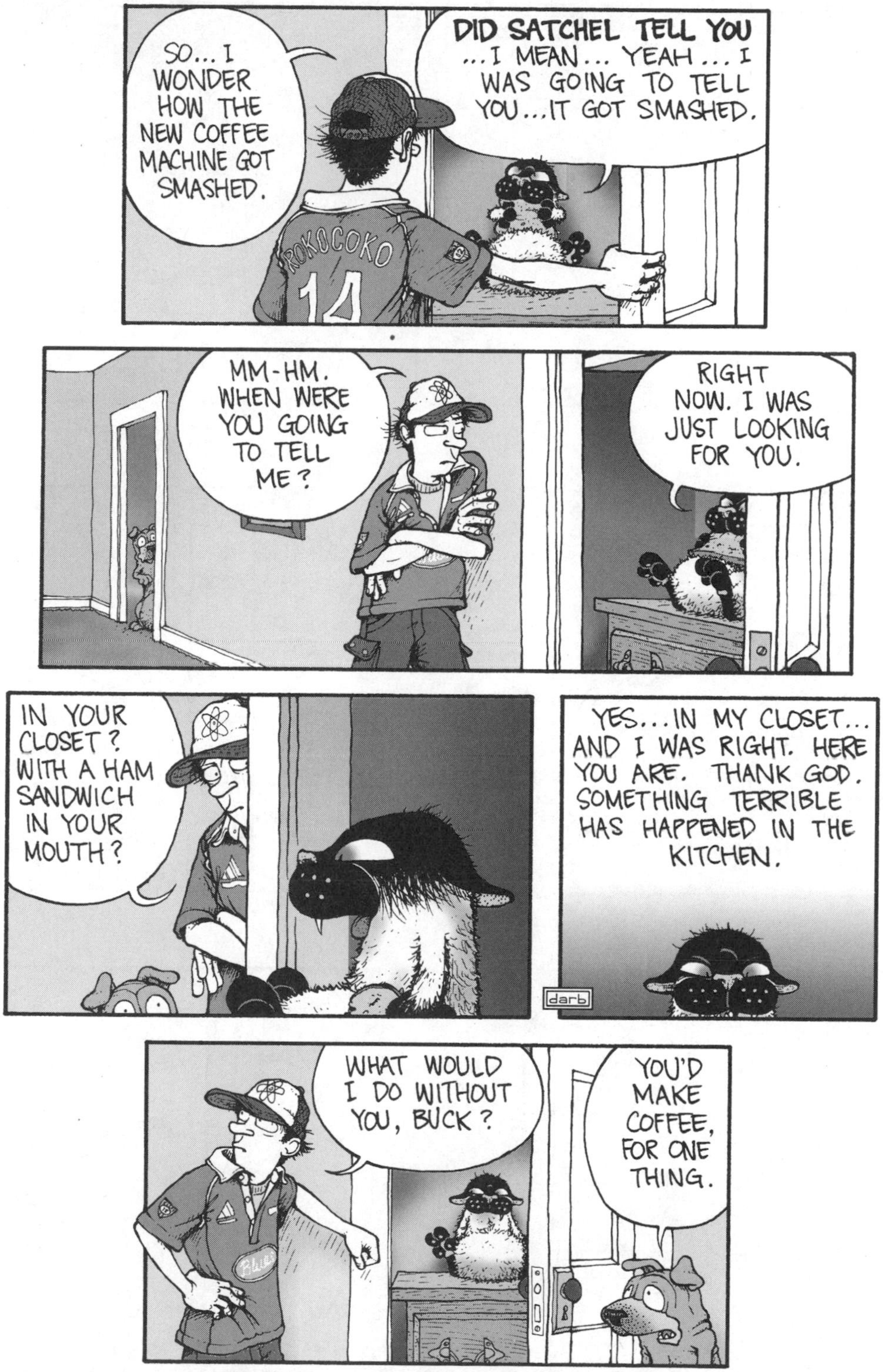
SO... I WONDER HOW THE NEW COFFEE MACHINE GOT SMASHED.
DID SATCHEL TELL YOU ...I MEAN... YEAH... I WAS GOING TO TELL YOU...IT GOT SMASHED.
ROKOCOKO 14
MM-HM. WHEN WERE YOU GOING TO TELL ME?
RIGHT NOW. I WAS JUST LOOKING FOR YOU.
IN YOUR CLOSET? WITH A HAM SANDWICH IN YOUR MOUTH?
YES...IN MY CLOSET... AND I WAS RIGHT. HERE YOU ARE. THANK GOD. SOMETHING TERRIBLE HAS HAPPENED IN THE KITCHEN.
darb
WHAT WOULD I DO WITHOUT YOU, BUCK?
YOU'D MAKE COFFEE, FOR ONE THING.

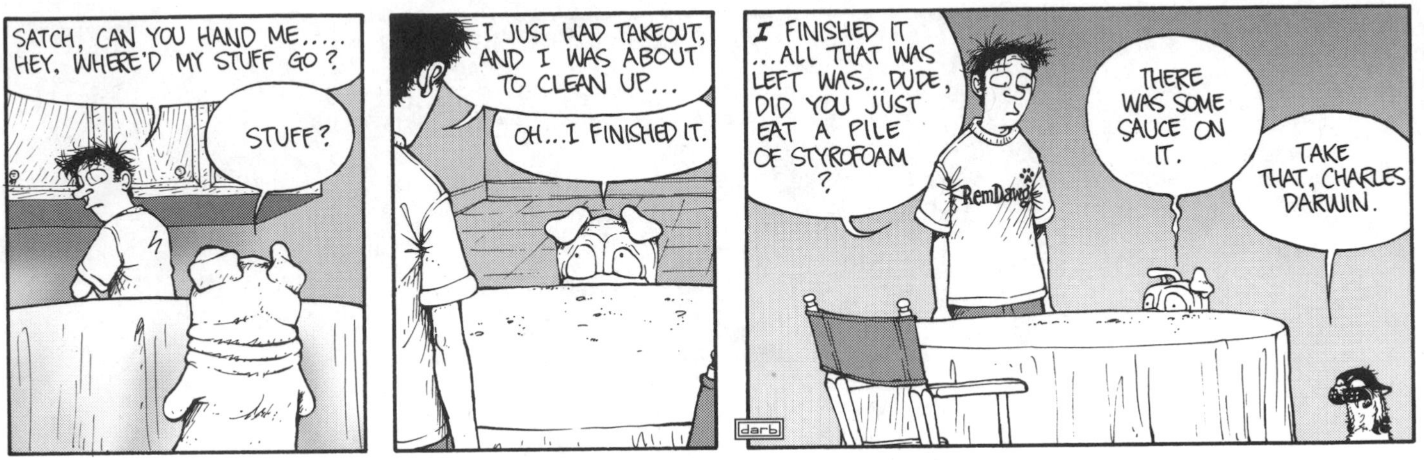
SATCH, CAN YOU HAND ME..... HEY, WHERE'D MY STUFF GO?
STUFF?
I JUST HAD TAKEOUT, AND I WAS ABOUT TO CLEAN UP...
OH...I FINISHED IT.
I FINISHED IT ...ALL THAT WAS LEFT WAS... DUDE, DID YOU JUST EAT A PILE OF STYROFOAM ?
RemDawg
THERE WAS SOME SAUCE ON IT.
TAKE THAT, CHARLES DARWIN.
darb

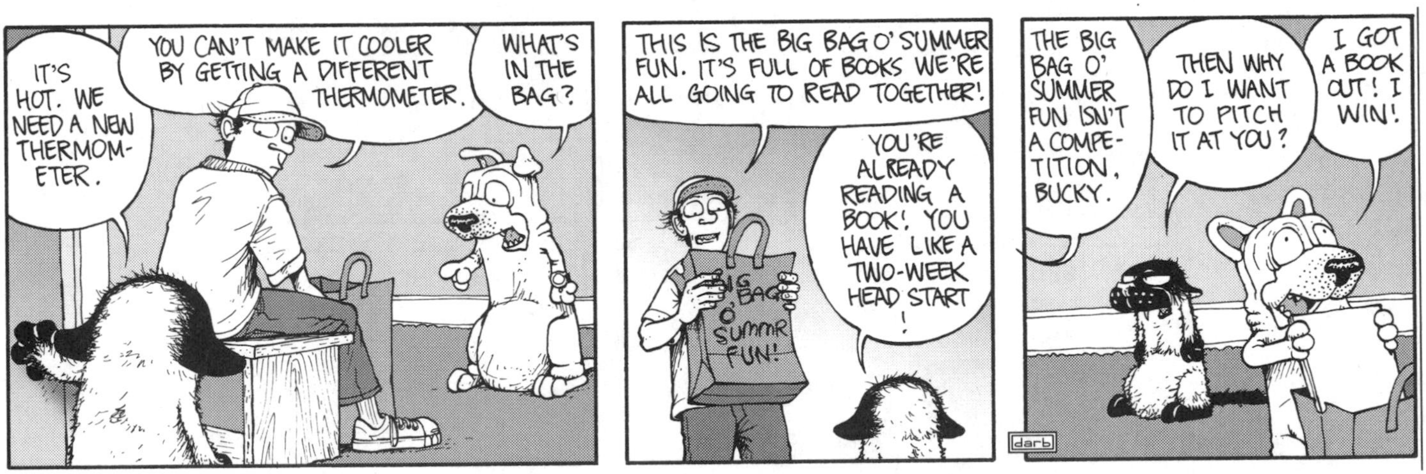
IT'S HOT. WE NEED A NEW THERMOM-ETER.
YOU CAN'T MAKE IT COOLER BY GETTING A DIFFERENT THERMOMETER.
WHAT'S IN THE BAG?
THIS IS THE BIG BAG O' SUMMER FUN. IT'S FULL OF BOOKS WE'RE ALL GOING TO READ TOGETHER!
BIG BAG O' SUMMR FUN!
YOU'RE ALREADY READING A BOOK! YOU HAVE LIKE A TWO-WEEK HEAD START !
THE BIG BAG O' SUMMER FUN ISN'T A COMPE-TITION, BUCKY.
THEN WHY DO I WANT TO PITCH IT AT YOU?
I GOT A BOOK OUT! I WIN!
darb

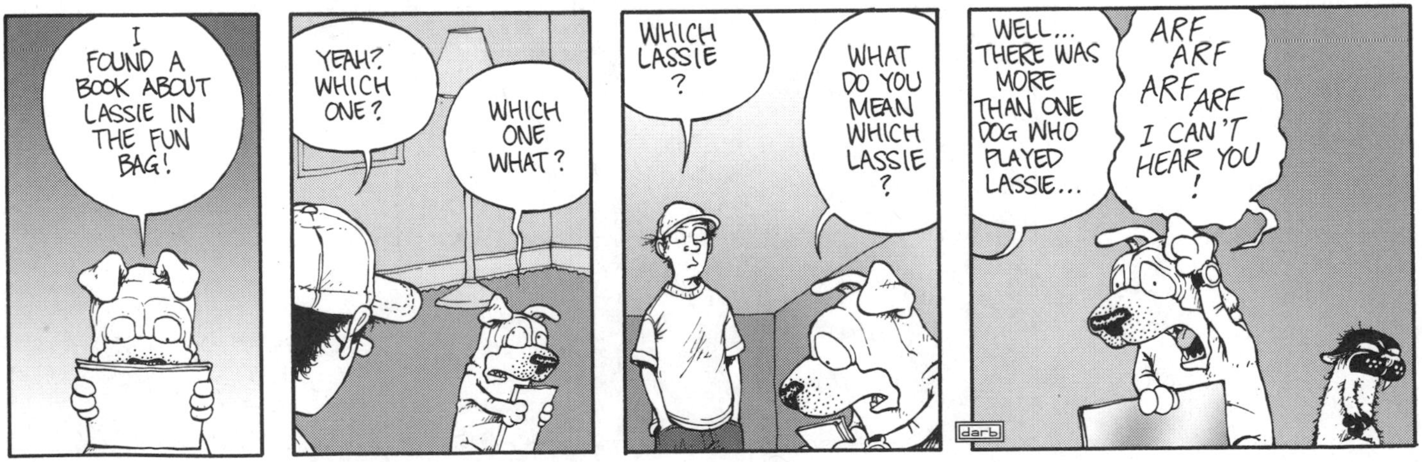
I FOUND A BOOK ABOUT LASSIE IN THE FUN BAG!
YEAH? WHICH ONE?
WHICH ONE WHAT?
WHICH LASSIE ?
WHAT DO YOU MEAN WHICH LASSIE ?
WELL... THERE WAS MORE THAN ONE DOG WHO PLAYED LASSIE...
ARF ARF ARF ARF I CAN'T HEAR YOU !
darb

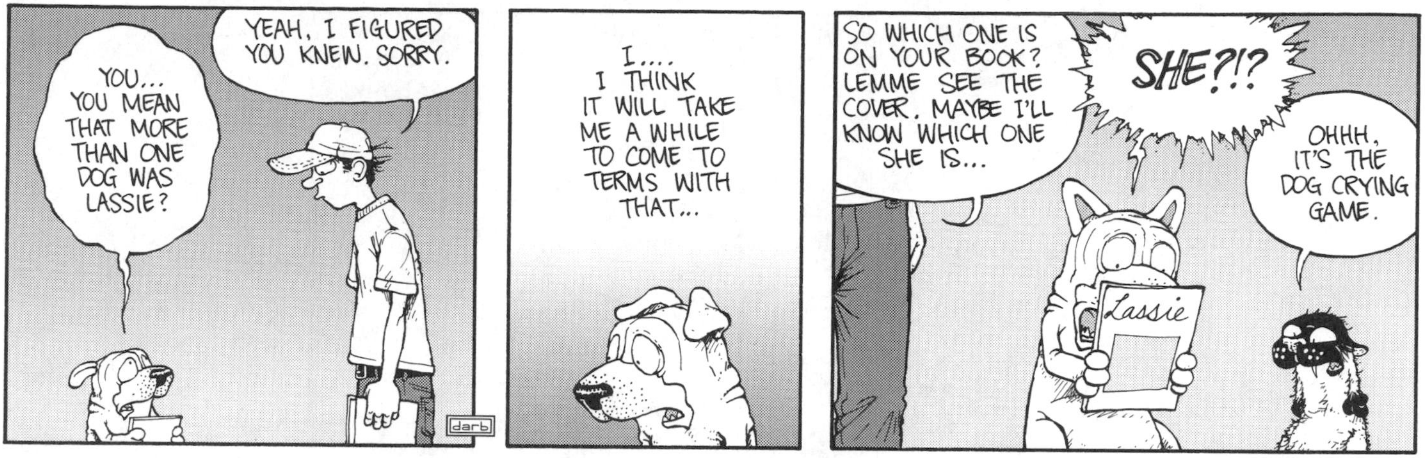
YOU... YOU MEAN THAT MORE THAN ONE DOG WAS LASSIE?
YEAH, I FIGURED YOU KNEW. SORRY.
darb
I.... I THINK IT WILL TAKE ME A WHILE TO COME TO TERMS WITH THAT...
SO WHICH ONE IS ON YOUR BOOK? LEMME SEE THE COVER. MAYBE I'LL KNOW WHICH ONE SHE IS...
SHE?!?
Lassie
OHHH, IT'S THE DOG CRYING GAME.

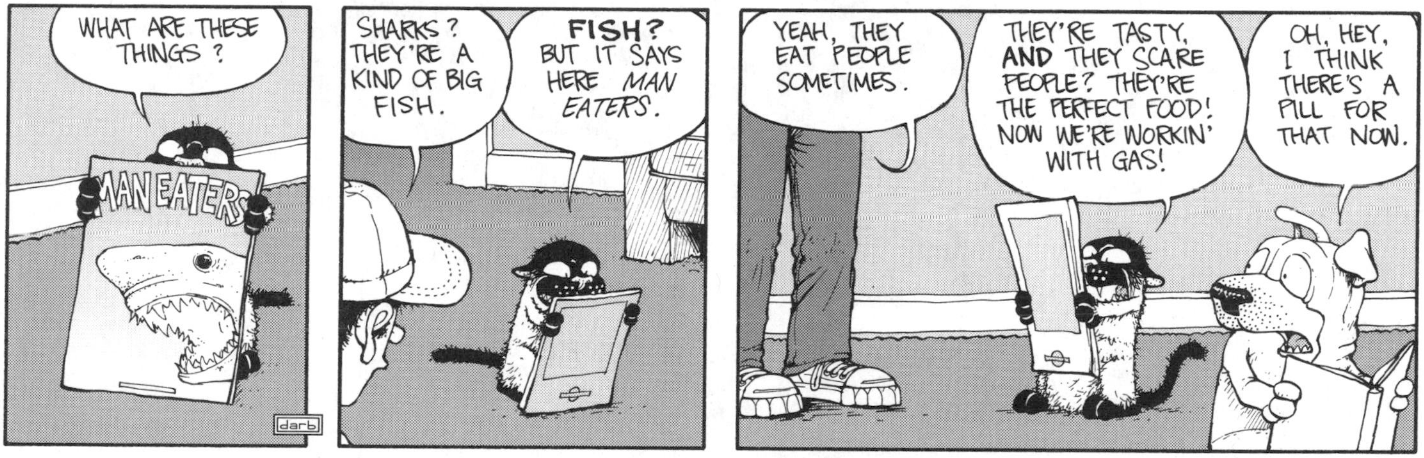
WHAT ARE THESE THINGS ?
MAN EATERS
darb
SHARKS ? THEY'RE A KIND OF BIG FISH.
FISH? BUT IT SAYS HERE MAN EATERS.
YEAH, THEY EAT PEOPLE SOMETIMES.
THEY'RE TASTY, AND THEY SCARE PEOPLE? THEY'RE THE PERFECT FOOD! NOW WE'RE WORKIN' WITH GAS!
OH, HEY, I THINK THERE'S A PILL FOR THAT NOW.

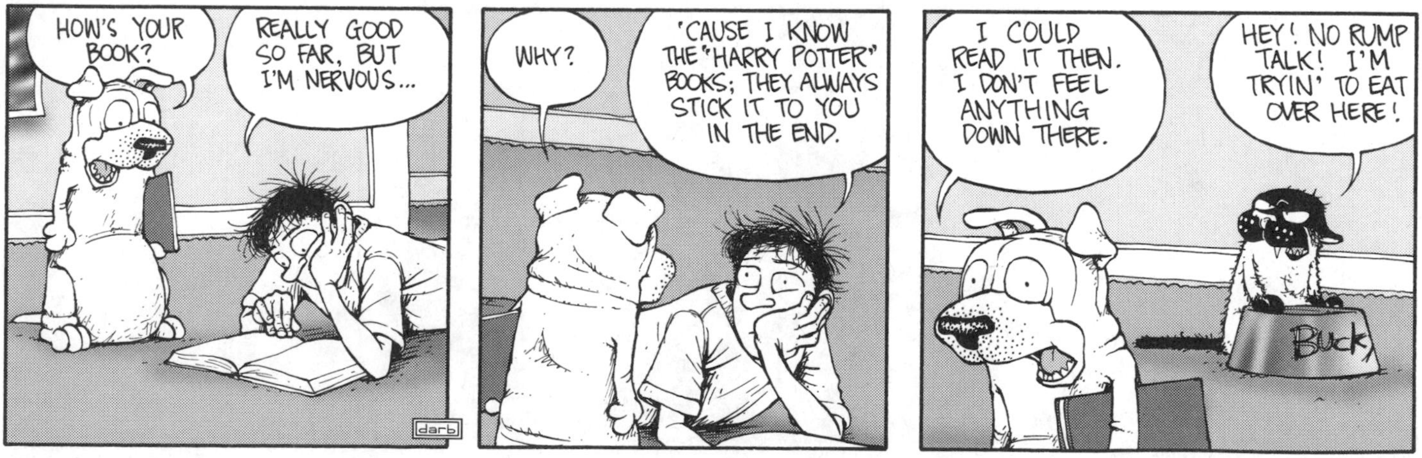
HOW'S YOUR BOOK?
REALLY GOOD SO FAR, BUT I'M NERVOUS...
darb
WHY?
'CAUSE I KNOW THE "HARRY POTTER" BOOKS; THEY ALWAYS STICK IT TO YOU IN THE END.
I COULD READ IT THEN. I DON'T FEEL ANYTHING DOWN THERE.
HEY! NO RUMP TALK! I'M TRYIN' TO EAT OVER HERE!
BUCKY

EXIT
WHAT DO WE DO NOW?
NOW WE BEAT ON EACH OTHER WITH THE BONKERS. I'M GONNA TENDERIZE YOU LIKE A PORK CHOP.
MEGABONKERS!
bonk your friends silly!
BUCS
darb
DO I HAVE TO USE THE MINIBONKER? I THINK IT'S JUST FOR SHOW. ...IT'S GOT A KEY CHAIN ON IT.
I TOLD YOU, THE OTHER MEGABONKER IN THE BOX IS MY BACKUP IN CASE I BREAK THIS ONE ON YOUR THICK HEAD.
BUCS
BUT I CAN'T PLAY WITH THIS ONE. IT WOULDN'T BE SAFE ENOUGH.
WHO SAYS YOU CAN'T USE THE MINIBONKER? WHO SAYS IT ISN'T SAFE?
BUCS
BONK!
IT SAYS RIGHT HERE ON THE BOX: *DO NOT PLAY WITH THE MINIBONKER. IT IS NOT SAFE.*
SHUT UP AND TAKE YOUR BONKING, PORKY.
bonk your friends silly!

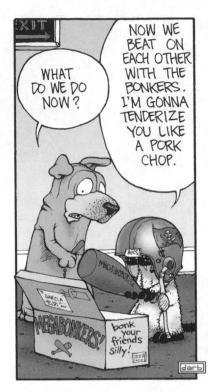

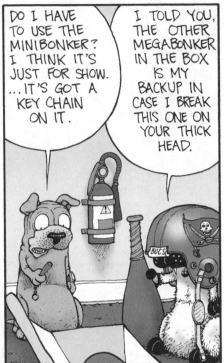

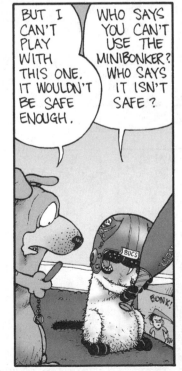

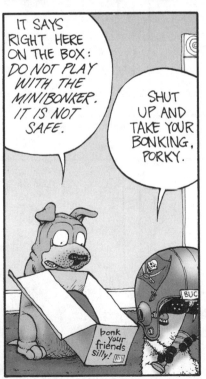

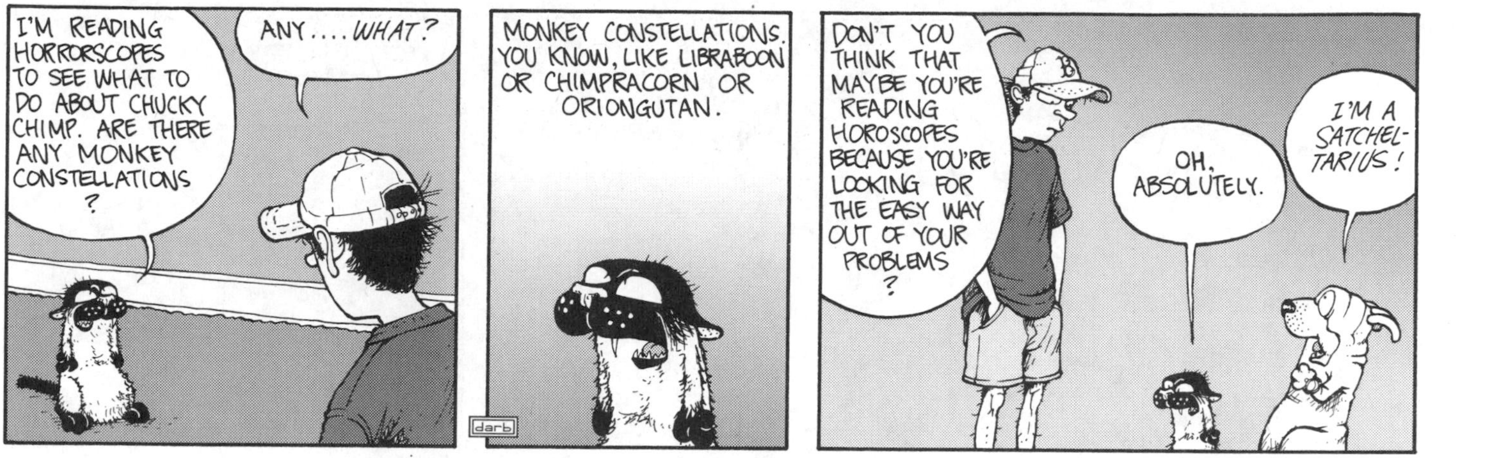
I'M READING HORRORSCOPES TO SEE WHAT TO DO ABOUT CHUCKY CHIMP. ARE THERE ANY MONKEY CONSTELLATIONS?
ANY.... *WHAT?*
MONKEY CONSTELLATIONS. YOU KNOW, LIKE LIBRABOON OR CHIMPRACORN OR ORIONGUTAN.
DON'T YOU THINK THAT MAYBE YOU'RE READING HOROSCOPES BECAUSE YOU'RE LOOKING FOR THE EASY WAY OUT OF YOUR PROBLEMS?
OH, ABSOLUTELY.
I'M A SATCHEL-TARIUS!

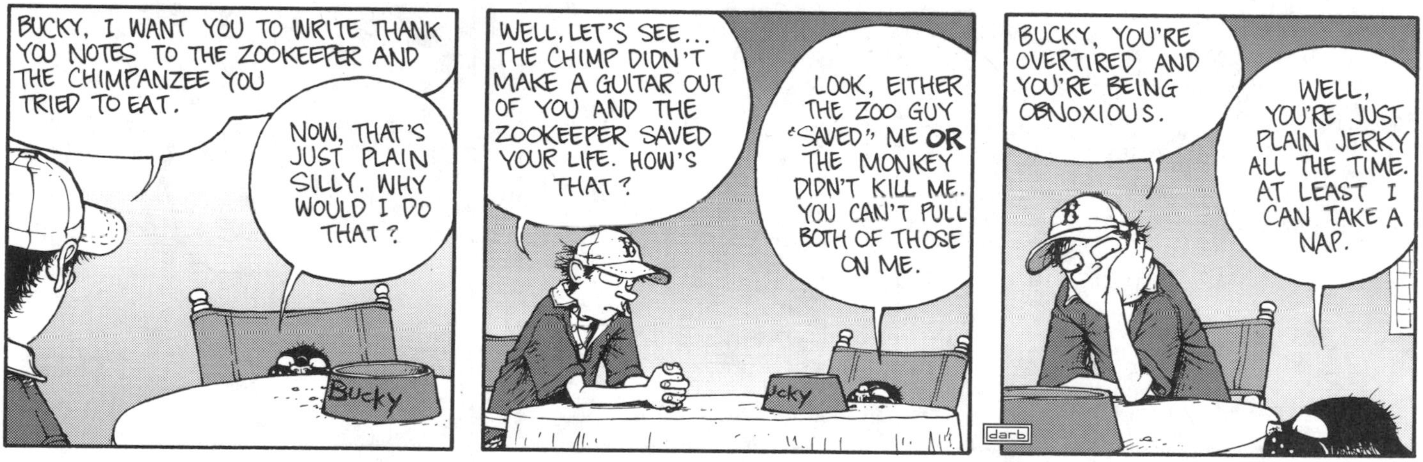
BUCKY, I WANT YOU TO WRITE THANK YOU NOTES TO THE ZOOKEEPER AND THE CHIMPANZEE YOU TRIED TO EAT.
NOW, THAT'S JUST PLAIN SILLY. WHY WOULD I DO THAT?
Bucky
WELL, LET'S SEE... THE CHIMP DIDN'T MAKE A GUITAR OUT OF YOU AND THE ZOOKEEPER SAVED YOUR LIFE. HOW'S THAT?
LOOK, EITHER THE ZOO GUY "SAVED" ME **OR** THE MONKEY DIDN'T KILL ME. YOU CAN'T PULL BOTH OF THOSE ON ME.
BUCKY, YOU'RE OVERTIRED AND YOU'RE BEING OBNOXIOUS.
WELL, YOU'RE JUST PLAIN JERKY ALL THE TIME. AT LEAST I CAN TAKE A NAP.

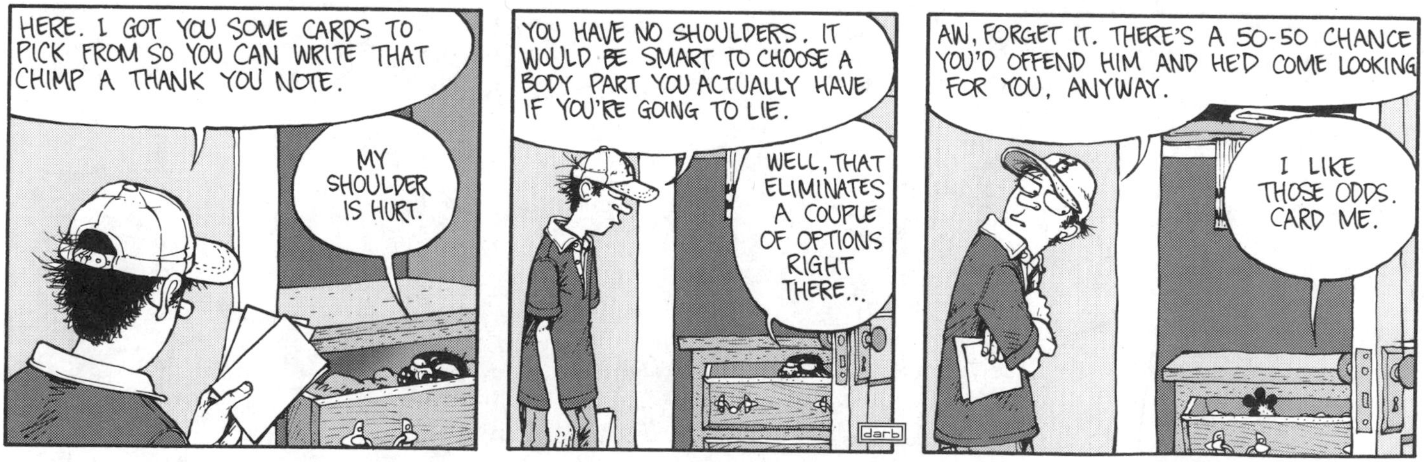
HERE. I GOT YOU SOME CARDS TO PICK FROM SO YOU CAN WRITE THAT CHIMP A THANK YOU NOTE.
MY SHOULDER IS HURT.
YOU HAVE NO SHOULDERS. IT WOULD BE SMART TO CHOOSE A BODY PART YOU ACTUALLY HAVE IF YOU'RE GOING TO LIE.
WELL, THAT ELIMINATES A COUPLE OF OPTIONS RIGHT THERE...
AW, FORGET IT. THERE'S A 50-50 CHANCE YOU'D OFFEND HIM AND HE'D COME LOOKING FOR YOU, ANYWAY.
I LIKE THOSE ODDS. CARD ME.

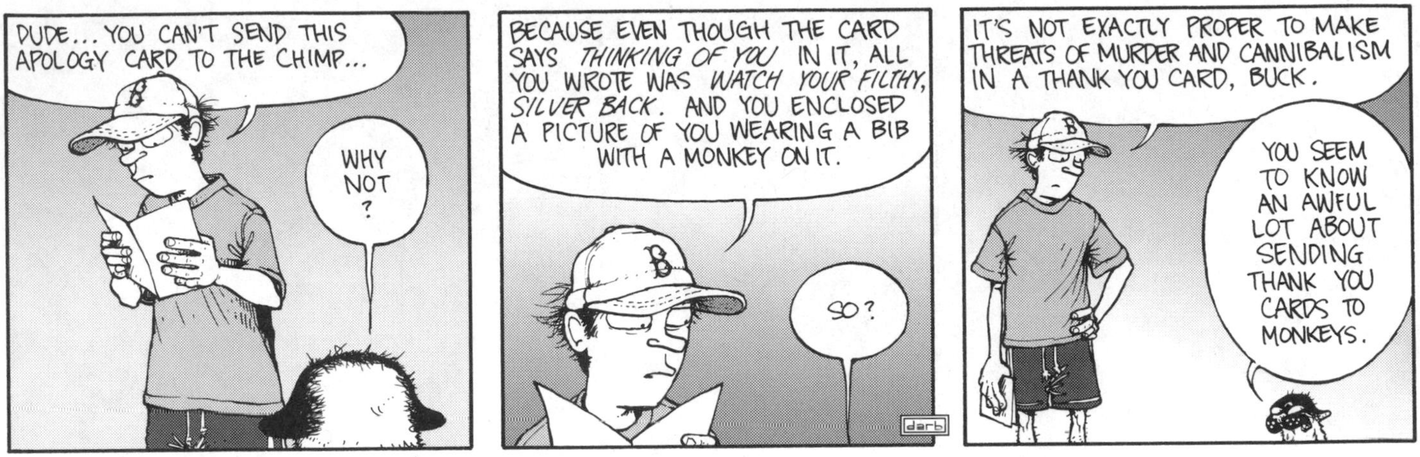
DUDE... YOU CAN'T SEND THIS APOLOGY CARD TO THE CHIMP...
WHY NOT ?
BECAUSE EVEN THOUGH THE CARD SAYS *THINKING OF YOU* IN IT, ALL YOU WROTE WAS *WATCH YOUR FILTHY, SILVER BACK*. AND YOU ENCLOSED A PICTURE OF YOU WEARING A BIB WITH A MONKEY ON IT.
SO?
IT'S NOT EXACTLY PROPER TO MAKE THREATS OF MURDER AND CANNIBALISM IN A THANK YOU CARD, BUCK.
YOU SEEM TO KNOW AN AWFUL LOT ABOUT SENDING THANK YOU CARDS TO MONKEYS.
darb

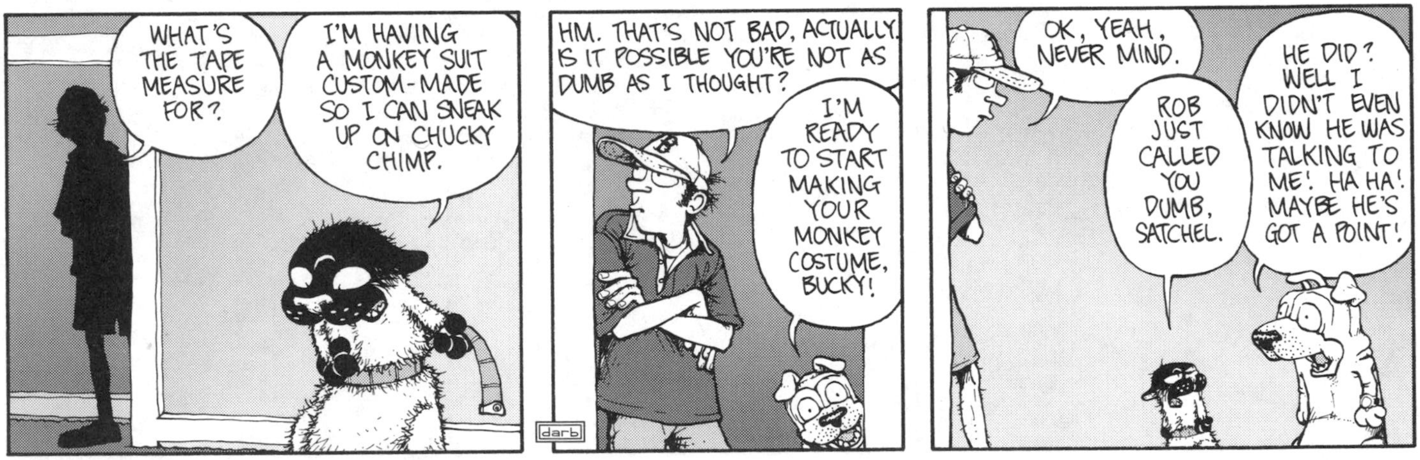
WHAT'S THE TAPE MEASURE FOR?
I'M HAVING A MONKEY SUIT CUSTOM-MADE SO I CAN SNEAK UP ON CHUCKY CHIMP.
darb
HM. THAT'S NOT BAD, ACTUALLY. IS IT POSSIBLE YOU'RE NOT AS DUMB AS I THOUGHT?
I'M READY TO START MAKING YOUR MONKEY COSTUME, BUCKY!
OK, YEAH, NEVER MIND.
ROB JUST CALLED YOU DUMB, SATCHEL.
HE DID? WELL I DIDN'T EVEN KNOW HE WAS TALKING TO ME! HA HA! MAYBE HE'S GOT A POINT!

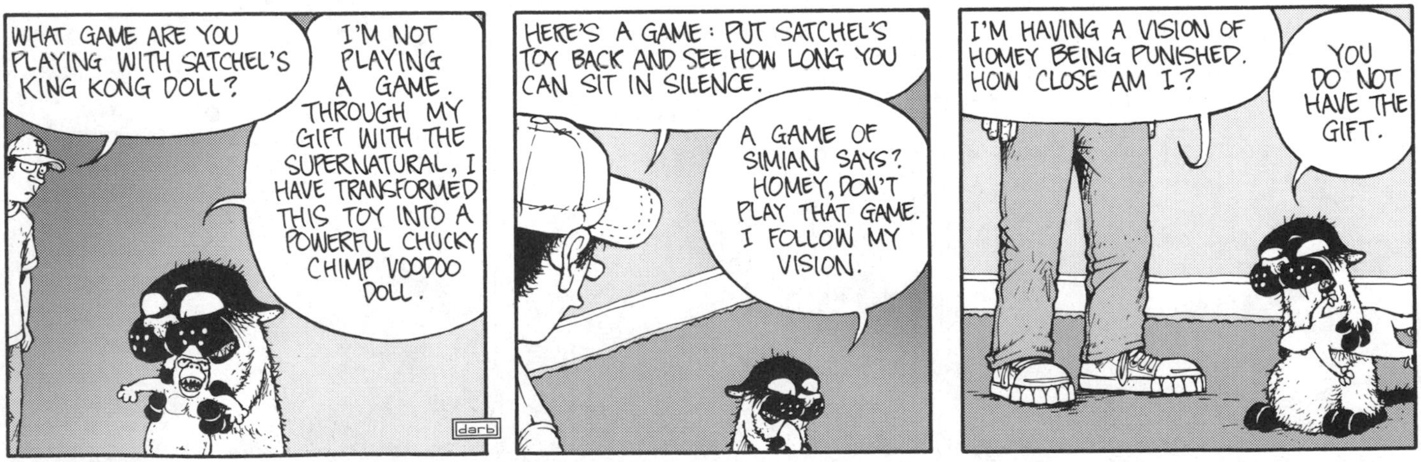
WHAT GAME ARE YOU PLAYING WITH SATCHEL'S KING KONG DOLL?
I'M NOT PLAYING A GAME. THROUGH MY GIFT WITH THE SUPERNATURAL, I HAVE TRANSFORMED THIS TOY INTO A POWERFUL CHUCKY CHIMP VOODOO DOLL.
darb
HERE'S A GAME: PUT SATCHEL'S TOY BACK AND SEE HOW LONG YOU CAN SIT IN SILENCE.
A GAME OF SIMIAN SAYS? HOMEY, DON'T PLAY THAT GAME. I FOLLOW MY VISION.
I'M HAVING A VISION OF HOMEY BEING PUNISHED. HOW CLOSE AM I?
YOU DO NOT HAVE THE GIFT.

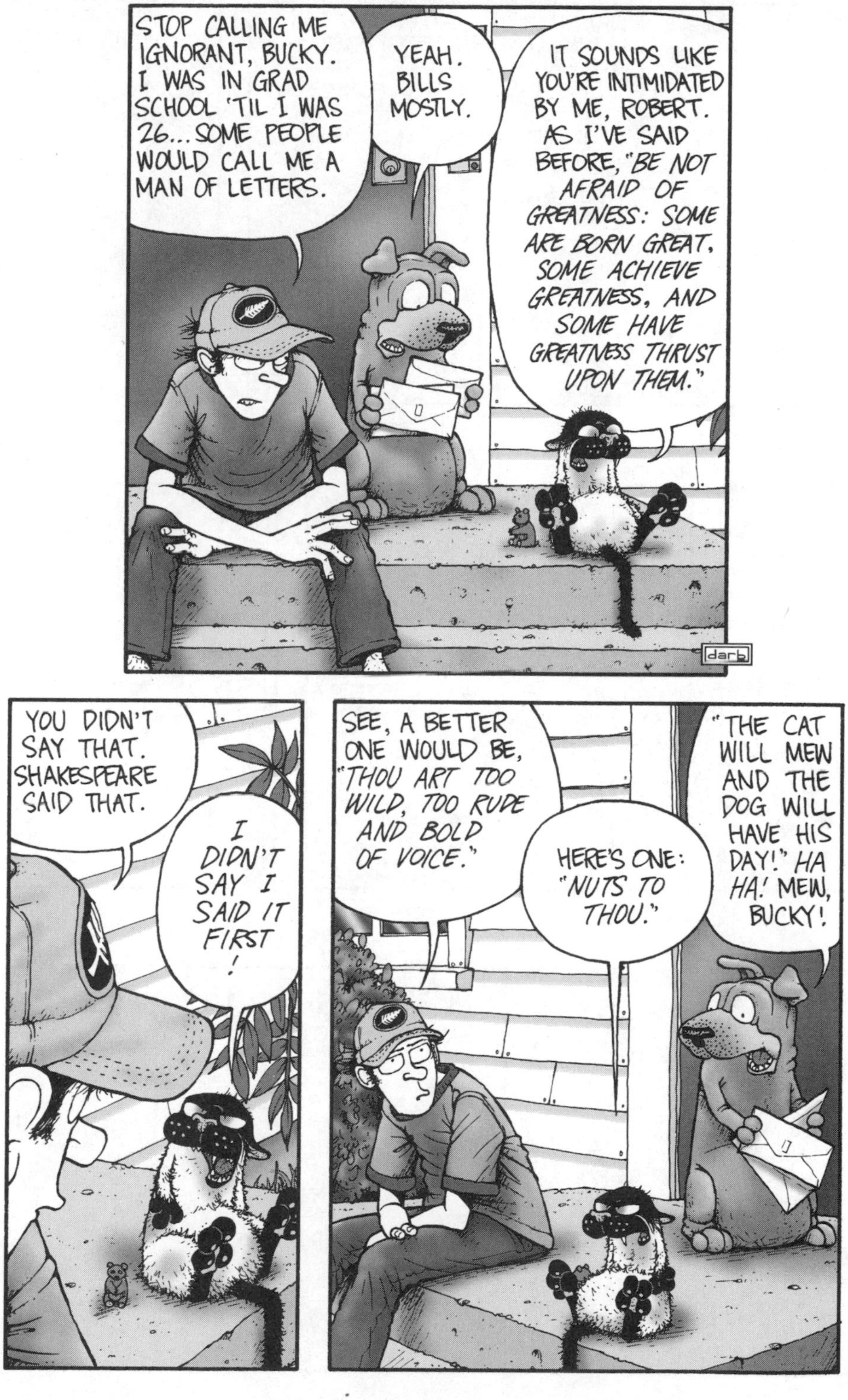
STOP CALLING ME IGNORANT, BUCKY. I WAS IN GRAD SCHOOL 'TIL I WAS 26... SOME PEOPLE WOULD CALL ME A MAN OF LETTERS.
YEAH. BILLS MOSTLY.
IT SOUNDS LIKE YOU'RE INTIMIDATED BY ME, ROBERT. AS I'VE SAID BEFORE, "BE NOT AFRAID OF GREATNESS: SOME ARE BORN GREAT, SOME ACHIEVE GREATNESS, AND SOME HAVE GREATNESS THRUST UPON THEM."
darb
YOU DIDN'T SAY THAT. SHAKESPEARE SAID THAT.
I DIDN'T SAY I SAID IT FIRST!
SEE, A BETTER ONE WOULD BE, "THOU ART TOO WILD, TOO RUDE AND BOLD OF VOICE."
HERE'S ONE: "NUTS TO THOU."
"THE CAT WILL MEW AND THE DOG WILL HAVE HIS DAY!" HA HA! MEW, BUCKY!

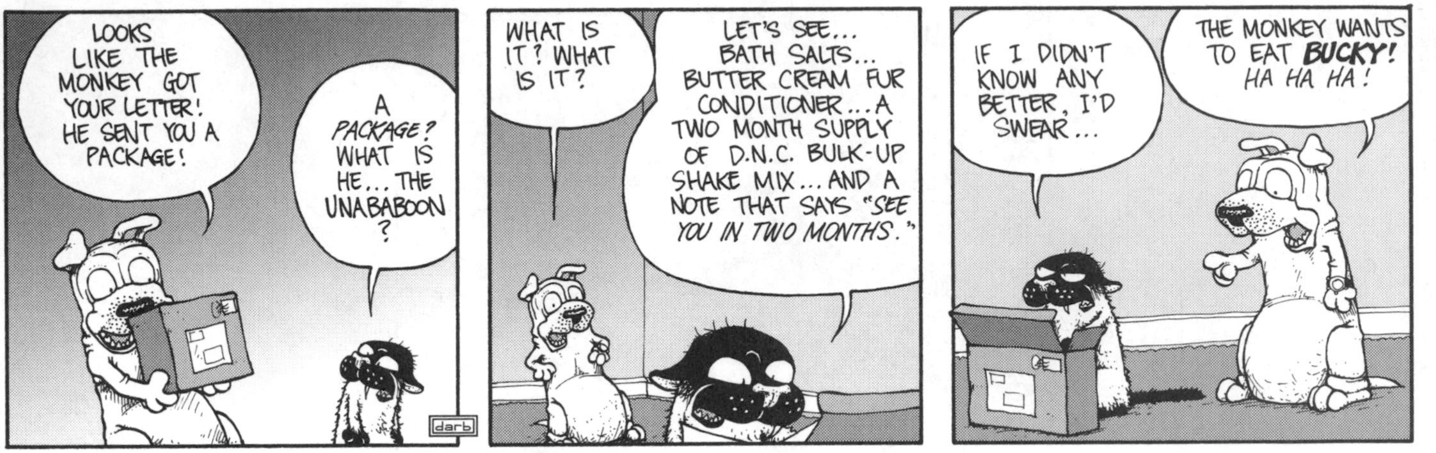
LOOKS LIKE THE MONKEY GOT YOUR LETTER! HE SENT YOU A PACKAGE!
A PACKAGE? WHAT IS HE... THE UNABABOON?
WHAT IS IT? WHAT IS IT?
LET'S SEE... BATH SALTS... BUTTER CREAM FUR CONDITIONER... A TWO MONTH SUPPLY OF D.N.C. BULK-UP SHAKE MIX... AND A NOTE THAT SAYS "SEE YOU IN TWO MONTHS."
IF I DIDN'T KNOW ANY BETTER, I'D SWEAR...
THE MONKEY WANTS TO EAT BUCKY! HA HA HA!
darb

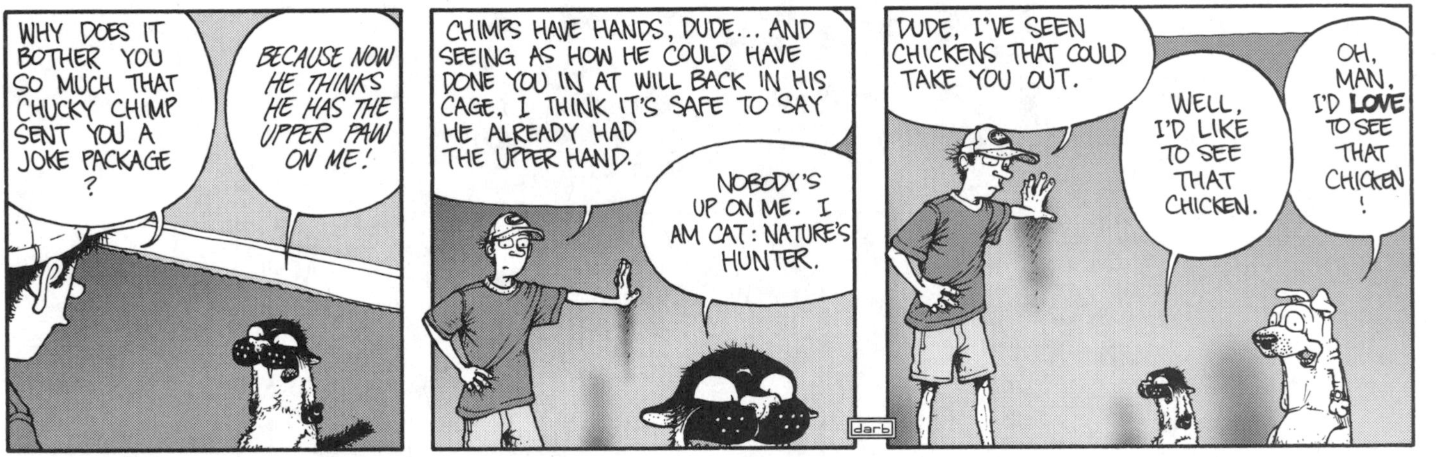
WHY DOES IT BOTHER YOU SO MUCH THAT CHUCKY CHIMP SENT YOU A JOKE PACKAGE?
BECAUSE NOW HE THINKS HE HAS THE UPPER PAW ON ME!
CHIMPS HAVE HANDS, DUDE... AND SEEING AS HOW HE COULD HAVE DONE YOU IN AT WILL BACK IN HIS CAGE, I THINK IT'S SAFE TO SAY HE ALREADY HAD THE UPPER HAND.
NOBODY'S UP ON ME. I AM CAT: NATURE'S HUNTER.
DUDE, I'VE SEEN CHICKENS THAT COULD TAKE YOU OUT.
WELL, I'D LIKE TO SEE THAT CHICKEN.
OH, MAN, I'D LOVE TO SEE THAT CHICKEN!
darb

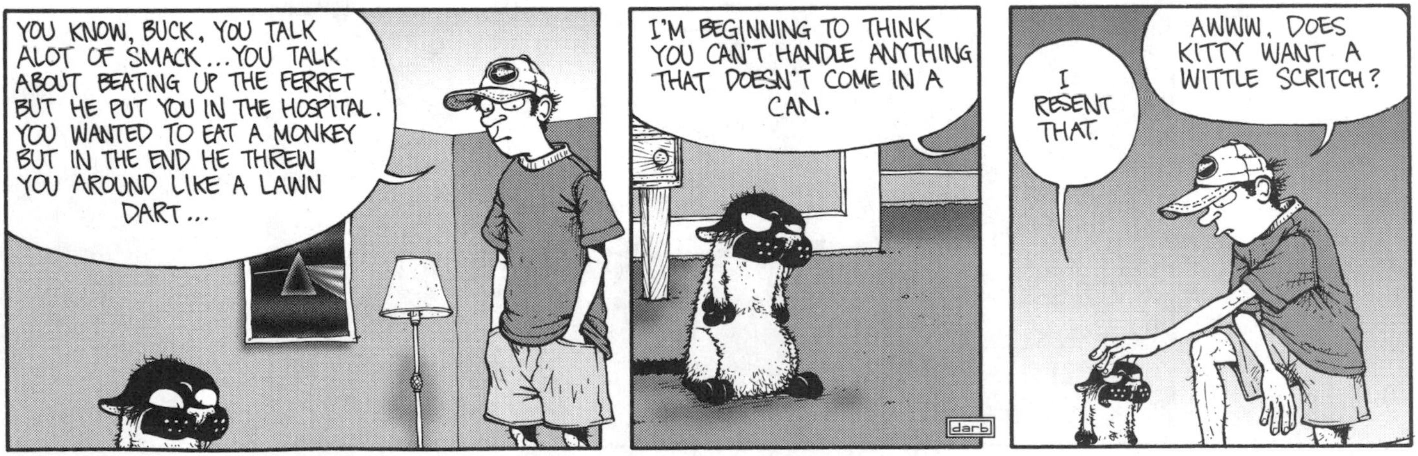
YOU KNOW, BUCK, YOU TALK ALOT OF SMACK... YOU TALK ABOUT BEATING UP THE FERRET BUT HE PUT YOU IN THE HOSPITAL. YOU WANTED TO EAT A MONKEY BUT IN THE END HE THREW YOU AROUND LIKE A LAWN DART...
I'M BEGINNING TO THINK YOU CAN'T HANDLE ANYTHING THAT DOESN'T COME IN A CAN.
I RESENT THAT.
AWWW, DOES KITTY WANT A WITTLE SCRITCH?
darb

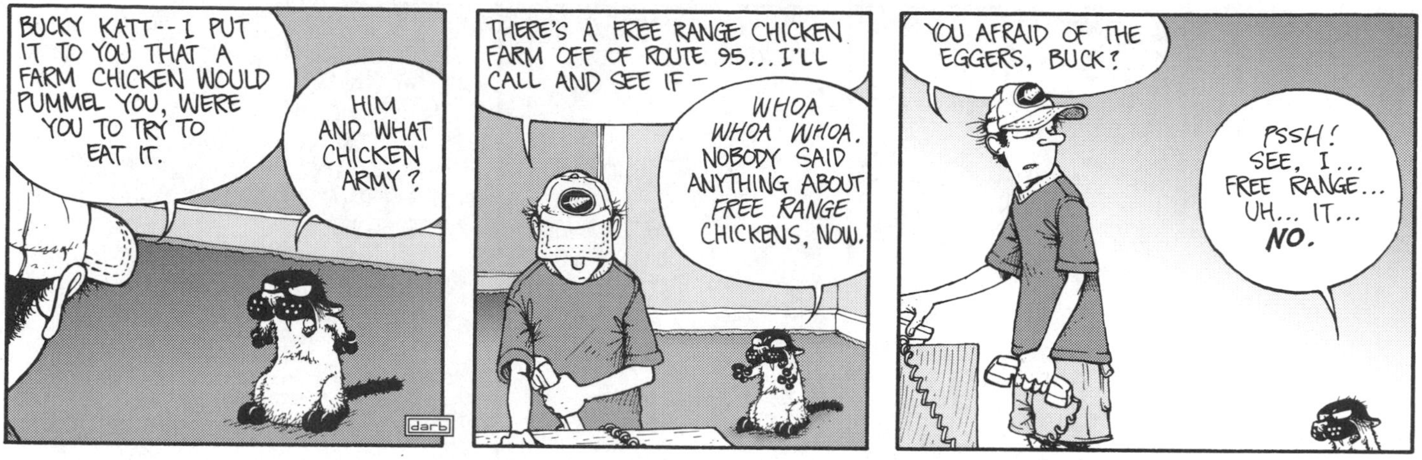
BUCKY KATT--I PUT IT TO YOU THAT A FARM CHICKEN WOULD PUMMEL YOU, WERE YOU TO TRY TO EAT IT.
HIM AND WHAT CHICKEN ARMY?
THERE'S A FREE RANGE CHICKEN FARM OFF OF ROUTE 95... I'LL CALL AND SEE IF –
WHOA WHOA WHOA. NOBODY SAID ANYTHING ABOUT *FREE RANGE* CHICKENS, NOW.
YOU AFRAID OF THE EGGERS, BUCK?
PSSH! SEE, I... FREE RANGE... UH... IT... **NO.**
darb

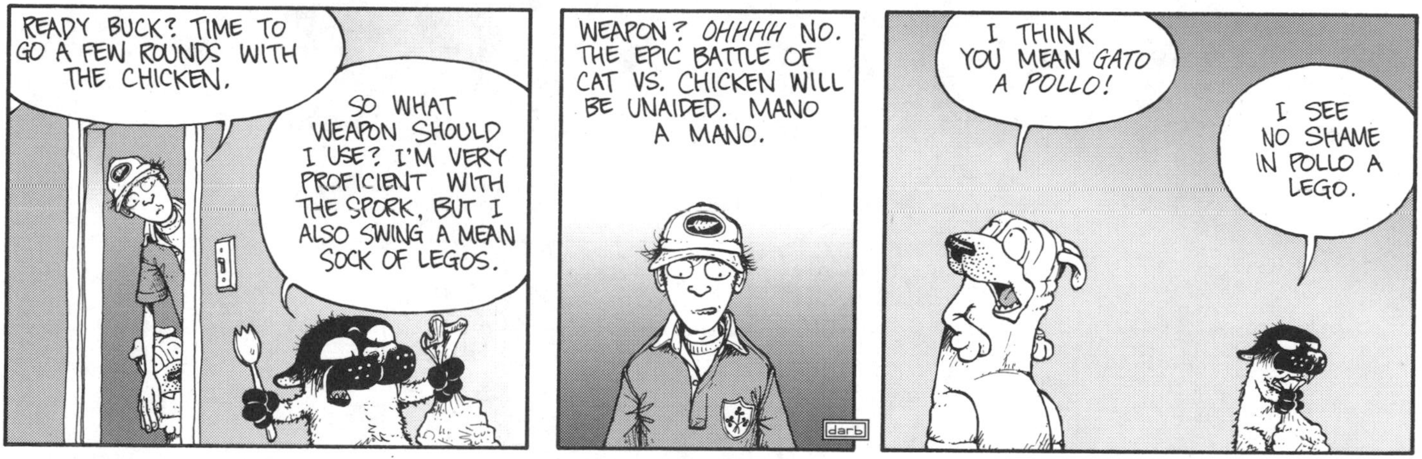
READY BUCK? TIME TO GO A FEW ROUNDS WITH THE CHICKEN.
SO WHAT WEAPON SHOULD I USE? I'M VERY PROFICIENT WITH THE SPORK, BUT I ALSO SWING A MEAN SOCK OF LEGOS.
WEAPON? *OHHHH* NO. THE EPIC BATTLE OF CAT VS. CHICKEN WILL BE UNAIDED. MANO A MANO.
darb
I THINK YOU MEAN *GATO A POLLO!*
I SEE NO SHAME IN POLLO A LEGO.

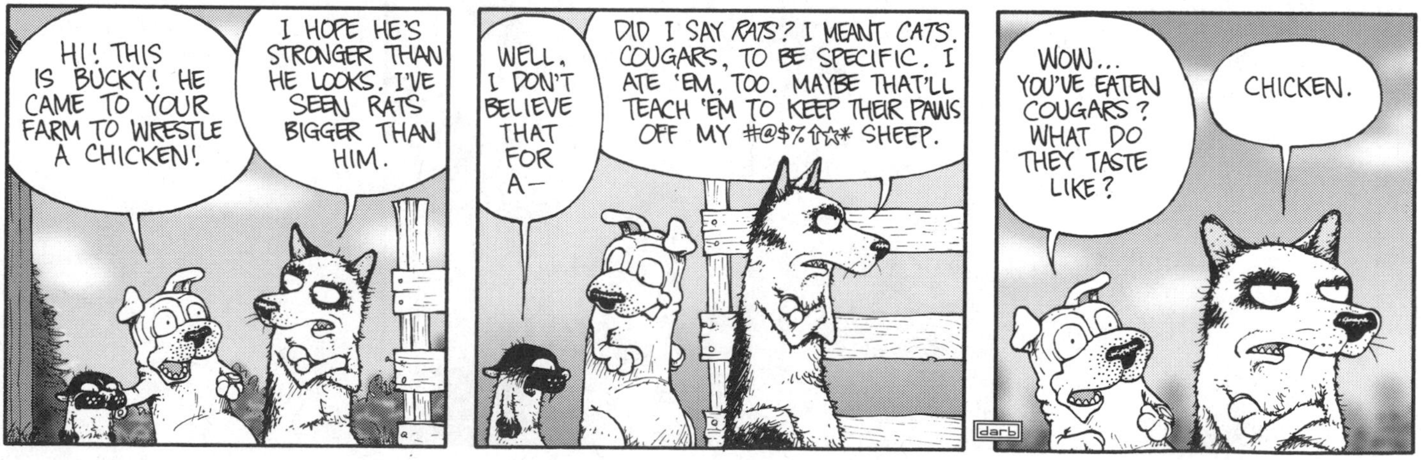
HI! THIS IS BUCKY! HE CAME TO YOUR FARM TO WRESTLE A CHICKEN!
I HOPE HE'S STRONGER THAN HE LOOKS. I'VE SEEN RATS BIGGER THAN HIM.
WELL, I DON'T BELIEVE THAT FOR A–
DID I SAY *RATS?* I MEANT *CATS.* COUGARS, TO BE SPECIFIC. I ATE 'EM, TOO. MAYBE THAT'LL TEACH 'EM TO KEEP THEIR PAWS OFF MY #@$%⇧☆* SHEEP.
darb
WOW... YOU'VE EATEN COUGARS? WHAT DO THEY TASTE LIKE?
CHICKEN.

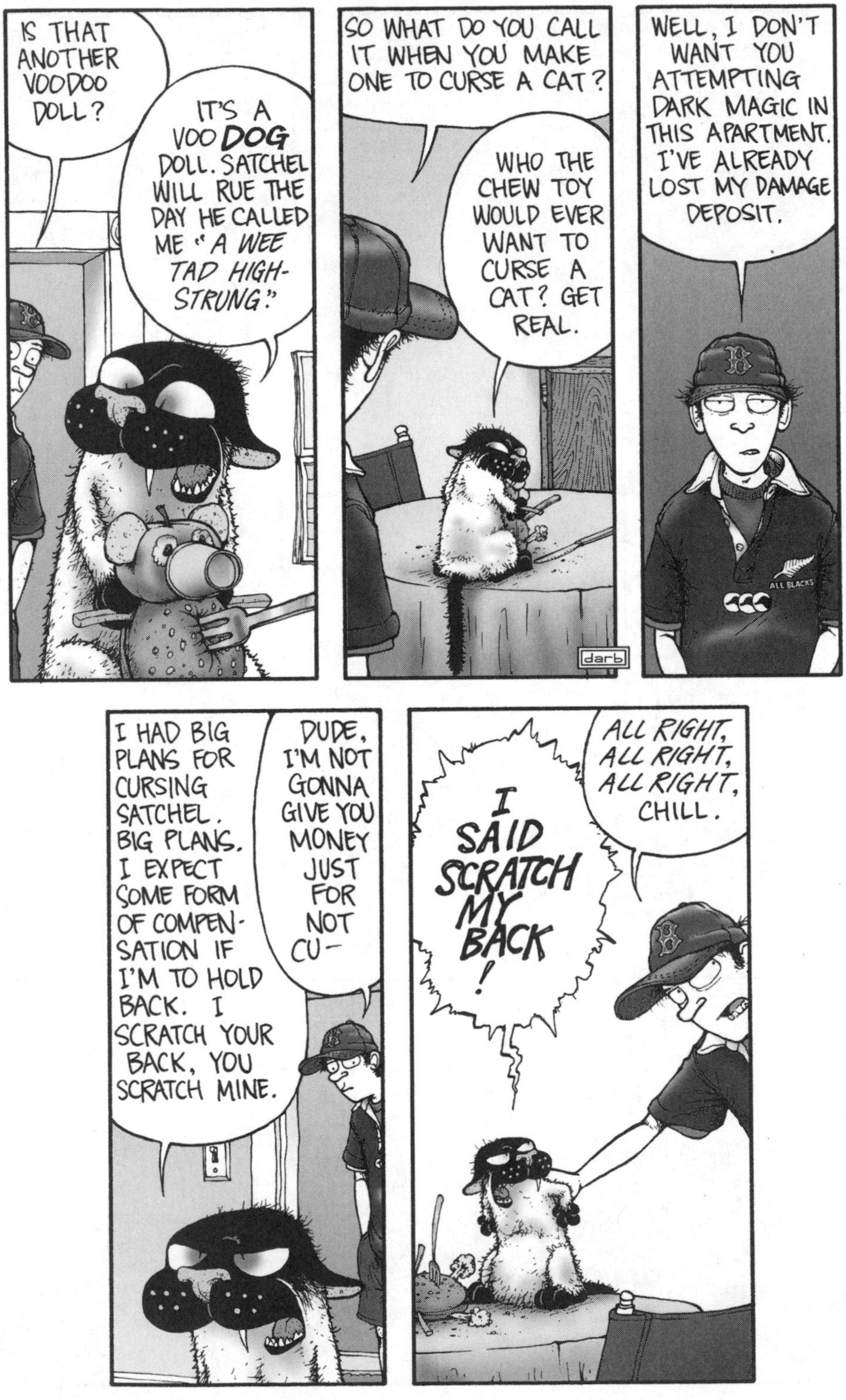
IS THAT ANOTHER VOODOO DOLL?
IT'S A VOO**DOG** DOLL. SATCHEL WILL RUE THE DAY HE CALLED ME "A WEE TAD HIGH-STRUNG."
SO WHAT DO YOU CALL IT WHEN YOU MAKE ONE TO CURSE A CAT?
WHO THE CHEW TOY WOULD EVER WANT TO CURSE A CAT? GET REAL.
darb
WELL, I DON'T WANT YOU ATTEMPTING DARK MAGIC IN THIS APARTMENT. I'VE ALREADY LOST MY DAMAGE DEPOSIT.
ALL BLACKS
I HAD BIG PLANS FOR CURSING SATCHEL. BIG PLANS. I EXPECT SOME FORM OF COMPENSATION IF I'M TO HOLD BACK. I SCRATCH YOUR BACK, YOU SCRATCH MINE.
DUDE, I'M NOT GONNA GIVE YOU MONEY JUST FOR NOT CU–
I SAID SCRATCH MY BACK!
ALL RIGHT, ALL RIGHT, ALL RIGHT, CHILL.